Season of Fire

The Confederate Strike on Washington

Season of Fire

The Confederate Strike on Washington

Joseph Judge

Rockbridge Publishing Company
Berryville, Virginia

cl

Published by

Rockbridge Publishing Company
Post Office Box 351
Berryville, VA 22611
(703) 955-3980

Maps Copyright 1994 by Katherine Tennery

Library of Congress Cataloging-in-Publication Data

Judge, Joseph, 1928—
    Season of fire: the Confederate strike on Washington / Joseph Judge.
        p.   cm.
    Includes bibliographical references (p.) and index.
    ISBN 1-883522-00-5 $30.00
    1. Shenandoah Valley Campaign, 1864 (May-August) 2. Maryland Cam-
paign, 1864. 3. Fort Stevens (Washington, D.C.)—History. 4. Washington (D.C.)—History—Civil War, 1861-1865. I. Title.
E476.66.J83 1994
973.7'378—dc20   94-15046
                                                           CIP

10 9 8 7 6 5 4 3 2 1
First Edition

For Phyllis

Contents

Valley of Fire

Invasion of the North

Foreword

Franz Sigel's advance up the Shenandoah Valley in 1864, David Hunter's subsequent abuse of the Valley's landscape, civilians and private property and Jubal Early's retaliatory raid on the nation's capital contain all of the ingredients for a Cecil B. DeMille or Steven Spielberg spectacle. It is the kind of all too human story that provided the themes for Greek mythology, the Old Testament, Senecan revenge tragedies, Christian morality plays, Arthurian legend, medieval romances and Shakespeare, and illustrates vividly that truth is not only stranger than fiction, it is often more interesting and dramatic.

Consider that a former vice-president of the United States, John C. Breckinridge of Kentucky, has recently lost a bitter presidential election to Abraham Lincoln, a virtually unknown candidate from a brand new political party, the G.O.P. The election, which hinged on violent, emotional issues of constitutional law, has cleaved the country in two. Consider further that Breckinridge is now at war with his former government in the Valley of Virginia. At New Market, he successfully leads a rag-tag but deadly collection of Palatinate farmers, Scots-Irish mountaineers, Irish-Catholic railroad workers and aristocratic undergraduates against a German-born general, Franz Sigel, his German-speaking staff and their army, which includes Italian and Irish immigrants, former policemen and firemen, as well as a member of one of the nation's richest industrial families, Henry du Pont, and a nephew of one of America's greatest poets, Charles R. Lowell.

Consider now that after the handsome Kentuckian has driven the infidels from the Old Dominion's sacred soil, the upstart president, himself a Kentucky native, sends a fanatic David Hunter (like Joshua) and his federal legions to raze the homes of the Valley civilians (Jerichoans), to defile their monuments and public buildings, including the Virginia Military Institute, and to turn their crop-laden fields into great conflagrations: the plagues of Egypt all over again.

And consider also that to avenge these Vandal-like violations, Robert E. Lee (a King Arthur himself) orders Jubal Early (descendant of Cain) to lead Stonewall Jackson's old corps (his Valley shepherds) in driving Hunter's army (Goliath and the

Philistines) from the Promised Land. That holy mission accomplished, Jubal and his barefoot Davids cross the Potomac (River Jordan) and enter the north (Holy Land), where they ransom a village (Hagerstown, Maryland) and then advance on Washington, D.C. (Jerusalem itself).

However, these heroes (or marauders, depending on your perspective) must first cross the Monocacy River, where they are challenged to a duel by a literally hobbling force led by an aspiring novelist, Lew Wallace, who will one day author *Ben Hur*. The resulting battle's pageantry rivals that of the climactic scene in Chaucer's *The Knight's Tale*. After hours of gory fratricide, the gray crusaders cross the river, burn a nobleman's palace (Montgomery Blair's) and prepare to storm the very gates of Fort Stevens (Nottingham Castle) in pursuit of the Holy Grail.

From the parapets, however, Lincoln (MacBeth or, depending on your perspective, Julius Caesar), observes the Army of the Potomac's VI Corps (Sir Guy's archers and foot-soldiers) drive Early's forces (Robin and his no-longer-merry-men) back into the Shenandoah Valley (Sherwood Forest and Birnham Wood). All the while, Oliver Wendell Holmes (a future Solomon), concerned over his sovereign's safety, implores Lincoln to "Get down, you damned fool!"

This is the allegorical gist of *Season of Fire*. Along the way, future presidents and congressmen become locked in mortal combat with future governors and senators, Virginians kill (West) Virginians, Marylanders wreak havoc on Maryland, a gray ghost, John S. Mosby, terrorizes the countryside, and cavalryman Harry Gilmor—a natural for the male lead in *Romeo and Juliet*—proves that he, and not an anti-Viet Nam War demonstrator, was the source of the phrase: "Make love, not war." *Season of Fire* tells a powerful American story; and best (or worst) of all, it is a true one.

JOHN P. MONAHAN, III

Acknowledgments

A book such as this becomes, in the end, a work of many hands. Scholars who labor in the vineyard of Civil War history have been most generous with their time and research, of which there is a prodigious quantity. Rockbridge publisher Kathie Tennery made her mind up very quickly to produce the book; its perceived quality is due entirely to her meticulous care, taste and pursuit of the best. I thank Mark Carroll, editor at Fulcrum Press, who took the initial interest in ithe manuscript and submitted it to Brian C. Pohanka, a thoroughly sound reviewer, who corrected many early errors. Other historians who reviewed the book—Robert J. Driver, Jr., Harold R. Woodward, Jr., John Heatwole, Ted Alexander, chief historian at Antietam, and Jay Monahan, who understands the power of the story—invariably left it better. Roger Keller straightened out the details about McCausland's raid at Hagerstown. John McDonough of the Manuscripts Division of the Library of Congress and his wife Dorothy (my sister) were unfailing as sources of support as well as information. Dr. Richard J. Sommers of the United States Army Historical Institute at Carlisle Barracks, Pa., was an infallible guide to the collections there, and to the great conflict itself. The staffs of the county libraries at Rockville and Potomac, Maryland, were always pleased to be of service.

On the ground, Antietam superintendant Susan Moore has been supportive from the start, and Monocacy Battlefield park historian Kathy Beeler has often been a knowing and patient guide to the field. Mark Stephens of the Association for the Preservation of Civil War Sites provided me with information on the Valley's battle-fields. Mr. and Mrs. Francis Kellerman, who now live in DeSellum's residence of Summit Hall, Gaithersburg, were kind enough to show me the premises and share the family history. The DeSellum papers are held by the Montgomery County Historical Society and its knowledgable librarian Jane Sween. Philip Cantelon, president of the Historical Society, and his wife Eileen McGuckian provided particular historical materials from the files of *Peerless Rockville*. The Mallet–Prevost family offered me inspection of still-standing "Uncle Tom's Cabin." Chief of Interpretation for National Capital Parks Al James was helpful in arranging visits to Fort Stevens and National Battlefield Cemetery. David Smith and John Daly of the National Capital Parks provided me with terrain maps of the Fort Stevens area. Thanks also to the staff at

Seneca Creek State Park, site of Woodlands. Many other made the life of a book writer much easier in one way or another: those Valley folk Sally and Richard Sessoms and the Drakes and McClungs of lovely Lexington, Virginia, superb hosts; Gerry Valerio of Bookmark Studios in Annapolis, a man of elegant ideas; and John Hightower of Berryville, an unflagging enthusiast for this project.

Introduction

A person who would find the Monocacy battlefield probably cannot, at least easily. I-270, six broad lanes of thundering trucks and whining sports cars, imbecilic CB talk and the occasional careening hub cap, lies across the heart of it. I do not know how this could have happened without evoking the damnation of the muse of history.

No clue alerts the hundreds of thousands of westbound drivers who each year descend 270's long slope down into the Frederick valley, that just here, as the huge road levels up before crossing the Monocacy River, perhaps a flash of brown or green in the corner of a distracted driver's eye, exactly here, beneath the piers of the road and in the fields beyond, men killed one another for cause. Exactly here was the union of states, the United States, preserved. For exactly here were purchased in blood the precious hours that saved the capital from capture by the Confederates and all that may have ensued—perhaps the taking of Lincoln and the Congress, recognition of the Confederacy by England and France, seizure of millions of dollars in negotiable bonds, of untold supplies of war matériel and release of eighteen thousand prisoners of war from Point Lookout, a fully-equipped entire corps to turn against Grant's back at Petersburg.

Monocacy was one of the hinges of our national fate, but it has been obscured. To find its all but hidden remnants, one has to continue into Frederick and then come back east on Maryland state route 355. About a mile before the Monocacy River, on the south side of the road, stands one of only four monuments that mark the events of July 9, 1864. Erected in 1914, the fiftieth anniversary of the battle, by the United Daughters of the Confederacy of Frederick, the square-cut granite boulder bears a bronze tablet that dedicates the monument to the "memory of the southern soldiers who fell there in battle."

What was once the first National Road continues east across the river. Just past the bridge a sharp right puts you on the old road, the 1864 Washington Road. After another bend left, on a ridge, is a grassy acre bearing a second monument. Unveiled on November 24, 1908, the thirty-five-foot pillar of Rhode Island granite stands on a base ten feet square, is surmounted by a polished ball of granite three feet in diameter, and recalls the bravery of the men of the 87th and 138th and other Pennsylvania units who fought here. Just beyond, at the corner of the Baker Valley Road and the old Washington Road, stands a third monument, a solid granite monolith with a bronze tablet in the shape of a Greek cross; the location, a triangle bounded with three granite posts, is near the position of the regiment it honors, the 10th Vermont.

The monument is directly across a steep little valley from the beautiful old house of Araby Farm, which stands with its weathered brick and high dormers, looking very much as it did a century and more ago, its fields still flowing away west toward the river and southwest toward the Worthington place. As one historian puts it: "Araby is the essential blood-soaked heart of the Monocacy battlefield."

The fourth of Monocacy's monuments memorializes the 14th New Jersey Volunteer Infantry: a twenty-four-foot high pillar bearing the figure of an energetic infantry soldier, his left hand holding the top of his grounded musket, his right hand reaching for ammunition at his belt. On July 11, 1907, 180 survivors of the regiment came down to Monocacy Junction for the unveiling.

On that occasion, Comrade (of the Reunion Association) Henry C. La Rowe of Brooklyn, New York, delivered himself of what were once regarded in days of oratory as "noble sentiments":

> We almost hear "a voice that is still," we almost "feel a touch of a vanished hand," a voice we heard and a hand we clasped for the last time forty-three years ago today. Memory recalls forms and faces that we shall not see again until we "pass over the river and rest with them under the shade of the trees."
>
> But after all, comrades, don't you think it paid to stay here? . . . What if men were maimed for life! What matters it if we reddened the sheaves of grain with our blood! Who regrets it now, in view of the undreamed of beneficent results of the Civil War.

Now that the National Park Service is at last moving forward with plans to preserve much of the battlefield (1994), it seems a fitting time to remember again the compatriots who stayed there, the boys killed amid the corn, who sprawled across the crashed-down wheat, hung on the rick-rack fences above the Monocacy, and stained the creek below Araby so richly crimson with their blood.

We think we know the larger "why" of their deaths, but not the smaller ones. Even if we find message in such sacrifice, a portent read in the broken bones, the knocked-off knee caps, the entrails spewed on the damp summer grass, we are slow to comprehend why these particular creatures came here to die on the shoulder of a warm hill above the meander of a Maryland stream named by an Indian in a language that none of them had ever heard.

By 1864 the Shawnees had been gone from this valley for a century, and the woods had been replaced with fields of rye and corn and nodding wheat, a checkerboard of growing crops set off by zig-zag rail fences entwined by sweet honeysuckle and Virginia creeper and poison ivy and bindweed with its white, trumpet-like flowers, against which the crimson of blood almost shimmers.

It was a stage set for tragedy. The quiet of this valley, so deep that farmers tending summer fields can hear a song sparrow from across the river or a hawk screaming from far above the hills, was shattered by the thunderous roaring and exploding and screaming and thudding and shouting and creaking and breaking and shattering and crying and crying out that happens when death is on the loose, blind death, blinded by easy pickings, swinging his huge scythe, left, right, left, right, and boys tumble about and fall down with their limbs torn and hearts stopped, the tanned boys from Georgia and the dark ones from Louisiana and the fair, blond ones from Pennsylvania and Ohio.

They had marched hard miles from far away to meet their destiny on this hot summer day, and those who survived would march many more, down the dirt roads to Washington City. Every man among them knew they were players in a drama that had been unfolding since spring came to Virginia. Already major scenes had been played out—at New Market, at Piedmont, at Lynchburg, at Leetown: infantry regiments in bare feet hurried mile after mile, like marathon runners, to grip and kill the enemy; cavalry troops dashed into broadsides of cannonfire, the great guns thundering flame and smoke, scattering death distantly in small, sudden blizzards of metal. Already many had passed from the stage—general officers who had proven themselves once again and always to be God's own arrogant fools. And once again the truly brave had been truly brave.

As the drama now moves on to the crashing climax, we must remind ourselves that it is useless to tell such a tale as this unless it makes us ponder, not the vast process of history but man's individual fate.

Potomac, Maryland
1994

BOOK ONE

VALLEY
OF FIRE

I.
Political Generals
in the Valley

Friday, March 4, 1864—Dublin, Virginia

He had been, at age thirty-five, the youngest vice president in the history of the United States, the nation he had now sworn to divide, and he looked the part. As he strode with purpose into the headquarters of the Department of Western Virginia, orderlies noted the square cut jaw, thin handlebar mustache and handsome features of the tall man, especially the clear, intense eyes, heard the sonorous voice that could spellbind, and pronounced to themselves the famous name—Maj. Gen. John Cabell Breckinridge. Vice President John Cabell Breckinridge. Almost president.

What was he doing in a God-forsaken hole like this railroad hamlet of Dublin, deep in the wintry mountains of southwestern Virginia?

Like so many confederate officers, Breckinridge was from patriotic American stock—an ancestor had signed the Declaration, a grandfather had been Jefferson's attorney general, another had been president of Princeton. As a very young man he had won Henry Clay's old seat in Congress from the Ashland district of Kentucky. Clay's grandson, Lt. James B. Clay, in fact, was his aide, and young James left his epitaph: "I can say with truth that he was the truest, greatest man I was ever thrown in contact with."

He had served in the Mexican War as well as the Congress, and was only five months eligible for the office when the Democratic convention nominated him to run with James Buchanan on the Buck and Breck ticket that won an easy victory in 1856.

By 1860 the nation was being swept toward war and Breckinridge, who had declared slavery an evil that must be eradicated, found himself identified as a southerner, however moderate. It was as a southerner that he sought a compromise to avert the oncoming crisis, but his own party split under the strain. In the belief that his acceptance of the presidential nomination of the southern wing would forestall the

Battles & Leaders

MAJ. GEN. JOHN C. BRECKINRIDGE

nomination of Stephen Douglas by the northern wing, he accepted. It was not to be. Douglas stayed in, and Abraham Lincoln defeated Breckinridge.

Reluctant, he stayed to the bitter end in the Senate to oppose Lincoln's war policies until, in the fall of 1861, federal authorities moved to arrest him as a traitor. He faced prison or the confederate army and chose the latter, serving gallantly with the Army of Tennessee at Shiloh, Corinth, Vicksburg, Jackson and Chickamauga, rising to major general in command of a corps. Then, like others before him, he crossed Braxton Bragg during the Chattanooga campaign, a feud that ruined his effectiveness in the west just at a time when a need presented itself in the east. It was almost as though the god of battles had called, a personal invitation to a moment of glory or humiliation, not transferrable, not refusable.

Only the day before, Ulysses S. Grant had received orders to report to Washington to receive his commission. He was coming east with extraordinary powers, and there was no doubt he would confront Robert E. Lee in Virginia come spring.

Dublin was headquarters for a department that covered a vast realm of mountain and valley in Virginia, eastern Tennessee, Kentucky, and West Virginia. Passing through it, and as vital as the Baltimore & Ohio was to the Union, the tracks of the Virginia & Tennessee ran from Lynchburg southwest through Dublin and Wytheville and on through the Cumberland Gap into the west.

But Breckinridge also had his eye on that other corridor and passage between north and south, the great Shenandoah Valley, the bread basket of the Confederacy, Lee's extended left flank as he faced Grant, a great prize in itself, and the doorway to eventual victory for either side. Through the Valley, he felt, would a strike from the north come. If there were destiny for his command, it was there.

That very day he mounted a small column to begin a four-hundred-mile tour of his department, every step on horseback, to inspect and rally his men—all five thousand of them.

Saturday, March 12—Revere House, Cumberland, Maryland

Col. David Hunter Strother had been waiting with the other officers in the parlor of the Revere House in Cumberland, Maryland, the headquarters of the Department of West Virginia, to receive their new commander, and despite all he had heard he found himself somewhat taken aback by Franz Sigel's appearance, "small in stature and ungraceful. . . . His hair and beard are tawny, his jaws and cheek bones square and angular, his eyes light blue, forehead narrow, and too small for his face."

Indeed, that small and angular forehead gave Sigel a reptilian look, enhanced by a high part in slick black hair. His brows seemed fixed with a perpetual frown balanced by the perpetual pout of a little Vandyke beard. Although smartly attired in the dress uniform of a major general, he wore a shabby field hat—perhaps to reinforce the impression of a man of some experience. He spoke to the men with a heavy German accent.

Battles & Leaders

MAJ. GEN. FRANZ SIGEL

Maj. Gen. Franz Sigel was, an everyone knew, incompetent. He was also, as everyone knew, an ethnic political appointee with powerful Congressional connections that made his incompetence irrelevant. The more than one million Germans in 1864 America made up a significant minority in the thirty-one million population and a disproportionately large segment of the federal army. During the war years, more than eight hundred thousand immigrants would flood into the young United States—233 thousand Germans, compared to 197 thousand Irish and ninety-five thousand English and Scots. Sigel had somehow made himself the general for Germans as well as "the German general," even though his record as a military commander on two continents was dismal.

As a young officer in Germany he had commanded a column of the German

Republican Army under August Willich and suffered such a crushing defeat at Frieburg that he fled to Switzerland. He returned to be defeated again the following year. When his troops demanded a new leader, the republican Lorenz Brentano promoted Sigel upward to secretary of war. Taking command of a part of the German army, Sigel lost again at Waghausel and fled, finally, to New York in 1852.

Following one stream of immigrant Germans out to St. Louis, he became director of schools and formed the Turnverein, a militant group that drilled against the day they would fight for a republican Germany. Thus, when war came to Missouri in 1861, Sigel already had in hand a disciplined force that he promptly placed in service to the Union, capturing rebel sympathizers at Camp Jackson on May 10 and skirmishing at Carthage on July 5—obscure events that catapulted him to national prominence simply because he was German. Cynically, Lincoln's secretary of war, Maj. Gen. Henry W. Halleck, promoted Sigel to brigadier general as an incentive to German enlistment, and three days later Sigel rewarded him with an incompetent performance in the battle at Wilson's Creek, where he left the field after a flanking movement had failed. He did better at Pea Ridge, or Elkhorn Tavern, in March of 1862, where he commanded two divisions under Brig. Gen. Samuel R. Curtis, who was declared the winner—a battle important in that it helped keep the Confederacy out of Missouri and interesting because of the participation, on the Confederate side, of three regiments composed of Choctaw, Chickasaw, Cherokee, Creek and Seminole Indians, who were falsely accused of scalping dead Yankees.

Unscarred and unfazed by defeat, Sigel continued to rise in the eyes of his admiring countrymen, speaking at German rallies and using his ethnic political clout to such effect in Washington that in 1862 he was promoted to the exalted rank of major general. Among the officers who served under him were Schurz, Von Steinwehr, Schimmelfennig, Von Gilson and Van Arusburg. Shortly afterward he was licked by Stonewall Jackson in the Valley and shared in the union defeat at Second Manassas. In danger of being reduced in command, he went on extended medical leave, during which he beat up a political storm over the shabby treatment he had received. German soldiers were taught a new song, to the tune of "The Girl I Left Behind Me," entitled "I'm Going To Fight Mit Sigel." The chorus ran: "Yaw! daus is drue, I shpeakes mit you, I'm going to fight mit Sigel."

There was a vulnerable target for such a campaign—Brig. Gen. Benjamin F. Kelley of the Department of West Virginia, who had been somnolent since taking command in the summer of 1863. Grant had plans for an offensive in the spring of 1864, and he doubted that Kelley had sufficient energy to lead it.

Grant himself was making new arrangements. On this very day Henry Halleck was stepping down as general-in-chief, a title Grant would assume along with the rank of lieutenant general, the highest in an American army since George Washington and revived by Congressional act for Grant. He had met Lincoln for the first time on March 8 and been given his commission the following day. He had taken command of the armies of the United States on the tenth and immediately gone to Virginia to see George Gordon Meade and the Army of the Potomac.

New affairs were afoot and plans in the air. In this atmosphere, military and political considerations decided the issue and Franz Sigel was named new head of the department. Col. Strother, whom Sigel would command, commented bitterly at the time that "the Dutch vote must be secured at all hazards . . . and the sacrifice of West Virginia is a small matter." Now Strother listened with astonishment as Sigel greeted his fellow officers with the remark, delivered in broken English, that he felt himself unequal to the task at hand.

Mid-March—In the Alleghenies

Breckinridge, on his long ride through his department, found three thousand infantry troops. Col. John McCausland, at the Narrows on the New River twenty miles north of Dublin, had about fourteen hundred, and Brig. Gen. John Echols, twenty miles farther on at Lewisburg, had a brigade of infantry, three regiments (22nd, 23rd and 26th, all Virginian) numbering about sixteen hundred. Although his roster sheet showed eight batteries of artillery, only three, Capt. George Chapman's, Jackson's under 1st Lt. Randolph Blain and Capt. John McClanahan's, actually had guns. One Parrott rifle, six three-inch rifles, six howitzers and three twelve-pound Napoleons—sixteen among them.

If several artillery units had no guns, the cavalry, like the 23rd Virginia under Col. Robert White, had no horses. The troopers were here, there and everywhere between Dublin and Beverly, and the horses were farmed out all over Tazewell County in search of fodder.

Breckinridge exhorted his troops as only he could, instituted two a day drills, and told the commanders to gather thirty days rations and prepare to send their baggage to the rear. Where they were going, and at the rate they would be going, they would not need it.

Mid-March—Department of West Virginia

So benighted was this Union backwater Department of West Virginia, which had not even existed prior to Robert Milroy's defeat at Winchester the previous June, that some considered any change was for the better. Among them was the young captain of artillery Henry A. du Pont, of the Delaware du Ponts, who wrote to his mother Louisa on March 19 that "we are all much pleased with the change."

And, in the continental tradition, Sigel could swagger about and direct drill and observe discipline in a soldierly enough way as to inspire confidence, however false the grounds. Like a boy playing soldier, he drew colored diagrams of his command down to the regimental level. And he very quickly lived up to his reputation as a political general by summoning cronies to his side. First came an old friend and classmate from Karlsruhe Military School, Brig. Gen. Max Weber. Next came thirty-eight-year-old

Maj. Gen. Julius Stahel-Szamvald, a Hungarian officer who had dropped his last name for American audiences and whom Strother referred to contemptuously as "a traveling clerk . . . a . . . fancy cavalry officer who has never done anything in the field and never will."

Nonetheless, Sigel named Stahel not only chief of cavalry but chief of staff.

The maps revealed the immensity of the department: it encompassed all of West Virginia, all of Maryland west of the Monocacy, all of the Shenandoah Valley and Loudon County in Virginia. What the maps could not show adequately was the soaring ridge and plunging river valley landscape that made all movement difficult for the 23,400 men and 118 pieces of artillery scattered through it, principally along the tracks of the Baltimore & Ohio Railroad, the protection of which was the department's chief and continuous duty.

A considerable force of thirty-five hundred was with Maj. Gen. George Crook in the Kanawha Valley. Sigel had difficulty training his men because there seemed no way to bring them together without stripping the department bare, but he hoped to have twenty thousand ready for "active service in the field" when spring again brought movement to the great Valley.

Mid March—Mount Crawford, Rockingham County, Virginia

Brig. Gen. John D. Imboden was the official confederate guardian of the Shenandoah Valley, since July of 1863 commander of the Valley District, everything west of the Blue Ridge and north of the James, a separate territory created especially for Stonewall Jackson.

Imboden had felt so little menaced since the previous summer that he held the territory with only three thousand men. His command was lean and also lithe, having only one brigade of infantry, Brig. Gen. Gabriel C. Wharton's (which was away on loan) and a six-gun battery under John McClanahan. The rest were horse soldiers, ready to move instantly and move far: the 18th and 23rd Virginia Cavalry and 62nd Mounted Infantry, as well as John H. McNeill's Rangers, and two small but colorful cavalry battalions that often operated like partisans and were commanded by officers from Maryland, Thomas Sturgis Davis and Harry Gilmor of Baltimore.

The forces had been in camp at Mount Crawford during the winter, stirring themselves in December to fend with Gen. William Wood Averell. As Imboden put it, to "shy him off" from the valley during his cavalry raid.

Breckinridge found this Imboden to be an unusual man. A native of the valley, he was, as he said, "acquainted with nearly all its leading inhabitants, and perfectly familiar with the natural features and resources of the entire district." He looked as though he could have dealt cards on a river boat with a neatly trimmed mustache and fine, thick hair that rose from his forehead in a combed and polished wave. But he knew his own abilities, and declined to be considered for a major generalship with the remark that "I really feel that I have as high military rank as I am qualified for."

He was comfortable as well with his own little private army, the 18th Virginia Cavalry. It was made up of companies from Imboden's own 1st Virginia Partisan Rangers; his brother George was colonel in command. Brother Frank, big six-foot, three-inch Frank, was captain of Co. H. Brother James was a sergeant major. And a fifth brother, seventeen-year-old Jacob, was with the cadet corps at the Virginia Military Institute in Lexington, handy in case of need.

For all the family around him, John Imboden felt he was being worn away by the years of warfare, and confided to a friend that "I have but few intimate personal friends, and the number is perhaps growing less as I grow older."

For the foreseeable future, however, he would not have time to worry about it. Like everyone else in Breckinridge's department, he was nervously watching the build-up of union troops at Martinsburg and in the Kanawha Valley. He wrote to Robert E. Lee, "I have little or no doubt that we shall have a big raid here some time this month."

Battles & Leaders

BRIG. GEN. JOHN D. IMBODEN

Tuesday, March 29—Cumberland

Maj. Gen. Edward O.C. Ord arrived in Cumberland with a letter from U.S. Grant outlining his strategy for the spring offensives. While he would be attacking Lee along the Rapidan in May, Crook would lead a column south of Charleston to attack the Virginia and Tennessee Railroad, turn eastward to destroy the works and mines at Saltville and Wytheville in southwestern Virginia, and then move northward, on Staunton. A second column would assemble at and move south from Beverly in West Virginia and hit the V&T tracks near Covington, in western Virginia, and then turn eastward, toward the Shenandoah and Staunton and beyond, to the important base of Lynchburg. This column would be commanded not by Sigel but by Ord, although

Battles & Leaders

GEN. WILLIAM W. AVERELL

Sigel was asked to assemble eight thousand infantry and fifteen hundred picked cavalry with ten days rations and be ready to move in ten days. Beyond that, his role that was of supply sergeant. He would carry necessary supplies up the valley to meet Crook and Ord at Staunton.

As Grant told Gen. William T. Sherman, probably with a laugh, "If Sigel can't skin himself, he can hold a leg whilst some one else skins."

But Sigel would not hold the leg. Infuriated that Grant had made his plans "as though I did not exist at all," he informed Ord, "I don't think I shall do it."

Despite his reputation as "one of the kindest and most unselfish of men," Ord flew into a rage at such insubordination and asked Grant to relieve him of command.

Sigel, for the record, noted he had done his utmost to comply with Grant's orders, but he could find only sixty-five hundred troops that could be spared, and the roads to Beverly were all but impassable, even for empty wagons, because of incessant rains. According to Sigel, Ord "became so diffident in regard to the whole matter that he asked . . . to be relieved."

Wary of a political storm just prior to the spring campaign, Grant reluctantly complied with Ord's wishes on April 17. On that same day, Lt. Col. Orville E. Babcock arrived in Cumberland with a new plan, this one to be worked out with Sigel's assistance.

What they did was remove Ord's column. Crook, with added men from Brig. Gen. Jeremiah C. Sullivan's division and "the best mounted cavalry," was to advance as scheduled from the Kanawha Valley, but now with ten thousand men. To command the cavalry, Crook would have with him, by Grant's order, William Averell, who had led four thousand cavalry in a sweep behind North Mountain in December. Prevented from entering the Shenandoah Valley, Averell instead struck the V&T line sixty miles west of Lynchburg and destroyed army stores. It was the kind of thing Grant liked. It worked.

Sigel himself would assemble a full division of infantry, the remainder of Averell's cavalry and five batteries of field guns at Martinsburg and then move south before May 2, through Winchester to Cedar Creek, threatening the valley.

Grant, with more important things on his mind, said, "All right, but be ready to go by May 2."

As that day approached, Sigel became more and more withdrawn and inaccessible. Those around him noticed "something reserved, even morose, in his mien." Openly paranoid, he continued replacing Kelley men with his own. Strother's criticism was scathing, calling Sigel "a military pedagogue, given to technical shams and trifles, . . . narrow minded and totally wanting in practical capacity."

That was demonstrated beyond any doubt when Sigel, wanting two cavalry regiments returned to him from Grant, sent his request not to Grant but to Congress! Halleck intercepted the telegram just in time and showed it to Grant, who exploded.

Battles & Leaders

GEN. GEORGE CROOK

Congress or no Congress, he told Sigel to get the hell in line.

Wednesday, April 27—Martinsburg, Inspection

At two P.M., per orders for the day, Sigel's army, which on this date comprised six regiments of infantry and eight of cavalry, stepped out onto the parade ground at Martinsburg for what was billed as a "grand review" prior to the commencement of the campaign. It turned out to be, quickly enough, more of a comic pantomime.

"Such a time as we had finding our places in the line," bemoaned one participant, "was never seen before."

An enraged Sigel was appalled by the confused milling about. He considered two of his three Ohio regiments—James Washburns's eight-hundred-man 116th and Horace Kellogg's seven-hundred-man 123rd—to be "entirely useless." The third Ohio unit, Lt. Col. Gottfried Becker's seven-hundred-man 28th, was above censure; it was entirely German and made of troops who could speak so little English they could not communicate with the other regiments.

He found the cavalry to be "in wretched condition."

When the 18th Connecticut marched in on the following day, Sigel looked it over and gave it a vote of no confidence.

It was difficult for the union sympathizers of Martinsburg to understand the union army commander after his final remarks to them, in which he praised "the greatest general of the age"—Grant, of course. No, Robert E. Lee!

With all of that, Sigel's army stumbled out of Martinsburg about nine A.M. on April 29, three hours late, and moved slowly southward to Bunker Hill, eleven miles away, which they required no less than eleven hours to reach.

Friday, April 29—Washington, D.C.

Halleck to Sherman:

> It seems but little better than murder to give important commands to men such as Sigel.

II.
The Valley
of Virginia

Sunday, May 1, 4:30 P.M.—Winchester

Once more a union army was marching into Winchester, that cockpit of war in the lower valley, fought over a dozens of times, with two major battles in the spring of 1862 and summer of 1863 recorded as union defeats. This was an uncertain, footsore army led by a German martinet and politician who had drilled his men the previous day for three hours on legs and feet made weary by negotiating the macadam surface of the valley pike, packed gravel that was anything but uniform and presented a hard and often sliding footing under marching men.

As they toiled southward from the camp at Bunker Hill, going up the valley as it gradually rose toward distant Lexington, the day was fair but the landscape chilling. The gravel road led straight between stone walls and rail fences and the high sun cast a shadow from small stones and markers in the fields beyond; William Hewitt of the 12th West Virginia may have exaggerated, but not much, when he noted that there was "not a mile of the whole route ... which there could not be seen a soldier's grave."

Four miles north of town the pike led past Stephenson's Depot, where Milroy had met disaster the previous June, opening the way to the Potomac and Gettysburg. The horrid spectacle of the partially buried and still unburied remains of some of their former comrades quieted the columns filing by. No doubt this beautiful valley was a place of fear for men in blue.

May 1, Afternoon—Valley Pike Near Bunker Hill

As Sigel's army marched away over the southern horizon, he appeared—the legendary Gray Ghost, he of the firm mouth and calm and even gaze—Col. John Singleton

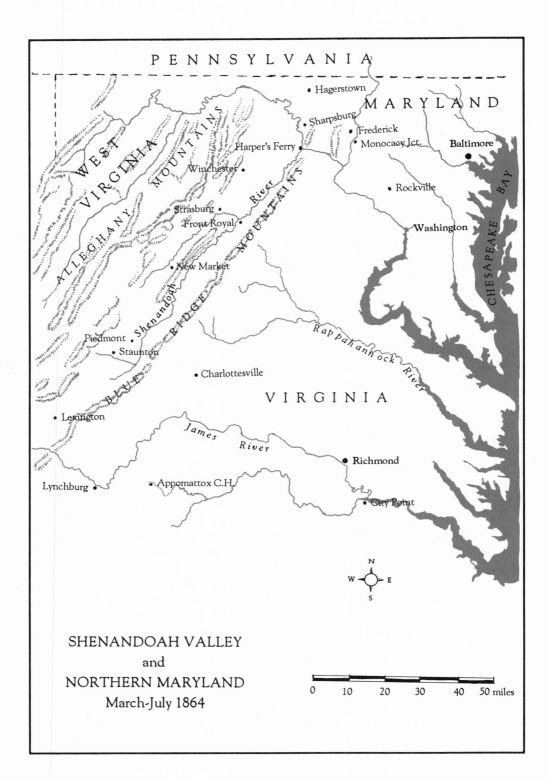

SHENANDOAH VALLEY
and
NORTHERN MARYLAND
March-July 1864

Mosby. He had spent the first years of war riding with J.E.B. Stuart, until in January 1863 he organized his own command, technically the 43rd Battalion Virginia Cavalry, but actually Mosby's famed and feared partisan rangers. No action could take place in the northern valley or mountain passes without his presence; it was a region he held so securely that it was known as "Mosby's Confederacy."

The Confederacy's borders ran from modern Bluemont (known before 1900 as Snickersville) for twenty miles down the crest of the Blue Ridge to Linden, then east for twenty miles, exactly along the route of modern I-66, to modern route 15 beyond The Plains, then north along the Bull Run Mountains to Aldie, and northwest to Bluemont. Rich and rolling piedmont encased in

USMHI-MOLLUS

COL. JOHN SINGLETON MOSBY

mountains, it encompassed what is now the blooded horse country of Loudon County, including the wealthy communities of Middleburg and Upperville.

From here, Mosby's men ranged west across the northern Shenandoah and east to the southern outskirts of Washington. They were a constant intrusion across the Potomac, raiding as far as Poolesville and Offutt's Cross Roads, modern Potomac, Maryland.

Now, in the late afternoon, south of Bunker Hill, as a train of eight supply wagons labored after Sigel's army, Mosby and a band of ten men materialized and took them—thirty-four horses and twenty prisoners were sent to the rear under guard.

When a new detachment of twenty men galloped up, Mosby led them north to Martinsburg, which they reached after the dark. Making prisoners of the guards, they found the officers' tents at Sigel's former headquarters empty, the men gathered somewhere to party (relieved that Sigel had finally gone?). They took the officers' clothes and fifteen horses and vanished into the night.

May 1—Dublin Depot

Lee to Breckinridge:

It will be impossible to send any reinforcements to the Valley from this army.

Monday, May 2—Mount Jackson

Before breaking camp at Mount Jackson, Imboden ordered Gen. William Harman at Staunton to have the reserves of Augusta, Rockbridge and Rockingham counties at the ready. That meant all men over forty-five years of age and young men between sixteen and eighteen. Gen. Francis H. Smith, commandant at the Virginia Military Institute, was alerted that his corps of about 250 cadets, all under eighteen, might also be called. Imboden then led his forces northward, toward Woodstock. His effectives present in the column numbered 1,492 and he had a few hundred down the valley scouting both in front of or behind Sigel. He was confident that his little command was "in splendid condition for hard service." They would, before long, see all of the hard service they wanted.

Signal stations on mountain peaks far into western Virginia reported to Breckinridge and Imboden on the movements of Crook and of Averell, who was at Logan Court House with eleven infantry regiments and eight of cavalry. They so threatened Breckinridge's rear and flank that it might prevent him from moving quickly to Imboden's aid should Sigel attack. They knew they had to divert Sigel's attention, threaten his own rear, and the best and fastest way to do that was to strike at the B&O. For Imboden that meant getting along with that other legendary partisan leader, Capt. John H. McNeill. Imboden may not have thought himself smart enough to be a major general, but he knew enough about how armies are supposed to work that he had hauled McNeill before a court-martial in Staunton to try to break him of the habit of accepting deserters from other units, no questions asked. Now every man counted, and such niceties as desertion were put aside so long as a man was willing to fight.

Tuesday, May 3—Evening, Old Field

The sun goes down at different times and places in West Virginia; light lingers along the spines of the ridges that angle for hundreds of miles northeast-southwest long after it has been extinguished in the deep valleys.

McNeill's camp was at Old Field, in the valley of the South Branch of the Potomac, between three-thousand-foot South Branch Mountain and Mill Creek Mountain—a valley so cramped it was called The Trough. To the west lay the wash-board landscape of Patterson Creek Mountain, then Patterson Creek Valley, then three-thousand-foot Knobly Mountain and then a steep, long decline down the western Allegheny front, called Great Backbone Mountain, into the valley of the North Fork of the Potomac.

The way between Old Field and the Potomac Valley was through twelve-hundred-foot mountain passes like Greenland Gap and Doll's Gap through Knobly Mountain.

It was after dark in the valley at Old Field when McNeill gave the signal and his column of sixty moved out at a trot, quickly swallowed in the ink of the valley night. Riding at their head, "Hanse" McNeill looked like a hell-fire preacher with glinting eyes and a beard so dark and fulsome he seemed to be peering over a broom. They were to be met along the way by Capt. John Peerce with a column of partisans, and together, guided by starlight, they would pass through the western passes toward the North Fork, which enclosed the railroad tracks that connected the Union east and west.

May 3, Midnight—The Army Moves

Gen. U.S. Grant:

> Soon after midnight, May 3rd-4th the Army of the Potomac moved out from its position north of the Rapidan, to start upon that memorable campaign.

Wednesday, May 4, Evening—Dublin Depot

Jefferson Davis to Breckinridge:

> Information received here indicates the propriety of your making a junction with General Imboden to meet the enemy on his movements toward Staunton. Communicate with General R.E. Lee and General Imboden.

Clearly, the choice had been made between defending the Department of Western Virginia against Crook and Averell and rushing to the north to help Imboden defend Staunton against Sigel. Lee's left, as he faced Grant across a Rapidan suddenly afire with combat, was to be the primary consideration. Lee was convinced that Sigel intended to cross the Blue Ridge and hit his flank. He must be stopped.

Breckinridge immediately wired Lee for instructions and considered the difficulties of a rapid move northward. The rail line that ran southwest from Staunton terminated in about fifty miles at Jackson's River Depot (modern Clifton Forge) from which his army could move quickly on trains. The problem was getting there. Echols, at Lewisburg, was thirty-five miles from the depot, and Wharton, whose brigade had come in only three days before and been sent up to relieve McCausland at Narrows, was more than sixty.

Once at Staunton it was back to foot cavalry, since the rail line ran east, over the Blue Ridge, and Sigel lay north, down the valley—a long way north, another two days' march up to Woodstock, where Imboden was last seen.

After nine hours, Lee's reply came in at five A.M.: "Hit Sigel."

Thursday, May 5, Dawn—Piedmont, West Virginia

McNeill sent Peerce's command of ten men down the road to Bloomington, a mile west of Piedmont, West Virginia, with orders to apprehend any east-bound train. McNeil then crossed country to the rail line above Piedmont and caught the first west-bound train and sent it into Piedmont with a demand that the garrison, a detachment of the 6th West Virginia, surrender. He followed the train to ensure compliance.

The strategy of the war in the east can be interpreted as a game of railroads and trains that could not only move entire armies to gain tactical advantages but also carry the bulk of the material necessary for fighting. Thousands of men were set into motion time and again for the sole purpose of cutting a railroad line, and rail road centers and junctions were apt to be battle sites.

Now McNeill had one such center at his mercy—Piedmont, with its roundhouse and machine shops and storage sheds. In the railyard he found no less than fifteen engines. Nine were wrecked where they stood, but six others were steamed up and launched, one after another, racing down the track westward, like a series of insane bowling balls hoping to hit something, anything. The buildings and sheds were set ablaze, and Piedmont was becoming an inferno as a union column, alerted by wire, made an appearance and opened fire with their lone field gun, killing one man.

A messenger from Peerce said a line of retreat through Bloomington was open. When McNeill arrived, he found Peerce holding a train with two cars of federal troops, all armed, none with ammunition. The capable Peerce had galloped down the platform and captured 115 troops by himself, armed only with his pistol.

They paroled the prisoners, burned the trains and vanished back into the mountain passes. Within hours, the secretary of war in faraway Washington, Edwin Stanton, knew what had happened and blamed Sigel for it, just as Imboden had hoped.

May 5—Winchester

Sigel could not have cared less about Piedmont. He declared it "insignificant." His mind was churning with other, more important matters—like avoiding real war by playing at war in Winchester. On May 5, in the very hours that Warren and Ewell were locked in mortal combat at the Wilderness, the first great battle of 1864, Sigel was playing games in the fields outside of town. His mock battle was conducted in movements that were unfamiliar to his infantry brigade commanders, colonels August Moor and Joseph Thoburn, and baffled his regimental commanders.

Sigel and his staff choreographed, often in orders impossible to understand, the advance and retreat and charge of the eight infantry regiments hither and yon over the fields for no divinable purpose.

"There was never anything seen half so ridiculous," said one participant. "It was the funniest farce ever witnessed anywhere," said a soldier in James Washburn's 116th

David Hunter Strother
Virginia State Library & Archives

GEN. SIGEL REVIEWS HIS TROOPS

Ohio, and he should have known, since the 116th was advanced to the right, then to the left, and finally sent off on a charge that Sigel forgot to end. They went so far off the field that officers had to be sent to find and retrieve them.

Col. George Wells's 34th Massachusetts fared even worse. It was still on the field, pretending to skirmish "over fences, through swamps, across ravines and in woodland," long after dark, since no one had bothered to order it back. When it was finally retrieved, Wells was furious. When orders were posted that the game would be repeated on May 6, Wells feigned illness and turned over his command to Lt. Col. William Lincoln, saying "I've lost all interest in it, and in the service. . . . I won't serve under such fools."

The feeling was general that "it bred in everyone the most supreme contempt for General Sigel and his crowd of foreign adventurers."

But those who still could laugh at the absurdity of it all must have howled at Lincoln's crack when he heard the day's summary: "Killed, none. Wounded, none. Missing, the 34th Massachusetts Infantry."

Unfortunately for him, Wells's resolve did not stick, and when the 34th finally moved out of Winchester on May 9, he was again at its head.

Friday, May 6, 6:00 A.M.—Lewisburg

As mist still shrouded the mountains roads before them, John Echol's brigade formed up at Lewisburg for the march north. Their commander had stressed the gravity of the situation in the valley, and they knew they had no time to lose.

Echols was impressive mentally and physically. A graduate of both VMI and Washington College in Lexington and the Harvard Law School, he had been a practicing attorney for twenty years when war came. He was huge by army standards— over 250 pounds on a six-foot, four-inch frame. Someone that big and bright stands out in any crowd, and Echols had been elected colonel of the 27th Virginia in the Stonewall Brigade and led that regiment from First Manassas until Kernstown in 1862, where he was wounded. Recovered, he was now a brigadier with sixteen hundred men in one regiment—Col. George S. Patton's 22nd Virginia—and two battalions, Lt. Col. Clarence Derrick's 23rd Virginia, and Lt. Col. George Edgar's 26th Virginia.

He was determined to take those men to Staunton before Sigel could get there; Breckinridge had promised him that trains would be waiting at Jackson's River Depot. But Echols was not well. His heart was bothering him, and he feared the exertion might kill him, but he kept it to himself, and his men stepped out in good spirit.

May 6, Dawn—Narrows

Gabriel Wharton had twice the distance to cover to the depot at Jackson River. His cavalry units, about four hundred fifty men under Col. George Smith in the 62nd Virginia Mounted Infantry and a small but agile force of sixty-two, Capt. Charles Woodson's Co. A, 1st Missouri Cavalry, had to move at the pace of his infantry, three hundred fifty men of the 30th Virginia Battalion under Lt. Col. J. Lyle Clark and seven hundred in John Wolfe's 51st Virginia Regiment.

Breckinridge saw them off from Narrows, on the New River, and then trotted ahead with his headquarters staff at a fast pace. He knew that Grant had crossed the Rapidan. If Sigel moved now, they would be too late to relieve Lee.

Saturday, May 7—Winchester

Sigel could be nonchalant about Piedmont, but sooner or later he would have to do something about McNeil, and Mosby, too. It was Kelley's opinion, back in Cumberland, that McNeill had to be killed, captured or driven out of the country before "we can expect . . . safety."

On Saturday, Col. Jacob Higgins led the five hundred men of the 22nd Pennyslvania Cavalry and the 15th New York Cavalry toward the passes through North Mountain and Wardensville in the Lost River Valley. From there the road led west, through Baker to Moorefield and the South Fork valley and Old Field, where he hoped to find and defeat McNeill. His movement would clear the army's right flank as it moved south. Sigel also intended to clear his left, "especially against Mosby," and for this he sent Col. William H. Boyd with three hundred "select horsemen" eastward into the Luray Valley.

May 7, Evening—Jackson's River Depot

The Virginia Central had reached the banks of the Jackson River in 1861, after years of track-laying from Charlottesville through the Blue Ridge to Waynesboro and across the Valley to Staunton. The intention was to take it west to the Ohio, and a roadbed had been graded for that purpose, but years would now pass before it was utilized.

Echols's brigade had marched steadily for two days to cover the thirty-six miles from Lewisburg, and they were relieved to reach the depot and the anticipated train ride to Staunton.

Breckinridge had covered the sixty miles from Narrows in the same two days, and he was waiting at the depot with the worst of tidings: no train.

He was going to ride on toward Staunton, and he advised Echols to rest his men and follow along next day.

That evening Wharton's weary column made camp in a mountain meadow some twenty miles to the south. Since leaving Narrows, they had walked forty miles in two days.

Sunday, May 8, Early Afternoon—Massanutten Signal Station

Imboden's signal corps lookouts on twenty-three-hundred-foot Shenandoah Peak, the northernmost knob of Massanutten Mountain, had a magnificent view to the west, beyond North Mountain to the billowing ridges of western Virginia; to the east, across the Page Valley to the Blue Ridge; and to the north, toward the distant Potomac Valley and Maryland. In the foreground, they looked directly down upon Strasburg.

Early on Sunday afternoon they picked up the distant movements of cavalry columns, estimated at an exaggerated one thousand men each, one moving westward over North Mountain toward the Moorefield road (modern route 55) and the other passing eastward through Front Royal and taking the road toward Chester Gap in the Blue Ridge (modern 522). It was Higgins and Boyd.

Quickly apprised of this, Imboden could hardly believe his good fortune. Sigel was obviously testing both his flanks before moving south. That might take days. Imboden could hold up Sigel's entire army if he could interfere with these cavalry columns "as far from Strasburg as possible and delay their return as long as possible."

He called Col. George Smith of the 62nd Virginia Mounted Infantry and told him to keep his five hundred men in front of Sigel. Then, as a precaution against any spying "Union man," he spread the word that he had to move camp closer to North Mountain to find better fodder for his horses. In the next few hours, Imboden quietly collected a strike force—his own 18th Virginia Cavalry under his brother George, along with McNeill's Rangers and two of McClanahan's guns.

Leaving Woodstock around four P.M., the fast-moving column vanished in the falling light toward a narrow pass in North Mountain that they called "The Devil's Hole" and we know as Wolf Gap.

May 8, 4:00 P.M.—Near Moorefield

Just as Imboden was setting out from Woodstock, his quarry, Higgins's troopers, pulled up to water their horses a few miles from Moorefield. As the tired men dismounted, shots rang out from the nearby mountainside. Several horses reared in pain, and one man fell dead. The column quickly remounted and rode into Moorefield.

They went through the little town carefully, in a tight column. On the other side, in a field, their horses peacefully grazing, were McNeill's partisan rangers. As Higgins formed up, drew sabers and pistols, McNeill's men scrambled up a hillside, firing a volley as they went.

Higgins seemed content to have run them off, since he broke off the pursuit and camped at Moorefield that night and the entire next day as well.

May 8—Staunton

Breckinridge reached his destination on Sunday evening, after three days in the saddle and a ride of 145 miles. He was relieved, and probably flabbergasted, to find that Sigel was still in Winchester. What could he be waiting for?

News from the south was of an entirely different color. Crook was closing on Dublin. Brig. Gen. Albert Jenkins and Col. McCausland were going out to meet him and promised to give him a "warm reception." But it was clear the bargain had been a bad one for the department. As its commander rushed to aid Lee by supporting Imboden in the Valley, the mountains and tracks behind him were falling to an advancing enemy.

Monday, May 9, 7:00 A.M.—Winchester

Finally, Sigel began to move. At daybreak the cavalry started south in two long columns. Behind them tramped the infantry, in growing heat and dust. By early afternoon they had covered the fifteen miles to Cedar Creek, where the advance guard came upon a platoon of Confederates in the act of destroying the bridge. They were unable to save it, and the army had to fall out and wait for the engineers. While they were waiting, the tired men were drilled by Sigel.

May 9—Cloyd's Mountain

Jenkins and McCausland had entrenched the top of Cloyd's Mountain north of Dublin to protect the road to the important railroad bridge over the New River. On Monday morning George Crook sent one of his brigades on a flanking movement through thick woods and another, led by a future president, Col. Rutherford B. Hayes, straight up the hill and into the teeth of the guns—a courageous act that pried the defenses open and led to fierce hand-to-hand combat that lasted almost two hours and cost more than five hundred confederate and seven hundred union casualties, including Albert Jenkins, who died within weeks of his wounds.

Now in command, McCausland led his survivors through Dublin and out to the bridge, but he could not hold it, so he crossed to the other side to await the inevitable.

May 9, Evening—Goshen

Goshen Pass, where the Maury River, known as the North River in 1864, cuts a four-mile-long gap through the Appalachians Mountains, is one of the loveliest places in Virginia, its towering rock walls flaming in this season with mountain laurel and rhododendron. This well-known passage to the west was used by John Lederer as early as 1670. Nearby was a large Indian burial mound. The old frontiersman and pal of Daniel Morgan, Maj. John Hayes, was buried on Jump Mountain—overlooking the mound—at his request, it was said, so he could see if the Indians rose with the rest on Judgement Day.

But Echols and his brigade were interested in neither the history nor the scenery, only in provisions and forage—or, rather, the lack of them—as they went into camp at Goshen. In two days out of Jackson's River Depot, they had walked forty-five miles and still had thirty-five to go to Staunton.

May 9, Night—Jackson's River Depot

A mile from the depot, Wharton's exhausted brigade could walk no farther and fell into camp while he rode ahead to locate the promised train. Like Echols two days earlier, Wharton felt his heart sink when he discovered there was no train. But he showed real pluck in his report to Breckinridge in Staunton: "We will reach Staunton," he wired. No modifiers.

Fortune smiled on his courage when, in the middle of the night, the unmistakable sounds of an arriving train woke the brigade, and they soon were pouring into the cars—Wolfe's and Clark's Virginians and Thomas E. Jackson's three twelve-pound Napoleons and a Parrott rifle. Woodson's company of Missouri cavalry and George Smith's mounted infantry would have to follow as best they could. But with Wharton on the way and Echols at Goshen, it was beginning to look as though Breckinridge

GEN. GABRIEL WHARTON

would have something to fight with other than his file clerks.

May 9, Night—The Valley Pike

The lone horseman galloping up the valley turnpike through the windy dark of a spring night, following the moonlight on the road, was a piece of work. The pampered son of wealthy Baltimore business-man Robert Gilmor III, Harry Gilmor had learned to ride in the emerald pastures around his country home north of Towson. But he had turned to the unpampered life of home-steading in Wisconsin and Ne-braska before the war brought him back—in time to be ar-rested in Baltimore for his southern sympathy. Upon his release he rode his favorite mare, Bessie, down into Virginia and joined Turner Ashby's famous Cavalry in 1861. (Never, however, did he ride Bessie in a fight, "for fear of getting her killed . . . she was so foolish.")

During the Antietam campaign in 1862, Gilmor had been captured and jailed again, this time for five months. Once more he donned confederate gray and fought at Brandy Station, where both Fitzhugh Lee and J.E.B. Stuart singled him out for mention. He was provost of Gettysburg during the battle, and later was allowed to form his own unit of partisan rangers, the 2nd Battalion of Maryland Cavalry.

There was a lot about war he seemed to like; he once compared an action in which he almost lost his life to "a good fox hunt." At that—the chase, the hunt, the kill—he was superb, dashing among enemy horses, dashing across a swollen river, dashing through the night to a dawn attack.

Sometimes too dashing. Gilmor had been in Staunton for a negative reason. During a guerilla raid a few months earlier on a Baltimore and Ohio train west of Harper's Ferry, one of the passengers, a Judge Bright of Indiana, complained that his watch had been taken. When told that his men had robbed the passengers, Gilmor offered to shoot anyone caught in the act.

Lee ordered the charges of not respecting private property aired at Staunton in April.

Even though a panel of cavalry officers had fully acquitted Gilmor of "every charge and specification," he still had to await Lee's personal review.

One of Breckinridge's first acts after reaching Staunton was to call up Gilmor and review the trial records himself. He told the cavalier to get back down the valley to his command, to get in Sigel's rear and harass him in every way possible.

This inspired in the superb equestrian Gilmor the highest compliment he could think of. He called Breckinridge, a "most thoroughbred gentleman."

Gilmor left Staunton at two P.M. on May 9 and rode down the valley to New Market, forty-five miles away. He was overjoyed to be back in the game.

USMHI-MOLLUS

MAJ. HARRY GILMOR

Tuesday, May 10, Dawn—the Moorefield Road at Baker

Higgins, returning to Sigel, had been riding since nine the previous evening. During those dark hours, John Imboden had carefully set a trap, positioning his command along the slopes of a mountain gap outside Baker and leaving a few riders out on the road as bait. Just at daybreak, Higgin's advance, from the 22nd Pennsylvania Cavalry, came into view, and the bait sprinted toward the gap. The union column charged after them for perhaps a quarter of a mile. As they galloped past, Imboden opened fire.

The shock of the ambush ignited one of the most insane retreats of the war. Higgins and a nine-man escort dashed away first, not toward Winchester and Sigel but northward, up the road to Rio and Kirby and Romney. The 22nd Pennsylvania Cavalry and 15th New York came galloping after them at breakneck speed, followed by a whooping 18th Virginia Cavalry. Up the dirt roads they dashed, "nip and tuck," as one rider recalled, "head up and tail up." He called it "the hardest, longest race during this war."

They ran all morning, not lagging until noon, when exhaustion forced them to stop and attempt to rest and water the horses. But in ten minutes Imboden was after them again. They lost their wagons, some burned, others abandoned. They threw away equipment and weapons to help them travel faster. They killed horses that could not keep up.

They ran for almost nine hours until panting and sweating and trembling they reached Romney in mid-afternoon, where they thought themselves at last safe. There McNeill hit them and captured the town in the matter of a minute, and the federal cavalry ran north for another nine miles, crossing the suspension bridge over the South Fork to Springfield.

Here Higgins rode off alone to Old Town, across the Potomac in Maryland. His disgraced troopers trailed after him, completing a rout and leaving behind them for *sixty miles* a trail of broken and captured wagons with their ammunition and supplies, fifty wounded, five dead.

May 10—Cumberland

Kelley to Sigel:

> Rumor says that your cavalry were attacked this A.M. near Wardensville by a superior force under Imboden and McNeill and were totally routed.

May 10, 9:00 P.M.—Virginia Military Institute

Rat-a-tat-tat. Rat-a-tat-tat. The urgency of the drum's quick tattoo awakened every sleeping cadet. They scrambled into clothes and ran down to the parade ground to form into ranks. They stood breathlessly at attention as the adjutant read a message by lantern light, which cast long shadows up the castle-like walls of the great barracks. It was from Gen. Breckinridge in Staunton. The union army under Sigel was moving toward Staunton and was even then as far as Strasburg. Said the commander of the valley's defense to the cadet corps: "I would be glad to have your assistance at once."

Cadet John S. Wise recalled that "the air was rent with wild cheering at the thought that our hour was come at last."

Wednesday, May 11—Belle Grove Plantation

Two miles below Middletown and a half mile off the pike, Isaac Hite's colonial estate, Belle Grove, stood along Cedar Creek. Sigel made his headquarters there. The old house of dressed limestone raised four chimneys over a broad hip roof; although only a single story on a high basement, it gave Strother the impression of being "baronial in size." Tents were pitched on the front lawn "under an immense lilac hedge in full bloom. A most beautiful and fragrant shade."

Belle Grove represented a different America, one that was rapidly sinking in this conflict of brothers. The rebellion against England was still forty-four years in the future when Joist Hite led sixteen families out of Pennsylvania in 1732, bound for the Valley of Virginia. Crossing the Potomac at Pack Horse Ford, they moved south to Winchester and settled on land owned by Thomas, Lord Fairfax. A few years later they came to know Fairfax's surveyor, a lean, freckle-faced, red-headed sixteen-year-old from the lower Potomac named George Washington.

George Bowman married, successively, two of Joist Hite's daughters, Anna Maria and Mary, and built for his family a stockaded stone house near Cedar Creek. One son served as a colonel in the Revolution and two others made the long journey west with Lewis and Clark. In 1794, not far away from Fort Bowman, later called Harmony Hall, Joist's grandson, Maj. Isaac Hite, built Bell Grove for his bride, Nelly Conway Madison, James's sister, and it was here that the future president and *his* bride, Dolley, spent two weeks of their honeymoon.

It was a house with much history. "[I]n the garret," said Strother, "we found barrels of old papers . . . some autograph papers, receipts, and business letters of Thomas Jefferson and George Washington. . . . As the house was only occupied by a poor family of tenants, our officers helped themselves to these literary mementoes."

May 11, 6:00 A.M.—The Valley Pike, Strasburg

The army got under way at six A.M., as armies are supposed to do, and crossed the repaired bridge over Cedar Creek, with cavalry preceding, as before. Almost at once the chatter of small arms sounded from up the road as Sturgis Davis's tiny troop of Maryland horseman, twenty-six in all, annoyed Sigel's cavalry advance. Other shots were heard during the long, hot march as bushwhackers took pot-shots of the passing lines. Finally, around four P.M., Sigel captured Woodstock simply by walking into it.

And there a major prize awaited him. In the telegrapher's office, gathered for Imboden, were all of Breckinridge's dispatches. As Sigel read them, he knew that his enemy was still in Staunton, at least two days' march to the south, and with a force not yet fully assembled. He knew he could reach the Luray road at New Market before Breckinridge could stop him, and by turning east be over the Blue Ridge and on Lee's flank in a matter of a few days. No one could stop Franz Sigel from winning the American Civil War but Sigel himself.

Faced with these enormous possibilities for attack, Sigel hunkered down at Woodstock and awaited Breckinridge's next move.

May 11, 7:00 A.M.—Lexington

From a distance they looked like any other body of soldiers, clad for battle in confederate gray, muskets shouldered, 222 VMI cadets marching out in four companies, with two three-inch rifles pulled along by fine-looking horses (actually Margaret Preston's carriage team, among others, impressed only that morning), and the fellow leading them, Col. Scott Shipp, though somewhat pudgy, looked martial enough with his glowering eyes and straight back.

May 11—Staunton

While the battle of Spotsylvania was raging to the east and Gen. J.E.B. Stuart was falling mortally wounded in a clash with Sheridan at Yellow Tavern, Breckinridge was counting his blessings. The surprise train from Jackson River was on its way, scheduled to arrive by two P.M. with Wharton's advance infantry. Echols, who had walked the whole way, would be there by evening.

When the VMI cadets came in, he had already decided, he would move north.

May 11, Late at Night—Mount Jackson

Imboden had been riding almost nonstop for eighty miles from the Lost River Valley when he found his command back in Mount Jackson, to which George Smith had prudently moved from Woodstock. He immediately wired Breckinridge in Staunton that he had left his regiments behind as they were "much jaded, and camped tonight on the head of Lost River." He promised they would be on line in the valley by late afternoon of the following day, by which time Sigel would again be coming forward, his cavalry advancing directly toward Mount Jackson.

"By what hour can I expect support here?"

Thursday, May 12, 1:00 A.M.—New Market

Harry Gilmor reached New Market and found a place for a few hours sleep. He awakened before dawn and went to Imboden's headquarters on Rude's Hill, asking for the 2nd Maryland. Half of the command had been left in Staunton, but the best mounted, eighty-five men in all, were up front, he was told, holding up Sigel's army. Their picket line was spread clear across the valley between Massanutten and North Mountain, and they could not be assigned other duty until the 18th and 23rd Virginia cavalries came in from Lost River that afternoon. Gilmor went to William Ripley's farm near the pike and sent word for his men to meet him there as they came off the line.

May 12, Midafternoon—Staunton

At the Bloody Angle of Spotsylvania, one of the fiercest battles in American history was raging all this Thursday. In the valley, in Staunton, a footsore but game Corps of

Cadets reached Breckinridge's headquarters after two forced marches of eighteen miles each. They came into town stepping smartly to the fifer playing "The Girl I Left Behind Me," but the grizzled veterans of Wharton's brigade taunted them about war being for men. Scott Shipp set up camp a mile from town and restricted his corps to their tents—happily enough for them to be out of the rain that had been falling since morning.

May 12, 4:00 P.M.—Hawkinstown

Around fifty or sixty of his troopers had come in to Ripley's farm by four P.M. when Gilmor heard "sharp firing at a short distance," and Sturgis Davis charged up and told him there were fully five hundred union cavalry coming their way. Gilmor could do nothing but drive in their pickets and retreat under heavy fire. "They ran us handsomely for two miles . . . into Hawkinstown," where Gilmor decided to counter and suddenly gave the order: "'By fours, right about wheel, march—charge!' and we went at them with a yell."

But he quickly realized that these were good cavalry he was against, for Maj. Charles Otis and his 21st New York anticipated the counter-charge. Otis wheeled his advance, just as Gilmor had, and greeted Gilmor's charge with a volley from his carbines. Once again, the Marylanders had to fall back.

A mile beyond Hawkinstown, Gilmor and three men hid behind a small house and waited for Otis's van to pass. When it did, Gilmor "sprang out into the road and fired at the foremost man, wounding him. The next shot brought down a horse; and I began to retreat, firing as I went."

Then occurred one of those slow-motion events that happen under extreme pressure. As Gilmor wheeled about fifty or sixty yards up the road to give another shot, he saw "an officer dismount, seize the carbine from a man, rest it on a post, and take deliberate aim at me. I *felt* he was going to strike me, wheeled, struck the spurs into my horse, and dashed off at full speed . . . it seemed to me an age until the carbine cracked . . . the ball struck me in the back, within two inches of the spine, on the upper part of the right hip bone. The force with which it struck nearly knocked me over the front of my saddle, and made me deathly sick; besides, I felt a sort of paralysis of the spine, and right hip and leg."

He somehow kept his saddle, expecting "to fall every minute" and hoping to regain his column. Just outside Mount Jackson, Gilmor began to recover somewhat and found his troop there, waiting in good order. When Otis came up, he looked the situation over and withdrew, content to have run Gilmor off.

Only then did Gilmor examine his wound. He realized with relief that the bullet had struck the crupper of his saddle and hit him a glancing blow; "the bullet had cut clean through everything, and laid the flesh open to the bone," but it was far from mortal. He remounted with difficulty and made his way to Mount Airy, which Imboden called "the celebrated Meem plantation," home of militia general John G. Meem, at the foot of the Massanutten, where he felt "at home, for such it had always been to me, like my father's house in Maryland." Mrs. Meem and other ladies were anxiously waiting on the lawn as Gilmor rode up, "quite stiff and in much pain but so anxious to hide the place that I dismounted almost as well as ever and walked into the house without assistance."

However, Mrs. Meem, sitting near the door, saw the ragged hole in the major's pants and "soon after I heard a roar of laughter and some one say, 'That is a funny place for Major Gilmor to be shot in!'"

Friday, May 13, 6:00 A.M.—Staunton

Breckinridge later wrote, "Being convinced that the enemy was advancing in comparative confidence, I determined not to await his coming but to march to meet him and give him battle wherever found."

At daybreak on Friday morning, he went looking.

May 13-14—Theatre of War, Fort Valley, Page Valley

A soldier walking south along the banks of the Shenandoah River from its junction with the Potomac at Harper's Ferry would find the wall of the Blue Ridge on his left the entire way. He would see occasional niches in the wall, where a valley opened toward a pass or, as it was then called, a gap. The first gap was Snicker's, above Snicker's Ferry on the river, then Ashby's, then Manassas, through which a road ran down to Front Royal, then Chester, on a more southern Front Royal road, then Thornton, above Sperryville.

Ahead, he would find the vast valley of the Shenandoah, with its checkerboard fields shadowed by passing clouds, opening between the Blue Ridge and the long wall of North Mountain, the first great ridge of the Alleghenies to the west.

But this immense valley is itself divided by a long and narrow mountain, which also divides the river. Thus the soldier could continue southward at Front Royal, along a river now called the South Fork, or he could walk westward from the little town, along the second arm of the river, the North Fork, which, too, would soon carry him southward. Between these parallel streams, as between the tangs of a tuning fork, rises the singular mountain, Massanutten. Its northern end seems to ride like a huge prow over Front Royal. Shaped like Noah's ark, Massanutten stretches southward for fifty miles to Port Republic.

Thus are two valleys formed—the eastern, narrower one between the Blue Ridge and the eastern flank of Massanutten, and the western, wider one between the western flank of Massanutten and North Mountain. The eastern valley is called Page or Luray, and the western is the great Shenandoah, with its stairstep of towns rising southward.

There is a geographical secret tucked away in the Massanutten itself. As the soldier might follow the North Fork from Front Royal around toward Strasburg, Woodstock,

Mount Jackson, New Market and points south, he might notice a stream, Passage Creek, issuing from the mountain to join the North Fork, just as he passed under the brow of Shenandoah Peak. Were he to turn into Passage Creek and cross its tight little meanders twenty-six times, he would find a narrow cleft, beyond which opens a lovely and green little valley, four miles wide, called Powell's Fort or, simply, Fort Valley.

Powell had been a counterfeiter who made silver coins from a local ore, and there were furnaces in the valley.

So secure is this entrance from a military view that George Washington intended in extremity to take his Continental Army into Fort Valley, where they could have held out for years.

Beyond the "Mouth," as the cleft was called, a road led past log cabins and barns to hamlets like Burner's Springs, a three-story resort with adjacent cabins with fireplaces operated by Solomon McIntruff and his "presentable" daughters.

Burner's Springs was a favorite of Harry Gilmor, who appreciated not only the quarters, the provender, but also the ladies and the fact that "it was impossible to surprise me there." Indeed, once inside Fort Valley, the only exits were back through the Mouth or over difficult mountain trails, unsuitable for large forces, eastward into the Page Valley and westward toward Woodstock and Edinburg in the Shenandoah.

May 13, Morning—Mount Jackson

When Sigel's forward pickets probed toward Imboden's advance near Mount Jackson, the tired troopers who had just relieved Davis the previous afternoon gave way and fell back down the pike toward New Market. They stopped four miles north of the town, at Rude's Hill, a hundred-foot height that commanded the road northward.

Imboden wired Breckinridge that he would hold at Rude's Hill until Sigel brought up artillery and infantry. When could he expect to see the army?

Even then, that army was on its way, "all in high spirits," with Wharton's mighty marchers in the lead. As clouds rolled in from the western mountains, however, rain began to fall in torrents. During the afternoon there was a terrific crack of lightning, and the column seemed to explode where the 23rd Virginia was marching; eleven bodies were hurled outward from the blast, several badly burned and none to fight again in this campaign.

May 13—Fort Valley

Imboden was worried about the whereabouts of the column of cavalry somewhere to his east. It had been two days since Col. William Boyd had left Sigel's army with his three-hundred-man 1st New York (Lincoln) Cavalry and two mountain howitzers and disappeared eastward, toward the Blue Ridge. He could cross as far north as Ashby's Gap, or at Manassas Gap, or farther south at Chester Gap, and thence down the road to Sperryville, west across Thornton Gap into Luray, and then across New Market Gap to appear in force exactly on Imboden's right flank.

Or he might have cut the corner a lot closer and slipped into the Page Valley and even now be in Luray, ready to move on the unready Confederates.

Imboden asked Gilmor to take a look in that direction. Helped into his saddle at Mt. Airey, Gilmor led his troopers over the Massanutten into Fort Valley. At Caroline Furnace he heard that Federals were down the road at Burner's Springs. He came upon the tracks of a troop of horses, not Boyd's three hundred, but perhaps fifty, he thought. His estimate was correct.

Sigel also wanted to know where Boyd was and knew where he wanted him, back at Woodstock. He had sent out a troop of 20th Pennsylvania Cavalry under Lt. Norman H. Meldrum to find Boyd and bring him back. Meldrum was taking a short cut through Fort Valley. As Gilmor followed his tracks, the day dimmed and dark clouds threatened one of those valley summer rains that come quick, pour steady and stay awhile.

May 13, 4:00 P.M.—New Market

Imboden to Breckinridge:

If [Sigel] comes on, I will fight him here.

But Sigel was not coming on. His army was still squatting in Woodstock, and by late in the day his advance had even pulled back from Mount Jackson. He was going the wrong way.

May 13, 4:00 P.M.—New Market Gap

It was one of the war's more memorable sights. Just as Imboden was wiring his determination to fight, soldiers in camp on Shirley's Hill, southwest of town, noticed a glimmer of movement in Massanutten's mountain pass, but their observations were dimmed by the falling rain. Soon afterwards, troopers of the 23rd Virginia Cavalry on Rude's Hill, looking southeast toward the mountain, were greatly surprised at the sight of hundreds of horsemen in blue filling up the Luray road through the gap. "We sat and watched as they came down the mountain, only a couple of miles from our camp."

It was Boyd. He had slipped east of the Blue Ridge over Chester Gap, had crossed back into Page Valley by way of Thornton Gap and was now moving confidently toward New Market over Massanutten, as though fully expecting to find Sigel's entire army cheering him on.

Imboden exploded into action. The boy Elton Henkel ran to the front of his house when he heard the racket and saw troopers riding down the pike "neck and neck, the horses hooves hammering the pike, the scabbards of sabers rattling, and the cavalrymen giving the rebel yell." Reaching Strayer's Corner, the troopers turned eastward and galloped off toward Massanutten, dragging two of McClanahan's field guns.

May 13, 4:00 P.M.—*New Market Gap*

Scanning the misty scene with his field glasses, Boyd could look down on the whole Shenandoah from well south of New Market, north to beyond Rude's Hill, where there was an encampment of several hundred troops. The pike was alive with movement, a train of wagons with white cloth tops and a column of soldiers moving south from Mount Jackson. What troops were they? He called his officers into conference.

They are the enemy, was the consensus.

"No, they are ours," said Boyd.

But, if ours, where are they going?

"Moving south from Mount Jackson to New Market. Sigel is on the move against Imboden."

But, if that is so, why does he have his baggage wagons *in front* of his infantry?

Boyd scoffed at such common sense and sent Capt. James Stevenson on ahead, down the mountain, to scout. Presently, Stevenson reported that a column of cavalry and a section of artillery were moving rapidly toward the base of the mountain below them.

"Sigel's," said Boyd. "Push on."

At the bridge over Smith's Creek east of New Market, Stevenson came upon a few union pickets dressed in blue, who melted away. The head of his column was no sooner across the bridge than Stevenson saw the bluff ahead explode with fire and he heard a shout: "Now we've got the damned Yankees! Give 'em hell!"

It was Robert White's 23rd Virginia Cavalry, lying in wait. As they fired into the milling column ahead, Boyd tried to form a charge against them but he realized it was bad terrain, with the bridge as a fatal bottleneck, and started to retreat up the Luray road.

There Imboden and the 18th Virginia Cavalry and McClanahan's guns were waiting for him. They had slipped across Smith's Creek south of the bridge and moved into position between Boyd and the gap.

They opened fire. Trapped and desperate, the Germans from New York ganged up in a charge against the 18th Virginia, and eighty of them crashed through the firing line. The rest of the troop galloped through the opening, but as they went up the steep incline toward the gap, McClanahan's guns began blowing horses and riders off the road, causing those behind to veer into the thick woods.

Stevenson, trying to rally his men, was losing his saddle. As he stopped to tighten it, Boyd rode past him, shouting that the enemy was right behind them. Stevenson threw himself on his horse as a party of the 18th Virginia rode up, yelling at him to surrender. He fired his pistol at them and hung on as his horse struggled upward. A bullet hit his scabbard. Another hit his blanket roll. Another knocked his hat off. "[O]ur men were . . . running in all directions on foot, their horses . . . given out or

USMHI-MOLLUS

MAJ. GEN. JULIUS STAHEL

got fast among the rocks . . . some of the horses rushed along wildly, without riders, the saddles under their bellies."

Then the heavens opened. The rains came in gushing sheets, the road turned to slippery mud. Men tumbled into thick pine woods and lay panting, hoping for dark. And when dark came, the extent of the disaster was evident—another complete, dumfounding rout. Boyd's entire column was gone, broken into knots of shivering survivors, who huddled in the drowned woods or felt their way through the dark forest toward Fort Valley and the way back to Sigel's army, knowing that in the morning they would be pursued all the way to Woodstock.

That night Imboden wired Breckinridge: "They are wandering in the mountain tonight. . . . Boyd was wounded. We have his horse and he is in the bush."

In four days, in actions fifty miles apart, Imboden, a man who knew his limitations, had obliterated Higgins and Boyd, Sigel's flanking cavalry, eight hundred men, a third of the entire union cavalry force.

May 13, Night—Fort Valley

Gilmor found his quarry, Meldrum's messenger force, keeping out of the weather in a large barn, the horses tied around it, and a few pickets huddled miserably over damp fires which went out as the rain began to pour again. Knowing "the place could have been taken," Gilmor opted not to pay the price in casualties. In the morning, though, as he waited at a crossroad to confront him, he found to his astonishment that Meldrum had at daylight taken the mountain path out of Fort Valley toward Milford in Page Valley, a "frightful" road.

With thirty picked riders, Gilmor followed. From the crest he went even farther ahead with his favorite officer, Lt. William H. Kemp, and five others. They came to the farm of an agitated man named Santemeyer, who told them that the Federals had taken two of his best horses and beaten him on the head for protesting. Gilmor and a small party sprinted far ahead of his column and found the union cavalry dismounted at a ford across the South Fork of the Shenandoah River, held up by very high water.

"This," said Gilmor, "was the worst managed affair I ever undertook. I must have lost my senses; for the moment we came within seventy-five yards of them, I and Kemp, who was as crazy as myself, dashed down among them with a yell, calling upon them to surrender."

A brave union sergeant, seeing his companions raising their arms, cried out, "Don't surrender to five men!" and Kemp pointed his revolver and killed the man. The rest leaped to their horses

GEN. AUGUST MOOR

and began to fire their pistols. "[T]he whistling of the bullets brought me to my senses," said Gilmor. "I wheeled and got out of there as fast as my horse could carry me."

He noticed, however, that the leader of the band was "mounted on a beautiful black stallion." The chase led them through a "deep and ragged ravine," at the end of which Gilmor found the rest of his column coming up with a yell. The ravine was so narrow that he couldn't turn his horse around until he had dashed out into a field.

The federal cavalry retreated toward the river, where some tried swimming across. After a "short and bloody" fight, Gilmor counted two of the enemy killed, nine drowned, eleven men and thirteen horses captured, and seven horses killed—"among them the lieutenant's noble black."

Saturday, May 14, 9:00 A.M.—Stahel's Headquarters

Both generals Sigel and Jeremiah Sullivan were already there when Col. Moor arrived for a conference with Gen. Stahel. Moor commanded the First Brigade, three Ohio regiments and one from Connecticut, about twenty-five hundred men, and expected to receive orders concerning them. Stahel explained to him, however, that he was to conduct a reconnaissance of Rude's Hill in force, using, in addition to his own 123rd Ohio, the 1st West Virginia and the 34th Massachusetts, regiments that normally reported to Col. Thoburn. Although believing this to be "a great mistake," Moor played the good soldier—though his troops considered him a poor one—and assented to the order.

Rude's Hill? Moor confessed that he "had no knowledge of the place at all," and his request for a map was greeted by blank stares. Perhaps scouts should be sent forward to guide the way?

Maps? Scouts? "Nobody," Moor later recalled, "could furnish either."

May 14, 10:00 A.M.—New Market

The word that Imboden had waited so long to hear finally came. Breckinridge was nearing New Market and would reach Lacy Springs, ten miles south, by noon. Leaving George Smith of the 62nd in charge, Imboden saddled his horse and headed down the pike to meet his commander.

May 14, 11:00 A.M.—Woodstock

He had no scouts ahead, but August Moor had a cloud of cavalry with him as he marched in falling rain out of Woodstock with Jacob Weddle's seven hundred West Virginians and George Wells's five hundred Bay Staters. Riding ahead were 170 troopers from the 20th Pennsylvania Cavalry and 130 from the 15th New York Cavalry, both under Col. John Wynkoop of Stahel's Second Cavalry Brigade. Up the road at Edinburg, they picked up Horace Kellogg's seven hundred Ohioans. A cavalry force of six hundred men under Maj. Timothy Quinn, made up of units from the 1st New York (Lincoln), 1st New York (Veteran) and 21st New York cavalrys, had left that morning for Mount Jackson. Moor had guns—four with Alonzo Snow's Marylanders and two with Chatham Ewing's West Virginians.

In fact, Moor had a full third of Sigel's entire force—2,350 men. Sigel had divided his army and was sending a third of it ahead by twenty miles. David Strother, agonized by the debacles with Higgins and Boyd, thought Sigel was "courting destruction" and commented acidly that Sigel was now "sending detachments of his force so far from the main body as to be destroyed in detail."

May 14, Noon—Lacy Springs

Breckinridge appeared right on time, welcomed Imboden, congratulated him on the victory over Boyd and invited him to stay for dinner, which was being prepared in a nearby house. Both men were certain that Sigel's army was still in repose in Woodstock.

May 14, Early Afternoon—Rude's Hill

North of Rude's Hill lay the wide, flat, sometimes marshy meadowland known as Meems Bottom, where the valley pike crossed the North Fork of the Shenandoah on a wooden bridge that was a constant target of fighting throughout the war.

When Quinn arrived early in the afternoon, he saw that George Imboden's 18th Virginia Cavalry had torn out the bridge's planking. The confederate lines were clearly visible on the crest of the hill to the south, beyond the river. Quinn quickly repaired the bridge and sent fifty men across, then sixty, then brought up his entire command of six hundred.

Almost as a gesture, George Imboden launched an attack down the hill, quickly brushed aside by Quinn. With only one hundred men, Imboden had to fall back.

May 14, Afternoon—Lacy Springs

Imboden and Breckinridge were still at table when a courier rushed in with the news: twenty-five federal cavalry had taken Rude's Hill and were pressing toward New Market. Smith had formed a line of battle just north of town to protect Col. Imboden's retreat. Even as he spoke, the leaden sky reflected to earth the distant booming of artillery fire and return fire.

As Gen. Imboden mounted his horse, Breckinridge asked him to "hold New Market at all hazards until dark." Then, if forced, he should fall back four miles, and Breckinridge would bring his army up in support.

May 14, Afternoon—Road to Rude's Hill

As the sodden hours and miles slogged by, the mood of Col. William Lincoln of the 34th Massachusetts, riding in the advance, reflected that of the whole force. "The air is oppressively hot and close; the men are faint. . . . Mount Jackson comes into sight; is reached; is passed; still our leader cries only 'Forward!' Still on; beyond support; past hope of help, . . . as if we left hope behind."

They encountered a forlorn and bedraggled soldier walking down the road toward them. They could hardly believe it was Col. Boyd, wishing himself dead, walking to Woodstock from the disaster at New Market Gap. Behind him came a straggling parade of defeated cavalrymen, some with tuckered-out mounts, most on foot.

Forward!

With every mile taking them farther and farther from any possible support from Sigel, they would walk, on this steamy afternoon, for seven hours, with one break of ten minutes, and cover twenty-one miles, almost, but not quite, to New Market.

May 14, 4:00 P.M.—New Market

Arriving on a panting horse, Imboden saw instantly that Smith had done well. His line ran from halfway up the hillside northwest of town, across the pike, and east toward Smith's Creek, disappearing into some woods. McClanahan's guns were well positioned on the extreme left, high on Manor's Hill, several hundred feet higher than the federal batteries—Snow and Ewing, who had been brought forward—with which it was exchanging fire. Riding to the battery, Imboden had a full view of the field to Rude's Hill. He saw no infantry and concluded there would be no attempt to "dislodge us that evening." He was wrong.

May 14, Evening—Woodstock, Sigel's Headquarters

As the sound of the cannon reverberated down the echoing valley, magnified by the lowering clouds, Sigel had grown anxious and again divided his command, sending Maj. Henry Peale's 18th Connecticut forward to Edinburg, to back up Moor. All afternoon a stream of local people had been passing through Woodstock, getting out of harm's way and telling Sigel that Breckinridge had arrived with thousands—fifteen thousand, twenty thousand! He was going north into Maryland.

An aide found Sigel pacing back and forth "as restless as a chained Hyena." Finally word came from Moor. He had taken New Market. That was it. That opened the way for an advance to Mount Jackson and control of the Meems Bottom bridge. Sigel issued orders: the army would move at five A.M. on the following day, Sunday, the 15th of May, toward Mount Jackson and New Market.

May 14, 9:00 P.M.—Lacy Spring, Breckinridge's Headquarters

Imboden's message was all too brief. Federal forces were in New Market. Breckinridge issued orders: the army would move, not at five A.M., as originally planned, but at one A.M., "with the intention of attacking the enemy early in the morning."

Night clouds of white mist piled up, raced under darker ones, formless but for the suggestion of a figure, vast, sky high, hooded, great and grey and grim. Men in bivouac looked up briefly and looked away.

III.
The Battle at
New Market

Darkness, rain, and exhaustion caught up with Gen. Imboden about four miles south of New Market, and he simply camped by the side of the road and went to sleep. In the still of the night, about two hours before dawn, he was awakened by the light of a tin lantern shining in his face and "was immediately accosted by Gen. Breckinridge. He informed me his troops would reach that point before sunrise."

Behind the general, his troops were slogging in sucking mud through the darkest night any of them could remember. The veterans that afternoon had been having fun taunting the cadets: "You better get home to mammy!" But there was more to it than age and innocence. This was, by and large, an army of Virginians. Between them Wharton and Echols had six Virginia regiments. They were mainly farm boys from hard-scrabble backgrounds, who would go back to that life if they survived the war. The cadets had the look and the reality of privilege. Among them was the son of the recent governor of Virginia, John Letcher; Breckinridge had two cousins in the corps; both Secretary of War Seddon and Gen. Jubal Early had nephews there, as did Robert E. Lee himself.

Nor was there that much difference in age between the veterans and cadets. The gray-eyed John McClanahan was from Victoria, Texas, but the boys in his Staunton Horse Artillery, McClanahan's Battery, were Virginia lads, many in their late teens and early twenties. Cpl. Samuel Shank of the 62nd Virginia, which was assigned to companion the cadet corps, had fought at Gettysburg. He was sixteen years old.

It was more than soldierly joshing, then, when Wharton's soldiers inquired whether the boys wanted rosewood caskets lined with satin. One waved a pair of shears toward the cadets, asking which ones wanted a lock of hair sent home to his family after the Yankees killed him. Others took the impending battle far more seriously. With a

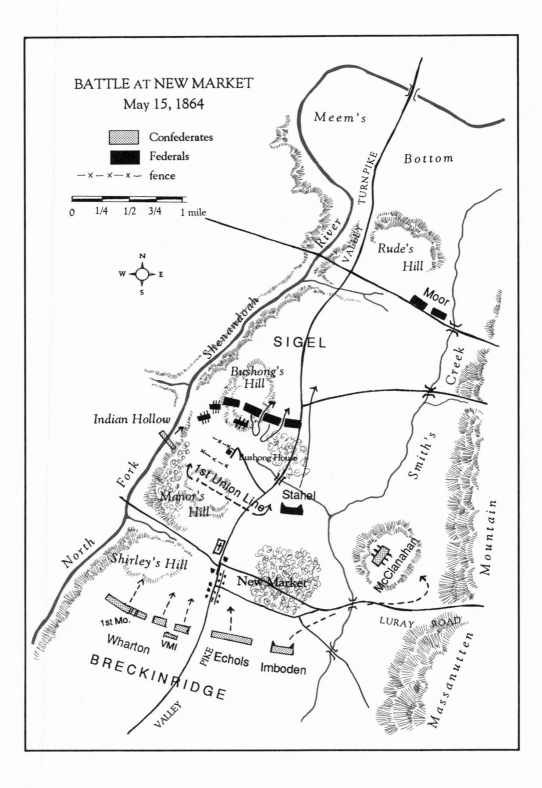

BATTLE AT NEW MARKET
May 15, 1864

Confederates
Federals
— x — x — x — fence

0   1/4   1/2   3/4   1 mile

solemn face and a chill, cadet Jacqueline Beverly "Bev" Stanard told his friend John Wise he had a feeling he would not be marching back with him. And it was not a jest when Shipp instructed them, as they were falling into marching column at one-thirty A.M., that when they engaged the enemy, no one was to stop but the stretcher bearers.

May 15, Dawn—Shirley's Hill

Imboden described for Breckinridge the ground ahead. Before them was the valley, framed by nature: to the east, Smith's Creek and the wall of Massanutten, and to the west, the North Fork, running parallel to the mountain. Thus both flanks for both armies were "out of bounds," protected by the streams.

Dividing the scene, the pike ran straight ahead, north and south, passing through the small red-brick town of about seven hundred inhabitants. New Market boasted two streets and a crossroad where the road to Luray ran east and a road to the North Fork ran west through a ravine called New Market Valley. Between the pike and the North Fork, from a few miles south of town to a few miles north of it, four hills occupied the rolling land—Williamson's, Shirley's, Manor's and Bushong's—with vales between them, and, between Shirley's and Manor's, the ravine. The land to the east sloped down to Smith's Creek at the foot of the mountain.

Thus the ground determined that the battle would be fought west of the pike, from hill to hill, man to man, artillery clearing for infantry in a classic cover and attack advance.

Believing that Sigel was moving toward him, Breckinridge made defensive arrangements. Because infantry would soon bog down in the low and marshy ground to the east of the road, Breckinridge sent Imboden with the seven hundred mounted cavalry troopers to hold that ground, backed up by McClanahan's four guns. He then looked for the highest ground on which to place the rest of his guns, sixteen counting VMI's two, all under Maj. William McLaughlin. He found it on Williamson's Hill to the west of the road. Between the guns and Imboden, he drew his defensive line—on the left and along the slope Wharton, then Echols across the pike, with the cadets and the 26th Virginia Battalion in reserve, which some resented since they felt they were tending the corps; it was common knowledge that Breckinridge told Imboden he would keep the cadets and the 26th together, and he "did not wish to put the cadets in if he could avoid it."

They waited. An hour went by. Nothing happened.

Breckinridge asked Imboden to draw Moor from his position in the town by feinting advance and retreat, but Moor would have none of it. He stayed put, waiting for help.

Moor may have thought he was still facing Imboden alone. On the previous afternoon, after Quinn had taken Rude's Hill and pressed on toward New Market, Moor's panting column had finished its forced march of twenty miles and come up behind Quinn. The batteries of Alonzo Snow and Chatham Ewing had arrived on the scene and been put to work at once, exchanging from Bushong's Hill with McClanahan, who was positioned on Shirley's Hill, two miles away. The booming of the guns seemed to summon the armies toward battle. Moor's column marched past the roaring artillery, the 34th Massachusetts in the lead, formed into line of battle and advanced toward New Market. By six P.M. it was over for the day. Imboden had appeared and, by Breckinridge's order, pulled his forces out of town.

Now Moor was still lodged there.

May 15—Sigel's Headquarters, Woodstock

David Strother: "While the troops were moving . . . General Sigel came out of the house at full run toward the camp of teamsters and Negro servants. His high boots were hanging down and altogether he cut a very absurd figure as he ran, exclaiming at every jump, 'By Got, I vill catch dot dam tief.' It seems that in the moving he had lost a favorite brandy flask and was accusing everyone he met of stealing it. Our hostess, Madame Cheney, appearing at the time was flatly accused of stealing it. She was horrified and indignant. She got Captain [Thomas] Putnam aside in a room and, after stating her wrongs, lifted her hands to heaven exclaiming, 'May the vengeance of the Almighty follow that man. He has wounded my feelings too deeply for healing or apology.'

"We at length got off in the mud and rain as gruff and uncomfortable as we could well be."

May 15, 11:00 A.M.—Shirley's Hill

Hill to hill. Breckinridge sent a section of McLaughlin's guns forward from Williamson's Hill to the top of Shirley's Hill, and then he himself rode up to watch the result as they opened on the town. After a time, he called Imboden and other officers to the top of the hill and they conferred.

"I have offered him battle," Breckinridge said to George Edgar, in command of the 26th Virginia, "and he declines to advance." He turned to Imboden and said, "We can attack and whip them here," and added, perhaps to posterity, "and I'll do it."

As soon as McLaughlin positioned eight guns at the very top of the hill and opened fire on the federal line, Breckinridge ordered everyone else "to advance as rapidly as possible."

Wharton's command (John Wolfe's 700-man 51st Virginia, J. Lyle Clark's 347-man 30th Virginia) came down from Williamson's Hill, formed in column, amd marched rapidly up the pike toward New Market. At Shirley's Hill, they marched by the left flank and began to ascend the back slopes. To the right of the 30th, Breckinridge now moved the 448 men of Smith's 62nd, the left wing of which was the company from Missouri, the seventy men of Co. A of the 1st Missouri Cavalry under Capt. Woodson, also on foot.

That filled in the front almost to the pike. Breckinridge continued the line with the 315 men of White's 23rd Virginia Cavalry, also dismounted, and, some two hundred yards farther south, Patton's 580-man 22nd Virginia and Derrick's 579-man 23rd Virginia.

Behind the center were placed Shipp's 226 cadets, to the right of the 425 men of Edgar's nursemaid 26th Virginia, now complaining loudly about their reserve position, saying the "bombproofs" next to them would not fight.

By eleven A.M., this line of not quite thirty-seven hundred men was ready to advance. Imboden, with his seven hundred troopers and four guns, had already started out for the bridge over Smith's Creek.

Breckinridge had a job for him, to slip across Smith's Creek and follow it around the union left flank to Mount Jackson, where he was to destroy the bridge and the union escape route. He sent identical orders across New Market gap to Gilmor, who was back at Caroline Furnace. Breckinridge told Gilmor he expected to fight Sigel that morning, and that he would whip him and capture his whole army, trains and all, if Gilmor could get that bridge.

May 15—With the Baggage Train, Valley Turnpike

As he stood at his assigned position with the wagons, with orders to retire to a place of safety if the army retreated, seventeen-year-old cadet John Wise, whose father was with Lee at Petersburg, gathered the four-man guard and told them:

"Boys, the enemy is in our front, . . . but I have an enemy in my rear as dreadful as any before us. If I return home and tell my father that I was on the baggage guard when my comrades were fighting, I know my fate. He will kill me with worse than bullets." Whereupon the four cadets turned the guard over to the wagon driver and ran for the front, one to his death.

May 15, 11:00 A.M.—Manor's Hill

In New Market, Maj. Gen. Stahel had arrived with the rest of the union cavalry and, ranking Moor, took command. He soon was a spectator to Breckinridge's occupation of Shirley's Hill, which commanded the town from the southwest, and quickly decided he would have to abandon it and withdraw toward Sigel, who had been advised to come forward with all due speed.

Stahel selected for his defensive line a stone wall that ran beside a road from St. Matthews Church, at the northern end of town, up the slope to the top of Manor's Hill. Moor's regiments—the 123rd Ohio, 1st West Virginia—took position behind it. He put his guns at either end, Snow in the cemetery behind the church and Ewing all the way over the crest of Manor's, in a stand of cedar trees overlooking the little vale along the North Fork the natives called Indian Hollow. Near Ewing was John

Wynkoop's cavalry with the 34th Massachusetts in support.

Wharton thought he could take the wall and Moor's line, but he was concerned that his command, while marching down Shirley's and up Manor's hills, would be caught in the cross-fire from the union batteries. So he issued orders that when the advance came his men were to run, not march, to the bottom of the hill. Once in the ravine they would be safe from Stahel's guns because their fire could not be depressed to that low an angle.

May 15, 11:05 A.M.—Wharton's Swarm of Bees

Not quite on the hour, the army began to move. The complainers of the 26th felt somewhat better when Co. B was posted all the way on Wharton's left, in cedars near the North Fork, and told to hold that flank. Then Lt. Col. Clark's 30th Virginia jumped up and ran down the hill toward the federal pickets in the ravine between the hills.

At that point the rest of Wharton's brigade rose and went forward over the crest of Shirley's Hill and downward "rather pell-mell," as instructed. Watching from Manor's crest, Ewing's gunners followed Clark's skirmishers as they leaped and dodged down the hill. Their eyes then went back to the crest of Shirley's, and with a start they saw that the long fence across the hill was moving, and with a greater start realized that what they were looking at were not fence rails but bayonets. An army was coming at them "like a swarm of bees."

"A cold chill run down our backs," said the gunner.

May 15, Noon—The Earth Rocked

Somehow Shipp did not get Wharton's word, or got it wrong.

As the VMI fifer struck up a tune, Shipp ordered, "Attention! Battalion forward! Guide—center-r-rr!" and Sgt. Maj. Jonathan Woodbridge stepped out forty paces to the front of the colors as directing guide. Cadet Oliver Evans, who was a major target at six-foot, two-inches, unfurled the institute's colors, and "every cadet in the institute leaped forward, dressing to the ensign."

The cadets, along with the 26th Virginia, came over the crest of Shirley's Hill and started down through the rain, not at a run, as Wharton had ordered, but, as he said watching them come, "as tho' going to dress parade."

It was, in its own way, splendid as well as stupid. From the ravine, George Smith and his 62nd watched them advance and were moved to admiration. "Nothing could have been handsomer than the perfect order in which they moved."

But the shells that could not reach the ravine rained now on the hillside, and gaps began to appear in the cadets' line. A smoking hole appeared where cadets Govan Hill, Charles Read, Pierre Woodlief and James Merritt had been marching a moment before. Miraculously, though all were injured, none were killed.

John Wise, who had left the wagons far behind, left a vivid memoir of his experience, running down the green slope, "answering the wild cry of our comrades as their musketry rattled out its opening volleys," and then "a sound more stunning than thunder. It burst directly in my face; lightnings leaped, fire flashed, the earth rocked, the sky whirled round. . . . My gun pitched forward, and I fell upon my knees. Cadet Sergeant William Cabell looked back at me sternly, pityingly, and called out, 'Close up, men,' as he passed. I knew no more."

Even as gaps in their line opened, the cadets closed up like veterans and came on into the valley and safety. There Breckinridge let his troops rest for a half hour while he prepared for the assault on the next hill, Manor's.

As McLaughlin's shells burst around Moor's West Virginians and Ohioans, regiments new to the battle began arriving on the field in response to urgent messages sent back to Sigel. A battery came rumbling up the pike, Capt. Alfred von Kleiser's 30th New York, which unlimbered its guns along the road, a few hundred yards behind the Manor's Hill line. Von Kleiser was not much older than the VMI cadets; he had been at war since he was eighteen and in command of the battery at age twenty-one; the unit was one of those attracted into service by men like Sigel; it was entirely German.

More guns came clattering toward the developing field of battle—the six three-inch rifles of Capt. John Carlin's D Battery, 1st West Virginia Light Artillery. After spending the early spring in Hampshire and Hardy counties skirmishing with Thomas Lafayette Rosser's confederate cavalry, they had joined Sigel at Martinsburg, feeling confidently veteran. This was to be their first large scale battle, a disastrous distinction they would soon discover.

Soon Maj. Peale's 350 men of the 18th Connecticut came up the pike after a forced march from Edinburg and arrived on the field as the artillery barrage was in progress. They began to take a position near von Kleiser, but Moor sent them forward, on the line, to the right of the 123rd Ohio and 1st West Virginia. No sooner were they there than Clark's Virginians came bounding down Shirley's Hill before them, and Peale ordered Capt. William Spaulding to take out two companies and take on the rebel skirmishers in the valley.

There was a brief and fierce struggle. Spaulding was shot in the stomach and carried back to the wall. His question—"Are they driving us?"—was his last.

May 15, Noon—Sigel Arrives

Breckinridge rested Wharton's Brigade for a half hour while he studied the advance on Manor's Hill. To do this, he rode into New Market, "looking every inch a fine confederate general," and climbed to the roof of Martha Henkel's house. No sooner had he poked his head out than the roof was peppered with bullets. He then remounted and rode west to St. Matthews. As he paused to observe, a shell hit a gatepost a few feet away, but failed to explode.

He had seen enough. He moved ten guns—George Chapman's four twelve-pound howitzers and two three-inch rifles, a section of two three-inchers under Lt. Carter Berkeley of McClanahan's Battery, and the two VMI three-inch rifles—from Shirley's Hill, down to the pike, and up to the outskirts of town, where they would have a good angle to fire on Moor's line as his infantry advanced.

He left that infantry pretty much as it was, with the exception of moving the entire 26th Virginia into the line on the far left, leaving the cadets alone in reserve.

All of this had taken an hour.

Around noon, Wharton's men knocked over a fence along the valley road and started up Manor's hill through rain that was now falling harder. A figure appeared, leaping downward, yelling that the Yankees were one hundred yards ahead. One of the cadets remembered how ". . . our nerves were strung . . . our breath coming short . . . waiting the crash of musketry." As they took their turn advancing behind Wharton, Cadet Evans somehow managed to catch his flag staff with its drenched and limp colors in a cedar limb and had to struggle through the deeply muddied field to catch up.

As they struggled upward, the cadets passed three veterans wounded by federal artillery fire, lying on the field; one raised his hat: "Charge them, boys! Charge them! Give the Yankees hell!" In another instant there was the noise, glare and smoke of an exploding shell and all three bodies, hats and all, had been dismembered.

George Wells of the 34th Massachusetts watched Wharton coming and found himself admiring the discipline of the troops: "Nothing could have been finer." But he also watched his men begin to fall as "the air filled with bullets and bursting shells."

Stahel decided to pull back. Not only was he about to be overwhelmed on the field, he expected Sigel and reinforcements to arrive. As he prepared to withdraw, orders came to him—to withdraw. They were from Sigel, and within minutes the commanding general himself "came on the field with a great flourish."

As if in response, the confederate "front line cheered and rushed to the attack at a run." Without an order or command to do so, the 123rd Ohio got up and ran, leaving the 18th Connecticut isolated. Ewing quickly pulled his guns out and up the hill. Just as Wharton was about to close on the West Virginia and Connecticut infantry, Sigel gave orders and the Federals scrambled up the hill as Stahel's cavalry rushed to cover the withdrawal. Thus, when the cadets finally reached the crest of Manor's Hill, expecting to find combat, they were surprised and relieved to find Wharton in possession and the Yankees in retreat.

As Sigel approached the field, Maj. Theodore F. Lang, who had been supplying him with courier information all morning, asked him where the rest of the army was. Sigel replied they were coming. Lang looked down the empty road. In fact, much of Sigel's army was strung out behind him for many miles and goodly parts of it, Gottfried Becker's 28th Ohio and James Washburn's 116th Ohio and Henry du Pont's six-gun battery, would not see New Market on this fateful day. The last order they had received from their general was to move to Mount Jackson.

May 15, 2:00 P.M.—Bushong's Hill

Somewhere beyond Rude's Hill, and hurrying as best they could toward the cannons, were Jacob M. Campbell's 566 men of the 54th Pennsylvania and William Curtis's 929 West Virginians of the 12th infantry. To accomodate their arrival and easy insertion into the line, Sigel now constructed a two-tiered defensive position based on Bushong's Hill.

The 18th Connecticut and the unstable 123rd Ohio were left in front, with von Kleiser's six-gun battery straddling the pike to their left. A considerable distance behind them, far up the hill beyond the Bushong's farm residence, a second line was formed by the 34th Massachusetts and 1st West Virginia, with the massed guns of both Carlin and Snow, a dozen three-inch rifles, on the highest rise to their right, just at the edge of the bluff overlooking the North Fork.

The scheme seemed to work for the new arrivals; when the 54th Pennsylvania came up it was moved into line to the left of the 1st West Virginia, and the 12th West Virginia was motioned into reserve behind the 34th Massachusetts.

Sigel's entire left, from the pike to Smith's Creek, was occupied by 2,000 cavalry under Stahel, including William Tibbitts's First Brigade and John Wynkoop's Second. Between the cavalry and New Market was a small woods. Sometime after noon, as Breckinridge was moving through the town, John Daniel Imboden took a little ride through that woods to see what Echols's 22nd and 23rd Virginians would face on the other side. What he saw convinced him to send a courier to Breckinridge asking permission to make a diversion on his way to Mount Jackson. The general replied: "Tell General Imboden, as he knows this ground, and I don't, to make any movement he thinks advantageous." What Imboden had seen was "Sigel's entire cavalry force massed in very close order in the fields just beyond the woods."

May 15, 2:00 P.M.—East of Smith's Creek

Moving at a "trot march," Imboden "swept down Smith's Creek" with McClanahan's battery bouncing behind. He pulled up at the top of a little hill "less than a thousand yards from the enemy's cavalry" and the gunners quickly unlimbered and looked down their sights across the creek to the fields where Stahel's troopers stood "massed in column, close order, squadron front, giving our gunners a target of whole acres of men and horses."

As McClanahan opened fire, "the effect was magical." Thrown into fearful confusion by being fired upon at such close range, the riders realized they could not maneuver to face the guns without being cut down, so they simply ran off the field, this "rapid retrograde movement of the discomfited cavalry," as Imboden called it, being visible to both sides.

In the movement, von Kleiser's battery was uncovered. One of Carter Berkeley's guns from near town seized the moment and fired a shell into his position that knocked the wheel off one of his twelve-pounders. He tried at first to drag it to the pike, but had to abandon it as the battle continued to form.

May 15, 2:00 P.M.—Bushong's Hill

As Sigel's massed artillery began to thunder from the summit of Bushong's Hill, and both McLaughlin's from near town and McClanahan's from across the creek thundered in reply, the sky seemed to split as though rent by a great scythe, and the heavens rolled with an even louder thunder of their own, and a teeming rain began as Wharton's brigade rose once more for yet another hill to conquer.

Eye-witnesses spoke in similes. The confederate attack was "like an avalanche," "such a storm of shot and shell, so thick the air seemed alive."

Sigel's first line was receiving enfilading fire from McClanahan's guns as well as from the front, and it finally got too hot for the shaky 123rd, apparently still spooked by their previous fright. They stood, delivered a single volley toward the advancing ranks of gray, and again ran away, this time along a lane that led down to the pike. Its flank thus uncovered, the 18th Connecticut had no recourse but to follow. Von Kleiser's battery, less the busted field gun, pulled out with equal speed. As they reached Sigel's second line, most of the 18th Connecticut rallied behind it, but the 123rd Ohio kept right on going, headlong toward Mount Jackson. Officers were sent to chase down and rally them, if possible.

May 15, 2:20 P.M.—Bushong's Hill

Wharton's line had not yet gripped the federal defense, which had been falling back steadily before its advance from Williamson's through Shirley's and Manor's hills. Now it was moving along Bushong's in good order, more bothered by the pounding rain and thunder than by the enemy. The hill was whale-shaped, so the units on the left, walking along the western slope, Edgar's 26th and the left elements of Wolfe's 51st, could not see over the brow to their right the men of Clark's 30th.

From their position atop the whale back, however, Clark's men had a grand view of the field before them, where T.K. Bushong's substantial farm house occupied the center of the stage. To its left as they approached was the barn. Just beyond the house, to the north, was an orchard, leafing out now, and then a fence. Beyond the fence the land dipped into a swale which was filling with rain, then rose to a little plateau where von Kleiser's guns were mounted. Farther to the left, leading to the steep bluff overlooking the North Fork, the ground rose more sharply to the crest, where Sigel's massed guns were exchanging fire with McLaughlin's.

The paths of the 51st Virginia and 26th Virginia would take them directly into the artillery of Carlin and Snow. The 30th Virginia would have to cross the Bushong yard, pass on either side of the house, continue through the orchard to the fence and then descend into the swale before facing von Kleiser's guns. If they got past von Kleiser, the 30th would have to take on the 34th Massachusetts, which provided infantry support for the artillery. The course of the 62nd Virginia would take them to the right of the Bushong house and directly at the defensive line of the 1st West Virginia. To their right, the dismounted 23rd Virginia Cavalry was on the lower slope of the whale, down in the valley next to the pike, which they would guide on until the men reached the line of the 54th Pennsylvania.

It was 2:20 P.M. when federal gunners saw the gray line emerging from the rain and mist of the fields ahead. Figures appeared as if by magic from the empty horizon near Indian Hollow as the 26th and 51st rose into view. Other companies of the 51st and the 30th had reached the fence beyond the orchard and stepped into the field below the cannon. Still others were dimly seen crossing the road between the Bushong house and the pike.

Double shotted with canister, the guns opened on the phantoms before them and turned the world into virtual hell. Maj. Peter J. Otey of the 30th said his regiment was "cut up, shattered and scattered" in a moment. He himself fell when a minié ball crushed his right arm.

The right companies of the 51st, who were beyond the fence when the cannon opened, acted like men in shock. The rain clouds, the sky itself, seemed to shake above them and the air turn blue with fire and flying grape and shell. They were being mowed down by canister; only two were killed but almost one hundred were wounded.

When Wharton himself reached the 51st to direct the charge against Sigel's line, he found those who were still standing in the field dazed, drifting backward.

As the 62nd stepped onto the field, after passing the front of the Bushong house, it began to advance through the little swale and there the guns found them. Of the regiment's 450 men, ninety were suddenly gone, killed or thrashing on the ground. Seven of the twelve company commanders were down, four killed instantly and three crippled for life. Smith's entire color company lay dead or wounded; the colors went through six hands.

One of Carlin's gunners later wrote, "I cannot describe to you the scene, but it was awful; twelve pieces pouring canister into them at one hundred and fifty yards, and not moving them. At last they wavered."

Wharton's whole line was now stopped. Under terrible fire the survivors hung along the fence. Among them was Charles Woodson's small unit of Missourians.

Moving through the orchard on Smith's left, they found themselves directly in front of von Kleiser's guns and so close that the troopers began to fire their pistols at the gunners, the only instance in the war when pistols exchanged with cannon—six-shot Colts against twelve-pound Napoleon cannon. The Missourians could shoot. Five of von Kleiser's gunners went down, and seven horses. The retaliation was quick and merciless. Shells exploded furiously, shaking the trees and ripping away their leaves. Woodson was hit by a fragment. His first lieutenant, Edward Scott, experienced a series of terrible visitations, first Sgt. Will Day, coming to Scott with a chest wound and falling dead at his feet. Then 2nd Lt. J.W. Jones, hit in the head, also fell dead at his feet. A third man approached, saying, "Good-bye, Lieutenant, I am killed." As Scott bent over to attend the man, he himself was wounded by a flying fragment. The company of his 1st Missouri Cavalry was cut to pieces; forty of its sixty-two men were down.

Along the line, more than two hundred men had disappeared. To the federal gunners, it seemed the entire line had been eliminated. Where the 30th Virginia and the 51st Virginia had once been joined, there was now a vacant space. Carlin, Snow and von Kleiser had managed to blow a great hole directly in the center of Wharton's line.

May 15, 2:30 P.M.—At Chapman's Battery

When not riding the lines on his splendid Texas bay and rallying his troops, Breckinridge had spent the early afternoon beside the pike with Chapman's battery, moving it forward in support of Wharton's advance. It was there that Maj. Charles Semple found him and informed him of the gap in the line and stated his opinion that Sigel would surely charge through it, collapsing the whole left wing.

"Why don't you put the cadets in line?"

"They are only children and I cannot expose them to such a fire."

"General, it is too late. The Federals are right on us."

"Will they stand?"

"They are of the best Virginia blood and they will."

"Then put the boys in . . . and may God forgive me."

May 15, 2:45 P.M.—The Cadets Close the Gap

Almost as soon as they started forward to join the line, the corps began to take casualties. Before they reached the first fence at the Bushong house, Charles Crockett and Henry Jones were torn asunder by a shell and 1st Sgt. William Cabell, a cousin of Breckinridge's, was hit in the chest by a fragment. William McDowell was shot in the heart.

Once over the fence, half the corps ran around the front and half around the back of the house. Robert Cousins noticed the house was literally drumming from the impact of bullets and shell fragments. Then into the orchard and a fire so withering that to Col. Shipp "it seemed impossible that any living creature could escape." Jack Stanard's leg was broken by a fragment. Thomas Jefferson fell clutching his stomach. Then Shipp was knocked over by a fragment and thought killed. Capt. Henry Wise took command and hustled the boys the last thirty yards to the orchard fence.

They could see almost nothing through the fog of gunsmoke and rain, only the lower part of the wheels and the lower legs and feet of Sigel's gunners. Sigel would never forget how the "rain fell in torrents and the wind drove clouds of smoke from our own and the enemy's lines against us, giving the latter the advantage in distinguishing our position."

Now, on command, the cadets knelt on one knee, aimed their muskets north and slightly upward, and fired. A federal officer watched as "a streak of fire and smoke flashed across the field" and announced that Wharton's line, though badly hurt, was not broken.

May 15, 2:45 P.M.—Stahel Charges

Julius Stahel had lost eight hundred troopers to Imboden in the Lost River Valley and New Market Gap. He had been blown away from his position near Smith's Creek. His command, falling back, had taken a cramped position farther north between the pike and the creek and done nothing, but now it could do everything and be absolved of all its past sins. It could save Sigel. As Breckinridge's left under Wharton had come to a shuddering stop in the face of the terrible guns on Bushong's Hill, his right had also slowed and stopped when faced by Stahel's cavalry fire.

The rain-lashed day was in the balance. Despite the killing and the running and the victories and defeats, the day was still in the balance. A hard blow to his right would cripple Breckinridge, perhaps kill him, send him reeling back.

Stahel formed two thousand troopers, squadron front, a scene from the Napoleonic wars of fifty years before, and now from *Gotterdamerung*, the sky splitting as though the huge scythe had again ripped its dank air, hooded clouds leaning down toward earth until, at the moment the charge began, the day turned black, rent suddenly by huge streams of light leaping between cloud and ground and thunder crashing so loudly nothing could be heard, not even the guns.

At the bottom of the slope, they watched and moved. Breckinridge ran his artillery—Chapman's, Berkeley's section, the VMI section—up the pike to confront the wave of riders coming distantly through the downpour. George S. Patton calmly composed his 22nd Virginia in a different configuration: small groups standing back to back, ready to fire in any direction, like jetties in the face of an oncoming wave. (His younger brother William was, at that moment, a cadet sergeant standing his ground at the Bushong fence.)

To Patton's right, Clarence Derrick, not VMI but West Point, did the same with his 23rd Virginia infantry. Both regiments sent skirmishers running at an angle to the charging horsemen to hit them on the flanks. And, from across Smith's Creek, McClanahan watched, preparing to deliver another blow.

They came through the rain, bobbing somewhat over uneven patches of ground, sabers flashing: Col. Robert F. Taylor's veteran New Yorkers, Maj. Henry Roessler's New Yorkers, R.B. Douglas's Pennsylvanians. Onward they came, toward victory, until the cannon opened a single, massive, simultaneous barrage, hurling double-shot canister. McClanahan boomed from the east. The skirmishers closed toward the horses, firing, firing, firing.

The great charge was suddenly smashed as horses reeled and fell and bolted. The artillery loaded, fired, loaded, fired. The 22nd Virginia broke out of its squares and advanced toward the enemy, firing, firing.

Stahel's entire command was now halted, milling, falling, riding away from the field. The cavalry was "running back for their miserable life!" said one New Yorker. "I was ashamed to be in such an army," said Tibbits. "A disaster."

In a wave it had come down toward the confederate line, and in bits and pieces it was riding hell-bent back toward the rear. Stahel also was riding back, to find Sigel. When he did, he reported in apparent bewilderment: "Mein Gott . . . vare ish mein cavalrie?"

May 15—Mount Jackson

Vare, also, was Jeremiah Sullivan?

Sigel, writing after the battle, said that about noon he had sent two aides, captains Charles S. McEntee and Thomas G. Putnam, to Sullivan "with orders to bring forward all his troops without delay." Shortly thereafter, as Moor was withdrawing into the second line across Bushong's Hill, Sigel's staff aide, Capt. R.G. Prendergast, had reported to him that "all the infantry and artillery of Gen. Sullivan had arrived, the head of the column being in sight, and they were waiting for orders." Sigel then arranged his line the way he did only because he "supposed this report to be correct."

Sullivan, in fact, was where Sigel had last ordered him to be, at Mount Jackson. He had been there since ten A.M., having marched for five hours up from Woodstock. During the morning he had responded to intermittent orders arriving from New Market, first dispatching the batteries of Carlin and von Kleiser (their appearance probably being mistaken by Prendergast for the whole column). When orders finally came to bring up the infantry he did just that, leaving behind Henry du Pont's battery as he marched away with the 28th and 116th Ohio. Around two P.M., a mile from Bushong's Hill, Sullivan stopped, for reasons never adequately explained. He may have had a premonition that the place was about to burn down since he waited so close to the exit.

May 15, 3:00 P.M.—The Infantry Charge

David Strother had many causes for disdain and disgust while in Sigel's service, and here was another. After Stahel had reported on what was obvious, the panicky retreat of his entire cavalry, which was even then jamming the pike northward, Sigel became very agitated, said Strother, "and rode here and there with Stahel and Moor, all jabbering in German. In his excitement he seemed to forget his English entirely and the purely American portion of his staff were totally useless to him."

The German generals concocted an attack by their remaining right wing, a movement that, if made a half hour earlier when Wharton's line was staggering to a halt, might have won the day. The immediate cause for the decision, according to Sigel, was a report from Lt. Ephraim Chalfant of Carlin's battery, on the extreme right, that "he could not hold his position." Sigel instantly "ordered two companies of the 12th West Virginia to advance and protect the pieces, but to my surprise there was no disposition to advance; in fact, in spite of treaties and reproaches, the men could not be moved an inch!"

Perhaps Sigel was ranting at them in German. Whatever the cause, he reported that in his frustration "to save the guns, I determined to make a counter-charge of the whole right wing. . . . Bayonets were fixed and the charge was made in a splendid style."

Very far from the truth indeed. The orders for the charge were given in such a din of thundering noise from both the cannon and from the clouds that it was entirely uncoordinated. George Wells did not understand he was to charge with the 34th Massachusetts until he saw the 1st West Virginia on his left suddenly move forward. The same was true of Jacob Campbell and his 54th Pennsylvania, who saw the West Virginians move to his right and had to organize his own advance very quickly.

Because they were so far ahead of the rest of the line, the 1st West Virginia became the sole target of confederate fire, not only from the 62nd Virginia and the cadets in their front, but from Breckinridge's guns firing canister from the pike. They had not gone a hundred yards forward when they had had enough and turned back, leaving fifty men on the ground, passing the late-starting 54th Pennsylvania as it moved forward, uncovering the right flank of that unit. A "destructive fire" now poured into the Pennsylvanians from every quarter. The regiment would suffer thirty-two dead and 180 wounded on this day, most of them in these few minutes. Campbell could see Patton and Derrick hurrying along beyond the pike to his left, about to envelop him. He realized he would be destroyed if he remained, so he, too, turned back.

Nature joined the fray. From his position down on the pike, artillerist Carter Berkeley described "the most terrible storm I ever witnessed . . . a dark and angry cloud hung over the combatants, the forked lightning flashed through the blackness as if heaven were crying out against the horrid work."

As the 34th Massachusetts charged through the blowing smoke and rain, Wells saw with a start that they were alone. The West Virginians had disappeared from his left, and Campbell was vanishing from the far left. He tried to halt his regiment but could not be heard. They were now taking a terrific fire from the confederate lines and were falling like gathered wheat; in a few minutes, nearly half the command was shot away, thirty killed, 130 wounded. Finally, Wells rushed forward and physically grabbed the color bearer, turned him around. Only then did the men understand to withdraw, back to their line, stepping over their fallen comrades.

The line, however, was not there. The West Virginians had not stopped at their former position but continued to run away toward the pike. Watching them go, one of Carlin's gunners spoke for all when he said that "every man knew that we were whipped."

Carlin, as well as Snow and von Kleiser, had now received orders to limber their guns and retreat, but that was sooner said than done, since von Kleiser was in a position now entirely exposed in front of a fast-deserting infantry line, and both Carlin and Snow were isolated far on the right, subjects for intense enemy fire and even attack. And it soon came.

The entire confederate line surged forward. Wharton himself led the 51st, which was now intermingled with the 26th, both units running toward the guns and the lonely 34th Massachusetts. Alonzo Snow's Marylanders moved quickly, limbered their six rifles and made a getaway; in the entire engagement they suffered only four men wounded from their one-hundred-man battery.

Carlin, farther to the right, was taking greater punishment from a company of the 26th Virginia firing from the cover of Indian Hollow as well as those rushing toward him. He ordered everyone out at once, but it was all but too late. Five horses from a single gun were killed almost simultaneously; the gun would have to be abandoned. Three horses went down at another gun as a shell cracked half its carriage, still they managed to drag it backward until three more horses went down. A few hundred yards farther and a third cannon became hopelessly mired in a mud hole. Its horses began to drop. The men tried to pull it out by hand. A fresh team was brought up and shot down. The gun was left. Carlin, his ammunition caissons bouncing away down the pike, struggled from the field of battle, leaving behind every artilleryman's disgrace, three guns and seventeen dead horses.

Carlin's entire battery might have been destroyed or captured had not the brave 34th Massachusetts stood its ground yet again. As it ran back to its position, Lt. Col. William Lincoln was hit, and he watched the subsequent events from the ground. Sigel, as though drawn to this display of courage as a compensatory event for all of his fatal blundering, appeared behind the 34th, riding back and forth amid the blizzard of shot and shell that was pruning the cedar trees behind him. Wells, watching him, later said, "How he escaped is a mystery to me."

Being hit by flanking fire from the cadets on their left and the 51st and 26th ahead and on their right, there was no escape for the 34th unless they moved out now, and they did so in good order, not running, keeping formation, moving toward the pike. Sigel had ridden out ahead of them.

It was at the center of the field that the day's most remembered, indeed now legendary, action took place. As the VMI cadets moved out from the Bushong fence with the rest of the line, they came to the swale that was now a lake of mud. Many had their shoes and socks sucked off their feet as they struggled through. They began to come under fire from the 34th Massachusetts and some West Virginia infantry who had not run. Charles Randolph fell. Frank Gibson was hit in the leg, thigh, cheek and hand. John Upshur's right leg was smashed. Ahead of them, on the rise, lay von Kleiser's guns, three hundred yards across a green field of young wheat.

"Exhausted, wet to their skin, muddied to their eyebrows with the stiff clay through which they had pulled—some of them shoeless after their struggle across the plowed ground—they nevertheless advanced." Cadet captain Henry Wise shouted the command to charge, and the whole line advanced at the double-quick, swarming toward the battery placements.

Madness. Through the driving rain, the wind-blown smoke, the rolling clouds of musket fire, in a deafening theater of sound of angry yells, human screams of pain and fear, the thunder of powder and crackling of rifles, until: "A wild yell went up," Imboden recalled, "when a cadet mounted a caisson and waved the Institute flag in triumph over it." It was Cadet Ensign Evans. Something like taking the opponent's goal, but this was no game as the victorious troops looked behind them and saw "the ground was strewn with their dead and wounded."

Literally. Of Shipp's 226 cadets, ten were killed and forty-six wounded on that day, most charging the cannons. Except for the Missouri unit, which lost forty of its sixty-two men, the VMI cadets suffered the highest percentage of killed and wounded of any confederate unit in the battle.

Hagley Museum Library

CAPT. HENRY A. DU PONT

Von Kleiser had made off with his remaining four guns and joined the stream of survivors clogging the pike. The retreat was becoming a rout. Strother and others patrolled the fields with drawn sabers to halt and rally running men. A small sketch of the lunacy of battle occurred as Strother raised his sword to strike a soldier for cowardly retreat, and a bullet hit the man and killed him. Then Strother was hit, but the stray had lost all its momentum and simply thudded against him. He also made an exit to the north, where Stahel's cavalry, recovered somewhat from their own previous cowardice, stood against the line of retreat with drawn sabers. But nothing stopped the runaway army.

May 15, 4:00 P.M.—South of Rude's Hill, du Pont to the Rescue

There was nothing to protect that army's rear, either, until the straggling column neared Rude's Hill, and there, by the side of the pike, they saw a battery preparing to fire at the confederate lines behind them. It was Capt. Henry du Pont, at last in action, and in action with a plan.

Coming upon the routed army as he hurried to the battlefield had not surprised him; he had in fact "been anticipating something of the kind all along as everything has been so mismanaged." His plan was simple and effective. Posting two guns well in advance, he told them to fire until they feared being overrun, and then retreat to the rear. A second section of two guns, five hundred yards behind the first, would then open on the Confederates and continue until threatened, and thus the sections leap-frogged backward, holding Breckinridge in check as Sigel's army passed safely behind them. Du Pont and his guns probably prevented the annihilation of Sigel's army. Not for nothing had he graduated first in his class (1861) at West Point.

May 15, 5:00 P.M.—Rude's Hill

As he approached, Sigel saw "a dark line on Rude's Hill"— Sullivan, with the 28th and 116th Ohio. What passed between the two generals was not recorded. Sigel positioned Sullivan's regiments on the hill with du Pont's six guns to cover their movement as "disgraceful fleeing masses of cavalry and straggling infantry" passed down through Meem's Bottom toward the bridge.

May 15, 5:00 P.M.—Three Miles North of New Market

Harry Gilmor could not reach the bridge at Meem's Bottom in time, and Imboden's column had been unable to recross Smith's Creek because of the exceedingly high water. Imboden now went looking for Breckinridge to report and found him on the road to Rude's Hill, standing in a grassy orchard about a hundred yards behind McLaughlin's guns, covered with mud. He had been "much of the time off his horse during the whole day, mingling with and cheering his brave, tired, hungry, drenched, and muddy infantry and artillery to whose lot had fallen the hard fighting."

Imboden was told by Breckinridge that his men were completely out of ammunition and had been for an hour. They had been running after the Feds with empty guns, hoping the supply wagon, traveling the hard surface of the Valley road, would catch up. As they talked, several shells, du Pont's, whistled in and exploded in the orchard. Imboden told his commander that by moving one hundred yards left or right he would be out of the line of fire. Breckinridge laughed and said he was standing on the only dry place and would rather risk being hit by a shell than "wade in the mud again," which was, Imboden noted, "all the way up to our horse's knees."

The wagon arrived, the guns were reloaded, and Breckinridge said to Carter Berkeley, "Go at once; charge down the pike and drive them off the hill."

Berkeley remembered that "we put out at a run, every man yelling as loud as he could. . . . It looked as if we were going into the very jaws of death." The two guns disappeared from federal view as they went into a dip in the road, and Berkeley rode ahead to find du Pont's guns limbering and "the whole line breaking in confusion . . . the long bottom before us filled with refugees . . . the poor, panic-stricken wretches were flying before us in easy range of our guns and relentlessly we poured the shot and shell into them. . . . We put in our deadliest shots as they were packing like frightened cattle across the bridge."

May 15, 7:00 P.M.—Bridge at Meem's Bottom

It was seven o'clock before the trailing unit was over and Henry du Pont, the last man to cross, burned the bridge, unleashing the last column of smoke to rise into the rain of that dark May day.

May 15, 8:00 P.M.—Battlefield

Carter Berkeley was making his way back to New Market when he came upon Sandy Stuart, a VMI gunner, "wringing wet . . . his hands and face . . . black with powder."

"Lieutenant," said Stuart, "the blot on the institute has been wiped out today by the best blood of Virginia."

"Sandy," said Berkeley, "I never knew that there was a blot on the institute."

"Your boys tried to put a stigma on us this morning, calling us bombproofs and wagon dogs."

A boy cried out from the field, and Berkeley found a wounded cadet seated with a wounded companion in his arms.

"Sir, do get me a doctor; my friend is wounded."

"My poor boy," replied Berkeley, "your friend is dead."

Monday, May 16, Dawn—Woodstock Hotel

David Strother awakened on a sofa, still "booted, belted, and spurred, stiff with mud and soaked with rain." Outside he saw that the traffic was still moving on the pike—cannon, wagons, stragglers. After a "wretched meal," he looked in the barroom and found "a long pine box containing the body of a dead soldier, stiff in his bloody garments. On another cot lay a soldier with the death rattle in his throat. On a third lay one mortally wounded in the bowels. . . . A fourth had just been carried out."

May 16—Flag of Truce

When Harry Gilmor came into New Market on Monday, Breckinridge asked him if he was afraid to swim the swollen North Fork near the burned out bridge, and Gilmor, of course, said of course not. Breckenridge told him that a long train of ambulances was going up the valley turnpike, and he wanted Gilmor to harass it and cause Sigel any discomfort he could.

Gilmor arrived at the river bank at midday, and for a moment he had second thoughts. The current seemed so swift that "a horse could not possibly live in it." He was on his great gray, however, and that magnificent animal entered the river and "made his way nobly to the other bank." Sixty of Gilmor's men followed him over, with only three being swept downstream.

On nearing Mount Jackson a mile and half up the pike, the Marylanders saw a white flag of truce coming toward them in the hand of none other than Maj. Charles Otis of the 21st New York Cavalry.

He bore a request from Sigel for the body of a Capt. Mitchell, killed at New Market. Gilmor sent a courier back across the river with the message and, "in accordance with military rules," had to suspend his operation and await the return, which did not occur for hours. The answer was negative; Breckenridge could receive no communication from Sigel, and Gilmor was to push on down the valley as instructed. When Gilmor relayed this news to Otis, he also said that he himself would mark the grave so Mitchell could be recovered at some future time.

Early that morning Breckinridge had sent a flag forward to Sigel asking for a federal burial detail to help collect the union dead, and Sigel had refused.

Gilmor's column moved out with both Gilmor and Otis riding at its head. As they neared Hawkinstown, Otis suddenly looked at Gilmor's gray with the shock of recognition.

"Were you in a skirmish a few days ago, just about here as a matter of fact?" he asked.

"I was," said Gilmor.

"Were you not wounded?"

It was now Gilmor's turn for a shock as he saw the look on Otis's face. "Yes. Are you not the man who shot me?"

Otis seemed amused and smiled broadly as he replied, "I am. I am truly surprised to see you riding."

"It's nothing," said Gilmor. "A bruise."

When they got to the tollgate, Otis showed Gilmor the post on which he had rested the carbine.

"I bear you no ill will," said Gilmor, "but I should be happy for the occasion to show my respects in the field."

"I would be happy to meet you there, Major, and show you the best in my shop."

As Gilmor and Otis rode on side by side at the head of a confederate column, the Marylander found his companion "full of fun."

The bridge at Edinburg had been burned, so the troopers had to swim Stony Creek. As they pushed on toward Woodstock with no sign of the enemy, Otis asked Gilmor what his options were if they hit Sigel's rear guard and a fight ensued.

"You may show your flag and stand by the side of the road. Or, if you prefer taking a part to playing spectator, you may gallop over to your friends and have a part in the game."

"I prefer the latter," said Otis.

At Woodstock, Gilmor discovered Sigel was farther still down the road ,at Strasburg, and decided to stop. He approved of Otis puting up at the hotel in Strasburg while he himself camped out. The next day, near Fisher's Hill, they hit Sigel's pickets, which Gilmor drove in. "As soon as the firing commenced, I bade the major good-bye and turned him loose. He started off at a gallop, opened his white flag as he passed by my advance, and rode on."

They never met again.

New Market—Aftermath

The fierce fighting had taken a toll of both armies, as casualty lists were being composed and burial details reported. Of the five thousand men he had at New Market, Sigel had lost more than 840 killed, wounded or captured, along with 170 horses and five guns. The regiments he had sent forward on that suicidal piecemeal infantry charge had suffered ; both the 34th Massachusetts and 54th Pennsylvania had lost about half their complement—sixty-two killed outright and more than 310 wounded. During the aborted cavalry charge, the 1st New York (Lincoln) had twelve killed and twenty-six wounded.

Breckinridge's greatest losses had been taken when Wharton's line stepped into the artillery fire beyond the Bushong fence—more than ninety wounded in the 51st Virginia, more than eighty in the 62nd Virginia, more than seventy-five in the 23rd Virginia Battalion. Altogether, the confederate casualties were about 530 from a force of 4,000.

The cadets had also suffered disproportionately, with ten dead and forty-five wounded of their 226.

Each armies had lost about thirteen percent of its fighting forces, but how unequal was the result. Breckinridge was regarded by the people of the valley as a veritable god of war, another Jackson. Had he not won New Market on the first anniversary of Jackson's funeral? Was it not a Sunday, Jackson's usual day to fight? But Lee was not sentimental about heroes. He wired at noon on the 16th, "I offer you the thanks of this army," and he wanted Breckinridge either to pursue Sigel all the way into Maryland, if possible, or join him before Richmond.

Late in the afternoon of May 16, Breckinridge rode up to Staunton to gather his hard-used army for service with Lee. He received encouragement to do so when word came from McCausland, down south, that Crook and Averell were withdrawing from their raid. At five A.M. the next day, Echols and Wharton followed him to Staunton. He also took Smith and the sorely damaged 62nd; Lee needed infantry, however badly hurt. By May 19 they were boarded on Virginia Central Railroad cars and on their way over the Blue Ridge toward Richmond. Behind them the people of the Valley of Virginia were dismayed, angry and despondent at their departure. They were left once more with Imboden and his thousand men as their protectors, left to confront an army "we had with so much difficulty defeated," one that they knew would return.

Sigel started to lie about what happened almost before it stopped happening. He informed the War Department that he had been "greatly outnumbered" and had to withdraw, but "the retrograde movement was effected in perfect order. The troops are in very good spirits and will fight another battle if the enemy should advance against us." The clever and caustic David Strother made a quip that quickly made the rounds: "We do good work in this department. Averell is tearing up the . . . railroad while Sigel is tearing down the . . . turnpike."

Unaware of Sigel's movements, and absorbed with his own at Spotsylvania, Grant had asked Henry Halleck, the chief of staff, to order Sigel to advance to Staunton. Now he was surprised and infuriated at Halleck's reply at midnight on May 17:

> Instead of advancing on Staunton, he is already in full retreat on Strasburg. If you expect anything from him you will be mistaken. He will do nothing but run. He never did anything else.

Already Sigel had become the butt of jokesters singing not, "who fights mit Sigel," but "who runs mit Sigel." Clearly, he had to go. Halleck suggested Maj. Gen. David Hunter. Grant concurred. "By all means, I would say appoint Gen. Hunter *or anyone else.*"

Hunter reached the army headquarters at Cedar Creek on May 21. His cousin Strother was waiting for him. "We can afford to lose such a battle as New Market," said Strother, "to get rid of such a mistake as . . . Sigel."

They waited on the porch until Sigel appeared, and then they went inside to negotiate the German general's future. He was, after all, still a political figure with a strong following and could not simply be turned out. He agreed to accept the command of the reserve division at Harper's Ferry, thus bumping Kelley once more. On May 23 he was on his way north, telling his staff that "it were better to have died on the battlefield than suffer this disgrace" and never dreaming that he would once again have the opportunity to face Breckinridge.

Hunter looked things over and reported that the army of the Department of West Virginia was "utterly demoralized and stampeded . . . and the three generals with it, Sigel, Stahel, and Sullivan, not worth one cent."

IV.
Vengeful Generals
in the Valley

Tuesday, May 24—Hunter

Maj. Gen. David Hunter had a scowling visage, baggy eyes and a baggier jaw under a pursing mouth covered by a straggly mustache. Outwardly as unperturbed as an Indian chief, which, with his straight black hair and swarthy complexion, he somewhat resembled, he boiled with fierce emotions that often exploded. That seemed especially ugly from a man of his age, sixty-two, which was old for the time.

As Sigel had been considered a political asset by the Lincoln administration, Hunter had already proven himself a liability, a loose cannon repudiated by the president himself. Years before, early in his career, he had almost been cashiered from the service for challenging his commanding officer to a duel. His complaining letters to Lincoln about his assignment to Kansas prompted Lincoln to tell him that he was his own worst enemy. "You are adopting the best possible way to ruin yourself."

It turned out that Hunter had even better ways, however. Transferred from the Department of the West to that of the South, he issued orders from Hilton Head that created the 1st South Carolina Volunteers, the first black regiment of the war. This led to a furious confederate government declaring him unprotected by the usual rules of warfare, a man who would, if caught, be executed as a common felon.

Hunter took it a giant step farther. He began freeing slaves within his department. Lincoln knew this would so provoke the entire South that it might destroy whatever chance for a negotiated settlement still existed. He had no choice but to countermand the order and recall Hunter to Washington, where he sat and steamed until Sigel's fall.

Henry du Pont sized him up as a man "dominated by prejudices and antipathies so intense and so violent as to render him at times quite incapable of taking a fair and unbiased view"—and not only of military affairs.

Battles & Leaders

MAJ. GEN. DAVID HUNTER

One of those antipathies was toward slave owners. It was Hunter's policy, wherever assigned, to visit the wrath of God upon the persons and property of slave holders. He desired intensely to bring the destruction of rebellion right into the parlors of civilians. Like David Strother, he was from a fine Virginia family, but he thought Virginia merited destruction because of its secession and slave holding.

So fervent was this opinion that he did not spare his own first cousin, Andrew Hunter, a prominent lawyer of Jefferson County whose grand home stood near Charles Town, about eight miles from Harpers Ferry. Andrew had been named for Hunter's father, but the general regarded him as Confederate in sympathy. He not only arrested his cousin and threw him into a common jail without charges but ordered his mansion burned to the ground with all its contents, including his wife's and daughter's clothes. He then camped his cavalry on the beautiful grounds.

Wherever he went, David Hunter left a trail of flame, smoke, and destruction. On May 24, he issued an order:

> For every train fired or soldier assassinated, the house or other property of every secession sympathizer residing within a circuit of five miles shall be destroyed by fire; and for all public property taken or destroyed, an assessment of five times the value of such property will be made upon the secession sympathizers residing within a circuit of ten miles around the point at which the offense was committed.

May 24—Newtown

A wagon train passing through Newtown had been fired on and a sergeant wounded. Hunter was determined to visit fire and sword upon the perpetrators. On May 23, his adjutant, P.G. Bier, commanded Maj. Quinn of the 1st New York Cavalry to "detail from your command two hundred men . . . to proceed to Newtown to-morrow morning at three o'clock for the purpose of burning every house, store, and outbuilding in that place. . . . You will also burn the houses, etc., of all rebels between Newtown and Middletown."

The New Yorkers were more selective. They burnt three houses—that of the parson, the Rev. John Wolff, a "sentimental Secessionist"; that of a Mr. White, "a rich Secessionist" living in Lexington; and that of a Mr. Harmon, "a bushwhacker."

Wednesday, May 25—Below Middletown

David Strother was pleased with himself. Not only was he rid of Sigel, of whom he had been contemptuous, but he had shined up enough to Hunter to be named the new chief of staff. In this capacity he now rode down the pike to Middletown to meet a delegation from Newtown—four men who did not want their town burned down. Strother handed them Hunter's order and told them "vengeance would surely fall upon the country if these robberies and murders continued." They could, however, protect themselves by revealing the names of the partisans.

Well, they allowed, there was a certain Capt. Sheerer of Winchester who was among them. And a Capt. Glenn who headed a unit of young men from Maryland. And in Newtown they often met at the house of a Mrs. Wilson.

Hunter ordered Mrs. Wilson arrested. That afternoon a column appeared at her house in Newtown. When the soldiers made preparations to burn the place, the widow Wilson informed them it was rented. They then carried all her furniture out. "She and her daughters assisted in the removal with great alacrity, thanking the officer for his consideration. Her astonishment and grief was great when the heap of furniture instead of the house was set fire to and consumed. The woman herself was then arrested and trudged six miles to a guard tent."

That morning, at President Lincoln's request to "retain the Dutch in some position if possible," Hunter has assigned Max Weber to Harpers Ferry and Franz Sigel to Cumberland, where he would command "the railroad reserves."

Thursday, May 26—Moving South Again

The reinforced army moved out of Cedar Creek about eight-thirty, "the road muddy and the world gloomy." Beyond Strasburg, when they halted for rest, the men looked back at "a volume of smoke rising from the house of Boyden, a farmer, . . . said to be

Virginia State Archives

COL. DAVID HUNTER STROTHER
(self-portrait)

a rendezvous for bushwhackers."

That night they camped at Pugh's Run, north of Woodstock. Maj. Theodore Lang rode forward to visit the Cheney house. Mrs. Cheney inquired, "Is that wretched Dutchman with you?"

"No, Madam. Gen. Sigel has been reassigned," said Lang.

"Thank you, God," said Mrs. Cheney. "I have never prayed for vengeance against anyone that the prayer has not been granted."

When Strother later saw Sullivan in his quarters in Woodstock he gave him some advice: Conduct yourself so as to secure the blessing of Mrs. Cheney.

Friday, May 27—Woodstock

Strother found "the whole town squalling with women, children, chickens, and geese. The feathers were flying like a cloud." His conscience was bothering him. He had decided to "have no more social intercourse with the people of the country because of the outrages and distresses which awaken my sympathies but which I could not prevent." Case in point was a letter delivered to Strother in Woodstock. It was from the pastor in Newtown whose home had been burned—and something more. Strother, it appears, had not been honest with himself or his diary when he referred to "the Reverend J. Wolff, the parson." Now, with the letter in hand, he admitted to himself that the parson was "my old schoolmate, John Wolff, . . . asking to meet me at the pickets. It was written simply and no doubt truthfully and I am sorry I did not see him, . . . but I could not have helped him."

Saturday, May 28—Woodstock

Strother: "[Lt. John R.] Meigs went out scouting and burned the house of a man who had assisted in killing and capturing stragglers during Sigel's retreat."

Sunday, May 29, Sunrise—Woodstock

Hunter had been in touch with Henry Halleck in Washington and was ordered to proceed to Charlottesville and destroy the Virginia Central Railroad. Once east of the Blue Ridge, he expected support from Sheridan's cavalry. His intention was to cross at Rockfish Gap above Staunton after joining forces with Crook and Averell who were "in fine condition and advancing with sixteen thousand men." A weird thing had happened to Averell at New River. He had been hit square in the forehead by a stray bullet that had just enough energy left to reach him and inflict only a slight bruise.

Rising at four, the army was under way by sunrise. As it passed through Woodstock, Hunter had the jail searched but found it empty. To Strother, "He was evidently seeking an apology to burn something and proposed to set fire to the Hollingsworth Hotel, but I told him that our wounded had lain there and had been well cared for."

May 29—Newtown

Having been asked by Imboden to get into the federal rear beyond Cedar Creek and make all the mischief he could, Harry Gilmor had taken his command "down the crest of the Blue Ridge" to near Front Royal, where he swam his horses across the Shenandoah and began operations between Middletown and Martinsburg. On the 29th he received word that a train of twenty-two wagons carrying medical supplies, guarded by 175 cavalry and eighty infantry, was on the road from Winchester to Newtown.

He waited in a thick wood near Bartonsville. When the train came into view, there were horsemen ahead and behind, and Gilmor suspected the infantry were all inside the wagons, waiting to give his troopers a broadside. He waited until the train began to enter Newtown, then divided his fifty-three men into two squads and charged from the rear. "Every man of us yelled as loud as possible and kept on yelling," hoping to stampede it. The rear guard held Gilmor long enough for the defenders to overturn two wagons across a bridge at the south end of town while the rest made a run for Middletown.

At that point, Gilmor lost control of his horse. With saber in hand, he could not "turn his head to the left or right." The big gray leaped through the overturned wagons and ran after the train. Passing the home of a Dr. McLeod, Gilmor saw that the Yankee cavalry were all drawn up, prepared to hit the pursing Confederates in the flank; so astonished were they when Gilmor flashed by alone that all shots fired at him missed.

"I passed the whole party," he recalled, "and got among the wagons, still going at full speed." He cut the ear off a wagon master, shot a sergeant through the neck, (whom he recognized as being from the 18th Connecticut, the regiment that once guarded him as a prisoner), ranged up alongside the leading horse of the train and "rising in the stirrups, gave him a hard blow on the crest, just behind the head strap. This brought him down and tied the whole team in a knot across the road, with all the rest piled up behind them."

Gilmor then "plunged in his spurs, cleared the fence on my left into a large open field and hastened back toward Newtown to see what the boys were doing." The boys, in fact, had driven off the federal defenders and were even then capturing the piled-up train. They took forty prisoners, including six officers going to their commands, and seventy horses. The wagons contained material for a large field hospital. Gilmor ordered them burned and rode into Newtown where Dr. McLeod was attending the wounded, including a Capt. Brett of the 1st New York cavalry, who died in Gilmor's presence.

The people of Newtown were alarmed at what Gilmor had done and what Hunter would do to them in return. They told him that because of his actions, "We shall be houseless before tomorrow night." Gilmor was incensed. He wrote a note to Gen. Hunter. When a three-hundred-man federal cavalry regiment arrived as predicted on May 31 under command of Maj. Joseph A. Stearns, Gilmor's note was delivered. Gilmor told Hunter that he held forty men and six officers from the wagon train, and upon receipt of the news that Hunter had burned down Newtown, he would *hang every one of them and send their bodies to him.* And, said Gilmor, *Hunter knew that I would do it.*

Stearns spared the town. Gilmor heard that his two captains, Battersby and Bailey, had actually shed tears at "the inhuman order with which they were charged."

When Gilmor paroled his prisoners, he found that one of them was a Marylander, a Lt. Smiser, newly commissioned.

"They told me not to go up in this valley," said Smiser. "They told me that sure enough Harry Gilmor was going to get me. They said—you can count on it, Harry Gilmor's going to get'cha."

"Who told you that?" asked Harry.

"Your brother Charley."

Monday, May 30—Middletown

John Mosby came upon still-burning wagons on the road between Middletown and Newtown that he recognized as Gilmor's very recent work. Beyond blazed a barn fired by Stearns that day.

While the fires burned, Mosby calmly awaited a union wagon train that soon appeared on the Winchester road. It was simple work: two Yankees killed, five prisoners and eight wagons taken.

May 30, New Market

Hunter's army returned now to the scene of their disgrace. A ghastly sight awaited them as they marched past the battlefield with the partially exposed remains of their comrades who had been too hastily buried. A work detail sent out to rebury them counted only about sixty bodies.

When a scouting party came back from North Mountain with a prisoner, Hunter wanted to hang him but was talked out of it.

Tuesday, May 31—New Market, Intense Heat

After the torrential rains of the previous weeks, summer fell suddenly upon the Valley, arriving, as it so often does, full blown. By noon it was so hot that the army could do nothing but seek shelter and doze. They awaited word from Crook.

Wednesday, June 1—Near New Market

Imboden: "On the 1st of June Hunter . . . drove me out of New Market with my handful of cavalry and six guns. . . . I again reported the perils of the valley to General Lee. Over eleven thousand men were driving me before them up the valley. Generals Crook and Averell, with ten thousand more, were known to be rapidly coming down upon my rear from Lewisburg, and would form a junction with Hunter at Staunton within five or six days. . . . General Lee directed me to call out all the reserves and to telegraph Brig. Gen. William E. Jones . . . to come to my aid with all the men he could collect. . . . Jones responded promptly that he would join me via Lynchburg and Staunton by the 4th with about three thousand men."

Thursday, June 2—Mount Crawford

During the afternoon, Hunter's army waited in the hills within sight of the town while its advanced cavalry drove Imboden through Harrisonburg. He had no place to put up a good defense until he reached the North River, a tributary of the Shenandoah's South Fork, at Mount Crawford, eight miles south of Harrisonburg and seventeen from Staunton. There, Imboden took position on the south bank and waited for help.

Friday, June 3—Harrisonburg

The demands of the federal army for meat and flour created "great consternation and disgust." Strother noted that "the soldiers...are plundering dreadfully from all accounts."

Stearns returned from his journey to Newtown and had to report his failure to burn the place out. Hunter was furious. Stearns said the people there had made a general submission and taken an oath of allegiance. Hunter was still angry.

He had other things to ponder, however. Strother convinced him to avoid meeting Imboden at his strong North River position and instead strike out for Port Republic, cross the South Fork and take Waynesboro, to the east of Staunton. That would cut the railroad, isolate Staunton and open the way to Rockfish Gap.

That night, rockets rose over Harrisonburg, the most ominous of all warnings to Imboden and his reserve soldiers, for these were meant as beacons, guiding Crook and Averell to the fateful rendezvous.

June 3, Night—Mount Crawford

They began to dribble in, Jones's quickly gathered men, for they arrived just as they had been dispatched—small units spread along the railroad line. Imboden and his staff were up all night, organizing them and the reserves, the old men and boys from surrounding counties, into two rough brigades.

Saturday, June 4, Sunrise—Brig. Gen. William E. "Grumble" Jones

At sunrise, "Grumble" Jones and his staff rode up to Mount Crawford, followed an hour later by Brig. Gen. John C. Vaughn and his brigade of a thousand Tennessee cavalry.

Jones was called Grumble because that was his normal disposition, as his troops knew only too well. He appeared to be half-mad, with small, piercing, suspicious eyes and a protruding lower lip rising through a full beard. And many thought that he *was* half-mad, made so by the tragedy that had befallen him in 1852 when, while returning from his honeymoon in California, their ship had run into a gale. His bride was swept from his arms and drowned.

His spats with Jeb Stuart had turned to enmity. During the famous review of Stuart's cavalry at Brandy Station, Jones had been found nonchalantly lying on the ground instead of being seated prim and proper in the saddle. During the battle that began the next day, Jones had detected a federal movement on his right flank. Stuart's reply, when informed, was: "Tell General Jones to attend to the Yankees in his front and I'll watch the flanks."

On hearing this, Jones said, "Well, let him alone; he'll damn soon see for himself." As he did.

As Lee's army was planning its move into Maryland during the Gettysburg campaign, Stuart had decided to leave Jones's Brigade behind, along with Beverly H. Robertson's, and the chance for glory went to Wade Hampton, Fitz Lee, and "Rooney" Lee. It was suspected that Stuart's personal animus entered into his decision. Roberston, of prior

commission, was told to "in-
struct Gen. Jones from time to
time as . . . events may require."

Then, in September, after
the defeated army had re-
turned, there was an ugly inci-
dent between Stuart and Jones.
Stuart had Jones arrested for
disrespect to a superior officer;
a court martial found him
guilty. Neither man would ever
say what had passed between
them and the records are simi-
larly silent on the matter. Lee,
who valued both men, had no
choice but to turn Jones's brigade over to another officer and
exile Jones back to his home
turf of southwestern Virginia,
where he took over the confederate cavalry forces.

William Turner Collection

BRIG. GEN. W.E. "GRUMBLE" JONES

He then served with distinction under James Longstreet in
Tennessee, and now he was
back in Virginia. Breckinridge
had left a vacuum. Jones asked
Richmond, "Must I assume
command?" and the answer, after a few days to think about it, was "Yes."

Saturday, June 4—Road to Port Republic

Hunter's army sent a regiment of cavalry under John Meigs toward Mt. Crawford to
screen his flanking advance toward Port Republic and Waynesboro beyond. The move
would have taken Smith and Imboden by surprise, but Hunter lost his opportunity
when the column reached the South Fork at Port Republic and found that "no one of
the engineers . . . understood how to put up the canvas pontoons" for the bridge. A
cavalry trooper tried to cross, but he was swept from his saddle; a half dozen men
stripped and leaped into the river to save him, but he disappeared downstream, never
to be found. By the time the bridge was finally pieced together it was six in the evening
and the army had nothing to do but march a mile south and bivouac in line of battle.

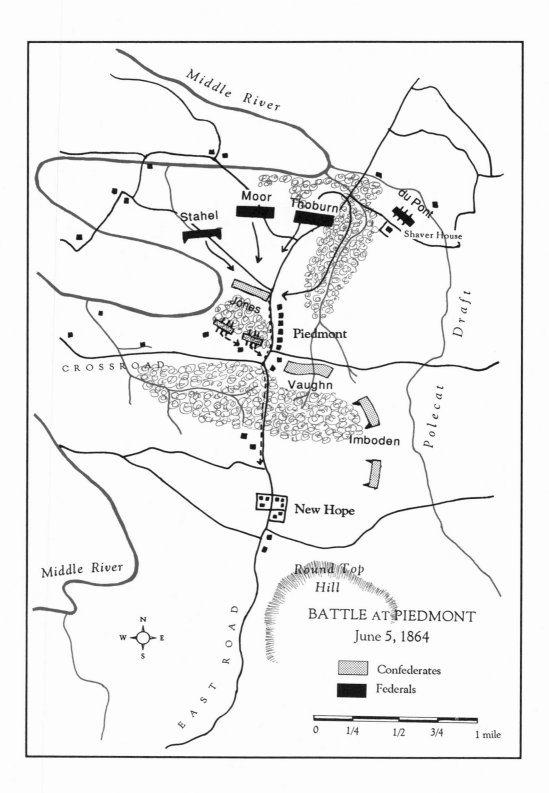

BATTLE AT PIEDMONT
June 5, 1864

V.
The Battle at Piedmont

Sunday, June 5—Piedmont

After the war, when John Imboden came to write about Piedmont, his bitterness about that day was reflected in what he said and the way he said it. "On the 5th our forces were concentrated about half a mile north-east of the village of Piedmont. Without going into details it suffices to say now that battle was joined. After repelling two assaults, our left wing was doubled up by a flank attack, Jones was killed, and we were disastrously beaten. Our loss was not less than 1500 men."

Period. No elaboration.

Many things stuck in Imboden's craw about Piedmont. He knew the ground and had recommended to Jones that they take their stand at Mowry's Hill, down the road from the little hamlet, hardly a scratch in the dirt with its small row of wooden houses. Jones preferred a position anchored on Piedmont.

All morning Imboden contested Hunter's advance from Port Republic, sparring with the 1st New York (Lincoln) and 1st New York (Veteran). Imboden's family enterprise 18th Virginia was joined by the 23rd Virginia and by a ragamuffin collection of old men and boys mounted on the family animal and called the Rockingham Reserves. They did well, giving Jones time to come up behind and start digging in at Piedmont.

At Mount Meridian, the 18th Virginia Cavalry hit up against Maj. Joseph Stearns's stalwart 1st New York, who "made a fine charge, driving the enemy pell mell." Badly outnumbered and outgunned, the 18th gave way, but not before it lost seventy men captured, including Capt. Frank Imboden.

As the remainder of the 18th fell back, John Imboden sent a rider down the East Road and asked that a section of guns be sent forward; they arrived so promptly that he realized Jones was already in position at Piedmont—but still he did not like it, and especially did not like what had happened to the 18th that morning. He and Grumble Jones argued openly as the battle swiftly approached.

Jones placed his infantry at the edge of a rolling woods northwest of the village, with its left anchored on a sixty-foot bluff overlooking the Middle River. Strother thought the position "strong and well chosen . . . on a conclave of wooded hills commanding an open valley between and open, gentle slopes in front . . . log and rail defenses very advantageously located in the edge of a forest." The federal approach to that line in the woods was up a smooth, open hill "so that troops moving over this hill could be mowed down by musketry . . . at short range."

Across East Road and east and south of the village, John Vaughn's Tennessee cavalry and Imboden's tired survivors from the 18th formed a wide semicircle south-ward to New Hope and Round Top Hill, insurance that Hunter could not flank the Confederates from the east. These arrangements displayed a glaring flaw, a large gap between the infantry's right and the cavalry's left, which bothered Jones not at all, as he believed cavalry could quickly close it.

When Hunter's advance appeared northward along the road in the form of Stahel's horsemen, Imboden recalled in a more fulsome memoir, "Lieut. Carter Berkeley [of McClanahan's Battery] dashed up with his guns and reported to me for orders." Though Jones, commanding, was nearby, Imboden "directed him to unlimber and open fire at once." Thus the formal battle opened, as Stahel's cavalry scattered out of harm's way in confusion.

And a change came over Gen. Jones, who "almost immediately calmed down as soon as the firing of Berkeley's guns began, for he was brave to a fault, and I believe enjoyed the roar of the battlefield."

Hunter, too, was conducting himself with energy. As his infantry hustled to form battle lines, Hunter assembled the 18th Connecticut, which had behaved so badly at New Market and "told them the enemy was before them and they would presently have a chance of retrieving their reputation." But, Strother reported, "they didn't seem much elated with the prospect and scarcely got up a decent cheer."

Augustus Moor's First Brigade, including the cheerless 18th Connecticut, now formed a line of battle opposite Jones's left, between the road and the river; to Moor's left, and also west of the road, Joseph Thoburn's Second Brigade moved into line— among them the hard-used 34th Massachusetts and 54th Pennsylvania. A regiment of the 5th New York Heavy Artillery, armed as infantry, had joined Hunter, and they took position with Moor.

Henry du Pont, ever inventive and now commanding Hunter's entire artillery, massed all of his twenty-two guns in one place, on the ridge behind the Shaver house, where Hunter had his headquarters, and deliberately began to select targets for their combined firepower, beginning with Carter Berkeley's advanced guns.

Shortly thereafter, Hunter's men were strongly reminded of their recent past when Moor advanced vigorously on Jones's line, only to be thrown back by a confederate counterattack that resounded to the cry of "New Market! New Market!"

Berkeley's section had found the range among Hunter's retreating infantry, but now du Pont selected Berkeley and rained down on his position such a terrific bombardment that the young lieutenant sent word to Imboden that all his horses soon would be killed, and he would be unable to withdraw. Jones ordered him to pull back. As Imboden relayed the order, he brought to Jones's attention the gap between the infantry and cavalry. Jones now filled it with artillery: McClanahan's remaining four guns, two of the Staunton Reserves's under Capt. James C. Marquis, and two of Capt. Thomas A. Bryan's Battery. Some of these guns were placed behind the infantry positions, and Bryan's four long range guns were placed far left.

As though by instinct, du Pont now concentrated his fire on the separate batteries. Marquis's guns were manned by boys aged sixteen to eighteen. He pounded Marquis and then Bryan.

"In a comparatively short time," he reported, "the concentrated fire of the . . . batteries was too much for these guns, which were compelled to abandon their position and fall back . . . down the road and beyond the village. The withdrawal . . . made in great haste, . . . I next concentrated the fire of my twenty-two pieces upon McClanahan's battery immediately in front of the village of Piedmont, with the result that some of the houses were considerably damaged. . . . [B]efore long it likewise limbered up and went to the rear."

While du Pont was chewing up Jones's artillery, Moor's brigade was making repeated attempts to overrun the infantry line along the front of the woods. The 18th Connecticut was behaving bravely; charging with the 5th New York heavies, it had been caught out on the open hill and was taking casualties under a regimental flag tattered with thirteen bullet holes and three cannon rips; the entire color guard, save one, killed or wounded.

By eleven-thirty, du Pont's guns had silenced the confederate artillery and he swung his guns toward Jones in the forest edge, "knocking the rail pens to splinters with great slaughter." As this slugging went on, Moor's brigade, exhausted by 150 casualties, began to pull back. The Confederates rose up and came after them "with ear-splitting yells" and made what du Pont called "a most determined assault upon our whole line."

Now Hunter began to waver. He ordered his wagons turned around, just in case, but the confederate attack, riddled by du Pont, slowed and then ceased. And the armies were where they had been all morning; neither side having been moved.

Hunter decided on one last attempt to break the confederate line, one suggested by the topography. East of the road, a long and wooded hollow or ravine ran from the northeast directly toward the village; it came out exactly where a gap again existed in the line with the removal of the confederate artillery. Hunter, leaving skirmishers in place to mask the movement, pulled the veteran 34th Massachusetts and 54th Pennsylvania out of line and sent them across the road and then down the ravine toward Piedmont.

At seven hundred yards from the confederate line, the 54th Pennsylvania fired a volley and "charged into the woods on the right flank and rear of the enemy's entrenched position." Col. Jacob Campbell reported that "a most desperate struggle took place, bayonets and clubbed guns . . . many hand to hand encounters." Behind them, the 34th Massachusetts came out of the ravine a mere twenty yards from the line and "advanced cheering" as "the enemy broke back into the woods in . . . confusion."

It was a brilliant stroke, and it had worked. Jones's infantry flank had been driven in and turned. The confederate line began to flake off and crumble.

Jones had intended all along to plug that gap in his line with cavalry, and he now sent a courier to tell Vaughn and Imboden to attack the left flanks of the federal regiments. Meanwhile, a child of battle, he himself rushed forward and swept up two reserve regiments that he had posted in the road and told Berkeley to follow along with his guns as he headed for the enemy.

Berkeley later commented on the action. "How vain the attempt to rush untried soldiers through a stampeding line of battle. . . . We were soon surrounded by our own flying men and in sight of the Yankees . . . Jones became desperate, rushed impetuously to the front, followed by many of Harper's men."

Harper was Col. Kenton Harper, who had been the first colonel of the 57th Virginia in the Stonewall Brigade. Too old to fight, he was sent home and placed in charge of the Reserves of Augusta, Rockbridge and Rockingham counties—and here they were, charging along after the inspired Jones, "right on the Yankee line of battle."

Doubtless Jones was brave. And his bravery proved deadly for the 34th Massachusetts, which had paid so dearly at New Market and now, said William Lincoln, in "less than five minutes we lost our major, adjutant, senior captain, and fifty-five men killed or wounded."

Whatever furies drove him, Jones rushed onward until a ball hit him squarely in the head, and he grumbled never again.

At the same time a troubled life was ending at one end of the line, an improbable hero was being born at the other—Julius Stahel, whose cavalry had been kicked around and who had been widely regarded as a Sigel-like phoney.

Many of Stahel's troopers had been dismounted and added to Moor's brigade for yet another attempt on the confederate left. As they advanced, Stahel, still mounted, was hit in the right arm and knocked to the ground. Bravely he had himself lifted back into the saddle. A soldier handed him his saber, which he lifted as he led a charge against the disintegrating confederate line. For this action, Stahel would later receive the Congressional Medal of Honor.

When Strother visited Stahel, however, the Hungarian told him "it pained his arm too much to ride."

An intoxicating sense of victory now seized the entire army. Strother recalled that "the earth shook with the roar of guns and musketry, and the . . . cheers rose with the smoke. . . . Back rolled the cheers from the front. Stretcher men, ambulance drivers, wounded men, butchers, bummers and all took up the shout."

As the dead and defeated Jones's infantry flooded past, running for their lives, Vaughn and Imboden and their combined command of two thousand cavalry troopers sat and watched. Their orders had never arrived. Now Imboden mounted his men and galloped toward the road, determined to make a stand at Mowry's Hill.

As Berkeley moved his guns southward along the road, he passed through the woods that surrounded Piedmont and came upon Lt. Park Collett "standing in the road limbering up and evidently oblivious of the critical condition. . . . I called out to him . . . that the Yankees were right behind us." Berkeley wheeled his section around to line up with Collett, "but it was too late, for . . . the enemy burst out of the woods, with yells of triumph, sabering, shooting, and riding down our poor fellows."

When Berkeley yelled at Collett to fire, one of his men replied, "[W]e will kill our own men."

"They would have been over us in a minute more. . . . I jumped off my horse and made a grab for the lanyard. . . . [T]he gunner . . . pulled it off himself."

Gen. Imboden was a witness to the extraordinary scene as he approached. "[W]e could even then distinctly hear the bugle notes of Stahel's cavalry brigade sounding the 'charge,' with which they came sweeping through Piedmont towards us, and the heavy thud of hoofs on the solid road from more than two thousand excited horses, . . . though we could not see them for the . . . woods."

Also appearing on the scene were about eighty Tennessee and Carolina riflemen under Maj. William Williams Stringfield of the 69th North Carolina. Imboden asked if they would still fight. Stringfield replied, "Yes, like hell."

"The enemy appeared in close column, platoon front, at a gallop." The cannon roared. The Tennessee muskets banged. Berkeley remembers that "the whole head of the Yankee column seemed to melt away." Imboden said that "the crashing of the shot on men and horses could be plainly heard. The head of the column . . . went down in a mass of groaning men and horses."

It was the end of the pursuit. Strother noted that the cavalry "got a round of grape and canister in their faces which drove them back." Berkeley said, "Collett saved everything."

June 5, Evening—On the Battlefield

Strother went forward with Maj. Theodore Lang on the now quiet field of battle to find and confirm Grumble Jones's death. He came upon "a body coarsely clothed in a dirty gray suit without any trappings or military insignia." But the corpse was wearing "a pair of fine military boots well worn and fine woolen underclothes perfectly clean and new. His hands were small and white, and his features, high white forehead, brown beard, and long hair indicated the gentleman and man of the upper class."

Maj. Lang "visited his pockets" and found a notation giving the total of his forces—seven thousand men and sixteen guns—and a letter from Imboden, but its contents will never be known.

That night Vaughn and Imboden led the survivors through New Hope to Fishersville, where they wired Lee. To defend Staunton, they said, they needed reinforcements. None were coming, replied Lee. The generals then decided to move toward Waynesboro and the railroad through Rockfish Gap, which they knew they must hold at all costs.

They had left on the field at Piedmont six hundred killed and wounded, and a thousand others fallen into federal hands. For the first time in the war, the upper

Shenandoah was under federal control. For the first time, a confederate army had been run out of Jackson's valley.

Hunter set up headquarters in "a small cottage in the village of Piedmont" and "had a good supper and a triumphant evening. The bands played and the men sang and shouted. The army was intoxicated with joy. Verily, they had wiped out the disgrace of New Market."

Monday, June 6—Staunton

Piedmont was a calamity for the confederate cause. It turned Lee's strategic flank. Yet it remains one of the war's under-reported battles. One loser, Jones, did not live to defend himself; the other loser, Imboden, wished to forget it. The winner, Hunter, became fully occupied with other less sanguine matters. It was a defeat that no one wished to describe and a victory that got old too soon, but it had an immediate, profound result.

On June 6, Hunter decided against Strother's advice to pursue Imboden and assault Waynesboro and took instead the road to Staunton, that long desired prize. As the column approached the city, "a dozen or more girls in their Sunday dresses stood by the roadside . . . and presented us with bouquets, . . . whether sincere or meant as a propitiation of the demons I could not tell."

Their entry into the city was made in grand style, with two bands and a vivid color guard. They paraded the main streets, playing "Hail Columbia" and "Yankee Doodle." The audience, "a few skinny sallow women, peeped from between half-closed window blinds, but generally the houses were closed."

Late in the day, Hunter went to the Staunton jail and "released all its inmates, thieves, spies, forgers, deserters, Irishmen, union men, Yankee soldiers, confederate officers, murderers, and rioters generally" and had to be restrained from burning it down.

Tuesday, June 7—Staunton

Strother: "[E]verything in shocking confusion. They were burning the railroad property and public stores and work shops. A mixed mob of federal soldiers, Negroes, Secessionists, mulatto women, children, Jews, and camp followers and the riff raff of the town were engaged in plundering the stores and depots. . . . At the Virginia Hotel Hospital, the provost guard were knocking the heads out of numerous barrels of apple brandy. The precious stream was running over the curbstones in cascades and rushing down the gutters with floating chips, paper, horse dung and dead rats. This luscious mixture was greedily drunk by dozens of soldiers and vagabonds on their hands and knees and their mouths in the gutter."

June 7—Lee's Headquarters, Cold Harbor

Grant's charge at Cold Harbor on June 3, a truly terrible assault in which his men were killed at the rate of a thousand per minute, had staggered both armies. In three days fifty thousand federal troops, half those present for duty, had been utilized in the attack, and twelve thousand of them had been killed or wounded. Of Lee's sixty thousand, half had been in the lines. His losses were less than half of Grant's.

Brave Breckinridge had led his brigades into action at the North Anna and at Cold Harbor. There, on June 4, his trusted horse, Old Sorrel, had been killed, crushing Breckinridge in the fall. Thought at first to be dead, he had partially recovered but still could not walk.

Able or not, Lee needed him back in the Valley. On June 7, Breckinridge was asked to lead his command westward once more, even if from the back of a wagon.

June 7—Staunton

Hunter had already started his cavalry eastward toward Waynesboro, intending to move on Charlottesville, when, upon hearing that Crook and Averell were at Buffalo Gap to the west, he took the rest of the army in that direction. After marching a few miles and hearing from scouts that the gap was empty, he halted. Other scouts then reported confederate cavalry moving to the south, toward Waynesboro. "Perceiving that we were marching away from the enemy, we faced about and returned to . . . Staunton." There Hunter finally received the tidings that Crook was only ten miles away, moving down the Virginia Central Railroad line from Goshen. He had with him twelve regiments of infantry, two batteries, and cavalry.

June 7—Cold Harbor

Lee to Jefferson Davis:

> If we cannot restrain the movements of the enemy in the Valley, he will do us great evil.

June 7—A "Favorite Rendezvous"

Harry Gilmor had been up in Clarke County, east of Winchester and well north of Front Royal, where he narrowly escaped a party of Jessie scouts—federal soldiers who wore confederate uniforms—and had to swim the Shenandoah again to rejoin his unit, reduced by now to about thirty, at "a favorite rendezvous." There a courier arrived: "Hunter has defeated Jones and Imboden, killing the former, at New Hope. He has pushed on to Lexington. . . . Come immediately."

Gilmor went to Fort Valley to collect his mare Bessie and then rode on to Mount

Airy and found what Hunter had left. The Meems's house had been "ransacked from top to bottom" and Hunter's men had been "killing all the hogs, sheep, poultry except for a few defended by a lady with a revolver."

He went on southward, behind Hunter's army, and caught up with Imboden and Vaughn at their perch on the mountainside beyond Waynesboro.

Thursday, June 9—Council of War, Staunton

Averell agreed with Strother that the future campaign should "follow up the Valley via Lexington and Buchanan and thence by the Peaks of Otter road to Liberty [now Bedford] and Lynchburg." But Crook was less sanguine about it. "What do you propose by this plan?" he asked Strother.

"To drive Lee out of Richmond by seizing and threatening his southern and western communications and sources of supply."

"Can you do this with our present force?"

"We can easily beat all of the force the enemy has in the Valley and West Virginia combined. Even if Lee details a division, which seems doubtful the way he is pressed by Grant, we have Sheridan cooperating with us. He will cut it off."

Crook stroked his huge, forked beard. "You may take Lynchburg, but you can depend on it that Lee will not let you hold it for long. If you expect to do it, you must do it now, and quickly."

"At the moment, we haven't the ammunition."

"Speed is more important than ammunition, more important than numbers. Besides, I have plenty of ammunition. Let me take my division and I will march on Lynchburg."

When Strother passed this along to Hunter, the commanding general commented that a good deal of delay was inevitable. (It takes time to burn houses, he might have said.) Nonetheless, he assented to the general plan of movement, and Strother drew up orders of march for the following day.

Crook's Army of the Kanahwa, as it was termed, added twelve thousand infantrymen to the Army of the Shenandoah's eight thousand. Thus the newly-minted Army of West Virginia, as Strother coined it in his orders, would march toward Lexington with twenty thousand men, thirty-six cannon and five thousand cavalry.

The wounded Stahel was replaced by another European, the French officer Alfred N. Duffié. Col. Moor's enlistment was up, and he had had enough with both Sigel and Stahel now gone; he was told to take his regiment, the 28th Ohio, and escort the mob of prisoners and refugees to Buffalo Gap and Beverly on his way home. Moor's command of the First Brigade, 1st Infantry Division, was given to capable George Wells of the battered 34th Massachusetts

Coming up to join the army was a supply train of two hundred wagons, many carrying ammunition, escorted by two regiments of infantry and several cavalry squadrons. What the Union had devoutly wished was about to happen—a large and powerful federal army was loose in southern Virginia, capable of closing on Lee at Richmond.

*Friday, June 10—The Road to
   Lexington*

Behind them, as they departed,
Staunton burned—several
woolen factories, a thousand
stands of arms, a thousand cavalry saddles, shoes and leather,
confederate gray cloth, all going up in gray smoke. Before
they left, however, there was "a
rather undignified scene" when
Lt. Col. William E. Starr caught
a fellow trying to steal his horse
and hauled him before Hunter,
who "cuffed and kicked him
around the tent" before releas-
ing him. Following this, Hunter
was reported to be in "high
good humor."

They moved out in four columns. Duffié took his cavalry
division eastward, toward the
Blue Ridge, slipping through
Tye River Gap in a wide flanking movement on Lexington
and hoping to cut the Charlot-

David Hunter Strother
Virginia State Library & Archives

"TIGER JOHN" MC CAUSLAND

tesville-Lynchburg rail line en route. Sullivan's infantry division, accompanied by
Hunter, took the pike for Mint Spring, Greenville, Steele's Tavern, Fairfield and Timber
Ridge, beyond which lay Lexington. Averell and Crook moved out by more westerly
mountain roads, through Middlebrook, Newport, Brownsburg and Cedar Grove.

There was nothing and no one in front of this federal force of twenty thousand men
but the thousand-man cavalry of "Tiger John" McCausland.

Like du Pont, McCausland had finished first in his class, but at VMI (1857). Like
du Pont, he had a good head—was a math teacher at VMI and later at the University
of Virginia. While du Pont's family was one of the most prominent in the United States,
McCausland's father was an immigrant from Ireland. Ever since the disaster at Cloyd's
Mountain (with Jenkins's death, he had been promoted to brigadier general),
McCausland had been clinging to Crooks' flank and duelling Averell. As they moved
toward their rendezvous with Hunter, McCausland stopped them at Panther Gap
beyond Goshen and then fell back along the track through Bell's Valley and Buffalo
Gap, where, on June 6, he heard about Piedmont and realized that he was all of the
confederate force left in the Valley.

He led his troopers across country to the Middlebrook road—this was the column reported to Hunter as he moved toward Buffalo Gap on June 7—where he took up a position on Arbor Hill, a few miles outside Staunton. If Hunter moved eastward, toward Waynesboro, Rockfish Gap and Charlottesville, McCausland would be after him like a hound dog; but if he moved southward, toward Lexington, there would be no need to pursue.

Sgt. James Zechariah McChesney, Co. H, 14th Virginia Cavalry, saw the dust cloud billowing over the trees as Averell's horses came down the Middlebrook road near Arbor Hill. He and a companion, having sent their horses to the rear, were crouching behind a barricade of fence rails which McCausland's pickets had thrown across the road. When the leading rider came within a thousand yards, McChesney opened fire with his Enfield, causing an abrupt halt of the federal column, which put out a skirmish line, not knowing what was in their front. McChesney and his companion then ran for it, a half mile, regained their horses and retreated.

June 10—Newport, on the Greenfield Road

Capt. Thomas Lewis Feamster, 14th Virginia Cavalry: "Commenced firing on Pickets early and we are driven back to the main column after a sharp skirmish, . . . dismounted & form a line of Battle the enemy approach us and flank us both on the right & left. Have a severe little fight & are driven back."

James McChesney, 14th Virginia Cavalry: "[H]ad quite a spirited skirmish, losing several men, but inflicting greater loss. . . . [S]lowly retreating, [McCausland] contested almost every hill top until we reached . . . Newport, when the rear guard under the command of Captain . . . Bouldin and Joseph Wilson charged and killed a number of enemy."

Capt. Edwin Edmunds Bouldin, 14th Virginia Cavalry: "In this charge an Irishman belonging to the Churchville Cavalry . . . & I were right in front, & he said to me, 'Now, Captain, don't you go too far—if you do they will get ya.' . . . When we started the charge we gave the rebel yell, & that warned McCausland of what was going on. He quickly stationed . . . dismounted men along the road & when the Yankees followed us back they poured the minié balls into them."

Crook's halted column had had enough of this. At Newport, Averell split off and rode westward to the Walker's Creek Valley and then by way of Hays Creek toward Brownsburg, hoping to get behind McCausland. The movement failed.

June 10—Brownsburg

At the beautiful hamlet of Brownsburg, McCausland received unexpected and welcome support when three guns of Thomas E. Jackson's battery of horse artillery suddenly showed up. They had been on the move all the way from southwestern

Virginia and had almost been cut off and captured by Averell's cavalry. Gathering up his entire strength, Tiger John McCausland retreated again to Cameron's Farm on a hill outside Lexington.

June 10, Late Afternoon—Hays Creek

At the Culton farm, young Calvin and a black companion were playing when they heard the cry, "Yankees!"

With a second Culton boy, they raced into the woods on horses they wanted to save, carrying hams that they hid in a sink hole and covered with rock. They tied their horses and waited anxiously through a long night.

Behind them, Averell stopped his column and made his headquarters at the farm called Bellvue. To the east was Brownsburg, where Crook arrived and camped not long after McCausland had gone.

June 10—Lexington, VMI

Leaving his command at the Cameron farm, McCausland continued on into Lexington. The road dropped down a steep bank, crossed the North (later renamed Maury) River on a wooden bridge and then climbed a bluff into town. The barracks of the institute, like a medieval fort, dominated the skyline. Beyond them, on the same ridge, were the white columns and red brick classrooms of Washington College. He went to the home of superintendent Francis Smith of VMI where Scott Shipp joined them. His message was simple: he could not defeat nor even stop Hunter, not even with the help of the cadets. They agreed to move a howitzer to the North River bridge and to ready bales of turpentine-soaked hay to fire it when the time came. That would be, they knew, only a matter of hours.

Saturday, June 11—Bellvue

When the Culton boys saw the Yankees mount up and ride away, they crept out of the woods with the hams and horses. A terrifying sight greeted them—the body of an old man hanging from a tree behind Bellvue.

David S. Creigh, charged with murdering a union soldier during one of Averell's raids, had been arrested and made to walk to Brownsburg all the way from Greenbrier County, across the mountains to the west. A slave had told on him and shown the Yanks the man's grave.

A drumhead court martial was summoned at Bellvue. Creigh readily admitted killing the man for cause. "He was a drunken straggler," he said, "and I found him robbing my home contrary to all rules of warfare." Later versions of the testimony said the man was molesting Creigh's daughter.

"Hang him," said Averell, despite the protest of several of his officers. It was believed that Hunter had approved the order. On the following dawn, Creigh, the father of nine children, was hanged from a tree behind the house. Two of his boys, Fred and Cyrus, were serving with the 14th Virginia Cavalry under "Tiger" John McCausland.

June 11, 10:00 A.M.—Lexington

At ten A.M. on June 11, the VMI corps of cadets was once more bugled into position and began standing to arms as word came that Hunter was only a dozen miles to the north. Cadet Henry Wise led a company onto a nearby hillside, while others were assigned to carry the turpentine–soaked bales of hay down to the covered bridge over the North River.

Soon they came, McCausland's harried little brigade, which swiftly passed, and then the rear guard, spilling down the ravine through which the valley road descended to dead end at the river road that took the traffic southeast to the bridge. The last of the mounted men clattered over, and the cadets applied torches.

Hunter's forward scouts were only a half-mile behind. By the time they appeared at the crest of the road, the bridge was a tunnel of flame, and McCausland had the howitzer down by the river and Jackson's battery up on the hills above VMI opening on the federal advance.

Federal artillery quickly appeared. Henry du Pont's battery of six guns was stationed to the east of the road, on the highest hill of the Cameron farm, offering a splendid view of the beautiful little red brick town nestled in the valley below, the church spires of Grace Episcopal and Thomas U. Walter's Lexington Presbyterian, the belfry of the old courthouse in the town center; the barracks of VMI with its battlemented walls and beyond, on a bluff to the west, the red and white buildings of Washington College against a green hill, the whole scene framed by flat-topped House Mountain and its companion heights. A dozen guns—Capt. Daniel W. Glassie's battery from Kentucky and Lt. George P. Kirkland's from Ohio—took up position to the west of the valley road, on the ridge above Joseph Shaner's apple orchard.

When they opened fire, shells rained down on Main Street and its shops, businesses and hotels. One fell at the entrance to Craft's Blue Hotel, another blew up Rhode's Tin Shop. Two fell against the old city jail and county buildings, one on Dr. Barton's office. Achilles J. Tynes, one of McCausland's exhausted staff, was sitting on the steps of the Lexington Hotel when, he said, "the rascals on the other side of the river got the range of the street . . . & let fly a shell. . . . [I]t passed over our heads about five feet, passing up the street about a hundred yards."

Rose Pendleton, the wife of Gen. William N. Pendleton, recorded the attack. "The wretches shelled the town for hours. Shells fell everywhere —in Col. Williamson's yard, into Mr. John Campbell's house, into Miss Baxter's House. One struck Colonel [Andrew] Reid's front door and almost struck his daughter."

Fannie Wilson reported that "we were standing in the front door when the ball passed over our heads . . . another struck the rafter, exploding with a thunderous noise . . . knocked nearly all the plastering off . . . made a great many holes . . . two pieces perforated the ceiling of grandpa's room just above the head of his bed where he was lying at the time in a doze."

Bricks and mortar began to fly from the VMI barracks as shells pounded the walls. About one P.M. the cadets were told to move out as shells exploded against Col. Shipp's house and began falling at the west end of the parade ground. The boys marched away from Lexington by the Fairgrounds Road, intending to cross the North River at its mouth and camp at Balcony Falls. Said Wise, "It galled and mortified us that we had been compelled to abandon it without firing a shot."

The shelling went on until midafternoon, when McChesney, on vidette duty at Mulberry Hill, Col. Reid's farm in the rear of Washington College "saw a large body of cavalry . . . descending a distant hill from the direction of the Barrens." Averell, coming from Brownsburg, had crossed the North River at Rockbridge Baths and was about to flank McCausland and trap him between two forces. McCausland saw the danger at once.

Rose Pendleton observed his withdrawl and Hunter's arrival. "[F]or two hours there was one continuous stream of cavalry, riding at a fast trot, and several abreast, passing out at the top of town. A quarter after four the vile rabble came over the hills in swarms."

As McCausland fell back to Broad Creek near Fancy Hill, ten miles south of Lexington, he crossed and then burned the bridge across the stream.

When, several miles outside of town, the cadet column halted, young Wise looked back and saw "the towers and turrets of the barracks, mess hall, and professor's houses in full blaze, sending up great masses of flame and smoke." Black Dave Hunter must have been in a truly fine mood.

June 11, 4:00 P.M.—Lexington

The cavalry and artillery crossed the North on a pontoon bridge, and most of the infantry crossed on the charred skeleton of the covered bridge, upon which the engineers had laid lumber from nearby buildings. But still others had hop–skipped across while the embers were still warm, so eager were they for plunder. By the time Strother and Hunter and the staff arrived at VMI they found "the sack already far advanced, soldiers, Negroes, and riffraff disputing over the plunder." One soldier took "one hundred dollars in gold" from the trunk of a cadet. Others "came out loaded with beds. carpets, cut velvet chairs, mathematical glasses and instruments, stuffed birds, charts, books, papers, arms, cadet uniforms, and hats in most ridiculous confusion."

Hunter took the superintendant's home on the parade grounds for his headquarters, "an elegant establishment" where the staff was "served at a table by an old-fashioned Virginia house servant named Robinson."

First, however, Hunter had stopped by the house of professor and major William Gilham and told Mrs. Gilham to get out her furniture, as he intended to burn the house in the morning. She politely offered him some applejack, icily apologized for its quality and began moving her furniture to the lawn.

The town was now swarming with troops. Miss Maggie Preston said, "They began to pour into our yard and kitchen. I ordered them out . . . half a dozen at a time. . . . They heeded me no more than wild beasts would have done; swore at me; and left me not one piece [of meat]. They broke into the smokehouse, raided the cellar of its butter."

Rose Pendleton, too, was "soon overrun by the thieving wretches," as were many, many others.

The army was marched through to the east of town, passing Stonewall Jackson's grave on the way. This they treated with respect, baring their heads and marching slowly and respectfully past. Some picked clover from the grave as a mememto.

June 11, Evening—Lexington

The home of the former governor of Virginia, John Letcher, stood at the corner of Main Street and Boundary Street, the lane dividing the VMI and Washington College campuses. Mrs. Letcher had been asked to board two officers, one of whom was Capt. Towns. Towns assured his hostess that her home would be spared, despite rumor to the contrary, and later brought her personal assurances from Gen. Hunter himself.

Sunday, June 12—Lexington Aflame

When asked by Hunter, Strother had given his opinion that VMI was "a most dangerous establishment where treason was systematically taught," and mentioned "what a list of capable military officers had been there raised up against the government of the country." Strother had a point. McCausland was only one of several dozen officers that VMI provided to the Confederacy. In fact, the institute provided one lieutenant general, three major generals, eighteen brigadiers, 160 colonels, 110 majors, 306 captains and 221 lieutenants.

Hunter's mind had long been made up. Early on Sunday he gave the order to fire everything, all the buildings and outbuildings. This order flushed the looters who were still at work. "One fellow had a stuffed gannet from the museum, . . . others high-topped hats. . . . Meigs came out with fine mathematical instruments, and Dr. Patton . . . with a beautiful human skeleton."

Something else turned up in the debris. Said Hunter, as a justification for his action, "I found here a violent proclamation from John Letcher, lately governor of Virginia, inciting a guerilla warfare upon my troops, and I ordered his property to be burned."

On the campus, fires were set.

"The burning of the Institute made a grand picture," wrote Strother, "a vast volume of black smoke rolled above the flames and covered half the horizon."

Hunter, recalled a cavalry officer, "stood looking at the burning building, saying as he rubbed his hands and chuckled with delight, 'Doesn't that burn beautifully?'"

June 12—The Letcher Home, Main Street

Capt. Matthew Berry, Hunter's assistant provost marshal, arrived with a squad and rang the door bell.

"General Hunter has ordered this house burned," he told Mrs. Letcher.

"But that's impossible. I have the general's own assurances. There must be some mistake. May I see your order, Captain?"

"The order was verbal, ma'm."

"You must wait until I see General Hunter."

"The order is preemptory, ma'm. You have five minutes to leave the house."

"But I must gather my mother's, and my children's, and my sister's clothing!"

"Sorry, ma'm, there is no time for that."

Whereupon Berry made his way past her, poured camphene on the parlor floor, and set it ablaze. He spotted Lizzie Letcher leaving by the back door with an armful of clothing and took it from her and cast it into the flames.

Mrs. Letcher ran upstairs and snatched her sleeping baby from the cradle and rushed from the house, "leaving everything she had to the flames."

The governor's seventy-eight-year-old mother lived next door, and Berry next set fire to her stable. As the sparks flew the forty feet toward her home, remembered young Sam Houston Letcher, then a lad of sixteen, "a Negro servant tried to extinguish it, and the soldiers threatened to shoot him."

Capt. Towns then arrived, presumably in a fury that his assurances had been so meaningless, countermanded the order and made the men form a bucket brigade to put the fire out.

Strother and Maj. Charles Halpine, the assistant adjutant, and Gen. Averell had walked to an opposite hill "to view the scene which was grand, although the burning went on very slowly."

Cornelia McDonald found "Mrs. Letcher . . . sitting on a stone in the street with the baby on her lap sleeping, and her other children gathered around her. She sat tearless and calm, but it was a pitiable group."

June 12, 2:00 P.M.—VMI

The institute burned out about two P.M., and, Strother reported, "the arsenal blew up with a smart explosion. The General seemed to enjoy the scene."

Strother had admired the bronze statue of Washington that stood before the institute and suggested that it would make a nice trophy of war—in Wheeling. Lt. John Meigs, to whom fell the job of having it crated, insisted it go to West Point.

"Whatever," said Strother.

The homes of Col. Thomas Williamson and Maj. Gilham next were torched. Mrs. Gilham sat on the parade ground in the midst of her belongings "firm and ladylike."

June 12—Bushwacker

As Crook advanced toward Lexington. Job Thorn, of Rockbridge, acted as his guide.

Matthew X. White, Jr., a captain of the 1st Rockbridge Dragoons in 1862, had left the war because of ill health, but had reenlisted on June 10 to face Hunter. On picket for the 14th Virginia on June 11th, he shot and killed Thorn.

On the following day, White went to his home in Lexington to secure some property before moving out, and there he was arrested. Hunter ordered him shot as a bushwhacker. He was taken across the river to the Cameron farm and shot eight times in the back. The Cameron daughters stayed all night with the body.

June 12—Lee's Headquarters, Near Richmond

Because the rheumatism that he contracted during the Mexican War and the minié ball that smacked into his chest at Williamsburg in 1862 had conspired to bend him permanently forward, Jubal Anderson Early appeared thinner, smaller and older than his 170 pounds, six-foot height and forty-seven years. His hair flopped in waves over outsized ears and his beard bristled, giving him an unkempt, disheveled look that made him easy to caricature—Old Jug Ears, the troops called him, Old Jube, Old Jubilee.

He was brave. His high pitched, raspy voice was easily distinguished from other voices over the sounds of a battle that competed with it, as when he burst from the woods into the open before federal cannon at Williamsburg and most people within earshot heard: *Follow me!*

He was known to curse, drink, chew tobacco. His temper was irreligious, sarcastic, at times sardonic. He was inclined to distrust his subordinates—all qualities that kept him a lifelong bachelor (when asked to speak to several ladies, Early said he had trouble speaking to one) and made him distasteful to the likes of his aide-de-camp, handsome Henry Kyd Douglas, who summed up his boss as "arbitrary, cynical, with strong prejudices, he was personally disagreeable; he made few admirers or friends either by his manners or his habits. . . . If he had a tender feeling, he endeavoured to conceal it and acted as though he would be ashamed to be detected in doing a kindness."

Yet those thick, black eyebrows shadowed striking dark eyes that glimmered with intelligence, the sharp look and cutting mind of what he had been, a commonwealth's attorney in rural Rocky Mount, Franklin County, in the hills south of Roanoke, Virginia.

The county still reeked of the frontier. It had been named in 1785 for Benjamin. Three years before, Jacob Boone, Daniel's cousin, had come up the Carolina road and built a mill and cabin on the banks of Maggodee Creek. Sited a few miles west of Rocky Mount, the Hill home along Pigg River was still called "the Indian fort," and folks recalled that two of Robert Hill's sons had been killed by Indians and one by a panther.

The first court, convened in 1786, was held in a house of logs which was still in use when Jubal Early was fifteen years old and the town had grown to thirty dwellings. The records of that court refer to the Early family in several guises. The old Washington Iron Works, which made arms during the Revolution, ended up in the hands of Col. Jeremiah Early;

Battles & Leaders

MAJ. GEN. JUBAL ANDERSON EARLY

the man who sold it to him, Col. John Donelson, moved on down to Tennessee where his daughter Rachel married Andrew Jackson.

In 1811, five years before Jubal was born, a marriage bond on January 7 gave notice that one Joseph Hix intended to marry the widow Polly Early. Her relatives were outraged, since Hix worked for Polly and was her social inferior. On the wedding night the couple entered their bridal chamber—and found awaiting them on the bed the exhumed coffin of her first husband.

Old Jube, a clever country boy who understood the strange, wild ways in which frontier people, deprived of so much, sometimes acted, knew he was very different in background and personality from the graceful sons of the eastern planter society with whom he served. He was a cob. He would never be a hero.

In fact, Jubal Early had far more in common with plebeian Ulysses Grant than he did with patrician Robert Lee. Early's backwoods childhood wasn't much different than Grant's out in Ohio, and both went to West Point because it meant a continuation of education. Both men served in Mexico, and both resigned their army commissions. Both knew hard times. Before the war called them out, Grant farmed a piece of ground he called Hardscrabble, a hand-me-down from his wife's family, and Early practised law in Rocky Mount, where he had a lot of clients who couldn't or wouldn't pay.

They could have ended up serving together, since Early was strongly against secession. In the end, though, his feelings of patrimony narrowed themselves to Virginia, and the pressure of the political community in which he lived decided him. He became a member of the Virginia Secession Convention of 1861.

He wasn't Jackson. But here he was, commanding Jackson's old II Corps, and Lee was content to have him do so because this cantankerous country lawyer with the isolated personality had another fundamental virtue that he shared with Grant—he would fight.

Lee was not taking a half measure. He was sending out an entire corps of eight thousand veterans that had been attached to his army and seen every major action since Cedar Mountain in August of 1862. Not any corps, but the Second Corps, which included Jackson's old brigades that knew the Valley of Virginia like the back of their hands. Lee knew that something had to be done about Hunter, but he was not content to drive him off; he was going to smash him, obliterate him. Because he had something else in mind. He and Early examined a large scale map of Virginia and Lee's finger ran up the Valley of Virginia, northward.

Monday, June 13, 2:00 A.M.—Camp at Cold Harbor

The initial conversation between Lee and Gen. Jubal Early was not noted later by either man—simply the result. The II Corps was in the rest area behind A.P. Hill's III Corps lines at Cold Harbor. Early left Lee's headquarters around midnight. At two A.M. men passed quietly between the campfires, and there was a vast heaving rustle like a wind through oaks as an army roused as quietly as possible and took formation on the roads, with murmured orders and whispered speculation. It was Early's desire to slip away unnoticed from the Richmond front, to disappear until he was suddenly on Hunter's back.

June 13—Lexington

Hunter decided to spare Superintendant Smith's house. "I suppose he feels that the roof which has sheltered us and the house where we have been entertained should be saved." Out of respect for the "Father of His Country," he also spared Washington College.

Word came from Averell that he was driving McCausland's two thousand men toward Buchanan. Duffié, "all sunburned and dusty," appeared in person and reported that he had led his troopers past Waynesboro and through the Tye River Gap to the east side of the Blue Ridge, where they destroyed five miles of the Charlottesville-

Lynchburg track, took seventy prisoners, seven hundred horses, three hundred wagons—a report that Strother, who tried to confirm it with others, found "greatly exaggerated."

He also displayed a package containing "several millions of confederate money" and said, "Eh, bien, General. I gob all dis monnoie."

June 13—Lynchburg

How Duffié had missed Imboden, and vice versa, is a mystery. From Rockfish Gap, Breckinridge had told Imboden to go after Duffié and to "overtake, engage, and whip him." Imboden had led his command up the South River and found the Mount Torry furnace burned. Turning toward Lexington, he found the Buena Vista furnace also burned. Without further ado, he turned back through White's Gap and followed Bent's Creek into Lynchburg, arriving on the 13th and immediately going into camp to rest his men and horses. He had neither overtaken nor engaged Duffié, much to Breckinridge's annoyance. Imboden obviously thought that Lynchburg came first.

June 13—Buchanan Bridge

As Hunter pressed on and McCausland fell back there were frequent clashes between van and rear guard, and a certain dangerous familiarity arose. Capt. Feamster of the 14th could not help but notice a particular officer riding "a splendid charger, iron gray. Again and again had we seen this gallant officer in front as the Yankees came in sight, day after day. He would get on some high point . . . & look at us thro' his field glasses."

When the moving columns reached the crossing of the James at Buchanan, Feamster set an ambush while McCausland fired the covered bridge. As usual, the gallant officer on the iron gray was in front, and, as usual, Feamster was the last man of the retreating column. Suddenly, they found themselves in hand-to-hand combat. Feamster knocked the officer's hat off, and "would have captured or killed him if he had not made his horse jump the fence." So impressed was Feamster with his opponent that he learned his name—William H. Powell.

June 13—The Road to Charlottesville

Early's corps had moved off through the dark of night along the Mechanicsville pike, toward Richmond, and the men speculated that they were moving to head off Grant from east of town. But as they crossed the Chickahominy River, the columns turned right, westward. Could they be going back to their beloved Valley? Their hopes rose even more when they turned west again, up the old Three Chopt road, named for the triple blazes that marked out the original route.

For Sgt. John Worsham, this was a most fortuitous turning, for he had relatives who lived only a mile from the route of march. He was, as his memoirs are titled, "one of Jackson's foot cavalry," in Co. F of the 21st Virginia Infantry. Despite such plebeian hash marks, Worsham's father was a successful merchant tailor, had blue Virginia blood tracing to 1640, was married to a lady whose father and grandfather had fought in the great American wars—1812 and Revolutionary. His compatriots in Co. F were Richmond's "young men generally of wealth, education, and refinement."

T.C. De Leon, recalling the city's war years in 1890, remembered Co. F through a haze of affection as containing "the brilliant advocate, the skillful surgeon, the man of letters, and the smooth-faced pet of the Mayday gatherings—all that made the pride, the boast and the love of Richmond."

That morning Worsham peeled off from the column and arrived at his relatives' home to find "all the ladies of the family and two of Richmond's belles assembled on a large porch." The dining room servant brought out a platter with ash cakes and a huge glass of buttermilk and ice, and one of the belles waited on John. Thirty years later he still recalled the scene vividly and fondly. "I can see those belles now, eating their ash cakes and drinking their buttermilk [to the sound of] distant cannon from Lee's and Grant's armies and the cheers from my own corps, marching we knew not whither."

He draws a vivid picture: the swirling crinolines and graceful skirts, the drawling, lilting conversation in the upper keys playing against the distant, muffled boom of artillery in the lower ranges, the dust from the marching column, the sweat running down the icy glass, a strange interlude of peace, civility with ash cakes and buttermilk instead of muddy water and beef jerky—then the brave good-byes, and dainty linen handkerchiefs waved from the porch, and they were gone.

II Corps made twenty-five miles that day and camped at Ground Squirrel Bridge over the James.

Tuesday, June 14—Maj. Gen. John Brown Gordon

On the morning of June 14, as Early's corps was tramping along, Gen. Gordon rode by on his horse.

"Hey, boys," he called out, "don't you want supper? You keep marchin' this fast you're going to wear out the wagon mules back there and that's the last you'll see of supper!"

If ever there was a soldier, it was Maj. Gen. John Brown Gordon of Georgia. Coat off, sleeves rolled up, wearing a savage Antietam scar on his left cheek like a chevron, his seat was ram-rod straight and his commanding voice could be used as a weapon.

A lawyer by training, Gordon had been a successful business man in the coal industry of northern Georgia and father of two children. He hesitated to enlist until his wife resolved his dilemma; she left the children with Gordon's mother and went to war with him, managing always to be near the front.

Elected captain of a ragtag bunch of local boys who called themselves, after the caps they wore, the Raccoon Roughs, he was soon named colonel of the 6th Alabama. At Seven Pines in 1862, the regiment made a brave attack, during which it lost all of its field officers and had its flank company "torn to a bloody fragment." It suffered forty-four casualties from its fifty-five officers and men, a total of sixty percent casualties, including Gordon's brother. During the charge, Gordon's horse was killed under him and his coat was riddled with bullet holes, but he was untouched.

He fought as bravely at Gaines's Mill and led Rodes's division at Malvern Hill, but he was remembered best in the army for his role at Antietam. Positioned in what came to be known as the Bloody Lane, he was exhorted by Lee to hold his ground or endanger the whole army. Gordon replied, "These

Battles & Leaders

MAJ. GEN. JOHN BROWN GORDON

men are going to stay here, General, until the sun goes down or victory is won." He was hit five times, the last a head wound so severe that his hat filled with blood as he lay unconscious; only a hole in the crown prevented him from drowning.

Carried into Virginia bloody and disfigured, he rallied to greet his devoted wife with a sprightly: "[I've]been to an Irish wedding." He recovered only to be wounded four more times at Spotsylvania, where he stood the brunt of the federal assault at the Bloody Angle.

Now Worsham, seeing him ride by on this June morning, had to comment that "I will bear my testimony that he was the most gallant man I ever saw on a battlefield. . . . [H]e shrank from nothing in battle. . . . The skirmishers were devoted to him and they would generally do as he wished."

Said another veteran, "He's most the prettiest thing you ever did see on a field of fight. It'ud put fight into a whipped chicken just to look at him!"

After the battle of Fredericksburg, one of the soldiers asked that Gordon not be allowed to address them before a battle again. When asked why, he replied, "Because he makes me feel like I could storm hell."

Early, however, was not devoted to Gordon. It had happened at the Wilderness, on May 6th, when Gordon, to his great astonishment, found Grant's right flank in the air and his own command lapped so far to the union right that he felt he could roll the whole line and give Grant a devastating defeat. He pleaded with Richard Ewell and Early for permission to attack. Early believed that Burnside had fallen in behind Grant's exposed flank and opposed the attack. Despite Gordon's continual entreaties and offer to take full responsibility, nothing happened until 5:30 in the afternoon, almost sundown, when Lee himself rode up to Ewell's headquarters to ask for some action to relieve pressure on the other wing of his army. Gordon, speaking over the heads of his superiors, told Lee what he had seen that morning and how he had been asking for an attack. An angry Early stepped in and renewed his objections.

Lee considered. "Attack them, General Gordon," he said at length, "and wreck as much of their line as you can before dark."

It was tragic for the Confederates—not the fight, but the missed opportunity. Grant's line went down like dominoes, with no Burnside in support or relief—regiment after regiment, with darkness coming on, and Gordon knowing the whole time what might have been. He minced no words in his report. "[H]ad the movement been made at an earlier hour and properly supported, . . . it would have resulted in a decided disaster to the whole right wing of General Grant's army, if not in its entire disorganization."

Gordon knew that Lee and Early and Ewell and the rest all knew that James Longstreet had turned Grant's left that day; with both flanks turned, Grant's army would have been smashed and driven back across the Rapidan. The Wilderness could have been a Yankee Gettysburg.

Lee blamed it on Ewell, leaving room for Gordon and Early to ignore the matter. Movement and action have a way of postponing grievances, and Gordon, whatever was in his heart, managed his division under Early without protest or problem. He wasn't one to gnaw a grudge when he was thinking about tired mules and tonight's supper.

June 14—Buchanan

Hunter's staff arrived in Buchanan about sunset and took quarters in the Haynes Hotel. After supper Averell appeared and reported that he had been unable to save the James River bridge. They had caught a spy, one of McCausland's men trying to pose as a federal scout.

Hunter spoke. "Let him be hung forthwith."

"Well, no," Averell replied. "I had him shot yesterday."

There was another fatality at Buchanan, a black soldier who attempted to rape a white woman. He was shot dead on the spot.

Wednesday, June 15, 8:00 A.M.—Louisa Court House

Early had reached the Virginia Central tracks at Trevilian Station. From Louisa Court House he wired Breckinridge via Gordonsville:

> Will be near Mechanicsville, Louisa County, to-night, and near Charlottesville to-morrow night. What is the state of things in the Valley? Let me hear from you via Gordonsville.

June 15—Buchanan

McCausland's burning of the James River bridge had held Hunter up for a full day. Averell found a place to cross his horses, but the wagons had to wait while a temporary bridge was built, which so enraged Hunter that he ordered part of the town of Buchanan burned. Strother blamed the conflagration on McCausland.

On a high, wooded hill above Buchanan stood the baronial estate of Col. John T. Anderson (whose brother, Gen. Joe, owned the famous Tredegar Iron Works in Richmond). The great house, with its splendid library, was rich in antique furniture and works of art. Anderson himself was an old man; his wife was also white of hair. As Imboden said, "There was no military or public object on God's earth to be gained from ruining such a man. Yet Hunter . . . ordered the grand old mansion . . . to be laid in ashes." The huge fire could be seen from many miles away.

June 15—Across the Peaks of Otter

It was another of those epic settings in which the war was so often fought. The Peaks of Otter—four-thousand-foot Flat Top and thirty-nine-hundred-foot Sharp Top—are the signature of the Blue Ridge mountains between the Valley and Lynchburg. A rough road rose on dusty switchbacks to pass between the peaks.

As the federal army made its way across, William Lincoln of the 34th Massachusetts left a vivid portrait. "Far above our heads we catch occasional glimpses of the moving column, the heavy rumbling of the artillery carriages coming to our ears like the low muttering of distant thunder; far below us we see the wagon train as it winds along its slow and heavy way."

There was a resort hotel between the peaks, where Hunter's staff stopped while the cavalry escort "plundered the smoke house, getting a hundred pieces of bacon." The adventurous Meigs and some of the others climbed to the top of the south peak but got no sight of the enemy.

The mountain rhododendrons were still in bloom and some of the men broke them off and jammed them into their musket barrels so that Hunter's column, winding down toward Liberty, looked like "a moving bank of flowers."

June 15, Late Afternoon—Liberty

McCausland placed his three guns on a hill outside Liberty and opened fire as Hunter's advance came into view. He kept at it until it grew dark, when he once again limbered the guns and backed off toward Lynchburg.

Hunter made his quarters that evening at the "house of one Kelso, an old-fashioned brick house handsomely located in a grove of oaks with a full view of the Peaks of Otter."

When he was offered a horse of "extraordinary ugliness," Strother gladly accepted. "He may be useful to me, as we are going into the jaws of the enemy blind."

June 15—Breckinridge

Breckinridge to Lee:

> Enemy reported to be advancing, in force not known. The cavalry under Imboden doing less than nothing. If a good general officer cannot be sent at once for them, they will go to ruin.

Thursday, June 16—Lynchburg

Breckinridge's brigades, "bronzed and dirty-looking, . . . many of them bare-footed," walked at route step into Lynchburg after a sixty-mile tramp from Rockfish Gap. The general still was commanding from his bed.

Fortunately for him, another recuperating general officer and friend, Daniel Harvey Hill, was in town. Hill had taken up preparations for defense, starting earthworks to be manned by local militia, the survivors of Piedmont, invalids from the hospitals and the corps of cadets from VMI. With such forces, the works ran only about a mile around the western side of the city and were tucked very close to the city line. Hunter's assaulting artillery would have a free fire zone across the streets and homes of Lynchburg.

Lynchburg was an old, red-brick, dark-leaf-tobacco town that had grown "like Rome," they liked to say, over seven hills and bluffs on the south side of the James since John Lynch, a seventeen-year-old Irishman, opened his ferry there in 1757. By 1830, fifteen big dark-leaf tobacco warehouses stood along the riverbank; that year, five hundred barges ran down the James to Richmond. Ten years later, the James River and Kanahwa Canal reached Lynchburg, and in 1852 the first train of the Tennessee and Virginia steamed into town.

Now the place counted more than eight thousand citizens, was the major rail and boat transportation hub for deep central Virginia, had several confederate hospitals and an arsenal and produced enough war matériel for Grant to exclaim, "If only I could have Lynchburg in my hand for a single day!"

It looked as though he was about to have his wish.

June 16, Morning—Liberty

Strother: "Our troops, I fear, are plundering the town and misbehaving terribly as women and children are besieging the General's door for protection."

At Liberty, Hunter heard that Lynchburg was defended only by sick and wounded in works that were little more than shallow rifle pits. He started "horse, foot and artillery" forward.

This country was much different than that of the lush valley. "Water was not plentiful, the land was poorer. Grazing not near so good." Out of the cool valley, out of the shadow of the mountains, they found the day stifling.

There were two roads from Liberty to Lynchburg. The northern route went by way of Forest and was called the Forest road; the southern route, known as the Salem turnpike, followed the tracks of the Virginia and Tennessee Railroad through New London and crossed the Great Otter River before it reached Lynchburg.

Sullivan's infantry and Duffié's cavalry were sent along the Forest road, while Crook led his infantry and Averell's cavalry along the V&T tracks, destroying them as he went.

June 16—Charlottesville

At first light, Early had left his camp at Valentine's Mill and spurred on ahead of his marching columns to Charlottesville, where he found a reply from Breckinridge: Hunter was twenty miles from Lynchburg and closing fast.

At eleven-forty A.M., Early wired Breckinridge:

> Send off at once all engines and cars of the Orange and Alexandria Railroad to this place, including everything at its disposal. I will send troops as soon as I get cars. . . . See that there is no lack of energy in railroad management, and give me information.

An hour later he wired again:

> Let me know what the railroad agents can and will do. . . . [E]verything depends upon promptness, energy, and dispatch. . . . Take the most summary measures and impress everything that is necessary in the way of men or means. . . . I have authority to direct your movements, and I will take the responsibility of what you may find it necessary to do. I will hold all railroad agents and employees responsible with their lives.

Old Jube was going to commandeer the entire railroad, and anyone objecting or resisting might get shot.

Small wonder he was full of anxiety; his van was still coming into Charlottesville and other units would not reach Keswick Depot to the east until that evening, hot and worn out. He was sixty miles from Lynchburg and Hunter, rolling almost unopposed, was a mere twenty.

Early knew he was going to be too late, despite his frantic telegraphing. Hunter would have his artillery cowing Lynchburg within a few hours and his troops in her streets by that night.

He spent the day chafing and waiting anxiously as railroad stock began arriving from the south. Too little, he knew, and a day too late.

June 16, Night—Six Miles East of Liberty

Hunter's staff had stopped for the night in a large but deserted house six miles from Liberty, "built on a stylish plan but . . . never occupied" because it was said to be haunted. Certainly the atmosphere contributed to Strother's growing apprehensiveness. They were across the mountains, as Strother had planned, and close to having "our grip upon the vitals of the Confederacy." Now he noted in his journal that if Lee was unable to relieve Lynchburg, "the Confederacy is gone up."

That was the good news. The bad news was that they were also in an isolated, and thus precarious, position, with no line of supply or reinforcement. Strother admitted to "a vague uneasiness" and realized that if Lee *did* reinforce Lynchburg with a sizeable force, then "our situation is most hazardous."

At two A.M. Hunter wakened his staff with word from Averell that he had been in a sharp fight at New London, eight miles closer to Lynchburg. It was boots and saddles. Strother was sent to order Sullivan's infantry to advance on New London, but "the greater part of the sentries did not know where the headquarters of their regiments were." Strother fumed. "I never saw such damnable ignorance and carelessness."

Finally on the move after a two-hour delay, the column found the bridge over the Great Otter was not ready, and neither the artillery nor the wagon train could cross.

Friday, June 17, Noon—Quaker Meeting House

The maligned Imboden had been vigorously contesting Averell's advance through New London. About seven miles east, only five miles west of Lynchburg, he dismounted his command and put up a defensive line based on a Quaker meeting house that occupied a ridge commanding the Salem pike. It was a small, steeply-gabled stone building erected in 1798 that housed the South River Meeting (whose non-violent members had contributed to American culture by providing ancestors for Mark Twain, Francis Scott Key and Jefferson Davis).

Four of McClanahan's guns were posted behind the church. As a hot skirmishing fire rattled his advance, Averell had to stop while Crook, finally across the repaired bridge, brought up the infantry. This promised to be a nasty little affair.

Battles & Leaders

MAJ. GEN. STEPHEN RAMSEUR

June 17—Keswick Depot

Early's commanders had awakened exhausted troops at two A.M. and had begun loading them into the rolling stock, box cars and passenger cars, that had been sent up from Lynchburg, but it had taken hours to get it organized. Stephen Ramseur's division was put aboard first, followed by a part of Gordon's (including a lucky Worsham) before they ran out of cars. Robert Rodes's men and the rest of Gordon's troops were told to start hoofing it along the tracks and cars would be sent back for them. It was now daylight and the hours fleeting.

Chug. North Garden Depot. Chug. Rockfish Depot. Chug. Chug. Arrington Depot. Amherst Court House. McIvor's Depot.

As they drew nearer and nearer, the troops expected to hear at any moment the thunder of federal cannon, but there was only an ominous silence. Had Hunter captured the town already? Would they be met by volleys from ambushing union troops? Every eye strained forward. Chug. The train was over the James and the city's spires and steeples rose to view—and those were *gray* uniforms in the station to greet the train!

Pvt. James Scott Moore of the 14th Virginia Cavalry, one of eighteen Moores who served that regiment, was on hand to witness the arrival of the first of Early's corps. "The train came in full view, plastered over sides and tops with men. Then the halt was made, and out swarmed men like blackbirds, piling up their knapsacks into huge piles. Quickly forming a 'double quick' and moved toward the firing line. Up hill and down they rushed, eager to get there . . . several thousand. They cheered all the time, especially loudly when they neared our cavalry line and could hear the whistle of the bullets."

And how happy the Lynchburghers were to see them. "We were cheered to the echo," says Worsham, "... and the ladies waved their hands and gave us lunches and cool water as we marched through the city."

June 17, Afternoon—Crook Advances

As the day began to fade, the impatient Crook could wait no longer. He sent a detachment of cavalry to the east, flanking Imboden, while ordering the infantry to assault the position at the church. Imboden began to withdraw. Crook was certain he had Lynchburg at his mercy.

Battles & Leaders

MAJ. GEN. ROBERT RODES

June 17, Late Afternoon—On the Salem Turnpike

Early had hastened to Breckinridge's bedside, been briefed, and then set out with D. H. Hill for a look at the defenses and the approaching Yankees. They rode out the Salem turnpike, past a redoubt that had been thrown up about two miles out and armed with two guns, and about four miles along the pike they came upon the enemy. Crooks's troops were advancing against Imboden even as Early and Hill watched.

A courier went back in a cloud of dust to Ramseur with an order to move out, occupy the redoubt and continue forward. Soon after, Early himself followed the courier, looking for Ramseur. The position at the meeting house could not hold for long.

At some point past the redoubt, Early found Ramseur and hurried him forward, himself in the lead, waving his white slouch hat. When he came up to the guns he stopped and shook his fist at the enemy, yelling: "No buttermilk rangers after you now, damn you!"

No buttermilk rangers, indeed; this was the Stonewall Brigade—or what was left of it.

Pvt. Moore never forgot the scene. "Napoleon never looked upon his 'Old Guard' or Caesar his 'Tenth Legion' with more pride than I did that evening upon the advance of Early's men through those fields of golden grain. [Ramseur's van organized a line only] seven or eight hundred yards from the Yankee infantry and kept moving closer. . . . The enemy, too, was very stubborn and held their ground well, but in an hour or more they had been driven . . . back several hundred yards. From six-thirty to seven P.M., Crook's division engaged with musketry and artillery with great fury. . . . This handsome little affair cost us forty men killed and wounded."

And the fields to the north, toward the Forest road where McCausland was retreating slowly, began to fill with more blue coats. But it was still in the balance. By nightfall neither Rodes's troops nor the rest of Gordon's had yet arrived; the artillery was somewhere on the road from Charlottesville, along with the wagons, and Early could count no more than seven thousand effectives. He was still outnumbered better than two to one and in great danger of losing Lynchburg in the event of an aggressive attack.

June 17—Road to New London

A man named Leftwich, who was almost certainly a descendent of the famous Col. Augustine Leftwich who made a fortune in Lynchburg tobacco and who strutted about town in a white linen suit while a slave held a green umbrella over his head, told Capt. Thomas K. McCann that the Yankees were being whipped "both East and West." When communicated to Hunter, this news so enraged him, Strother reported, that "he had Leftwich arrested and ordered his house to be burnt. It was a very pretty country residence, and the man had a sweet daughter about sixteen and a nice family. The house was burnt and destroyed. [Maj. Charles G.] Halpine, [Maj. Samuel] Stockton and myself rode away saying nothing, but we did not wish to look upon the scene."

June 17—Battlefield

All of the generals—Hunter, Crook and Averell—gathered at the home of a Maj. Hutter, a former paymaster in the old union army. They were "much disposed to follow on into the town," but Hunter demurred and decided to wait for morning.

John Prather, a private with the 91st Ohio, summed up the army's reaction: "The curses that greeted this order were long and deep and loud."

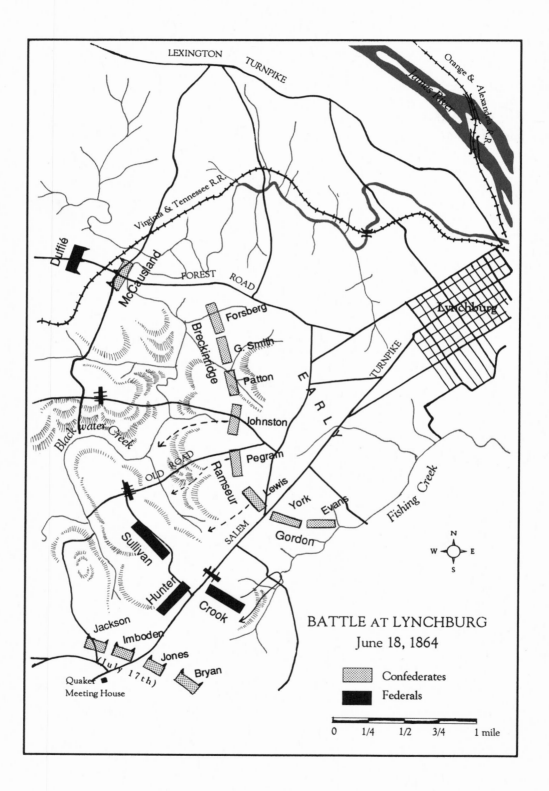

BATTLE AT LYNCHBURG
June 18, 1864

Confederates
Federals

0   1/4   1/2   3/4   1 mile

VI.
The Battle
at Lynchburg

Saturday, June 18, 1864

All night, Hunter and his army had listened to the constant huffing and chuffing of locomotives, to energetic band music, enthusiastic encouragement shouted by crowds of people, the rallying call of bugles and ominous roll of drums. They were convinced that Lee had sent an entire corps against them. Actually, it was a wonderful ruse, carried out with great élan—a single engine with a few box cars had shuffled back and forth all night, blowing steam and tooting while bands played and citizens screamed.

In the morning, Hunter ordered Alfred Duffié's cavalry division, out on the far left at the Forest road, to move forward. Duffié's two brigades numbered four New York regiments and two from Pennsylvania. He dismounted his troops and attacked McCausland, pushing him back through the long, hot morning beyond the railroad bridge of the V&T and then to the crossing of the Blackwater River, where confederate earthworks greeted him with heavy artillery fire. Around noon, the 1st New York (Lincoln) cavalry and two squadrons of the 20th Pennsylvania attacked the fortifications and were badly mauled. The 15th New York then tried the confederate left, with similar result. Duffié sent a note to Hunter, datelined *Hdqrs. First Cav. Div. Dept of West Virginia, In the Field, near Lynchburg, Va. June 18, 1864.* He said that he had been fighting per orders on the extreme left since twelve-thirty P.M. and found "the enemy's force much superior to mine."

In the center, Ramseur held his ground and had been joined by some of Gordon's regiments, who formed along his line across the Salem pike to his left. Opposite the Confederates, Hunter had placed du Pont's twenty-six guns on the pike, just in advance of Crook's line, composed of four Ohio and four West Virginia regiments. He then moved Jeremiah Sullivan's infantry brigades—led by the battle-tested 34th Massachusetts, 116th and 123rd Ohio, and 18th Connecticut—into line to Crook's left.

There was a new and intimidating sound in the din of battle—"the frequent report of telescopic rifles. . . . The heavy balls came whistling back among the staff, one passing between the General and Stockton as they sat talking on horseback."

That new weapon meant only one thing to Strother: "Richmond troops among the defenders."

He rode forward to find everyone on the ground, including Sullivan and the Second Brigade commander Col. Thoburn, who were "lying . . . on some boards" while rifle balls whacked the trees and scattered bark around them. That Early's ruse had worked was evident when Sullivan told Strother that "he had heard the railroad trains coming and going all night, also cheering and military music which indicated the arrival of troops."

Was he prepared now to resume the attack?

"I am ready to attack if ordered," said Sullivan, "but be assured it will end in disaster."

And Thoburn? He "spoke in the same strain and in somewhat more decided language."

But if they *were* ordered to attack, where should it be? Neither man would answer.

After reporting this to Hunter, who seemed unhappy but still ordered no advance, Strother, exhausted, lay on a board himself and fell into a deep sleep.

Late in the morning, Hunter decided to flank Early and sent Crook's infantry, supported by Averell, through a stand of woods to their right with the intention of turning Gordon. But Early had not been born yesterday. As soon as Crook vanished into the summer darkened woods, recalled du Pont, "the Confederates attacked us with great violence. Leaping over their defenses, the enemy's infantry, with terrific yells, assaulted the union left and center."

Strother was awakened with a start by "an uproar of musketry and yells. . . . The storm of yells and musketry rapidly approached and groups of fugitives began to appear through the woods. The General and staff drew their swords and rushed in. . . . The storm of musketry shook the earth."

Crook was quickly recalled and "hurried in to the left, regiment after regiment, and the fire was tremendous." This movement slowed the attack. Soon, the brave 34th Massachusetts and 116th Ohio counter-attacked. "[A]fter swaying back and forth, our entire line finally made a charge and drove the enemy into and over his first line of works." For a brief moment, "the Stars and Stripes, borne by the color bearer of the 116th Ohio, were seen waving from the enemy's breastworks." Strother heard "continued cheering from the front," but it was not to last, as "the word was given to withdraw."

There it was, in the balance. The day had become blistering hot and soldiers were gasping from exhaustion, fear, heat, dust. Yet the field invited a victory. Hunter had divided his army between Duffié's command along the Forest road and Sullivan and Crook on the Salem pike. Between them lay a huge and inviting gap. Early had merely to drive his cavalry through, turn Sullivan's left and follow with infantry, thus isolating Duffié, and Hunter would be bagged.

Yet Early hesitated; it would be less costly to do it in the morning, when he had his artillery up and his whole army at hand.

Hunter, too, had been given pause as prisoners came into interrogation after the federal attack. They were North Carolinians from either Robert Johnston's or William Lewis's brigade of Ramseur's division. They described their hike and railroad ride from Richmond, said there were thirty-thousand troops in Lynchburg. After this information, "all agreed we must get out if possible. Crook was cool and matter of fact. Averell was excited and angry."

At five o'clock the confederate line in front of Duffié opened a terrific fire. From Lynchburg, a mere two miles away, he heard martial music and train whistles blowing. His binoculars showed long columns of gray troops filing down the hills toward the Forest road—Rodes's division had finally arrived.

Day was failing. The lines remain stalemated. Now was the time, said John Gordon, to drive Hunter against the mountains.

Breckenridge, Ramseur, Rodes all agreed. Still Early hesitated. The artillery was still not up. He had a strong cavalry force on his right that might slip behind any offensive thrust, and an unknown quantity on his left, down along the Campbell Court House road. The attack would come in the morning.

That night the VMI cadets, who had been stationed all day in Spring Hill Cemetery behind Ramseur's lines, were moved up in dark so deep each had to hold on to the belt of the man ahead.

They filed into the redoubt and the weary men they replaced filed out "like the shadows of darkness" in silence.

Cadet John Wise recalled that "The place was horrible. The fort was new and constructed of stiff red clay. . . . There was no place to lie down. All that a man could do was to sit plump down in the mud, upon the low banquette, with his gun across his lap. I could not resist peeping over the parapet, and there, but a short distance from us, in a little valley, were the smouldering campfires of the enemy."

Wrapped in a blanket, Wise fell asleep, "hugging my rifle, never doubting there would be work for us at daybreak."

Sunday, June 19, Midnight—On Forest Road

Although Strother believed that "the troops were all withdrawn in silence," pickets of the 14th Virginia Cavalry out on Forest road had heard "a great stir in the union camp" around ten o'clock at night. McCausland believed that Duffié was trying to steal away and he prepared to follow.

June 19, 2:00 A.M.—Liberty

He left his skirmishers in place along the Salem pike until midnight to screen the movement, but Hunter had been withdrawing his lines since dark. Strother and the staff "had a pleasant ride by moonlight and by two o'clock in the morning got back to

Harper's Weekly

MAJ. GEN. ROBERT RANSOM

our old quarters in the vacant house five miles from Liberty."

Hunter did not plan to retrace his steps over the Peaks of Otter, however. With Early in command of the railroad, not only between Charlottesville and Lynchburg but between Charlottesville and Staunton, the confederate general could quickly move what Hunter believed to be twenty thousand men and cut off the entire federal force, deep in the upper valley, with no hope of support from the north. By dragging the two-hundred-wagon supply train along with him, Hunter had effectively annexed his own line of supply.

He decided to keep going westward on the Salem road, which crossed the Blue Ridge at Buford's Gap. Duffié was sent ahead to secure the gap and found it defended. Hunter told him to clear it at all hazards. At daylight, the army began moving through Liberty, leaving Averell behind to defend it.

June 19, 9:30 A.M.—New London

As it became light enough to see and Worsham's skirmish line finally advanced, they found that "Hunter had slipped out of the trap during the night and was in full retreat."

Early, his quarry gone, quickly mobilized the pursuit, and he had a new commander to lead it; in response to the plea of Breckinridge, Maj. Gen. Robert Ransom had arrived at Lynchburg to take command of the cavalry. Early could get along with Ransom because he had been commanding infantry, well-disciplined, home-state North Carolina infantry. They had behaved well at Antietam and Fredericksburg. Ransom had commanded the Department of Richmond and fought well at Drewry's Bluff. He was now cavalry only because this West Pointer (class of '50) had once been captain of the 1st U.S. Cavalry in the old army.

But whether he had seen the likes of an Imboden, a McCausland, a Gilmor or a Mosby in the peacetime service is to be doubted. These men literally thought by the seat of their pants as they rode into danger, ready to respond instantly to each situation as it changed. They knew that caution, almost always a friend of the infantry, was often an enemy of the cavalry.

Ransom landed in his new job in the saddle as he joined McCausland's brigade on a dash to Buchanan to cut off Hunter. They went by the Peaks of Otter road and brought McClanahan's guns.

Infantryman Early had no great faith in cavalry. Gilmor and Early had had an unpleasant exchange prior to his setting out after Hunter's retreating column. Early told Gilmor to "dash ahead, the enemy are all demoralized and you can capture hundreds of them."

"That's easy to say," said Gilmor, "but his rear guard is very large, well handled, and moving with precision, and I have only a handful of men here (250 Virginians and forty Marylanders). They are all overworked, as are their horses. The day is intensely hot and the roads several inches deep in dust. Harassing a rear guard means charging in rapidly and retreating hastily, extremely hard work."

Early did not change his mind, however, As Gilmor noted, "Like all infantry officers, he thought cavalry ought to know no flagging."

In fact, Early's hopes to catch Hunter were with his horse soldiers. By nine-thirty A.M. he was in New London and wired to Lee:

> I made arrangements to attack this morning at light, but it was discovered that the enemy were retreating, and I am now pursuing. The enemy is retreating in confusion, and if the cavalry does its duty we will destroy him.

. . . if the cavalry does its duty. . .

June 19, Sundown—Near Liberty

Both Harry Gilmor and Kyd Douglas were riding with the advance under Ramseur. Douglas noted the "scene of desolation" as they marched westward from Lynchburg. "Ransacked houses, crying women, clothes from the bed chambers and wardrobes of ladies, carried along on bayonets and draggled in the road, the garments of little children, and here and there a burning house marked the track of Hunter's retreat. I had never seen anything like this before and for the first time in the war I felt that vengeance ought not be left entirerly to the Lord."

Gilmor also remembered that he had "within a mile counted four burned houses; and so it was on Hunter's track everywhere."

Around sundown, Gilmor came upon Hunter's rear guard, "a pretty heavy body," and charged them over a hill near Liberty. From its summit, Gilmor saw "nearly the whole of Hunter's army forming in line of battle" and two regiments of cavalry coming

Doug Bast, Boonsboro Museum

HENRY KYD DOUGLAS

his way; they chased him back about a mile, where he came upon a Virginia battalion. They made a stand, exchanging skirmishing fire. On the hill, Hunter's cavalry threw up a rail barricade. Ramseur came up with 200 sharpshooters and told Gilmor "to turn their left and hit them in flank and rear" while he charged their right.

The tactic was a success, but a ditch slowed Gilmor's pursuit. Dismounting his men for the advance across the ditch, Gilmor himself remained mounted, "even though it made an ugly jump." His horse "gathered finely and made a splendid offer" before the sod gave way under his hind feet and he crashed into the ditch. The pursuit tailed off as twenty men grabbed the horse's "head, legs, and tail and lifted, or rather slid him out of the ditch, covered with mud."

Early soon brought up a brigade and marched into Liberty.

As Douglas and Gilmor rode side by side through the town—"a beautiful little town . . . remarkable for the number of pretty girls"—six young ladies ran out of a house, one of them calling Douglas's name. The handsome young officers rode up to the fence to talk to the ladies, one of whom brought Gilmor a drink of water. Gilmor recalls "the ladies were all crowded around us, laughing and talking. I had just placed the empty glass on the gate-post when a bullet struck its top with a loud rap, and jarred off the tumbler. The ladies screamed and bounded off for the house."

Douglas remembers a young lady crying out, "Look there, the Yankees!" prior to the shot; he remembers seeing "the white jet of several rifles" coming from the stable, the ball hitting the gate-post, knocking off the glass. But here the memories are sharply divergent. After the excitement, Gilmor says that he "turned in upon the lawn for it was against orders to sleep in a house," but he spent "an hour or two on the portico . . . a soldier *will* make love wherever he goes. . . . On bidding my charmer good-bye next morning I promised to write to her."

Douglas, on the other hand, claims that after the snipers were driven off and "before the night was far spent I was back again for a more quiet visit. As for Gilmor, he was given something else to do."

The ladies never revealed the truth.

Monday, June 20, Dawn—Buford's Gap

Hunter's column had paused for dinner along the road, but "the firing was so rapid and approaching so near that the General left the table, ordered the staff to horse." The army turned to face its enemy, eating supper in order of battle, but Ramseur did not come up to confront them. At midnight they moved again, another all night march "in the full moon shining gloriously," reaching Buford's Gap at dawn and finding it "a rocky, muddy road. . . . Our cavalry looks very much used up and demoralized."

They stopped at Bonsack's Station, "a humble house," where Strother found "the General and Stockton lying on the floor."

June 20, 1:00 P.M.—Buchanan

When McCausland arrived at Buchanan after an all night march, he found the town burned and Hunter not there. Surely, he had thought, the incendiary Hunter would have had to retreat down the Valley to keep his army between Early and the north. The cavalry would have "done its duty" and bagged him at Buchanan—but Hunter was not there. McCausland heard that he was retreating toward the west, up into the mountains beyond Salem, toward the Kanawha Valley. Relentlessly, McCausland pushed exhausted men and horses southward, toward Salem.

June 20, 2:00 P.M.—Buford's Gap: The Crisis of Our Fate

At two o'clock Averell reported the enemy advancing on his rear guard in force. A half hour later, Crook reported threats on both his flanks. Hunter gave the word to saddle up and move on. Averell wanted to stop and fight. "This is the crisis of our fate," he said, "as this battle will save or ruin us." Strother noted the gap had many good defensible positions.

They went ahead, down into the great Valley. The trains were ahead of them, guarded by Duffié and some artillery.

June 20, Late Afternoon—Buford's Gap

Early wanted desperately to bag Hunter. He asked Gilmor to ride forward and ascertain whether Hunter was encamped in the Valley below Buford's Gap, and, if so, whether "a division of infantry could be placed on his rear."

Gilmor rode ahead with twenty men and a guide, who took them to the summit from which "we had an extensive view, and beheld Hunter's army . . . in the Valley, with large squads of cavalry moving in every direction, and, sad to tell, numbers of houses, mills, and barns on fire."

Included in the holocaust was the guide's own home. They watched as "flames burst forth from his dwelling" where his sister lay ill. He turned to Gilmor and said, "I will kill every one of them that falls into my power."

Sending back a courier with news that they had found a mountain road by which Early could move a division, Gilmor went ahead, looking for Hunter's headquarters and looking to take a prisoner. Moving on the flank, he "passed to the rear of his forces, except the trains, which were still moving on toward Salem."

June 20—Night March to Salem

Again, Hunter kept on the move all night, marching on the Salem road. Strother noted that "burning bridges and railroad stations lighted our way."

At sunrise they reached Salem, a sixty-two-year-old valley town surrounded by mountains—Fort Lewis, McAfee's, Catawba and others—that boasted the red brick court house of Roanoke County, the Virginia Collegiate Institute and a number of hospitable taverns for travelers passing along the Carolina road—the Old Time, the Bull's Eye, the Indian Queen and two from Shakespeare's London, the Globe and the Mermaid. Strother went into one, unspecified, threw himself on a table and went to sleep.

Tuesday, June 21, Sunrise—Salem

Strother's sleep was rudely interrupted by the sound of cannon fire— McCausland. He, too, had been riding all night for a second time, down the Buchanan road, and now McClanahan's guns were lobbing shells into the town. It had the desired effect. A rumor came in that Crook had been cut off. The wagon train "was hurried through town on the Newcastle road accompanied by a disorganized rabble of mounted men, Negroes, skulkers, and fricoteurs (harlots)."

Suddenly, the firing ceased. After Hunter had gone to the front to investigate, it was declared there was "no adequate cause for excitement, only some cavalry appearing in our rear."

Actually, McCausland had slipped past Salem, his eye on the artillery that was moving with the train. At Hanging Rock, four or five miles up the slope of Catawba Mountain, he caught them. Carter Berkeley recalled how they "stood there an hour or two looking at his column moving rapidly into the gap. McCausland will tell you how he urged Ransom to attack."

Finally Berkeley could stand it no more and "ran out a gun without orders and fired into the moving column. . . . About that time McCausland charged, but it was only the rear of the retreating column."

It may have been the rear of the train, but McCausland hit du Pont's guns hard. His troopers isolated and captured a dozen guns—half of the command—numerous wagons and thirty-five Yankees. He set fire to a caisson full of ammunition and blew it sky high. Sgt. Milton Humphreys of McClanahan's Battery thought a battle was on. He reported "a rapid cannonade ahead and a dense smoke rose among the hills." Many were killed in the explosion. An 18th Cavalry trooper saw "men tore in Pieces by shel I saw a mans arm Lying a hundred yards from his mangeled Boddy." When Harry Gilmor passed the place on the following day, he commented on "the blackened corpses."

Word reached Hunter by ten-thirty that "our artillery en route with the train had been attacked and was all captured." Averell and Sullivan were ordered to advance rapidly, but in Strother's opinion they were "getting into an ugly position, artillery gone and cavalry worthless."

It was, for all intents and purposes, over. Hunter kept going, day and night it seemed, over Catawba Mountain to New Castle, which he reached on the twenty-second, and over Barbour and Warm Spring mountains, through Sweet Springs, to White Sulphur Springs, which he reached at sundown on the twenty-fourth. Then he went up through Lewisburg on the twenty-sixth and Gauley to the Kanawha, every step taking him farther and farther from the war, until they reached Charleston on the thirtieth.

Capt. Edwin Bouldin of the 14th Cavalry, who had commanded a regiment at Gettysburg, called it the "worst rout I saw during the war." A winded North Carolinian said, "They outran any Yankees I ever traveled after." William Walker, the chaplain of the 18th Connecticut, remembered it as "one of the most difficult and dangerous retreats of the war . . . in the face of appalling dangers from starvation and death."

What made Black Dave Hunter run? He had proved himself a criminal in uniform, an arsonist on a binge, and, like all bullies, he had run when confronted. Said John Brown Gordon, "It was then and still is incomprehensible to me that the small force under Early seemed to have filled Hunter with sudden panic. His hurried exit from Lynchburg was in marked contrast with his confident advance. . . . He ran away without any fight at all . . . precipitately, and did not stop until he had found a safe retreat beyond the mountains toward the Ohio.

"If I were asked an opinion as to this utterly causeless fright and flight, I should be tempted to say that conscience, the inward monitor which 'makes cowards of us all' was harrowing General Hunter, and causing him to see an avenger wrapped in every gray jacket before him."

Tuesday, June 28—Gauley, West Virginia

Hunter wired Washington from Gauley, West Virginia, on June 28 that his army was "in excellent heart and health" and that his campaign into Virginia had been "extremely successful, inflicting great injury upon the enemy." Maybe he believed it. But in truth, Hunter had run so fast and so far in the wrong direction that he had delivered up Maryland and one last chance for Lee to win the Civil War.

BOOK TWO

INVASION OF THE NORTH

VII.
Early Heads North

Wednesday, June 22, 1864—Day Off

Thus had Black Dave Hunter delivered to Jubal Anderson Early the whole wide Valley of Virginia basking in summer warmth and heavy with growing corn and wheat and tomatoes and greens, running with milk and honey. The Confederates had only to stroll down it to the far distant Potomac.

But the pursuit of Hunter had so wearied man and beast that word came down from headquarters that the regiments could stand down on the 22nd. This was so difficult for the hard-driven men to believe that they soon were spreading a rumor.

Seems that Old Jube wasn't all the starched-up bachelor he was purported to be, the story went, and at one time had actually had a sweetheart—and damned if he didn't run into her going through Big Lick (today's Roanoke). Where do you suppose his headquarters is? Up at that girl's school, Hollins, where his old flame was a teacher. And what do you think Old Jube's doing up there at Hollins? In a *tête-a-tête* with his old girl. And whose idea do you think this is, to take a day off in the middle of a war? Hers, of course! Do you think Old Jube 'ud give you a day off?

For Stephen Dodson Ramseur's division (which used to be Early's) it was truly a holiday, for they found themselves camped at Botetourt Springs, a premier prewar resort for wealthy Virginians in a verdant valley outside Big Lick. The road-weary troops made the most of it, whooping it up in the refreshing waters as they washed away the dust and grime of a week of hard campaigning.

Thursday, June 23—On the Road to Lexington

On the morning of the 23rd, Early rode out toward the mountains to make sure that Hunter was truly gone. He was—truly gone, on an irreversible course toward the Ohio River at Parkersburg. By nightfall, Ramseur had his division across the burned-out

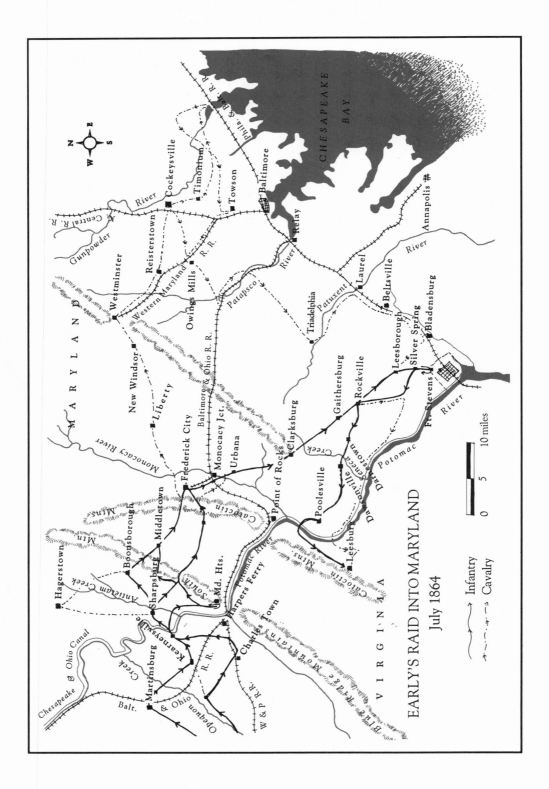

EARLY'S RAID INTO MARYLAND
July 1864

Infantry
Cavalry

bridge over the James at Buchanan, single-file over a temporary span of timber, and the rest of the army was coming up to camp nearby.

Friday, June 24—The Music Of the Spheres

Kyd Douglas got permission to do a little sight-seeing on the march north and used the opportunity to give vent to his romantic persuasions. As the army trudged down the Valley turnpike on Friday morning, Douglas led a number of troops several miles off the main road to visit the Natural Bridge, a bridge of stone ninety feet high that spanned a 215-foot gorge scoured out by Cedar Creek.

Thomas Jefferson had been so taken by the place that he had bought it, along with 157 acres, for the paltry sum of twenty shillings on July 5, 1775, in the midst of another war. He had built a cabin near the bridge, with slaves as caretakers and a guest book for visitors to record their "sentiments" on beholding the natural wonder.

Douglas had something else in mind. He brought several regimental bands to the gorge and was quite moved by "the solemn effect of their music as it rose and swelled in volume, and filled the great arch, and seemed to press against the sides of that cathedral dome, and then rolled along the high rocks that walled the ravine and died away in the widening wood."

What a strange war—a strangely innocent horror, a slaughter with sensibility, a mass murder with a certain modesty.

Saturday, June 25—Stonewall's Last Review

On Saturday morning, Rodes's division, Jackson's old division, marched away from the Valley turnpike and into the town of Lexington and up Main Street past the cemetery at the top of the hill where rested the remains of Stonewall himself.

"Not a man spoke," Douglas tells us. "Not a sound was uttered. Only the tramp, tramp of passing feet told that his surviving veterans were passing in review, while the drooping and tattered flags saluted his sacred dust."

"What hallowed memories it brought up!" exclaims John Worsham, "Many a tear was seen trickling down the cheeks of his veterans. How many of them had crossed the river and were then resting beneath the shade of the trees with him."

During Hunter's occupation of Lexington the grave had been desecrated by removal of the head and foot boards, leading Capt. H.W. Wingfield of the 58th Virginia Infantry to wonder how the Yankees had mustered up the nerve to do it to a man who "while living was such a terror to the Yankee nation." Now, however, it was covered with flowers.

Brigadier William Lewis, in a note to his sister, said that she could have "no idea what feelings passed over me."

Onward they passed in silence, muskets reversed, flags drooping. Lines from Tennyson's "Maude" flashed into Kyd Douglas's mind:

> They are here my own, my own;
> Were it ever so airy a tread,
> My heart would hear them and beat...
> My dust would hear them and beat
> Had I lain for a century dead!

Of such stuff was Stonewall's mystique made, and it lives yet.

Sunday, June 26—Headquarters, Army of Northern Virginia

Yes, Robert E. Lee *was* a genius, because he always saw a way out of the most serious difficulty and a way to attain victory when least expected.

The set of his mind is nowhere better illustrated than in late June of 1864. Hemmed into the Richmond-Petersburg trenches, outnumbered perhaps four to one, with a failing logistical support and the momentum of the war running strongly against him, Lee considered the fact that Hunter had escaped Early and the chance to kill off a federal army in the Valley had been lost.

Another bitter disappointment?

No, another opportunity.

Lee's mind flew over the landscape like a great invisible bird, up the valley pike, through all those little towns. With Hunter off to the west, an army could be well north of Winchester without opposition. Who is that in front? Franz Sigel—a joke. Max Weber—cannot hold us. Straight over Harpers Ferry and down into Washington City. He surveyed the forts, circling the city, unquestionably strong, on the highest points on every side, equipped with huge siege and coastal guns.

But inside? He looked to his own lines around Petersburg, the prisoners and the dead—heavy artillerists from Washington turned into foot soldiers. There was nobody in place along the Potomac. They thought they were perfectly safe.

Stop? No. Fly now down the dirt roads of southern Maryland to where the Potomac enters the Bay with eighteen thousand men who could turn the tide of war—freed, armed, organized, they could strike Grant in the back before he knew what hit him.

Lee picked up his pen:

His Excellency, Jefferson Davis

Mr. President—General Hunter has escaped Early.... If circumstances favor I should recommend Early's crossing the Potomac.... Great benefit might be drawn from the release of the prisoners at Point Lookout, if that can be accomplished; ... the guard there might be overpowered, the prisoners liberated and reorganized and marched immediately on the road to Washington.... [L]ittle or no opposition could be made by those at Washington.

June 26—Early's Headquarters, Staunton

They were making an army for the march north. The II Corps, Army of Northern Virginia, became the Army of the Valley District, Lt. Gen. Jubal A. Early commanding.

John Breckinridge, back on his feet, was named second in command and made a corps commander. The corps created for him comprised Maj. Gen. John B. Gordon's division, which pleased Gordon as it kept him away from Early; and Echols's division, which pleased Breckinridge since Wharton, Echols and Vaughn, who had been with him since New Market, were in it.

Gordon commanded a division rife with animosity and jealousy, a veritable powder keg of humanity. The remnants of the once-proud Louisiana brigades of Harry Hayes and Leroy Stafford were uneasily and unhappily combined under Brig. Gen. Zebulon York, a Yankee who had come to call Louisiana home. Brig. Gen. William Terry had a similar problem with the remnants of Virginia brigades, which included Stonewall's own "old first" brigade—the 2nd, 4th, 5th, 27th and 33rd Virginians—as well as the survivors of Edward "Allegheny" Johnson's division. "[B]oth officers and men," an inspector would note, "object to their consolidation into one Brigade. Strange officers command strange troops."

How strange this war, when neighborhoods insisted on the right to fight together.

The two other divisions, who reported directly to Early, had far fewer problems. Robert Emmett Rodes was a thirty-five-year-old VMI graduate and engineering professor, a native of Lynchburg whose bravery at Chancellorsville made him a major general. Rodes had intense eyes under dark brows but blond hair, giving him the look of a Viking with a drooping mustache that he was wont to chew in the heat of battle. In his four brigades were eleven North Carolina regiments, five Alabama and four Georgia.

The youngest general in the army, twenty-seven-year-old Stephen Ramseur, commanded the final division, with nine North Carolina regiments and five Virginia. The whole division knew his young wife was pregnant.

Late June—Shaping Up the Cavalry

Maj. Gen. Ransom had Imboden and McCausland under his wing. Early had developed a dislike for them both, since in his view they had let Hunter escape. Now a trusted cavalry force was added to Early's army when Col. Bradley T. Johnson reported with his one hundred-strong 1st Maryland Cavalry Battalion and was promptly promoted brigadier and given Grumble Jones's old brigade of five Virginia regiments. Harry Gilmor's Marylanders were added to Johnson's, and they would have the honor of the van as the army moved toward their home state.

But the cavalry continued to have low regard for Early. Andrew Hunter of the 17th Virginia Cavalry expressed an opinion that the tobacco chewing, hard swearing, opinionated, stooped, eccentric Old Jube was unfit to command a whole army. What he meant, probably, was that Early was unfit to command cavalry.

It is easy to understand from this distance that unappreciated feeling. The 14th Virginia and other cavalry had taken the mountain roads from Buchanan via Fincastle, Covington and Brownsburg to give the infantry plenty of room on the pike. Feamster of the 14th had only thirty-two men in his company, twenty-eight deemed effective.

Here was their weaponry: Three unarmed. One Austrian musket. Thirteen Mississippi rifles. Two Enfields. Ten Sharps carbines. Five Colt revolvers. Two sabers. Twenty cartridge boxes and belts. Five cap pouches. Of the thirty-two sets of tack, six bridles and saddles were private property. In effect, at least eight cavalry soldiers were riding to war with their ammunition and caps in their pockets.

As for the infantry, it was noted that half the troops had no shoes. This was fine, in fact, to be preferred by many, for marching off the macadamized pike, on the dusty back roads of the Valley that had not seen a drop of rain in twenty-three days. But on the paved roads of the north, it would mean a crippled army. Early sent a request to Richmond for shoes.

Tuesday, June 28—Potomac Bound

At three A.M. on the twenty-eighth of June, Early started his newly named Army of the Valley northward on the valley pike—almost fourteen thousand infantry, more than four thousand cavalry, more than fifty cannon served by a thousand gunners. It was as streamlined as he could get it. The forty best artillery guns had been selected and fully horsed with fresh animals; Maj. William Nelson, Maj. Carter Braxton and Maj. William McLaughlin commanded the battalions. Another ten guns traveled with the cavalry.

Corps headquarters had one six-horse wagon. Each division and brigade headquarters had one four-horse wagon. One four-horse wagon carried the cooking utensils for every five hundred men. If officers wanted fresh underwear, they had to carry it.

"We felt perfectly at home," says Worsham, "since nearly all the Valley from Staunton to the Potomac River was familiar to us and many of its inhabitants old acquaintances."

Having to cross the South Fork of the Shenandoah that day, the army made only eight or nine miles to Mount Crawford before encampment, but the next day they strode along twenty-four miles through Harrisonburg to Big Spring.

June 28—Charles Town, Duffield Depot

A few hours after Early put his army on the road outside Staunton, Lt. Col. John Mosby led four companies of his rangers with one howitzer through Charles Town to Duffield Depot on the B&O west of Harpers Ferry. On the road outside Charles Town, Mosby left Co. A to watch for Max Weber's Federals coming from Harpers Ferry. Some ladies from the town brought out bread, meat, pies and "an abundance of milk," and for a while the boys had "quite a picnic." Jim Williamson and Bill Walston had to watch it from afar, as they were posted as pickets on a nearby hill. Their "hearts and . . . thoughts were constantly turning back to the fair ladies of Charlestown and the rich fare" until a cloud of dust demanded their instant attention, and before long "a dark blue line fringed the edge of the woods."

Williamson hustled into town and reported to Lt. Joseph Nelson, who quickly rode out to assess the situation. He came back full of fight. "Boys, I can whip them if you will only stand by me!"

"A lot of the boys are in town, Lieutenant; we have only twenty-three men here. How many Yanks are there?"

USMHI-MOLLUS

MAJ. GEN MAX WEBER

"About sixty, but we can whip them. I know we can. Two of you men ride out there and draw them up the pike!"

Nelson formed up his two dozen riders behind a little hill until they heard the yells and shouts of the Feds pursuing the two rabbits up the pike. Nelson issued orders: "Draw pistols. Move out at a walk. By twos. By twos. Makes it look like they's more of us."

The gray line of horsemen kept to the edge of the woods that paralleled the pike and walked directly toward the enemy, who soon topped the hill and stopped in surprise, but only for a minute. They quickly raised their carbines and fired a volley—but firing downhill distorted their aim, and the shots did nothing more "than to shower a few leaves on our heads," Williamson recalled.

As soon as the shots were fired, Nelson yelled: "Now, boys! Now!"

The Confederates spurred up the hill and "before they could drop their carbines and draw pistols, we dashed with a yell in amongst them, firing in their faces. . . . [T]he whole body became panic stricken and retreated in the utmost disorder. Back over the hill they went, . . . a struggling mass of men and horses.

B&O Railroad Museum Library

JOHN W. GARRETT

"The pike was smooth and clear—a good road for a chase—and we gave them no time to rally."

One federal soldier was hit, and his foot caught in the stirrup as he fell. He grasped madly at the stirrup to release his foot but fell back. "The horse continued galloping on, and at every jump the soldier's head would bounce upon the road and strike against the horse, which would then kick him with its heels."

Williamson saw two soldiers standing by the road and shouted at them to stop the horse.

They threw their arms up in reply: "We surrender!"

"Catch that horse!" Williamson yelled, but it was too late. The horse was down the road. By the time he was stopped, the rider was dead.

At one moment, Williamson was charging down the road attempting to kill a man, and in the next moment he was trying to save his life. He was struck by the the strange attitude we have toward fairness, and later mused that "in the excitement of a fight we were accustomed to shoot and kill without . . . reflection, but in this case, to see a fellow creature dragged to his death in . . . an unnatural manner . . . made me forget . . . that he was an enemy, and my only thought was to save him."

Thus he hit on a tragic truth—that war falls on the "natural" side of the human equation; it is natural for men to wage war and deliberately, methodically kill one another, but when one dies by accident, that excites emotions of sorrow, terror, susceptibility not aroused by the wholesale slaughters of "fair" deaths in war.

When the expected train failed to appear on time, Mosby surrounded the station. The garrison gave up without firing a shot and were marched away as their camp and storehouses were set afire. When Max Weber added up his losses next day, he counted thirty-eight killed, wounded or missing from the fifty cavalry and three hundred infantry he had sent out. He estimated Mosby's force at four hundred and counted two guns instead of one. Mosby's report on this engagement, however, counted fifty prisoners from Duffield Depot alone, including two lieutenants, and nineteen prisoners and twenty-seven horses that Nelson had captured, not counting the several killed and wounded.

The rangers returned home by way of Paris early on the morning of the 30th, carrying "a large quantity of dry goods, coffee, etc. from the captured stores at Duffield Depot, and these looked charming to the eyes of the poor people of the 'Confederacy' who had not seen the inside of a store for two or three years."

Wednesday, June 29, 1:00 A.M.—Washington City

Washington City was asleep on that warm summer night when the first intimation of danger arrived, a telegram delivered an hour after midnight to the War Department, a large brick building on the Seventeenth Street side of the White House at Pennsylvania Avenue. The telegram was from a civilian, but an important and informed one—John Work Garrett, who ran the Baltimore and Ohio Railroad "hands on" as its president.

Garrett's offices were in Baltimore, and he had his ears tuned to the telegraph news that winked down the wires from Point of Rocks, Harpers Ferry, Martinsburg, and points west, and what he heard bothered him: rumors of large rebel forces up in the Valley of Virginia, of generals Breckinridge and Ewell moving up the Valley toward the Potomac with considerable numbers of well armed men. He wanted Lincoln's chief of staff, Henry Halleck, to realize that the situation demanded "the greatest vigilance and attention." He was wrong, of course, about Richard Ewell, who had been taken out of field command after Spotsylvania and sent to the defenses of Richmond. But that was all he was wrong about.

Friday, July 1, Morning—Frederick, Maryland

John Yellott—major, 1st Potomac Home Brigade, provost marshal at Frederick, fanatically union—picked up a whisper and sent it west along the telegraph wire to Franz Sigel's headquarters at Martinsburg, the Valley town strategically located between Winchester in Virginia and Hagerstown in Maryland. The B&O crossed into Virginia at Harpers Ferry, ran through Martinsburg on its way west.

Sigel's reserve division guarded the eastern approaches to the north in two scattered units. Benjamin Kelley's West Virginians, with Ohio and Maryland and Illinois troops mixed in, were stationed as far west as Clarksburg, Grafton and Buckhannon (all now deep in West Virginia) and others were concentrated around Cumberland at Green Spring, New Creek and Paw Paw and as far east as Sleepy Creek, near Hancock. Max Weber's command, headquartered at Harpers Ferry, picked up at Sleepy Creek and extended forty-five miles eastward, to the mouth of the Monocacy. He had troops at rail centers like Cherry Run and Point of Rocks, troops that counted men from seven different states—light artillery units from Pennsylvania, West Virginia and Indiana, infantry from Ohio and from New York.

The majority of the soldiers, however, were green, short-enlistment men and no match for "real" soldiers, that is, those who had faced Grant's killing machine along the Rapidan.

Said Yellott, "The wife of a confederate soldier has been heard to say that her husband will be in Martinsburg in two days' time. He is part of a significant rebel army, and when they get to Martinsburg they will break up the Baltimore and Ohio railroad."

Sigel had no reason to disbelieve it, and he asked the Independent Loudon County Rangers to ride south and take a look. Just as Maryland boys from Montgomery County fought for the Confederates, so did Virginia boys fight for the Union.

July 1, 1:30 P.M.—Halleck to Grant

At one-thirty P.M., Halleck passed along Garrett's concerns to Grant, down in City Point, qualifying them by adding, "There are conflicting reports about the rebel forces in Shenandoah Valley." But he was playing a guarded hand and went on to speculate that it "would be good policy" for the Confederates to attempt a raid into Maryland. If they did, Sigel couldn't hold them—and if he provided Grant now with the men he wanted, there would be none left to come to the rescue of Sigel.

Grant, angry that his appetite for new troops was going unmet, replied that Hunter should get back on the railroad line, where "he will have the enemy in front of him."

That was a laugh, with Hunter way to hell-and-gone out on the Ohio River and Early's army swinging along the valley pike just south of Winchester, having encountered no opposition all the way from Lexington and Staunton.

July 1—Along the Valley Pike

Summer was bursting full in that undulating green sea of corn and wheat framed in blue mountains, the Blue Ridge rolling with them to the east until the Massanutten stepped in closer and made a wall, and to the west, near Strasburg, the massive ridge of North Mountain announcing the Appalachians.

The beauty of the scene tugged at the heart of J. Kelley Bennette, a hospital attendant with the 8th Virginia Cavalry. "[T]he eye never wearies," he told his journal, "with looking at such a country." When he reached Fisher's Hill, just south of Strasburg, he gushed, "You have as pretty a landscape spread out before you as a poet or painter ever exulted over," the Shenandoah making "an hyperbole" as perfect "as could be described by the most exact mathematical rule, . . . hedgerows planted and dressed by the hand of art."

Even Old Jubilee felt a tug of promise as the miles continued to roll by and Winchester beckoned without opposition to his front. He wired Lee:

If you can continue to threaten Grant, I hope to be able to do something for your relief and the success of our cause shortly. I shall lose no time.

Saturday, July 2—Winchester

Winchester. Again.

More than a hundred engagements had been and would be fought in and around Winchester from the day in 1862 when Stonewall drove the Feds north. This time, after a brief rattling skirmish between a scattered local defense and George Booth's scouts of the Maryland cavalry—the Confederate Maryland cavalry, that is—Early's army pushed on through the town. "The good people of W. received us very kindly and enthusiastically," recalled Capt. Robert Park of the 12th Alabama.

Although the colors were the same, the "good people of

Battles & Leaders

HENRY HALLECK

W." could tell at a glance this wasn't the glorious Valley Army of Jackson. In the forty days following May 1, Lee's Army of Northern Virginia, outnumbered two to one, had lost twenty thousand men under relentless hammering by Grant's Army of the Potomac, which itself had sustained an incredible sixty-three thousand casualties—eighteen thousand at the Wilderness, thirty thousand at Spotsylvania Court House, seven thousand at Cold Harbor. Exchanging lives for real estate, Grant had driven Lee from the banks of the Rapidan in central Virginia into the defense of Richmond and Petersburg.

To replace his huge losses, Grant had stripped the Washington defenses of almost all of the artillery regiments who normally manned the big guns mounted in the ring of forts around the city. Heavy artillery units were twelve companies strong, trained in infantry tactics as well, and Grant had turned the heavy artillerists into foot soldiers. But, what Halleck had understood and thought to be "good policy" for Lee, that withdrawal had opened a window of opportunity for a strike at the now poorly-defended capital, and Early, with his patched-together army, was heading as fast as he could for that opening.

Battles & Leaders

GEN. LEW WALLACE

Patched together, all right, but still powerful. What was coming at Sigel in Martinsburg and Weber at Harpers Ferry was in aggregate sixty-seven regiments and six battalions of infantry; eleven regiments and nine battalions of cavalry; nine batteries, in three battalions, of field artillery; and seven batteries of horse artillery. At full strength on this march, Early's II Army Corps, Army of Northern Virginia, Army of the Valley District, numbered no fewer than eighteen thousand men.

Straggling and inconsistent reporting put his force at a probable fifteen thousand effectives, in these elements:

In John Gordon's division were Clement Evans's seven regiments of Georgians, Zebulon York's fragments of ten Louisiana regiments, once "Lee's Tigers," and William Terry's fragmented remains of fourteen once-proud Virginia regiments, including what was left of Stonewall's own first brigade.

Maj. Gen. Stephen Ramseur, that charming boy whose memory is surrounded by a halo of sorrow, had in his division five regiments of Robert Lilley's Virginians, four of Robert Johnston's North Carolinians and five of William Lewis's North Carolinians.

Maj. Gen. Robert Rodes's divison counted five regiments of Cullen Battle's Alabamians, five of Bryan Grimes's North Carolinians and four fragmented regiments of Philip Cook's Georgians. The fourth and final division, under Gen. John Echols, included four regiments of Gabriel Wharton's Virginians, three battalions of George Patton's Virginians and Brig. Gen. John C. Vaughn's collection of Tennessee and North Carolina mounted infantry.

Brig. Gen. Armistead Long counted almost forty guns in three battalions, all Virginia units, save one from Georgia.

Early's cavalry under Maj. Gen. Robert Ransom—Imboden, McCausland and Johnson—included units of field artillery. Johnson's was a unit of Baltimore light artillery, which would soon be facing a federal unit of the same name.

GEN. LEW WALLACE'S HEADQUARTERS IN BALTIMORE

These were men who had passed through the burning sieve of combat and lived to fight another day. Even in their fragmented state there was no question as to the plain hard-ass grit and weathered toughness of these veterans.

Sigel's scouts had returned to Martinsburg, and he reported to Washington that the enemy was in force in the Valley of Virginia—a force to be taken very seriously. Both Sigel and Weber, the German generals, began to scramble out of harm's way.

Saturday, July 2, 10:00 A.M.—
Wallace's Headquarters, Baltimore

About the time that Gen. Halleck in Washington was wiring Grant's thoughts to Hunter out in West Virginia about keeping the enemy in front, John Garrett's carriage was stopping at Gen. Lew Wallace's headquarters in Baltimore.

He wasted no time in informing Wallace, "There are confederates appearing along the line from Harpers Ferry west. You know and I know that Gen. [Christopher] Augur down in Washington doesn't have enough men to guard that city. You and he should get together and find out what is really going on out there and make plans for defense. Make sure the Rebels do not capture this railroad, especially the Monocacy Bridge."

Garrett had the full, kept look of a capitalist, that jowly but strong, full-necked, square-faced, narrow-eyed look that comes upon American business men in their prime. A lot of rye and port and steak and worry went into it. And throughout the confusing, contradictory events that would soon begin to accelerate, John W. Garrett leaves a record of knowing precisely what he was doing.

In contrast to the portly Garrett, whose large clean-shaven face was framed in white sideburns, Wallace was finely featured, with a thin, straight nose under dark, arching brows and a black explosion of mustache and beard.

And, unlike Garrett, Wallace lived with failure. A lawyer and prominent Democrat in his home state of Indiana, where he was the state's adjutant general, Wallace was a veteran of the Mexican War who entered the Civil War as a full colonel in command of Indiana's dashing 11th Zouave Regiment. He was promoted to general officer and saved Grant's career with a brilliant maneuver that won the battle at Fort Donelson in February 1862, and then fell afoul of Grant's temper and bad opinion for what Grant regarded as too slow a reaction to the confederate advance at Shiloh. (Truth be told, Grant himself was not even on the field when the advance began.) After that, this Democrat in a Republican administration, this volunteer general among West Pointers, had been shunted to administrative duties in Cincinnati and now Baltimore. He knew that Henry Halleck actively disliked both his politics and himself, and Wallace believed that Halleck was looking for an excuse to sack him.

Now here was John Garrett, sitting before him with news that could change his life.

But a confederate army would have to be in the lower Valley and able to cross the Potomac and take Frederick before they would ever come in sight of that bridge.

"I am telling you," said Garrett, "that a confederate army may be about to do just that. These units appearing at so many places indicate a large troop movement."

"I understand your concern, but I have a political problem in being more responsive. The boundary of my command is exactly at the Monocacy; I cannot proceed west of that stream."

"The bridge touches both banks."

"True. It should be well enough defended with that block house on the eastern bank, with two guns. But I take your point. I will do what I can."

Saturday, July 2, Afternoon—Winchester

Early was not a stupid man, and he knew he was looking at a classic offensive situation as he approached Martinsburg. Sigel was there with far fewer and far greener troops and a surfeit of goods and stores. He probably would not defend the place, and the only ways he could move the goods and the troops out were north by wagon toward the Potomac and east by train toward Harpers Ferry.

To prevent the hapless Hunter from sending help from his army in West Virginia, Imboden's cavalry was dispatched toward the western mountains to take out the railroad bridges over the South Branch of the Potomac, St. John's Run and Big Capon Creek.

Then the trap was armed by sending McCausland's horsemen to the northwest over the mountains and then northward toward the Potomac, around Sigel's right, with orders to burn the railroad bridge at Back Creek; thence he should move eastward along the tracks to North Mountain Depot and from there strike for Hainsville in Sigel's rear along the much-traveled dirt road between Martinsburg and the Potomac. McCausland moved out at sundown on July 2nd and disappeared toward the mountains.

The other claw of the pincer would be Bradley Johnson's cavalry dashing toward Leetown and the railroad crossing at Kearneysville, with Rodes's and Ramseur's divisions in support to discourage Sigel from moving toward help at Harpers Ferry. Johnson would carry the momentum of attack clear around to his left, west to Hainsville, where McCausland would be waiting.

Snap!

To prod Sigel out of Martinsburg and toward the trap at Hainsville, Early would send Breckinridge and Gordon directly down the Valley road from Winchester through Bunker Hill, Inwood, Darkesville and Pikeside to Martinsburg, with the 2nd Maryland cavalry under Harry Gilmor screening out front.

So it was, that at daybreak on a clear and warm July day, the long gray column, which had begun moving out of Winchester in the dark, separated at Brucetown, some seven miles down the road. According to plan, Breckinridge and Gordon continued on toward Martinsburg, with dashing Harry Gilmor galloping on ahead. Early stayed with the infantry of Rodes and Ramseur as Bradley Johnson led them to the right fork and the road to Leetown. All the elements were in place.

Sunday, July 3, First Light—Darkesville

It didn't work.

Harry Gilmor's Maryland troopers soon made contact with a line of pickets south of Martinsburg and quickly drove them in. The reserve line proved too stubborn, however, for a cavalry unit armed only with pistol and saber. Gilmor was ordered to hold up until the 9th Louisiana could send up some sharpshooters to help out. In the interval, Maj. Gen. Julius Stahel came out from Martinsburg with his full cavalry command of six hundred and took up a strong position "behind a rocky crest in a dense wood," as Gilmor remembered it, which Gilmor attacked at once and "met with a sudden and unexpected repulse."

Gilmor rode over to see Lt. Col. John Hodges of the 9th Louisiana and suggested a plan; if Hodges would move his command through a wheat field to flank the union position, Gilmor would attack as the enemy changed front. Hodges agreed and promptly moved his Louisianans toward the wheat. They were almost through it when Gen. Breckinridge rode up:

"What in the devil are you doing over there?" he thundered at Hodges.

"Major Gilmor asked me to turn the enemy's flank," he replied. "They are dis-

Battles & Leaders

BRADLEY JOHNSON, C.S.A.

mounted cavalry in the woods directly to our front, sir."

"Get your men out of that wheat field and back on the road," the general commanded. "Move up in column directly to the enemy and deploy and attack him when you find him. Gilmor is not commanding here; I am. Cavalry are fond of flanking tactics but it will take men on the ground to directly dislodge that force."

Gilmor was "very much mortified" by Breckinridge's caustic remarks. Several of his command rode up and said, "If he thinks we are afraid, let's charge them anyway."

"No," said Gilmor. "Let's just watch the infantry catch hell."

The column had hardly started up the road when the general's horse was shot and several men killed. A second regiment arrived on the scene and pressed forward. Gilmor took his horses around the flank and "charged in among them, driving them beautifully across three fields" toward Darkesville—but suddenly two columns of union horse charged out from behind the third field, causing Gilmor "to retreat rapidly." But the union charge was "feeble, and soon came down to a walk." Gilmor formed up his line while under fire from the Federals only forty yards away, then "scarcely waiting for the line to dress," he went at his enemy and drove him in utter confusion from the field.

What a piece of work was Harry Gilmor.

Breckinridge harassed Stahel's retreating cavalry with artillery fire until, at one P.M., Gilmor led the charge into Martinsburg.

Too late.

Earlier that morning, Sigel had thought fit to inform Lew Wallace, as Washington had not, of what was going on: "I have reports of an advance of the enemy in force down the Shenandoah Valley. His advance is now at Winchester."

Halleck passed Sigel's report of the previous day, about Early advancing on Winchester, on to Grant.

And all morning Sigel had been loading union stores and supplies on John Garrett's trains. By eleven-thirty A.M., his adjutant, Maj. A.T. Meysenberg, reported that "trains are out of Martinsburg. Everything . . . loaded and sent off." By that time Sigel was withdrawing in good order toward the Potomac fords at Shepherdstown—thanks to the Irish.

Bradley Johnson hit trouble worse than what Gilmor had experienced. Beyond Leetown he found a solid union force across his front. These were veteran soldiers of the 23rd Illinois Infantry, the "Irish Brigade" recruited in Chicago and led by a brave colonel with the appropriate moniker of James Mulligan—and Mulligan did not fear a fight.

He had proved that in the very earliest days of the war, when the Illinois Irish Brigade—not to be confused with the better-known Irish Brigade

David Hunter Strother
Virginia State Library & Archives

COL. JAMES MULLIGAN, U.S.A.

of the Army of the Potomac—was sent to relieve Thomas A. Marshall's cavalry regiment at Lexington, Missouri. As Mulligan later commented, "The trouble was not so much the getting into Lexington as the getting out," for an army of ten thousand men under Maj. Gen. Sterling Price came up rapidly and surrounded Mulligan and a few other units, who dug in around a college on a hill overlooking the Missouri River. For three days, September 18, 19 and 20, 1861, Mulligan's twenty-seven hundred men held off Price's now reinforced eighteen thousand until, out of food, out of water and out of ammunition, they had no choice but to surrender. All were paroled but Mulligan, who was held until October 30. With an escort of forty men under a flag of truce, he was exchanged in St. Louis and returned a hero to Chicago.

The unit that now faced Johnson had been in and around western Virginia since 1862, guarding the vital Baltimore and Ohio tracks. They had been through a hundred little skirmishes in that difficult terrain and its veterans had just come off a two-month furlough, so they were fresh. And they had shoes.

Johnson was still smarting from the affair years later when he recorded that he had contended that day with three thousand infantry and a six-gun battery that had stopped him cold at Leetown. He had just eight hundred in the saddle and a number of men whose horses had been shot, who tagged along on foot, hoping for a horse to show up.

Sigel sent reinforcements and word to Mulligan to hold on as long as he could and then withdraw toward Kearneysville and Shepherdstown. With a thousand dismounted troopers and fifteen hundred cavalry and two guns, Mulligan did not hesitate; he attacked Johnson's front and sent it reeling backwards. News of the fight spread quickly northward, all the way to Frederick, where people felt that first little thrill of adrenalin when they considered what might be coming their way.

As Mulligan drove Johnson toward Leetown, Sigel's command, in the form of a long wagon train and marching feet kicking up billows of red dust, was moving as quickly as it could down the road toward the Potomac.

July 3, 3:30 P.M.—Martinsburg

Gordon's Georgians tramped into Martinsburg around three-thirty P.M. and along with York's Louisianans quickly took to drinking and looting the place, despite Early's orders to Breckinridge to "prevent all plundering." Martinsburg was a union town, as Winchester was a southern one, and the victor took his spoils from one as he had not the other.

John Worsham never forgot it. Finding a friend of his in charge of the railroad express office, he exchanged his help in organizing the seized goods for a barrel of cakes which was carried to his unit. After awhile, though, he said that he must have something to eat, since "I hadn't nary mouthful for three days." He opened a box and his eyes burned on its contents: cakes, oranges, bananas, lemons and a bottle of wine! When last his eyes had rested on such viands he could not remember. "I got a chair, as the soldiers said 'a sure enough chair,' and sat down to my box and ate and ate until I could eat no more."

He also confiscated a pair of boots that he wore until the end of the war, and his small comment about them speaks volumes: ". . . the boots fitting me to a T when my feet were healed so that I could wear them."

July 3—Baltimore

Garrett to Stanton:

Breckinridge, Imboden and Early in command of Ewell's old Corps are north of Winchester with from fifteen to thirty thousand men.

July 3, 4:00 P.M.—Washington

Halleck to Grant:

> The three principal officers on the line of the road are Sigel, Stahel, and Max Weber, so you can judge what probability there is of a good defense if the enemy should attack the line in force.

July 3, 4:40 P.M.—Washington

Stanton to Garrett:

> [W]hat, exactly, is going on? We want to avoid being misled by stampede and groundless clamor. But if there is real danger we have to know. If you have any source of truthful information, you had better resort to it.

July 3—Baltimore

Garrett to Stanton:

> I have resorted to it and I am telling you that Early, Breckinridge and Imboden are north of Winchester with between fifteen and thirty thousand men, that they were fighting at Leetown this very afternoon, that Martinsburg has been abandoned with the telegraph and railroad line destroyed, that Hunter is too far away to be of any help whatsoever, that the garrison at Harpers Ferry cannot stop Early, that General Lew Wallace, who is in command of the Baltimore defenses, hasn't heard from Sigel since 10:35 this morning and we have no idea where he is or where he's been—but you can count on this, that he would not have fallen away from Martinsburg unless he was looking at a far superior force.

July 3, 5:00 P.M.—Headquarters, Army of the Potomac

Grant to Halleck:

> Early's corps is now here. There are no troops that can now be threatening Hunter's department.

July 3—Leetown

During the afternoon, frustration seized Bradley Johnson. His commander, Robert Ransom, had come up to survey the situation but could find no way to get through

Mulligan and seize the wagon train that was snaking closer and closer toward safety. They needed infantry.

When Johnson found it, though, it was Ramseur—and he was camped in Leetown and his men, completely played out after a gruelling, oppressively hot twenty-four-mile march, were going nowhere.

The game was up. Sigel was getting away.

Disgusted and angry at another opportunity lost by the cavalry, Early put up his headquarters tent near Ramseur and went to sleep.

July 3—Wallace's Headquarters, Baltimore

Worried about his conversation with Garrett, Wallace called in his adjutant, Samuel Lawrence, to discuss it. "Well," said Lawrence, "I saw in the newspaper this morning that General Hunter had crossed the mountains."

"Which ones?"

"Into the Kanawha Valley."

Wallace found a large military map of the eastern theatre of war in his office, and the two men studied it. "He is several hundred miles away from any action in the Valley of Virginia," said Wallace. "What is to prevent General Lee from sending a large detachment from Petersburg and seriously attempting the capture of Washington?"

"Nothing," said Lawrence, "if he sees the opportunity."

"He is reckoned among the great soldiers," said Wallace, "and I do not believe that we can count on him not seeing the opportunity."

Wallace to Brig. Gen. Erastus B. Tyler:

> Concentrate the 3rd Regiment of the Potomac Home Brigades at Monrovia, and if possible push it and any other troops you can raise on to Monocacy Junction. Send two companies to Monocacy Junction at once. You will order the guard at Monocacy Junction to hold the post and give immediate notice of the approach of the enemy.

July 3, 8:00 P.M.—Martinsburg

Brig. Gen. Max Weber commanding at Harpers Ferry to Maj. Gen. Davius N. Couch, commander, Department of the Susquehanna:

> Martinsburg is being evacuated in the face of a confederate force reported ten to twenty thousand strong with infantry, cavalry, artillery. Sigel is trying to reach Harpers Ferry but I have not heard from him since eleven this morning. The enemy are reported to be moving toward the Potomac.

RELAY HOUSE

July 3, 10:00 P.M.—Sigel's Headquarters

Sigel to Weber:

> The enemy took possession of Martinsburg about one P.M. today and are
> now reported to be marching on Williamsport and hard fighting at Leetown.

July 3—Relay House

The Metropolitan branch rail line that today links Washington with Frederick and
the west did not exist in 1864. Washington was connected to Baltimore by a spur of
the Baltimore and Ohio, from which another spur ran east to Annapolis. The artist
who drew "The Seat of War" in the early 1860s, offers a bird's eye view from over the
Potomac at the capital looking north ninety miles to Havre de Grace, Perryville and
Elkton and west ninety miles past Harpers Ferry and Martinsburg to Cumberland. The
only important places between Washington and Baltimore are the railroad junctions:
Annapolis Junction, where the Annapolis spur hit the main track a few miles north of
Laurel, and Elkridge Landing, where the tracks crossed the Patapsco at Relay House,
eight miles south of Baltimore.

Between 1833 and 1835, Benjamin Henry Latrobe II built what was in its day an
astounding structure—the largest bridge in the nation, the first multi-span masonry
railroad bridge and the first to be built on a curving alignment. Named the Thomas

Viaduct after the first president of the B&O, it is still in daily use, a beautiful sweep of track curving high over the deep Patapsco valley on eight huge arches.

Just to the north, on the Baltimore County side, rose a substantial hotel, the gabled and turreted Relay House. It was the first "railroad station," built for the convenience of passengers who, in the days before steam, had to wait during the change in the teams of horses that pulled the cars.

Relay was one of the roots of the B&O, and the B&O was the root of Maryland's wealth. From the day its tracks reached Wheeling on the Ohio River, New Year's Day of 1853, it had an open run from Baltimore to Cinncinatti and Chicago, and the wealth of the west began pouring through. Baltimore reflected it; the garden development of Roland Park, with its houses the size of steamboats, many built on steel girders, housed B&O officials, and president John W. Garrett lived in Evergreen, a great house now a part of Johns Hopkins University.

On May 4, 1861, when Benjamin Butler's 6th Massachusetts was attacked in the Pratt Street Riot in Baltimore, it seized Relay House, and ten days later invaded the city by train and "captured" Federal Hill, probably preventing a move for succession in the state.

From Relay the tracks ran north to the city and west toward Ellicott's Mills, Monrovia and Monocacy Junction, where they again divided, one branch continuing north into Frederick and another peeling away southward toward Harpers Ferry.

Relay was well guarded during the entire war but by increasingly greener troops as Grant devoured the veterans along the Rapidan and James. In early May of 1864, responding to a plea from Washington, Ohio raised several more volunteer infantry regiments for guard duty in the Washington theatre. The 144th Ohio, mustered in on May 11, served at Relay House and in Baltimore itself at Fort McHenry. The 149th and 159th Ohio, both mustered May 9, went into the Baltimore defenses and along the railroad bridges of the Philadelphia, Wilmington and Baltimore Railroad. These were among the units that Wallace had at his disposal when word came of Early's crossing of the Potomac, and he immediately began to move seven companies of the 149th and three of the 144th, along with a hundred mounted infantrymen of the 159th, toward Frederick and the Monocacy.

The Potomac Home Brigades had been formed at the start of the war by a governor of Maryland to guard the strategic communication points, the canals and railroad tracks and river crossings of the state. They were involved in many of the 145 officially reported skirmishes that occured in Maryland. In the summer of 1864, the 1st Maryland Potomac Home Brigade was assigned to the B&O, and Wallace could easily call it in to Monocacy. The third was equally at hand, at Annapolis Junction, Relay Station and already at Monocacy itself.

As Wallace's humble forces began to gather, Early's hardened corps of veterans, which Grant was so convinced were still in the lines at Richmond, was two hundred miles away and, on this Sunday night, about to be baptized in Potomac waters.

HARPER'S FERRY LOOKING DOWN THE POTOMAC
Maryland Heights (left) and Loudon Heights (right)

Monday, July 4—Harpers Ferry

It was a good day to cross George Washington's river. Young George had been up this way as a nineteen-year-old surveyor, when it was mostly Indian land with a few settlers like Thomas Cresap, and later he had dreamed of a canal linking Alexandria and Georgetown with the bountiful lands of the Ohio. He knew the fords at Shepherdstown and Nolan's Ferry and Conrad's and White's, but he never dreamed, we must assume, that his river, which he thought of as a binding umbilical cord tying the fertile Ohio country to the Potomac ports, would be the boundary between warring nations of Americans.

Early had a substantial breakfast at the home of a Maj. Hawks outside Leetown, then rode on into Charles Town ahead of his troops and continued on the road to Harpers Ferry. At Halltown, a small settlement beyond Charles Town, he encountered federal skirmishers who were obviously conducting a withdrawal in the face of the enemy. Early asked Ramseur and Rodes to come up with alacrity.

Ramseur took up the left flank and was in command of the B&O tracks west of Harpers Ferry by nine o'clock. Rodes went right and ahead and had Bolivar Heights in his hands about the same time. Those heights made up the third side of a triangle formed by the northeast-flowing Shenandoah and the southeast-flowing Potomac.

James Taylor
The Western Reserve Historical Society

POINT OF ROCKS

Inside the triangle was Harpers Ferry.

It was and is a lovely spot. Thomas Jefferson once remarked that the view from a Harpers Ferry hill over the conjunction of the rivers and eastward down the Potomac Valley was worth a trip across the Atlantic. A part of the subtle magnificence of the landscape is the framing of mountains over the river valleys. Across the Shenandoah and stepped somewhat back from the river, is a towering spur of the Blue Ridge, Loudon Heights, where Jackson had put guns in 1862. And across the Potomac, rising directly up from the river, the massive wall of Maryland Heights, commanding the landscape for miles around, including the whole valley and all of the streets of Harpers Ferry.

When Early trained his glasses on the Maryland Heights, he saw that they were occupied by very large guns—one hundred pounders. There would be no taking of Harpers Ferry and the easy road to Washington so long as the heavy federal guns were staring down on every operation. The town itself, in the valley below, was bustling with men moving equipment and supplies toward ferries shuttling to the Maryland shore below the heights. Weber was obviously going to run up there, and it was going to be very difficult to dislodge him.

Early knew he would have to go around. He would spend the rest of this fourth of July getting his army assembled for a crossing into Maryland, yet another summer and another crossing. He would go by way of the old fords below Sharspburg, and send his columns eastward, across South Mountain, by way of the old passes.

Always, along those roads, was death and disaster.

July 4, Morning—Point of Rocks

Mosby had assembled 250 of his rangers at Upperville on July 3 and marched them that day, along with a twelve-pound Napoleon, through Bloomfield to Wheatfield, where they camped. On the morning of the fourth they reached the Potomac opposite Berlin (modern Brunswick) and moved eastward along the bank to a ford about a mile west of Point of Rocks. They saw they were expected. Sharpshooters from two companies of the Potomac Home Brigade stationed at Point of Rocks had taken concealed positions along the wooded bank and on Patton Island in mid-river. Two companies of Loudon rangers were also at the point, and they were drawn by Capt. Daniel M. Keyes in a battle line just outside the little settlement. For a while the combatants traded long range volleys across the river. Mosby moved his cannon to a hill opposite the town and began lobbing shots over the river.

Mosby forced the issue, ordering his men to take the island, which they did, and then attack across the river, supported by the cannon firing onto the bank and dislodging the snipers. Capt. Adolphus E. Richards "then dashed into the river," leading his company in the face of fire coming from the shore ahead.

The defending home brigades "went scampering along the tow-path" with the Rebs in hot pursuit.

The scene of this action was one famous in the annals of American business—a forty-foot-wide shelf of land between the Catoctins and the river, the only convenient opening to the west along that whole mountain ridge. Both the B&O railroad, angling down along the old wheat wagon road from Frederick, and the Chesapeake and Ohio Canal, a big ditch along the north bank of the Potomac, had aimed for that shelf of land and that opening westward. The railroad won the race, and the canal, claiming prior rights to the right-of-way, sued in 1831; a protracted court struggle ended with victory by the canal. The railroad, as part of the settlement, bought twenty-five shares of the canal, and the state of Maryland worked out a physical compromise so that the canal and tow-path along which the soldiers were now running for their lives were separated from the railroad tracks by a fence, the barges and the locomotives each allotted their space with hardly a foot to spare.

A bridge spanned the canal near the settlement, and just beyond was the military camp and a protecting earthwork that offered a field of fire over the bridge. As the Federals fled over the bridge, they paused long enough to tear up the planking. They then piled into the earthwork and opened a brisk fire as Mosby's men pulled up on the towpath side of the destroyed bridge.

Lt. Harry Hatcher was nonplussed. As Capt. Richards told his men to tear down a shed for new bridge planks, Hatcher ran across on the supporting timbers, which had been left in place, and kept on going right into the camp, right up to the flagpole, where he hauled down the Stars and Stripes and returned with the flag across the bridge timbers—all in a continuous hail of minié balls that miraculously missed him during the entire performance.

That was all Richards needed. To hell with the planks. His men dismounted and charged across on the timbers and drove the home brigade out of its earthwork and back toward the mountains. By then planks were down on the bridge, and Mosby's whole command thundered over, burned the camp and a canal boat, cut down the telegraph poles and rifled the stores of supplies.

An unsuspecting train happened along the tracks from Harpers Ferry, and the Napoleon opened on it. It hit the cab and wounded the fireman, but the engineer managed to get her stopped, and then backed her all the way to Sandy Hook.

July 4—Washington

The 8th Illinois Volunteer Cavalry was Washington City's real police force, and it was spread all over the map. The commander, Lt. Col. David Clendenin, and his head-quarters were in barracks at Camp Relief on Seventh Street in Washington, but companies were in Alexandria, operating against smugglers at the huge cavalry depot at Camp Stoneman; in the city on funeral escort; and out along the Potomac at Muddy Branch, where they were guarding the canal and making an occasional foray into Virginia. On June 24, two companies had crossed the river at Conrad's Ferry, surrounded Leesburg and captured nine rebels and six horses.

On the fourth, Clendenin received orders from the War Department to take what companies were in camp (there were five) and get on out to Point of Rocks, picking up the two companies at Muddy Branch on the way.

These were not boys Clendenin was leading out. Most had been "veteranized," had reenlisted as veterans for another three years in exchange for a $300 bonus, a thirty-day furlough and free transportation to and from Illinois. (The free transportation had proven to be an unheated box car in which the men almost froze to death in Washington Station because the master had neglected to start the train.) In his memoirs, John Stewart Bryan recalls asking his grandfather, who had served with Mosby, whether or not all Yankees were cowards, and reports the old man's reply: "Son, no one who ever fought against the 8th Illinois Cavalry would have such an imbecilic idea as that!"

James J. Williamson, whose history of Mosby's rangers is level-headed and factual, states simply that in the summer of 1864 the 8th Illinois was "the best cavalry regiment in the Army of the Potomac," and Mosby veteran John H. Alexander called them "by considerable odds the best fighters we ever tackled."

Their battle streamers, from December 1861, when they arrived in Virginia, until April of 1864, when they finally left the field, are a virtual index of the battles fought by the Army of the Potomac. It was Capt. Marcellus E. Jones of the 8th Illinois, using a carbine he borrowed from Sgt. Levi Shafer, who is credited with firing the first shot of the battle of Gettysburg.

During its service, the 8th Illinois lost seven officers, its lieutenant colonel wounded and two majors killed, sixty-eight men killed or mortally wounded and another 175 who died of other causes.

The 8th was an extremely proud and self-sufficient regiment. When the long-anticipated thirty-day furloughs were suddenly terminated in February of 1864, there was no bitching and moaning. Col. William Gamble, commanding, issued an order remarking that "it is a high compliment to the regiment to be ordered back again inside of thirty days. . . . I expect that the regiment will . . . be ready to fight its way through as heretofore, without expecting or receiving any favor from any source."

Clendenin had moved out during the afternoon of the

Abner Hard

COL. DAVID CLENDENIN

fourth and pushed his command along the River road until one A.M., covering twenty miles to the camp at Muddy Branch. At dawn they were in saddles and on the move toward Point of Rocks.

July 4, Morning—Frederick Junction

Frederick Junction, on the west bank of the river, beyond the iron bridge, was where the B&O westbound track divided. One spur ran northwest three miles to Frederick, and the other turned south and paralleled the river for several miles before bearing southwest toward Point of Rocks and Harpers Ferry. Near the divide stood a two-story brick building the lower floor of which served as the railroad and telegraph office; the upper story were apartments for agent Frank Mantz and his family.

On this morning, the station was humming with the passage of men in blue—Potomac home guards and Ohio one-hundred-day men being collected on the Monocacy River by Gen. Erastus Tyler at Wallace's direction. One of the trains also

ARABY, THE THOMAS HOME

brought three young civilians who were on holiday: Sam Thomas, son of the owner of the nearby farm of Araby; Julius H. Anderson, who was dating Sam's sister Alice; and Hugh M. Gatchell, who was to be companion to Alice's best friend, Mamie Tyler. They were going to Araby for the Fourth of July and were in gay high spirits compared to the serious young men being marched away from the junction to nearby bivouac. There were muttered sentiments about rallying to the flag in time of war, and more than one envious glance followed the waiting carriage and driver who now carried Sam and his friends back across the river by a covered bridge and then up the steep watershed to Araby's long entrance drive.

July 4—Araby Farm

The noble old house was set in emerald lawns on a crest parallel to the high ridge that the Washington road followed. Handsome brick with the white dormer windows and a white Palladian doorway, a fine example of a Georgian country house, Araby had been built in 1780 for Scotsman James Marshall, whose descendants lived in it until 1860 when it was sold, along with the surrounding 240-acre farm, to C. Keefer Thomas, a Baltimore businessman who was native to the Frederick area. Thomas and his wife had another daughter and son in addition to Sam and Alice.

A great porch shaded by pines ran across the entire forty-foot front of the house and looked north and west toward the Frederick valley, the rail junction, Garrett's iron bridge and, closer to hand, the house of miller James Gambrill on the north side of the Washington road. Gambrill's mill with its big overshot wheel lay farther north, in the small valley carved out by Bush Creek, which joined the Monocacy in the three hundred yards that separated the iron railroad bridge and the covered bridge that carried the Washington road. Behind this triple geography of bridge-creek-bridge, the land rose abruptly into hills that looked out across the great Frederick plain.

The lads saw their pretty ladies on the big front porch, waving as the carriage approached. Beyond the house, the fields rolled away south and westward toward the river. On a small rise in that lower bottom land could be seen another farm, Clifton (or the River Farm), owned by Thomas Worthington. His large, two-story, L-shaped house had nine windows and a door on its front facade. Between the farms, the property line, which angled sharply from the river to the south, was clearly distinguished by a stout post-and-rail fence. A somewhat sunken road ran between Araby and Clifton, where it turned and became the very long entrance drive that followed the river's east bank until it hit the Washington road just at the foot of the covered bridge. This long entrance road gave Clifton its other name, River Drive Farm.

A more prosperous and peaceful landscape, with the big houses, bulging barns, fat fields and pretty girls in pastel dresses, could not have been imagined in the summer of 1864.

July 4, 11:35 A.M—*Baltimore*

Garrett to Stanton and Halleck:

> General Weber telegraphed me from Harpers Ferry, at 10:48 this morning that "the enemy are in sight. Two thousand cavalry and a force of infantry are in sight. . . . If they press me, I shall retire to the Heights." At 11:05, our agent at Harpers Ferry telegraphs: "Great excitement here. All citizens are leaving. Harpers Ferry is being evacuated."

Halleck was energized, and quickly organized a scratch force of Ohio militia, dismounted cavalry and light artillery armed as infantry, twenty-eight hundred in all, and sent them off to Harpers Ferry under command of Gen. Albion P. Howe, who ran the artillery depot in Washington. (Howe actually got through to Maryland Heights, riding the railroad as far as he could and hoofing it the rest of the way.)

July 4, 12:30 P.M.—Washington

Halleck to Weber:

> Everything should be prepared for a defense of your works and the first man
> who proposes a surrender or retreat should be hung.

July 4, 2:00 P.M.—Monocacy

Tyler to Wallace:

> Operator at Point of Rocks says the enemy have crossed one half mile west
> of that point. I have just sent another detachment in that direction. I have
> three companies and Gen. Weber one at this post. We can give them a sharp
> fight if they attack us in front.

July 4, 4:20 P.M.—Washington

Stanton to Horatio Seymour, Albany, New York:

> Mr. Governor: The President directs me to inform you that a rebel force,
> variously estimated at from 15,000 to 20,000 men, have invaded Maryland
> and that the public safety requires him to call upon the state executives for
> a militia force to repel the invasion . . . 12,000 men from your state to serve
> for one hundred days. . . . [Y]ou will with the utmost dispatch forward the
> troops to Washington by rail or steamboat, as may be the most expeditious.

July 4—Baltimore

A.A.G. Sam B. Lawrence to Gen. Tyler:

> Send no troops beyond the Monocacy without instructions from these
> headquarters.

Weber's reserves had caught their own deserter, and he informed Gen. Ben Kelley
in West Virginia, that it wasn't Ewell, but Early in command of Ewell's old corps and
pushing not less than twenty thousand infantry, ten thousand cavalry and sixty guns
toward Maryland.

July 4—Baltimore

Garrett to Stanton:

> Tell Tyler at Monocacy to stay awake; all wires west of Frederick have been cut.

July 4, Afternoon—Duffield's Depot

Breckinridge and Gordon had been late leaving Martinsburg, partly to enjoy a bit more plunder, partly because the troops had been hard used the day before. After burning the railroad bridges, they came down the tracks through Kearnesyville to Duffield's Depot, where they went into camp late in the afternoon of the fourth, some five miles from Early's lines.

Kyd Douglas noted that prior to the fateful crossing of the Potomac, Early had "spread his little army like a fan," sending cavalry units up and down the B&O line to hit as many places as possible and create the impression of a vast army on the move.

He certainly impressed Weber's scouts atop Maryland Heights, as he reported to Tyler, who relayed the news to Wallace in Baltimore, that "rebel cavalry under Major-General Ransom is said to be marching on Williamsport. . . . The enemy's strength is extravagantly estimated. It would be folly to give figures."

July 4, 7:00 P.M.—Harpers Ferry

Max Weber began to pull out of Harpers Ferry, taking his entire command across the Potomac and up to the top of the great hills on the Maryland side, burning the railroad and the pontoon bridges across the Potomac behind him—a treed racoon. Franz Sigel, who had been leading his Martinsburg refugees all day along the narrow, mountainous Maryland roads from the Shepherdstown crossing, arrived late that night and crawled up beside him.

No sooner was Weber out than the Rebs were in, Gen. Rodes himself leading his old Alabama brigade (now Cullen Battle's) in the search for commissary stores—and finding them.

"A universal pillaging of United States government property . . . was carried on all night," remembered Capt. Park of the 12th Alabama. What Morrow of the 8th Louisiana wrote to his father was that "our boys got the 4th of July dinner" that had been planned for the Yankee army, and he recounted the wonderful things: fruit, preserves, sardines, oysters, meat, wines and liquor. Artilleryman Henry Robinson Berkeley quoted a list more basic: sugar, coffee, hardtack, molasses. George Lester of the 38th Georgia gave the event an apt name: "The Dutch Generals' Barbecue." To add to the good fortune, shoes arrived by wagon from the south!

The strangest occurrence of the day had to do with Cpl. A. F. Henderson, who that afternoon had climbed into a cherry tree and, as he was reaching for a plump fruit, was hit out of the blue by a lucky minié ball or a stray piece of shell and carried away to the hospital.

July 4, Midnight—Camden Street Yards, Baltimore

Wallace knew that Halleck would have his ass for leaving his desk, so he kept his plans entirely secret from everyone but his immediate staff and John Garrett, who had the locomotive standing by and steaming in Baltimore's Camden Street yards when Wallace and an aide, Lt. Col. James R. Ross, climbed aboard soon after midnight; Garrett had sent word up and down the B&O line to make way.

He was off—a soldier under a cloud rushing for a second throw of the dice, to a hoped-for battle that could cleanse his name, standing in the lurching cab of a locomotive rushing under midnight stars through the honeysuckle-drenched darkness of the Maryland Piedmont, while a great army he will face sleeps under those same stars only a few miles up that rushing river of Potomac—and Kismet is moving the pieces around: some down, off the board, asleep, wounded, dead. Some febrile, fearful, rushing, alive, filled with dread. And lucky Lew Wallace in his locomotive, his adrenalin pumping, his heart pounding, the wheels clickety-clicking in the rushing dark.

It was not yet dawn when they screeched down to a stop just east of the iron bridge over the Monocacy. Wallace had a sense of hills fringing the dome of morning stars as an officer led him and Ross over to the blockhouse. He laid his head down on a bunk and a rooster bugled from the wide plain lying in darkness to the west, and another called from the hills beyond, and another from the valleys and hills lying toward the sunrise, and soon the footsore, tired men of the Confederacy, who were wrapped in worn-through blankets, awakened and listened to bright chanticleer, ears snapping in sweet memory; there were few roosters left in the blasted landscape of Virginia.

Tuesday, July 5, Morning—Bolivar Heights

Jubilee was up early and back onto Bolivar Heights, and he saw at once that Weber had stepped aside and would not contest the town. But Weber now held an all but impregnable position over the quick road to Washington, the one over the Potomac to Maryland and east along the railroad and canal through Point of Rocks and down the old Braddock road to the western forts of the capital. Jube would have to go around the hard way, through the South and Catoctin mountain passes that funneled his army toward Frederick city in her wide and fertile valley.

Ramseur and Rodes were told to demonstrate against the federal lines to hold Weber in place and then follow along.

Follow along one more time, boys, over that fateful Potomac!

Early himself trotted back to Halltown, on to Leetown, and then down the road toward Shepherdstown and the river, big and green in the warmth and fullness of July. Breckinridge had started Gordon's division from Duffield's Depot and they were already crossing the famous and familiar Boteler's ford a mile below the old settlement.

Shepherdstown, in fact, was the oldest inhabited community in western Virginia, its founding father, Thomas Shepherd, having arrived in 1732. Within a few years there was a grist mill, and a little town was laid out before the French and Indian war was fought. It was later incorporated under the name Mecklenburg in 1762 and was still Mecklenburg when a native son, James Rumsey, displayed one of his inventions, a device called a steamboat, in the slack water in front of the town on December 3, 1787. From 1798, however, its popular and official name were the same—Shepherdstown.

A mile to the east, an ancient Indian trail crossed the river at a shallows that later men, the Scotch-Irish and Germans moving southward along the trail from York, called Packhorse Ford. It was the only decent crossing for many miles in either direction. As population increased, the crossing became known as Wagon Road Ford, and finally, in 1765, a proper ferry was put into operation by Thomas Van Swearingen. Shepherdstown built a road from the town down to the ferry landing, and, on the Maryland side, Washington County built a road from Boonsboro through Sharpsburg to Swearingen Landing. John Blackford later bought Swearingen out and founded nearby the large farm he named Ferry Hill Plantation.

Inevitably a bridge was built, a fine covered bridge that replaced the ferry in 1850 and was burned by Confederates at the outbreak of war in 1861. So for the many armies that crossed this way, including Lee's entire Army of Northern Virginia, which took two days to cross following Antietam, it was back to the basics and into the shallows.

For poor Worsham, unable to wear the fine boots he had requisitioned in Martinsburg, the crossing became a literal torture: "I walked into the water and commenced to ford. About one-third of the way the bottom of the river was covered with large, round stones, then a smooth and level bed of granite which extended nearly to the opposite bank. I got along very well until I reached the level granite bottom which was covered with minute shells, adhering to the granite, so very sharp that they stuck into my feet at every step. I walked on them until I thought I could not take another step, stopped, but could not keep my feet still, thought of sitting down but the water was just deep enough to cover my mouth and nose if I had sat down. I thought I would turn back but I saw it was just as far back to the other side. Tears actually came into my eyes. I was never in as much torture for the same length of time in my life. Finally I got over."

July 5, Morning—Araby

It had been a happy holiday for the young couples and their friends at Araby, so merry that the Baltimore boys could not resist staying another day. The family was gathered on the cool porch after breakfast when they saw a detachment of soldiers turn off the

USMHI-MOLLUS

GEN. ERASTUS B. TYLER

Washington road and come marching toward the house along the shaded drive. A sergeant stepped forth and informed Anderson, Gatchell and young Thomas that they were under arrest.

"By whose order?" asked Sam's father, Col. Thomas.

"General Tyler."

"Upon what charge?"

"I do not know, sir."

"This is an outrage!"

"I think the General knows his mind, sir."

The three young men were summarily marched away and taken to the camp of the 11th Maryland, Col. William S. Landstreet's one-hundred-day men who had arrived from Baltimore, given muskets and told to fall into ranks with the other men.

Tyler not only believed that now was the time for all good men to come to the aid of their country, willing or not, it was thought he suspected these young men of having come out to Monocacy not for a holiday but to join up with Jubal Early.

July 5, Noon—Point of Rocks

When Clendenin arrived at Point of Rocks, he dismounted half his command and deployed them as skirmishers. Mosby had withdrawn to the Virginia shore and he now had his cannon and sharpshooters firing into Clendenin's position. He saw that Clendenin was preparing to follow him across the river and that the Illinois sharpshooters were making matters awfully hot in his own ranks.

The master of partisan tactics withdrew his command and drifted eastward, hoping to cross back into Maryland at Nolan's Ferry and get behind Clendenin, pinning him against the mountainside at Point of Rocks. But when he reached Nolan's, there was Clendenin waiting for him. Mosby calmly turned away and took his troopers on to Leesburg, and the 8th Illinois went into camp on the Maryland shore at Nolan's.

July 5, Morning—Harpers Ferry

Capt. Park of the 12th Alabama decided to go back into town with some partners, Capt J.P. Smith, Capt. R.M. Greene of the 6th Alabama and Sgt. A.P. Reid. "The enemy's sharpshooters from Maryland Heights fired pretty close to us repeatedly, and bullets fell so rapidly it was dangerous to walk over the town. But as we were on a frolic, resolved to see everything, we heeded the danger very little." When Park got back to the camp at Halltown, the effects of the unexpected change in diet caught up to him. He was sick enough that night to be carried off to war in an ambulance the following morning.

July 5, Morning—Monocacy Junction

After a few hours sleep, Wallace was roused, and Tyler gave him a status report. "The enemy numbers," said Tyler, "were somewhere between five and thirty thousand men, and the commanders were said to be Early, Gordon, Breckinridge, Ransom and Bradley T. Johnson. Position of the confederate army—unknown."

At Wallace's order, Tyler put a line of pickets out on the Best farm on the western bank. Wallace now scraped up what cavalry he could find on detached duty in and around Frederick: a unit of the 12th Pennsylvania Cavalry and a company of the independent Loudon County Rangers under a Maj. Thorpe. He found an additional ten men from Cole's independent Maryland volunteer cavalry under the Adjutant O.A. Horner, and he sent them all westward, across the Catoctin Range and toward the South Mountain passes.

July 5, Morning—Hagerstown

The horsemen in gray passing along the Sharpsburg turnpike on this July morning were McCausland's fifteen hundred cavalry troopers, who had failed to reach their rendezvous with Bradley Johnson at Hainsville. As the escaping Sigel headed northeastly for Shepherdstown, McCausland had followed with unusual orders from Early: cross the Potomac behind Sigel, but continue on to Hagerstown and hold the place for $200,000 ransom—or burn it.

McCausland had gone over the river on the fourth, as Sigel was running for Maryland Heights, and burned some canal barges at Slack Water, a smoke signal that alerted the Hagerstown garrison, a detachment of twenty officers and seventy-five enlisted men of the 6th U.S. Cavalry sent down from Carlisle, Pennsylvania, that trouble was coming their way. Lt. Hancock T. McLean acted promptly, putting out scouts and pickets, and the quartermaster began to move military supplies and more than five hundred horses north to Carlisle, Pennsylvania, and began to roll all moveable railroad stock toward Harrisburg.

On the morning of the fifth, on schedule, McCausland appeared at the outskirts of

Hagerstown and quickly drove the pickets back toward town. McLean sent a small unit of one corporal with four men out to taunt the Rebs and draw them into town. The ruse worked, and as McCausland's van reached the outskirts of Hagerstown, McLean attacked, capturing Lt. George M.E. Shearer and two troopers. Returning gunfire dropped two union riders and wounded six others as the Confederates spun around and retreated. As soon as they were out of sight, around one P.M., the garrison evacuated, leaving the town open, but McCausland had withdrawn to lick his wounds.

July 5, Midday—Washington

Anxiety was growing in Washington, to the point that the president himself sent a telegraph to Garrett:

> You say telegraphic communication reestablished with Sandy Hook. Well, what does Sandy Hook say about the operations of the enemy?

Grant to Halleck:

> If the enemy cross into Maryland or Pennsylvania I can send an army corps from here to meet them or cut off their return South. [Gen. Montgomery] Meigs should make arrangements for transport. We want now to crush out and destroy any force the enemy dare send north.

Grant to Meade:

> Send in one good division of your troops and all the dismounted cavalry to be forwarded at once. I will not send an army corps until more is learned.

July 5—Into Maryland

Meade put his finger on Brig. Gen. James B. Ricketts's Third Division, VI Corps, and all dismounted cavalry troopers from the cavalry corps's Second Division. That evening, Ricketts was in the saddle leading his command toward the wharves at City Point on the James at about the same time that Gordon was leading his Georgians toward the already bloodied ground of Antietam and Vaughn was leading Echols's division into the still battered town of Sharpsburg. Not only was the van of Early's army over the Potomac, Early himself was down on the C&O Canal near Antietam Furnace, helping his boys burn up some canal barges.

And Harry Gilmor, after a day's rest in Martinsburg, was in fine fettle, for his command had grown through new volunteers to 175. Sadly, he reported, "I left my gray at this place, well tired from hard service. He was captured by Hunter's forces returning to Harpers Ferry. . . . It was late in the evening when we crossed the Potomac, I riding a beautiful bay mare that cost me $350 in gold."

Good thing for Gilmor that his father was a successful business man.

Most units seem to have crossed the river in a serious silence, without the bands and fanfare of the summer crossings before Antietam and Gettysburg, when banners waved and bands played. But historian Glenn Worthington reports that in at least one unit "someone with a bass voice raised the song 'Maryland, My Maryland.' " It would have fitted Gilmor's band, this stirring anthem to succession and plea to join the Confederacy:

> *Come, for thy shield is bright and strong,*
> *Maryland, My Maryland!*
> *Come, for they dalliance does thee wrong,*
> *Maryland, My Maryland!*
> *Come to thine own heroic throng,*
> *That walks with liberty along,*
> *And Give a new Key to thine song,*
> *Maryland! My Maryland!*
>
> *I hear the distant thunder hum*
> *Maryland, My Maryland!*
> *The Old Line bugle, fife and drum,*
> *Maryland, My Maryland!*
> *She is not dead nor deaf nor dumb,*
> *Hurrah! She spurns the Northern call,*
> *She breathes! She burns! She's come, She'll come,*
> *Maryland, My Maryland!*

Even as the song died, the tide of gray flowed on, down the road from Shepherdstown and into the water and thence into the growing mist of the Maryland shore, the rising ghosts of the Valley army's violent past.

VIII.
Maryland Invaded

Tuesday, July 5, Night—Monocacy Junction

Three dismounted batteries from Monrovia arrived at Monocacy Junction. Capt. Edward N. Leib, a regular assigned to the 5th U.S. Cavalry, took command of the one hundred troopers of the 159th Ohio National Guard under Capt. H.S. Allen. At eight-thirty P.M a train arrived at Relay House below Baltimore to pick up the 11th Maryland Infantry under Col. Landstreet. When they arrived later at Monocacy, Wallace sized up these hundred-day enlistees at a glance: "a clean body of city men but, like their commander, green to a lamentable degree."

Wallace was right about that; this regiment of ten companies was greener than grass, having been mustered into service on the fifteenth and sixteenth of June, right off the streets of Baltimore, to serve for one hundred days and relieve "the same number of other troops," meaning real soldiers, for duty with Grant to hasten the end of Lee.

But here they were at the Monocacy, where a real battle was going to take place. Wallace put them to work digging an earthen embrasure on a nearby hill in which to protect the howitzer from the blockhouse; from there it had a wide field of fire to the west. Later he would put the 11th out on the middle of his right flank, where they might do some good guarding a ford and could be supported left and right by more veteran units.

A concentration of troops was growing slowly at Monocacy Junction, but almost all of them were green boys.

Bradley Johnson's and John McCausland's cavalry had been first over the river, and now Johnson awaited Gilmor at Boonsboro. When he arrived, Gilmor was given the 1st Maryland to add to his command, which pleased him greatly, for it was commanded by his "old friend and companion," Capt. Warner Welch.

Wednesday, July 6—Sharpsburg

On July 6, a warm and clear mountain morning, Jubilee Early officially moved his headquarters across the Potomac as he led the rest of the infantry across the symbolic waters.

Early's aide, Henry Kyd Douglas, was filled with admiration at the act. He wrote in his memoirs, "To invade the North with so few was a desperate thing to do, . . . so reckless that historians are still examining figures to see if it can be possible. Jackson being dead, it is safe to say no other General in either army would have attempted it against such odds."

As though rising from the mists of the river, a strange mood of nostalgia began to seep into the events and actions of this day. There was too much to remember here, beginning with Kyd Douglas, for he had been born and reared in the great house on the Maryland shore with the sweeping view, Ferry Hill itself, built by Col. John Blackford in 1813. Douglas had left the house three years before as the youngest staff officer under Stonewall Jackson and served on the staff of every officer succeeding to the command, which now belonged to Jubilee Early.

And he remembered a scene that had taken place on an autumn day of 1859, how hard it had been raining as he galloped up the road from the ferry and found an old man who called himself Isaac Smith at the foot of the steep hill, his two-horse team unable to secure traction because of the weight of the wagon they pulled. Kyd Douglas rode on to Ferry Hill Farm and brought back a team of carriage horses and their driver, a slave named Enoch, and together they pulled the wagon to the top. Only later did Douglas discover the true identity of the man and the nature of the wagon's contents—John Brown was hauling iron-tipped pikes to serve as weapons in a slave insurrection.

Kyd Douglas's father still lived at Ferry Hill Farm, and this July day he received a surprise visit from his son, who escorted a number of distinguished guests—Early, Gordon, Breckinridge and Ramseur. They all went sight-seeing, riding up through the two-year-old fields of battle above Antietam Creek. A strange and somewhat sad procession of general officers revisiting in their minds the carnage that had occurred in the peaceful scenes they now witnessed.

David Hunter Strother
Virginia Library & Archives

JOHN BROWN (aka Isaac Smith)
drawn two months prior to his death.

There stood the Dunkard Church, where Hooker crashed forward through the North Wood early in the morning against Early's command under Jackson, where he had stood and stood against it. The cornfield on Miller's farm that had changed hands fifteen times and was soaked in blood now nodded high again with a bountiful crop, as "high as your eye by the Fourth of July." The West Woods lay peaceful and dark, and it was hard to believe that Sedgwick's division, charging against Jackson, had lost twenty-two hundred men there in twenty-two minutes. The sunken road that came to be called Bloody Lane—was it possible that four thousand casualties happened there in four hours? Was it really possible that in this peaceful Maryland countryside, all those lives had been laid down in a single day—12,410 Federals, 10,700 Confederates?

Early passed quietly and slowly through these haunting scenes of the human mind and came out in an apple orchard near the town of Sharpsburg on this day of heat and high white clouds, and had the headquarters tent set up there.

For Capt. Park, the memories had been more explicit. After noting in Sharpsburg the "great holes, made by cannon balls and shells . . . in the houses and chimneys and trees," he had taken a refreshing bath in Antietam Creek, but "memories of scores of army comrades and childhood friends, slain on the banks of this stream, came before my mind, and kept away sleep for a long time. The preservation of such an undesirable union of States is not worth the life of a single Southerner lost on that memorable battle-field. Lt. John Fletcher of my company and Capt. Tucker commanding the 12th Alabama were killed [here]."

During the rest of the morning, and for the rest of the entire day, Rodes and Ramseur would be crossing Boteler's ford into Maryland.

July 6, Morning—City Point

Grant's army had created a new port city where the sluggish and shallow Appomattox River joined the stately old James, a city of sheds and tents and wooden barracks and docks and wharves and all manner of the coming industrial world.

This was the staging area for the siege of Richmond, and now the embarkation port for the units ordered north to cut off Early. Grant had told Meade to "send in one good division of your troops." Rufus Ingalls, chief of staff, now wired the quartermaster general, Montgomery Meigs:

> General Ricketts's division of about five thousand infantry are embarking here today for Harpers Ferry by way of Baltimore.

Rickett's soldiers, the third division of the VI Corps, had to march twelve miles through the heat and the dust from the Petersburg lines to reach the docks at City Point, and when they arrived "the blue uniforms . . . were thickly covered with the dust of old Virginia." By noon, first brigade commander Col. William S. Truex and his staff had shepherded aboard the steamer *Columbia* the 87th Pennsylvania and 14th New Jersey; she sailed down the James to Fortress Monroe, which she reached at nine P.M.

Behind them came more troops, including the 10th Vermont which reached the dock at three P.M. and sailed away at four. As Samuel Abbott explained, "It's quick work to load a boat in an hour, but Grant was there." And Grant had already telegraphed Halleck:

> A part of force directed by me to go north is already off and the whole will be in an hour or two.

What a change for the dog-faces! Wrote Abbott to his diary, "The contrast from marching through sand ankle-deep, as dry as an ash heap, with the air so thick with dust [that a person] only a few steps away is invisible, and being on the cool river is a great transformation we much appreciate—Hallelujah!"

At that exact hour, the 9th New York Heavy Artillery was just starting out for City Point. These heavies had been among the artillery-trained soldiers stationed in Washington tending the long-range guns that protected the capital when Grant had pulled them out of their comfortable quarters and made foot soldiers out of them. Now they truly were hoofing it, walking through "indescribable dust. Every face . . . looked like it wore a mask."

Before the end of the day they were all underway—*Columbia, Thomas Powell, Jersey Blue* and *Sylvan Shore*—with five thousand troops quite happy for the moment to drink in the clean bay air despite what lay ahead of them.

July 6, Morning—Hagerstown

McCausland probed at the defenses of Hagerstown in the morning and then rode into the undefended town. At the crossing of the National Pike running east-west and the ancient pathway running north and south through the Cumberland and Shenandoah valleys, Hagerstown in its Blue Ridge setting had been a lively and prosperous town from its founding by the Westphalian German Jonathan Hager. The population had reached twenty-five hundred by 1814. Merchants, farmers, businessmen and crafts-men, makers of shoes, hats, nails, rope and whiskey, crowded its streets and read its German-language *Country Almanack* and *Hagers-Town Town* newspaper. The town had several banks, one founded by native Nathaniel Rochester who moved to upstate New York and had a city named for him.

The acerbic Mrs. Anne Royall visited the place in 1827 and reported that "Hager-stown is principally settled by Germans and their descendants and, of course, retains many of their customs. The women are short and ill-shaped and have a vacancy of countenance which too evidently shows the want of proper schools." Her acidic tongue eventually did her in, and she was convicted in a Washington City court in 1829 for being "a common scold."

There were several things about Hagerstown that made it a fit candidate in Early's mind for retaliation and retribution for Hunter's deprivations in the Valley of Virginia: it was not slave-holding, and was, therefore, anti-secession; it was prosperous and could

Leslie's Illustrated Newspaper

INVASION OF MARYLAND—PILLAGING AT HAGERSTOWN DEPOT

afford a ransom; it was easy to get to and get out of. He estimated that the careful burghers could and would pay out $200,000 to save their town from the flames.

That's two hundred thousand.

He should have written it out in long-hand, because by the time McCausland drew up a regiment before the city hall market, a block north of the town square, and presented his demand to Matthew Barber, a bank official, a zero had disappeared. He wanted all government stockpiles, clothing to the tune of fifteen hundred suits, fifteen hundred pairs of shoes or boots and socks, fifteen hundred shirts and nineteen hundred pairs of underdrawers. This translated into a civilian wardrobe for every man of his command.

And $20,000 in cash. Whether there had been a mistake in the original transmission of the order, or whether McCausland had simply misread it, he would go back $180,000 short.

The city fathers were given three hours to come up with the money and four to bring in the clothing.

Perhaps McCausland thought that if things went truly bad up here among the Yankees, a civilian outfit carried in a saddle bag might make escape easier. In any event, the cash was forthcoming, put up by the Hagerstown Bank, First National Bank and Williamsport Branch Bank, but the clothes were not. Several hundred suits showed up, and McCausland's staff talked him into taking what they had and heading out. These soldiers were nervous about taking the war to civilians, and disapproving, despite what Hunter had done, and they were happy to leave the half-busted Germans behind and take the road to Boonsboro.

July 6, Morning—Antietam Furnace

It was a pleasant and an interesting camp along Antietam Creek, despite the sad memories of fallen comrades. What gave the place interest was its industrial history. A forge operated here as early as 1750, before Washington County was formed. Near the village of Antietam, a twenty-foot high dam had been built across the creek; below it the wheels of industry turned, including one of the country's earliest iron works, Antietam Iron Furnace, opened in 1765, supplied with local limestone for fluxing and local hardwoods for charcoal. Its bellows were powered by a waterwheel that was twenty feet in diameter and four feet wide, and it produced fifty tons of pig iron every week.

A dozen other mills gathered around the power supply, including a forge with a twenty-ton hammer operated by a sixteen-foot mill wheel, a nail factory whose sixteen-foot wheel drove nineteen nail and spike machines that turned out five hundred kegs of nails per week. This sneak preview of the coming Industrial Revolution soon counted mills for everything—rolling, slitting, grist, spinning, hemp, flour, saw, shingle, cooperage, woolen and stove.

But the engines of peace had been silenced by those of war, and the confederate troops along the creek found a bucolic calm and the chance to swim and bathe before shouldering their muskets once more and marching toward Maryland Heights, which rose to the southeast, hiding Harpers Ferry from view.

On the sixth, Gordon took his division toward the heights and sent Clement Evans and his Georgians to flush out some federal pickets, who retreated toward the heights and some formidable earthworks. The action confirmed that Sigel had joined Weber on Maryland Heights, leaving the road through Frederick undefended by any but a few soft and green hundred-day enlistees.

July 6, Morning—South Mountain

Bradley Johnson's van, on the fifth, had felt the first nettle of combat, the first sting of gunfire and whistling lead, when his advance had come upon some mounted men from Cole's Maryland cavalry at Keedysville, a spot on a map between Sharpsburg and Boonsboro. The Marylanders surprised their rebel cousins and sent them reeling back toward the protection of Ramseur's infantry, which was then crossing Antietam Creek.

This morning the confederate cavalry was probing the passes over South Mountain, as Early planned to use all three to move his army in flowing parallel lines. Ramseur, with the Marylanders Gilmor and Johnson in front, would move from Boonsboro to

Middletown in Pleasant Valley by way of Turner's Gap. To his south, Gordon would take his division to Middletown by way of Rohrersville and Fox's Gap. Still farther south, Rodes's division would cross the mountain at Crampton's Gap and come out at Jefferson, on the main road between Frederick and Harpers Ferry.

Parties were sent forward to secure the passes. On the afternoon of the sixth, the eighty-five scouts from Frederick ran headlong into a rebel picket post on the Middletown road. Adjutant O.A. Horner of Cole's Cavalry did not hesitate to lead his ten troopers on a dash at the pickets, who quickly fell back. Their reserve as quickly came up; Horner could see about twenty-five. So could Maj. Thorpe with his small unit of Samuel Mean's Loudon Rangers, and he turned tail toward Frederick, followed by the 12th Pennsylvania. They had come to find, not to fight.

That did Horner little good at the moment, as the Rebs were now coming right at his little unit. As he wheeled and whipped his mount to a gallop, the horse was hit and went down, rolling over and pinning Horner underneath, which is where he was when the Rebs rode up, removed the horse and made him a prisoner. Luckily, he was able to walk.

July 6, Afternoon—Monocacy Junction

Wallace had moved his command post to a small frame house south of the railroad tracks and on the east bank of the river; here he heard the news from Point of Rocks that Clendenin's 8th Illinois had chased Mosby back over the river at Nolan's Ferry. He immediately sent a message to Clendenin to report to him with his unit, and he sent a message to Chief of Staff Halleck asking permission to use the 8th Illinois, which officially reported to Gen. Augur in the Washington command.

July 6, Afternoon—Early's Headquarters, Sharpsburg

The tired rider who reined up in the orchard and was welcomed to Early's tent had been chasing the army for several days with a dispatch from Gen. Lee himself. The rider was none other than Lee's son, Robert, so the dispatch immediately assumed an awsome importance.

Early had been occupied most of the day by Gordon's "demonstration" upon Maryland Heights. This was a favored word for bluffing an attack. Another bit of jargon, "to develop the strength of the enemy," was a mask behind which many a false move later hid. A poor platoon chopped up in a murderous fire from a seemingly innocent enemy position was said to have been maneuvered "to develop the strength of the enemy."

Early read the message and asked the courier, "Do you know anything about this?"

"Nothing, except Father told me he does not have a great number of details about it; just the bare outline." He pronounced "bare" as "bayah" and otherwise had that soft, upper-class Virginia accent that settled around the tidewater and Richmond. By contrast, Early's somewhat gruff twang, expressed in his very high tone, had a lot of mountain Virginia in it.

Early went to his field desk and wrote out a reply for the younger Lee to take back to his father. He explained that he had intended to get across the Potomac at Harpers Ferry and take the easy road into the Frederick Valley and the Montgomery County roads to Washington, but he felt he could not squeeze his army past those big guns on Maryland Heights. Now, with word of this clandestine operation, he would definitely take the South Mountain passes eastward, and once he found out what the Yanks had planned for him, he would send a detachment of cavalry down to where Lee wanted them, at Point Lookout Prison in Delaware.

July 6, Late Afternoon—Maryland Heights

Sigel's scouts had been watching Boteler's ford ever since they climbed up on Maryland Heights, and he now told Stanton, who passed it on to Couch up in Pennsylvania, in case they were heading his way, that Early's army had now been passing over the Potomac's stones for forty non-stop hours.

Thursday, July 7, 4:00 A.M.—Monocacy Junction

Clendenin, down along the Potomac near Point of Rocks and Nolan's Ford, had spent Wednesday reconnoitering the river as far west as Sandy Hook; late in the day he received Wallace's order and set out at once, riding through the night to Monocacy, sleeping in his saddle. He arrived at Wallace's headquarters around four A.M., when the night was still deep, but lights were burning in the Mantz apartments over the station at the junction where Wallace was waiting.

Three hours earlier a courier had arrived at the camp of Frederick Alexander's Baltimore Light Battery with orders from Wallace, and Lt. Peter Leary, Jr., led out a section of guns—two three-inch Parrott rifles—and started in a clatter of hooves and creaking of cannon wheels for Frederick. They still had not arrived when Clendenin saluted Wallace.

"I appreciate your prompt response to my order," said Wallace, "especially since you are not under my command. I have wired General Halleck asking for the use of your cavalry in this extremity. The enemy is reported as very strong but we must know how strong and whether or not he intends an attempt on Pennsylvania, as before, or Baltimore, or Washington. If so, only Grant can save that situation by embarking troops. But we must know. We must know where, and how many. How soon can you start?"

"As soon as the men and horses eat."

"I have asked Frederick Alexander to send along two field guns to go out with you and to bring the rest of his battery up to this place. There is a unit of Loudon rangers that is prepared to go out with you as well."

"How many men have you here altogether, General?"

"The 11th Maryland, mostly green city men. Seven companies of the 149th Ohio National Guard. Three of the 144th. Four companies of the 1st Potomac Home Brigade and the entire 3rd. About a hundred mounted infantry of the 159th Ohio. Now your men. And, when it gets here, Alexander's battery. Call it about twenty-five hundred men and six guns, and one large howitzer that was here in the blockhouse."

"What is the estimate of the enemy's strength?"

"Sigel has been watching him cross at Shepherdstown. I understand it has taken him forty hours."

July 7, Dawn—Frederick

The steeples of Frederick were gleaming in the dawn light and roosters were again sounding the valley as the indefatigable Clendenin led 230 troopers of the 8th Illinois and two of Alexander's field guns out from Monocacy and passing through the sleeping streets of Frederick, took the Hagerstown road that ascended the Catoctin Ridge and passed through Solomon's Gap, offering a vista of the rolling green hills of beautiful Pleasant Valley beyond, framed by the blue wall of South Mountain.

Even that early in the day the valley smelled of damp heat and dusty roads, but as the column climbed the air seemed fresher and cooler. As it started down toward Middletown, it must have seemed quite good to be alive on such a morning.

July 7, 10:00 A.M.—Near Middletown

Harry Gilmor had been told to "advance slowly and cautiously toward Frederick, so as not to get too far in advance of the brigade," and he was doing just that when climbing the steep road two miles east of Middletown, he discovered on the other side of a bridge over a large stream "a column of cavalry and . . . two pieces of artillery in point-blank range."

Boom: Peter Leary's three-inch rifle prayed the Introit of the Monocacy.

Eight miles away, Wallace heard it as a messenger of fate and doom, flying downward from that place beyond the stars where history is made. "I heard the report of a distant gun, muffled to be sure . . . and distinctive in that it seemed dropped from the sky, high up, as I fancied it would come."

The shell exploded above Harry Gilmor's brother Richard, who was "sitting sideways on his horse when struck." A piece of shrapnel winged down and cut the calf of his leg. "I lost his services for the rest of this trip," Gilmor noted, "though he stayed with the wagons and took command of the cripples."

Gilmor dismounted his troops, waited, and, when no attack came, moved up, ordering Capt. Nicholas Burke to bring up Harry's own battalion, "with which we made a counter-charge and ran them back to within eight hundred yards of their guns," but they could advance no farther because of the bridge.

After a lot of firing back and forth, Gilmor sent Welch with two squadrons to the left, and he was about to go right when Ransom came up and asked what he was doing. Once again a Gilmor order was countermanded by a cautious superior.

Behind Ransom, Johnson's entire thousand-horse brigade was moving up the road from Middletown in a column of fours. Leary, from beyond the bridge, dropped an exploding shell into the third section, and nine bodies and horses were suddenly hurled about in the fire and smoke of the blast. Four men died instantly.

On the Monocacy bank, Wallace "started to my feet and listened. Then another gun! An interval, and then the third gun, echo-like and fainter because farther down the mountain side! There could be no mistake. Clendenin had found the enemy!"

Gilmor fumed as the opportunity to entrap Clendenin slipped away. "We should certainly have captured a large portion of them," he noted, and fumed even more when Ransom, after waiting an hour, told him to go ahead now and turn both flanks, as he had intended. But "before Welch and I could come together on top of the mountain, the Federals had seen the whole cavalry force in the Middletown Valley, and had fallen back toward Frederick."

July 7, 11:00 A.M.—Monocacy Junction

About three hundred yards downstream from the iron bridge that carried the railroad tracks, the Washington, or Georgetown road, crossed the Monocacy on a beautiful old covered bridge, weather-boarded and covered with a shingle roof. It was 250 feet long, fifty feet wide and sixteen feet high, with a line of heavy timbers running down the middle that divided it into two lanes.

An hour after Wallace heard the distant cannon fire, the bridge thundered with the passage of a galloping horseman, and a courier reined up at headquarters with a piece of paper, a leaf from a pocket notebook, on which was hastily written in pencil: "Catoctin Pass, July 7, 1864." That was all.

Half an hour later a second messenger arrived with word from Clendenin:

> I have abandoned the pass. Am falling back toward Frederick. A strong skirmish line of two hundred fifty men advanced on my skirmishers, which I could not spare force to meet, and protect my flanks at the same time. A mounted force of at least a squadron moved to my left and an equal force has gone through on Harpers Ferry pike. I will be in Frederick in two hours.

Clendenin was not bolting and running as the earlier scouts had; he was withdrawing through Solomon's Gap in good order in the face of a much superior enemy force, and when he backed off the mountain entirely and onto the valley floor, he immediately dismounted his troopers, put up a skirmishing line and positioned Alexander's battery on the outskirts of town, right in the intersection of the Harpers Ferry and Hagerstown roads, where it commanded a field of fire in both directions. Brad Johnson would have to come down into the teeth of his fire.

When Johnson did appear, about half past three, Alexander's guns greeted him with a precision of range that made his cavalry quickly scatter. The battery's unit historian later claimed that the marksmanship of these cannoneers, throughout the Monocacy battles, was due to their being duck hunters from up around the Susquehannah flats, used to drawing a bead, estimating range and speed and position.

But Johnson knew that all he had to do to defeat this small federal force was to run around both ends. And he knew every step the way. He was at home.

Thirty-five years old and a lawyer, not a professional soldier, he had worn the stars of a brigadier only since June 28, when he was appointed to take over Grumble Jones's command. But he sat his horse like a rider, for he was of bluest Maryland blood. One of his progenitors was that Thomas Johnson who had been a member of the Continental Congress from Maryland and who had, in fact, nominated George Washington to lead the Continental army. After that war, Thomas Johnson had been Maryland's first elected governor and later an associate justice of the supreme court. The Johnson family home, Richfields, stood then as it does now, amid rolling green acres in the valley north of Frederick.

Johnson had been in this war from the beginning. In May of 1861, the Maryland legislature held a special meeting in Frederick to debate secession. James Mason, a confederate agent, was in town looking for allies among the delegates. He assured Johnson that Maryland men would be welcomed in the south, and soon thereafter Johnson raised a company of local men and led them to Harpers Ferry, where they joined Stonewall. With other Maryland companies, they formed the 1st Maryland Regiment in the confederate army. They were at Manassas, where Pvt. John Swisher of Co. A became the first Marylander to die for the South.

In an earlier war, an earlier Bradley T. Johnson had recorded in his diary the arrival in Annapolis of Tench Tilghman's news from Yorktown: "In a minute the whole city was wild. Lights flashed in every window— men, women, and children poured into the streets. The State House bell rang out its peak, Liberty throughout the land to all the inhabitants thereof, and the American nation was born unto the world."

And what American nation was being born now, as another Bradley T. Johnson wearing Southern stars led his troopers, mostly men from southwest Virginia but a lot of Marylanders, too, through his home valley and against the capital of a nation his forebears had helped to create?

Wallace had the sense to know what was going on, and he sent Clendenin what help he could: Charles Gilpin with the 3rd Potomac Home Brigade of 700 men, 150 troops of the 159th Ohio Mounted Infantry and another of Alexander's guns. With Clendenin's 350 and the Loudon Rangers, there were about twelve hundred federal soldiers awaiting Johnson, about half of Wallace's entire strength. Gilmor estimated their strength at two thousand as he watched them form in skirmish line in the fields west of Frederick, between the Zimmerman and Rizer farms, their left flank resting on the Harpers Ferry-Jefferson road and their right extending just beyond the Hagerstown road. Alexander's guns remained at the junction of these roads, where they met at the city line and became Patrick Street.

It took Johnson until four P.M. to get his own artillery organized, forwarded, and positioned on two hills overlooking the valley and the union line, Prospect Hill above the Harpers Ferry road and Hagan's Hill above the Hagerstown turnpike. Those four guns, ironically, were manned by another Baltimore battery of light artillery, this one in the confederate service. Down below, his first line of skirmishers spread out on either side of the Hagerstown pike and, in concert with their artillery, opened fire on the union positions.

July 7, 3:40 P.M.—Baltimore

Garrett to Wallace:

> A large force of veterans has arrived by water and will be sent immediately. As Sigel's force remains on Maryland Heights, you are doubtless aware of the great importance of preserving Monocacy bridge. If it be damaged or destroyed, great delay will result in getting forward reinforcements to General Sigel. I trust you will be able to maintain your position and protect fully this most important structure.

Garrett and his goddamned bridge.

July 7, 4:00 P.M.—Frederick

Johnson considered the golden opportunity that lay before him to capture his native city for the Confederacy. The skirmish line in the valley cornfields was stubborn, which meant they would fight. But to fight they had to stay put, and while they were staying put, he would divide his eight-hundred-man command and send a column south to the Harpers Ferry road and thence across to the Georgetown road and then straight into the city by way of Market Street, while he took a second column north to the reservoir road, and then he, too, would swoop into town, bagging the whole Yankee force and taking Frederick.

To this end, when the column reached the turnpike tollgate at the hamlet of Fairview, Johnson detached a regiment under Lt. Col. Dunn and sent him down the country road that passed behind Prospect Hill to the Harpers Ferry pike. Dunn went right at it and "passed rapidly down the road in a sweeping gallop, and turning into the Harpers Ferry road, moved sharply toward the city, pushing his dismounted skirmishers as far as Rizer's barn, and across through Mount Olivet Cemetery toward the Georgetown turnpike."

This movement alone, observed from Frederick, was enough to send the wagons and carts packing along all roads leading east and away from the city. As stray confederate shells fell into the western part of the town, every house was deserted, but many of the people ran not away from the anticipated field of battle but toward it, seeking places in trees and atop fences to observe the action.

The skirmishing was stiff, with both lines probing and moving and firing at targets of opportunity. One such target, unfortunately for him, was the mounted silhouette of Lt. Charles S. Gilbert of Co. C, 8th Illinois, who was mortally wounded, the second man of the cavalry killed that day; another was the young bugler of Co. K, J.R. Baker. Five others were wounded. Gilbert was carried into Frederick still alive and left there to die when the town was evacuated.

The crackle of musket fire and the booming exchange of artillery had echoed in the valley for three hours, and the hot day was drawing toward a muggy close when Col. Gilpin roused up his troops and sent them charging toward Rizer's corn field, which they took from retreating Confederates and held.

July 7, 4:55 P.M.—*Monocacy Junction*

Wallace to Garrett:

> My troops are engaging the enemy to west and in the skirts of Frederick. Warm cannonading going on. I will hold the ridge at all hazards. Send the troops as rapidly as possible.

July 7, 5:00 P.M.—*Near the G. W. Smith House*

Johnson's bold plan of attack never happened. He and Ransom exchanged words at Johnson's headquarters on the range of hills near the George William Smith house.

"You can't do it," Ransom said. "You will be cut to pieces while entering the streets of that city."

"I know that city," Johnson replied. "You have seen the number of friends who have appeared here all day, informing us of the entire disposition of the enemy troops. They are all there in Zimmerman's field."

"Amateur suppositions. We are instructed not to lose touch with the infantry. If you start an action against Frederick and lose any considerable number of your command, what are we to do for the rest of this campaign? Besides, it is not necessary. When the infantry comes up, Frederick cannot stand. The risk is needless. I understand your feelings, being a native of the place, but when night falls, extract your people from the valley and take them back to the top of the mountain where we will wait for General Early."

Bradley Johnson was completely annoyed. Gilmor remembered that "Johnson several times asked Ransom to let him charge the enemy in the town in two columns, but he refused." Historian William Sharf says that Johnson "sullenly withdrew about nine o'clock . . . chagrined and mortified, [as he] saw a brilliant victory eluding his grasp."

Most historians think Johnson's plan would have worked, that Dunn's and Johnson's columns could have taken an undefended and unarmed Frederick in an hour and caught Clendenin and Gilpin's whole force. All it needed was imagination, daring and risk taking, and one suspects that the bad rap Early suffered for his use of cavalry may be based on the fact that Ransom led them.

Wallace did not understand what was going on between Ransom and Johnson, and when Gilpin's attack drove in the skirmish line to conclude the day's action, he was elated. He sent word up to Gilpin at the front: "You have behaved nobly. Compliment Lieutenant Colonel Clendenin and Captain Alexander for me. Endeavour to hold your ground. At one p.m. tonight eight thousand veterans will be here."

To his chief of staff back in Baltimore, Wallace was even more effusive: "Think I have had the best little battle of the war. Our men did not retreat but held their own. The enemy were repulsed three times."

July 7, 8:55 P.M.—Baltimore

Garrett to Stanton:

> General Wallace telegraphs that after a battle of four hours the enemy has been finally repulsed from Frederick.

Wallace's report: "After a sharp engagement of about four hours, during which the rebels threw a number of shells into Frederick city, our battery dismounted one of the rebel guns and silenced their artillery, and they were driven back to the mountain by a charge by the 3d Md. Potomac Home Brigade under Col. Gilpin. Our loss during the day was two men killed, one officer and seventeen men wounded; whilst the rebels reported loss was 140 killed and wounded. Thursday night Col. Gilpin's regiment, Col. Clendenin with the 8th Ill., Capt. [Edward] Leib's mounted infantry, and Alexander's Battery, resting on their arms . . . near the ground where they had fought."

July 7, Midnight—Frederick

Feeling anxious about Gilpin's position, Gen. Tyler around midnight sent his aide, Lt. Edward Y. Goldsborough, galloping into Frederick to find Gilpin and get a report. The lieutenant found the section of Alexander's guns at the head of Patrick Street with the 3rd Regiment of the Potomac Home Brigade "resting on their arms on the hill," and Gilpin sound asleep in the home of a Mr. Frederick Lambert nearby. A groggy Gilpin repeated the day's events. Goldsborough said that Tyler wanted to know his plans for further operations.

"That's more or less up to Early, isn't it?" the exhausted soldier might have replied. "I mean if he comes down that mountain in the morning with thirty thousand troops, my plans for further operations would be somewhat sharply curtailed, would they not? I will try to hold here for as long as I can, but there are not many of us."

When Goldsborough returned to Monocacy Junction, Tyler made plans to move reinforcements out in the morning.

Friday, July 8, 4:00 A.M.—*Monocacy Junction*

In Wallace's headquarters, that small frame house along the railroad near the Iron Bridge, there was a table. That's all. No chairs, no stools, no cots. To rest, the staff wrapped in a blanket and lay down on the floor, which is where Wallace was when an aide shook him.

"I hear a train, General."

"Which way?"

"From Baltimore."

Wallace scrambled to his feet. "We must get it stopped before those men get delivered to General Early!"

Lt. Col. Ross of Wallace's staff had been standing out on the tracks with a party with lanterns and flags, fully aware that Grant had ordered his troops to Harpers Ferry and that the engineer would roll right through Monocacy. At their urgent behest, the train hissed and slowed, grinding noisily to a shuddering stop, and a steamed colonel of infantry, William Henry of the 10th Vermont, bounded onto the ground.

"By whose order is this train stopped?" thundered Henry.

"Mine. General Wallace, commanding here."

"My orders [he gave it a Vermont shape—*aw-dahs*] from Grant, general, are to Harpers [*ha-pas*] Ferry."

"There is a bit of an obstacle between here and there, Colonel—General Early with Ewell's old corps, twenty to thirty thousand strong, with three infantry divisions, cavalry under McCausland, Imboden and Johnson, and artillery of several hundred guns. Coming right this way, right at us. They are just over there."

"I see. Well, whatever I can do for you, General."

"Order your men out for breakfast. When it gets light, we'll reboard and ride the cars up to Frederick. We must try to draw the enemy out and discover which way he is going."

As the 10th Vermont clambered off the train and lighted small camp fires beside the track to boil coffee, Wallace and Henry strolled down to the bluff.

"I have been so awaiting your train I could not sleep," said Wallace. "I hope many more are behind you."

"It is my understanding that the whole of the Greek Cross, the VI Corps, is coming. They are either in Baltimore this morning or moving up the bay on steamers. I think they sent us forward because we know the country. We spent a year here in '62, guarding the Potomac from Edward's Ferry down to Muddy Branch. We were camped at Seneca, Offutt's Cross Roads, Poolesville, White's Ford. My men called it the kind of country that would give a man proper burial."

July 8, Daybreak—Frederick

Soon after break of day, Gen. Tyler came up from Monocacy Junction to Gilpin's position in the fields west of town leading the three companies of the 144th Ohio and the seven of the 149th, all under Col. Allison Brown. They had marched up the east bank of the Monocacy and across the old Jug Bridge which carried the Baltimore turnpike. Named for a large stone ornament that stood on the eastern end, this third bridge over the river was three miles to the north of the iron railroad bridge and the covered road bridge nearby. When the Jug Bridge was finished for the turnpike company in 1807, so the story went, the celebrating engineer had sealed up a demijohn of whiskey in the stone jug.

The Ohioans were assigned to the positions from which the Confederates had been driven the previous evening. At nine A.M. the remaining three pieces of Capt. Alexander's artillery arrived, and then came Wallace riding on the train with the 10th Vermont.

The enemy, however, so aggressive the previous afternoon, had disappeared from the front. Tyler conferred with Clendenin and asked him to ascertain the position of the enemy. No questions asked, Clendenin sent one company southwest down the Harpers Ferry road and two others, B and C under Maj. John Waite, straight west, back up the Hagerstown pike; one of Alexander's guns went with them, since there was, without doubt, a large enemy force up there somewhere. Finally, he sent Co. M under Capt. John Morris northwest, to make its way around the confederate left by way of the Almshouse road and the mountain roads to Shookstown.

From the settlement of Braddock on the valley floor, the old road west wound upward for two and a half miles toward the narrow summit at Braddock Heights, a thousand feet in elevation. The width of the ridge at the summit was only 250 yards. On the right hand side, about halfway up, a mile from Braddock and a mile from the top, an old tavern owned by secessionist John Hagan was serving as Johnson's headquarters. (At this same tavern, during the Antietam campaign of '62, a party of confederate cavalry had stopped for a drink and been captured by a column of Yankees.)

Waite had the dash of a cavalry officer with his cape and a wide-brimmed hat with the right-hand brim snapped up, but he was a professional, and he made his way carefully along the road, with dismounted pickets out in the woods on either side. When they came upon Johnson's pickets, Waite hit them hard. As they withdrew, he followed very closely, and quickly brought the cannon right up to his skirmish line before any Confederate could see it. Unlimbering and loading in a hurry, the Baltimore battery fired a shell at short range that exploded at the tavern, causing "a general stampede."

Kelley Bennette saw a descending shell hit a rider at the shoulder and come out near his hip, "nearly severing his body in twain, thence through his saddle it finished its commission by killing his horse." The startled Rebs pulled back to the crest of the ridge and Waite was left firmly in command of the road; he kept his skirmish line stable through the woods on either side and held his ground.

Morris, meanwhile, had pushed up the Almshouse and Shookstown roads far enough to threaten to get behind Johnson entirely. Harry Gilmor was sent over that way to "clean them out." He moved by what he described as "a wood road" and "came upon them rather unexpectedly, and got them at a disadvantage." Gilmor's hard charge into the Illinois horsemen with pistols banging and riders screaming had its effect; it sent them reeling. Morris was hit by a ball in the hip. Other men were hit—Bryan, Overacker, Smith, Steenkie, Tofflemire. As Co. M fell back with the wounded crumpled in their saddles, Gilmor formed up to finish them off with a final charge.

In the woods watching all this was Sgt. Harrison Hakes of Co. B, who was positioned at Waite's extreme right flank; his unit was the end of the skirmish line based on the Hagerstown road. Hakes saw instantly, however, that he could also serve as Morris's left flank. He ordered a half dozen men to come with him on the double quick, and they ran toward the road down which the rebels were beginning to charge. They took up a position hidden by undergrowth and, as the gray horsemen dashed by, delivered a thundering broadside volley that knocked over twelve horses. Capt. James Clark's mount was hit by four or five bullets at once, and as he started to go down a bullet hit him in the chest. He lay in the road, expecting pain, but felt none. The bullet had bounded off a jacket button, making it concave but sparing him. After that, says Gilmor, "he was one of my pets."

Gilmor had no idea what was going on except that "we ran them rather too far, for we found ourselves among a line of infantry." He counted four men wounded but none killed, and was content to run the Yankees back down the roads to Frederick.

An hour and a half later, Morris, unable to ride farther, lay down and died. Abner Hard, the unit surgeon and also its historian, remembered that "he remained conscious to the last and died without a murmur, as he had fought without fear."

When the woods to his front began to fill with gray uniforms, Waite backed down the Hagerstown road toward Wallace's lines in the Rizer cornfield. He was not coming down unhurt, though. These two days of actions along the Catoctin ridge were costing lives. Thirty-five men in blue had been killed, wounded, or were missing from the 8th Illinois and Potomac Home Brigades. The artillery duel that lasted all day between the two Baltimore light artilleries was also deadly. One officer and an enlisted man were killed on the federal side, and seven wounded, while Wallace claimed "a number of their men and horses" had been killed on Hagan's Hill.

Col. Gamble had told his regiment back in Chicago that "the fighting reputation of the old Eighth must be retained without any fictitious puffs so much depended on by others."

No fictitious puffs needed here, on this hot July afternoon, on this green wooded mountainside with its dusty dirt roads. These men are, in reality, truly dead and wounded.

July 8—Pleasant Valley

Neither Waite nor Morris nor any other federal scout was in position to see the scene unfolding on the other side of the Catoctin ridge; a great, rolling army of foot soldiers with its teeming thousands was streaming down from the South Mountain passes and filling up the roads of Pleasant Valley. Ramseur, Gordon and Rodes were leading their men to Middletown or Jefferson, according to plan, and were currently moving through Turner's, Fox's and Grampton's gaps toward their goal. Only the narrow Catoctin ridge separated Wallace's little command of two thousand waiting in the cornfield west of Frederick from Early's eighteen thousand moving inevitably his way.

July 8, Afternoon—Frederick

It had been a quiet day on the line outside Frederick when the cavalry was catching hell on the hills to the west. As a federal officer, whose name was not recorded, reviewed the line that day, he called three men out of line.

"What are you doing here in civilian clothes?" he asked in astonishment.

"Because we're civilians," said Sam Thomas. "We were arrested and made to serve."

"This is neither the time nor the place to get to the bottom of this," the officer said, "but I want you off this field. You walk back down the Baltimore pike and report back to your camp."

The relieved young men were happy to oblige him.

July 8, Evening—Frederick

Sometime after three P.M. a column of confederate cavalry had come down the road, disappeared into a swale, and reappeared as dismounted skirmishers, closing to exchange rifle fire with the home guards and 10th Vermont. There sprang up a continuous exchange of cannon fire between the two Baltimore light artilleries. As the balls whizzed between the lines, an aide rode up to Wallace and pointed toward the road to town where crowds of people, including women and children, were hanging on the fences watching the action.

"Goods heavens," said Wallace. "Those people are within range. Ride down and get them out of there."

"They won't go, General. They've been there since yesterday. We tried driving them off then."

"No, no. They could be killed. Drive them off."

Several officers then galloped up and down the fence lines, brandishing warnings and ordering the folks to move off back to town. But none did. Perhaps among them was the wife of the soldier whose loose lips had first alerted John Yellott to the march of Early up the Valley. That seemed now a very long time ago. It also seemed that the inconceivable was becoming probable. The Confederacy was about to capture Frederick, Maryland, the wide-open back door to Baltimore and Washington.

Around four P.M., Wallace saw the first flows of lava from the erupting volcano to his west. He had "kept [his] glass busy searching the purpling face of the mountain," and now he saw "three long, continuous, yellow cloud lines, apparently on as many roads, crawling serpent-like down toward the valley. . . . What I saw were columns of infantry, with trains of artillery . . . strong columns of thousands and thousands."

He called over to Tyler, "Look yonder! That is what the fellows in our front have been waiting for!"

The sight of the descending columns of infantry was all Wallace needed to begin the withdrawal of his soldiers from their positions in the fields west of town.

Wallace and Tyler rode together back into Frederick.

"They think we will stay to be taken in," Wallace said, "but we will disappoint them. We will go back to the junction tonight. It's evident to me now that Early wants the pike to Washington, and he will soon get it. We must hold him back long enough for Grant to get a corps here. We must fight."

"I believe that we are badly outnumbered."

"True, but we must fight. At all hazards, we must fight."

July 8, Evening—Early's Headquarters, Middletown

Bradley Johnson arrived per orders at Early's headquarters just south of Middletown late on the evening of July 8th, thinking perhaps the details of the attack on Frederick were to be worked out. Instead he was handed an unwelcome surprise.

"General," said Early, "I suppose you know that General Lee's son joined us in Sharpsburg."

"I heard something of it, General, but I've been busy up front. As I hope you realize, we could have been in Frederick."

Early's toughened hand, palm up, waved the idea off. "I'm aware of your opinions, but your brigade is needed for other work than in Frederick. What Lee has brought to us is a plan that his father and Jefferson Davis have been hatching. There is that prison down at Point Lookout . . ."

Johnson took a long look at his superior. Bristly was the word for him, a "burly person . . . [with] neglected dress . . . swarthy features, and grizzled hair, cross-grained and fault-finding." But Johnson was a lawyer and unafraid.

"Don't tell me."

"Yes, that's it. They have twenty thousand of our men down there. That's a whole corps, General, one whole single entire goddam corps of veteran soldiers, if they can be got out. There is a commander in our Navy, an aide to Davis named John Taylor Wood, who thinks he can do just that. They are guarded by a lot of half-assed, half-shot veteran reserves and a bunch of no-account U.S. Colored troops. It's to be a joint operation. Wood is outfitting armed steamers in North Carolina, and he intends to effect a rescue and rendezvous with units from this corps. You're a Marylander, so Lee believes you can make your way down there more easily and effectively than anyone else. When you have our boys all rounded up, you will bring them up to Washington City, and I'll be waiting for you at Bladensburg."

Johnson was incredulous. "General," he protested, "that prison is at the mouth of the Potomac, about 150 miles from here. Washington City and all of its troops lies between us."

Early was unperturbed. "I'm fully aware of where it is. And that being the case, perhaps you should slip out of here first thing in the morning on the Libertytown road toward Baltimore and cut the railroad and telegraph lines north and south of that city, then angle on down to Point Lookout. I would appreciate it, though, if, as you are leaving, you would keep an eye on our flank at Frederick and see that we are getting along all right."

"And when do they expect me at Point Lookout?"

"On Tuesday next. The boats are supposed to get there on Tuesday to hook up with you."

"General, I am attached to you by my respect for your intellect and your manly character, but you know and I know that what you are proposing can't be done. It is utterly impossible for man or horse to accomplish the deed in less than ninety-six hours. We're talking about 300 miles of hard riding, taking out the wires and the bridges and cutting the rails."

"Well, Lee expects us to give it our best try. We are up here beyond the Potomac with no excuse for not trying it. Good luck to you, General. We will have to make our best attempt."

"I will do what I can. Whatever is possible for men and horses to do."

July 8, 8:00 P.M.—*Frederick*

Wallace was aware that he was turning Frederick over to sympathizers "bitter to vituperation" and abandoning to the mercies of confederate occupation "the legion devoted soul and purse to the Union," unionists who had left barrels of water on the street corners for the hot and weary troops. He said that leaving Frederick that night was one of the most trying events of his life. He stopped at eight P.M. to wire Washington:

> Breckinridge with a strong column moving down the Washington pike toward Urbana, is within six miles of that place. I shall withdraw immediately from Frederick City and put myself in position on the road to cover Washington.

Wallace piled stores and ammunition aboard trains and sent them down the spur track to Monocacy Junction, and then tried to remove so quietly that orders were whispered. Tyler, Gilpin and Clendenin's forces moved to the same place by the

Baltimore road, but a mad scene ensued as hundreds of citizens ran off or rode off with the troops, and almost every horse in town was led eastward. The collector of internal revenue put $70,000 on a train to Washington, and the B&O itself began moving its rolling stock out of harm's way.

Many southern sympathizers ran in the other direction, out the Hagerstown road, to tell Early the news. By the time his cavalry rode into town and hoisted the confederate flag over the court house, only the 8th Illinois cavalry stood between Early and the Monocacy.

Wallace left Tyler in command of the federal right wing at the Jug Bridge, with orders to defend it at all costs, and made his way, "stumbling through the dark, deepened by the trees

USMHI-MOLLUS

BRIG. GEN. JAMES RICKETTS

overhanging the road," back to his headquarters at the junction, arriving around midnight.

July 8, Midnight—Monocacy Junction

Wallace's aide, Col. Lynde Catlin, told him that trains had been coming in during the day, and that Col. Truex's first brigade of Ricketts's third division—about two thousand men—was on the ground. The infantry brigade–the 106th and 151st New York, 14th New Jersey and 87th Pennsylvania—also included the 10th Vermont, which even then was marching back from Frederick.

An hour later Ricketts himself arrived. A hardened regular Army officer, the forty-seven-year-old Ricketts had begun his career as an artilleryman and was commanding a battery when badly wounded in the leg and captured at the war's first battle at Bull Run. He was exchanged at South Mountain, and he knew the Maryland terrain well, having fought again, gallantly, at Antietam, where his division held the East Wood. In contrast to the angular, somewhat sad-looking Wallace, Ricketts was portly and direct. The first words out of his mouth were, "Is Jubal Early here?"

"Three miles that way, in Frederick City."

"With how many men?"

"Twenty to thirty thousand."

"What do you intend to do?"

"Fight."

"And how many men have you?"

"About twenty-five hundred. And you?"

"About five thousand."

"That's first rate."

"What do you hope to gain by fighting here?"

"If he comes this way, we know it is Washington he is after. He has marched all the way from Lynchburg, and we still don't know what his command consists of. I want to hold him up for at least a day to give Grant time to get troops to Washington. Grant is Washington's only hope."

"Very well. Here it will be."

"General Tyler has been given the right wing. You take up the left. I am putting you across the Washington pike because it is the post of honor. Early will almost certainly do his best fighting against the bridges here and the Washington road."

During the short night, the second brigade under Col. Matthew R. McClennan arrived, another twenty-five hundred men of three Ohio infantry, the 110th, 122nd and 126th, the 138th Pennsylvania and the 9th New York Heavy Artillery. Its colonel was William H. Seward, Jr., son of Lincoln's secretary of state.

From the trains they climbed up to a ridge where the Washington road ran. Truex had placed his New Yorkers, Pennsylvanians, New Jerseyites and Vermonters at the left of the line, in and around the intersection of the Washington and Baker Valley roads, and in the fields surrounding Araby. McClennan placed his regiments on the Thomas "hill field" atop the ridge and in a small valley behind it where Gambrill's mill stood. When the units had settled into place, a skirmish line was thrown out extending from in front of the hill field, overlooking the river, south and east to the Baker Valley road.

A part of the line overlooked the slow and shallow river, largely hidden behind its wooded shores but here and there winking silver through the summer night. It seemed to the tired troops that they had no sooner come to rest than a cool morning wind came through the trees to their rear. They looked out toward the steeples of Frederick in the distance and saw a vast butternut movement, rippling with the little lightening of sunlight reflected from sabers and bayonets and animated with the flutter of flags, flowing across the open fields toward them. Some of them, at least, had made their rendezvous with death.

Saturday, July 9, Dawn—On the Road

A night storm, typical of a Maryland July, had steamed the dark unstable air over the mountains and valleys until the piled-up clouds released pounding rains in quick showers, making sleep miserable for the confederate troops huddled in bivouac on the mountainside. In the small hours, the front had passed southward. At first light the army was stirring around campfires, still damp but preparing to march eastward, toward Frederick, and beyond it to the Monocacy.

Johnson's brigade was up long before light, and he led them out along the country roads toward the north of Frederick, toward Worman's mill on the old Liberty Road. In his long column were fifteen hundred mounted men—four cavalry battalions (1st and 2nd Maryland, 22nd and 32nd Virginia) and three cavalry regiments (8th, 21st and 36th Virginia) along with the 2nd Maryland (Griffin's) Baltimore Light Artillery. Only three men other than Johnson—his adjutant, Capt. George Wilson Booth, staff member Capt. Wilson C. Nicolas and the ranking man in the brigade, Col. W.E. Peters of the 21st Virginia—knew where they were going. As they trotted along on that glorious morning, they paused long enough to listen to the hollow booming of distant cannon to their south and determine that Early was "getting along alright."

The column moved rapidly along the road to Libertytown and through it for another mile to the junction with the New Windsor road. At New Windsor, the shop keepers had locked their doors and fled. The rebel cavalry reopened them, and while a general pilfering and looting was undertaken, Johnson sent Harry Gilmor forward six miles with twenty hand-picked men to capture Westminster.

IX.
The Battle at Monocacy

Saturday, July 9, 1864—Frederick Valley

Almost everyone remembered the unusually pleasant day. John Worsham, tramping along from Middletown with the 21st Virginia on the ninth never forgot it. "It was a beautiful day in this beautiful country. The sun was bright and hot and a nice breeze was blowing. . . . The air was laden with the perfume of flowers; the birds were singing in bush and tree; all the fields were green with growing crops. The city . . . looked as if it had just been painted. . . . [A] few floating clouds added effect to the landscape. It was a day and an hour to impress all. We marched along quietly, talking about the scene and the day."

Kelley Bennette remembered how the spires of Frederick, rising from the valley floor, "glittered like silver and gold in the burning sun."

Summer had truly smiled on the Frederick valley and its fields were golden with wheat ready for an early harvest. At Clifton, the Worthington farm, and adjacent Araby, the Thomas farm, four-horse wagons moved into the fields as the first light of day streaked the sky. While blue-clad troops in the fields above them dug rifle pits, the wagons moved as quickly as they could through the shocks of wheat, gathering them onto carriages, from which the wheat would be pitchforked into the loft of a barn.

William T. McDougal of the 126th Ohio was on picket up on the high Washington road, and he, too, found the day remarkable. "The morning dawned with a halo of sunshine and beauty," he later recalled. "The birds (which we had become so unaccustomed to hear during our late journey from the Rapidan to Petersburg) never appeared to be so joyful. The large farmhouse on the hill to our left seemed almost a paradise. . . . I remember the gathering of the wheat from the field."

Thomas Palm and John Ephraim Tyler Butler were slaves who had chosen to stay with the Worthington family. As they gathered the wheat, Butler looked skyward

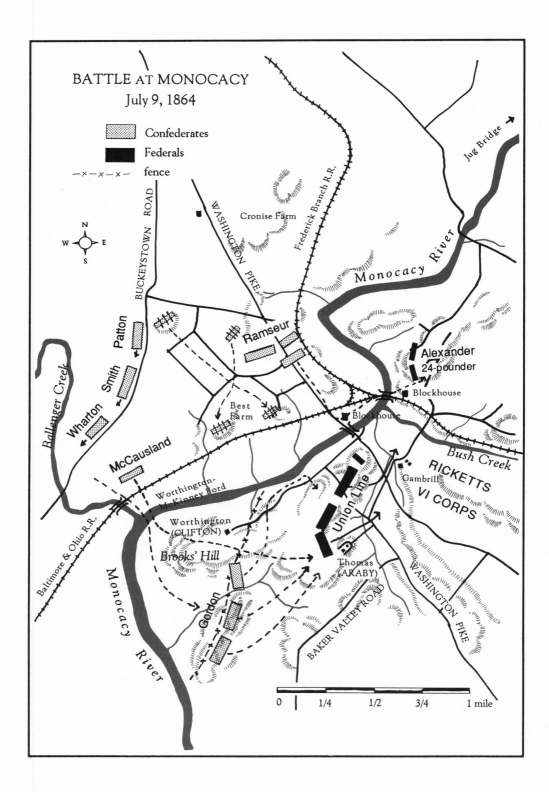

BATTLE AT MONOCACY
July 9, 1864

Confederates
Federals
—×—×—×— fence

N
W   E
S

Ballenger Creek

BUCKEYSTOWN ROAD

WASHINGTON PIKE

Cronise Farm

Frederick Branch R.R.

Monocacy River

Jug Bridge

Wharton Smith Patton

Ramseur

Alexander
24-pounder

Blockhouse

Best
Farm

Blockhouse

Bush Creek

McCausland

RICKETTS

Gambrill

VI CORPS

Baltimore & Ohio R.R.

Worthington-
McKinney Ford

Worthington
(CLIFTON)

Brooks' Hill

Union Line

Thomas
(ARABY)

WASHINGTON PIKE

Monocacy River

Gordon

BAKER VALLEY ROAD

0   1/4   1/2   3/4   1 mile

toward a kettle of turkey vultures that was beginning to form high in the morning sky, milling slowly upward on the warming air.

"Trouble comin, Thomas," he said.

"Comin' right here," said Thomas. And sure enough, about eight-thirty a deep rumble that was not a train was heard to the west, and then the distant rattle of musketry. John Worthington asked Thomas and Ephraim to unhitch the horses from the wagon and take them and all of the other horses in the stable, to Sugarloaf Mountain, a singular little mount, about five hundred feet high, some five miles to the southeast, and "tie them by their halters in the darkest and loneliest place you can find."

Keefer Thomas sent his horses to the same place.

Worthington moved heavy, two-inch oak boards against the cellar windows, which extended about three feet above ground, and carried several barrels of water into the cellar, just as though he were preparing for a great storm, a great thundering storm, with guns and blinding shot and shell and blizzards of lead and freshets of blood.

From his picket post on the Washington road, McDougal watched the refugees from Frederick streaming past "in great numbers—men, women and children, old and young, black and white, . . . moving with them all their household effects. . . . [W]e were told by the refugees that the Rebs were coming in great numbers."

July 9—Streets of Frederick

Ramseur's division was the first to reach Frederick town, to the cheers of the southern sympathizers who lined the streets. As Kyd Douglas, the first horseman in the column, rode down Patrick Street, an enthusiastic citizen (Peter Zahm, who later became a close friend) rushed into the street and presented him with a handsome pair of spurs.

Others were of an opposite sentiment. "Go ahead!" they yelled at the 6th North Carolina regiment, "You will soon meet regular soldiers!"

"Those are the fellows we are hunting for!" replied the marching men.

Capt. Park of the 12th Alabama, marching through town with Rodes's division, looked around for "the mythical 'Barbara Freitchie,' concerning whom the gentle Quaker poet, Whittier, erred sadly as to facts."

Ramseur pushed his three brigades—four regiments of North Carolina infantry under Robert D. Johnston, five regiments of Virginia infantry under Robert Lilley and the remnants of the 6th, 21st, 54th, 57th, and 1st Sharpshooters of North Carolina under William Lewis—down the pike running southeast to Washington, with Johnston leading and Lilley and Lewis in reserve.

Rodes, with his mixture of North Carolina, Alabama and Georgia troops, took the Baltimore pike that ran directly eastward from town, taking up Ramseur's left flank.

To Ramseur's right Breckinridge assigned John B. Gordon with Clement Evans's Georgians, Zebulon York's Louisianans and William Terry's Virginians.

July 9, First Light—8th Illinois Cavalry

The firing that Worthington's hands had heard was the 8th Illinois contesting the advance of the confederate army. After falling back from Frederick on the Baltimore road around two A.M., the 8th had circled back by a farm road to Monocacy Junction and two hours of rest. Now, as first light was streaking the summer sky, companies B and I were sent back toward Frederick along the Georgetown pike to confront the enemy. Capt. Leib and his mounted infantry were dispatched to the Jug Bridge to aid Allison Brown. Co. C, with Lt. John Sargent, was sent downstream to burn bridges it found and picket fords. Lt. George Corbit was told to take Co. B and guard a crossing near the Worthington house known locally as the Worthington-McKinney Ford. Maj. Waite was sent southward along the river in Sergeant's tracks with three companies, I, K and M, in search of bridges and fords. Clendenin himself took the rest of the regiment to the Baker Valley road to look for a force said to have crossed the river near Buckeystown and be moving toward Urbana and to take up the union left flank.

July 9, 8:00 A.M.—Cannon Call to Battle

Around eight A.M. Maj. William Nelson wheeled his three artillery units—Capt. Kirkpatrick's Amherst and John Massie's Fluvanna, both Virginian, and Capt. Milledge's from Georgia—onto a hillock on Simon Cronise's farm, which spread between the Washington pike and the railroad tracks east of Frederick. Massie took up a position between two trees, aimed his rifled gun precisely at the union center at the railroad bridge and with his very first shot killed two men of the 151st New York who were bending over their morning coffee pot. A second shell whistled down in the yard in front of the Gambrill house, where the 87th Pennsylvania was encamped, wounding three. So hot did this accurate artillery fire become that Wallace had to move his headquarters, scrambling quickly into the lee of a hill north of the tracks. The opening salvo had dislodged the enemy's central command. It had also spooked the engineer of the commissary train, who suddenly pulled out toward Monrovia with the VI Corps rations and supplies and Wallace's telegrapher—and with him all communications with the outside world.

July 9, 8:00 A.M—Wallace Sets the Defense

On a hill north of his headquarters and just to the east of the railroad bridge, Wallace had placed three of Alexander's three-inch rifles; they looked westward, toward the open valley and the approaches to the two bridges. Lying on the hill below the brow were eight companies of the 11th Maryland under Col. Landstreet. Nearby, from its embanked position, the big twenty-four-pound howitzer, which sounded like an explosion every time it was fired, anchored the center of the line. Alexander's other

James Taylor
The Western Reserve Historical Society

MONOCACY JUNCTION

three field pieces had been seconded to Ricketts and were placed on a hill southwest of the Georgetown pike.

In addition to the two major turnpikes that radiated from Frederick—the Baltimore pike ran due east and crossed the Monocacy on the Jug Bridge and the Georgetown (or Washington) pike ran southeast and crossed the river three miles farther south on the covered bridge—there were several farm roads that led to fords. The two that worried Wallace were Hughes's Ford, about a mile north of the Jug Bridge and Crum's Ford, about a mile to the south.

Because he was not sure which way Early intended to move, Wallace had to defend both roads and fords. This meant thinning his command along a front that stretched six miles, from the Baker Valley road east of Araby to Hughes's Ford. The right wing, under Tyler, was centered at the Jug Bridge, where he had six companies of the 149th Ohio. He also had a company of the 149th Ohio at Hughes's Ford, and Col. Gilpin with the 3rd Potomac Home Brigade and three companies of the 1st Potomac Home Brigade stationed along the base of a hill overlooking Crum's Ford.

Wallace fully expected the major attack to be aimed at capturing and crossing the wooden bridge of the Washington pike and the nearby iron railroad bridge. Following the shelling of the Gambrill's mill area, Ricketts' troops had been rapidly redeployed, stationed to bear the brunt when it came.

On a two mile front along the crest of the hills to the south of the bridge, thirty-five hundred men were formed in two lines of battle. William Truex's first brigade of infantry—the 14th New Jersey, 106th New York, 151st New York, 87th Pennsylvania and 10th Vermont—made up the first line, facing the river below, the bridge to the north and the plain beyond. McClennan's second brigade was marched into a parallel line behind them—the 9th New York heavies, 38th Pennsylvania and three Ohio regiments, the 110th, 122nd and 126th. On the far left, beyond the Baker Valley road, the end of the line was taken up and defended by Clendenin and his 8th Illinois Cavalry.

July 9—The Triangle

About a quarter mile west of its crossing of the Monocacy on the covered bridge, the Washington pike also crossed over the B&O tracks running south to Harpers Ferry. To defend this wooden overpass, a blockhouse had been built by the side of the pike similar to the one on the east bank that guarded the iron bridge. They were, in effect, log boxes with firing ports. The blockhouse and the deep cut to the north, through which the railroad tracks had been laid, provided good defensive cover.

Early in the morning, Wallace ordered various units over to the west bank to occupy the triangle of land formed by the Washington pike, the river and the railroad. Capt. Charles J. Brown (not to be confused with Allison Brown) led companies C and K of the 1st Maryland Potomac Home Brigade, some two hundred men, across the covered bridge to man and defend the blockhouse. Lt. George E. Davis of Co. D, 10th Vermont, followed with seventy-five picked men. Capt. Anson Wood led Co. M of the 9th New York heavies (with enough men from Co. E to make an even hundred) and Capt. Samuel Parker went with him, leading two companies of the 106th New York. This total force of about 350 men formed a concave line. Davis remembered it as 340 yards from railroad bridge to the overpass and 150 yards from there to the river, with a 400-yard baseline along the riverbank.

As Parker and Wood led their New Yorkers up the pike, Wood later recalled, he "discovered a union captain and learned from him that he had some sort of a skirmish line on the left of the pike, and that he outranked me. . . . He said that he thought I had better move up and reinforce his line. I did so and within five minutes the captain and the few men he had there disappeared from my sight and hearing forever."

Soon they came upon the squadron of the 8th Illinois backing down the road, with firing to their front. Wood had been more than a little naive as he "marched up the pike toward Frederick, anticipating a pleasant day on picket," when "suddenly a rebel skirmish line opened fire upon us." As his company moved quickly into defensive posture behind a rise of ground to the right of the road, there was a sudden fusillade of fire from the Confederates as they recognized the rank of a rider who had crossed through the covered bridge and spurred up to the front. It was Ricketts, satisfying himself as to the situation. He and a few of his staff rode up to visit with Wood. As the fire increased, he gracefully reined about and galloped back to his hilltop post. Wood noticed that the 106th New York had arrived and taken position on his left.

Hospital steward W. G. Duckett somehow became confused, wandered off and got himself captured and hauled before Brig. Gen. John Echols, who was moving to Breckinridge's orders on Early's right flank.

Then they knew.

"Damn that Sixth Corps!" Echols exploded. "We meet them wherever we go!"

Duckett led Echols to believe the entire corps was at hand and promised to help the general and his troops "to hospitable graves" before he was hustled off to detention.

July 9—The Jug Bridge

Three miles to the north, Erastus Tyler and Allison Brown had formed another salient at the Jug Bridge, putting out three companies of skirmishers from the 149th Ohio along a crest on the Frederick side of the river. Shortly after sunrise, Early's van—actually Robert Doak Lilley's Virginians, who would shortly be relieved and sent over to Ramseur—approached along the Baltimore road, scattered left and right into skirmish position and opened fire on the Ohio line, initiating an exchange that would continue for the next eleven hours. Coming up behind Lilley was Rodes's division led by Philip Cook's Georgians; in column behind Cook were William Cox's six North Carolina regiments, then Bryan Grimes's five North Carolinians and, finally, Cullen Battle's five Alabamians. With Lilley relieved, Cook's brigade formed skirmish lines to the right of the road, and Cox took position on the left.

July 9, 9:00 A.M.—Federal Line, Center

When the confederate shelling began, Tyler's three non-volunteers, Thomas, Anderson and Gatchell, still in their July 4 clothes, were placed with the others on a hill near the iron bridge. Here their saviour appeared; they never learned his name. He was an officer who rode up to them and said, "If you stay here you may be killed. If you are captured while fighting in civilian clothes, you will be shot. Gen. Wallace has more to worry about today than you gentlemen, so I advise you to get away from here as fast as you can."

Down went the muskets as the three dashed to the nearest refuge, the house belonging to Thomas's friend and neighbor, the miller James Gambrill. As they approached, they noticed that Gambrill, a man of their own age, had a visitor on his porch—General Ricketts! Just then Maj. Adam King galloped up, reported to the general, received instructions and rode away. In only a moment, it seemed, a squad of stretcher bearers appeared, carrying a badly wounded King.

Ricketts stirred himself and, seeming to notice the lads for the first time, said, "You boys get down there by that waterwheel and stay out of harm's way." And down they ran. They crawled under the big wheel, and there they stayed, civilians once more.

July 9, 9:30, A.M.—First Probes

Now Ramseur and Rodes both began probing their fronts in a more serious way. Rodes sent a cavalry unit a mile upstream from the Jug Bridge to force a passage at Hughes' Ford, which Capt. Charles McGinnis was defending with a single company, C, of the 149th Ohio. Allison Brown saw the movement and quickly sent Thomas Jenkins's Co. E of the 149th and Capt. Leib's mounted infantry galloping by a farm road to McGinnis's aid. They drove the enemy back from the ford.

About the same time, Ramseur advanced in force down the Washington pike. With Lilley and Lewis in reserve, Robert Johnston's North Carolinians pushed hard against Wood's position to the east of the road, and he fell back, but in good order. His troops, he proudly reported, maintained an excellent line, loading and firing rapidly and keeping the Carolina advance in check until they reached the cover of the railroad cut. He recalled particularly one soldier, "a schoolteacher from western New York named Wellon, who stopped and fired each time with great deliberation and excellent effect." As the 9th New York fell back on the rail line, Brown's 1st Maryland Home Guards came up in support and the line firmed and held, although Wood obviously never saw Brown; otherwise he would have recognized the disappearing captain.

Charles Brown realized the situation required veteran leadership, and in some agitation he turned to George Davis of the 10th Vermont and insisted he assume command, which Davis did "instantly and brought up my Tenth Vermonters." A severe firefight sprang up along the line of the railroad.

It now fell to the 23rd North Carolina under Col. Charles C. Blacknall to make an attempt on the blockhouse. Capt. V.E. Turner of the 23rd remembered the difficulty of the task since "a considerable force of the enemy were in a railroad cut and perfectly protected." As the Carolinians "made a dash for the blockhouse" they were "swept by a hot infilading fire" from the 10th Vermont in the cut to the east and the New York companies to the west. Alexander, from across the river, "also swept them with a raking fire." Capt. W.C. Wall, leading Co. F, was hit and went down; he would live. Blacknall himself had a vivid recollection: he "charged . . . within twenty feet of the house . . . but [found] it impossible to carry it by storm." At that moment he "was stunned . . . by the impact of a bullet on the head, which fortunately did not penetrate." The regiment fell back.

July 9—Jug Bridge

Affairs were heating up in front of Tyler as well. A force of sharpshooters from Rodes had made their way along a ridge five hundred yards to the west of the skirmish line and found a log house owned by a man named Simpson. They punched out firing positions in the chinks between the logs and in perfect safety began to rake the Ohio line so hotly that the men could not lift their heads.

July 9, 9:30 A.M.—Monocacy Junction

As the shells flew toward them, the federal soldiers stationed around the Mantz house and the railroad station at Monocacy Junction thought they were having a vision as they watched two "extremely attractive young women" make their way across the dangerous iron bridge. They were obviously practiced at it and must be local, the men believed. The ladies soon came into the camp and asked for Gen. Wallace. They were "obviously in deep distress over something," one orderly recalled, but the general was not there—or he was hiding.

The distraught ladies were Alice Thomas of Araby and her friend Mamie Tyler, upset because Tyler had kidnapped their fiancés. In the days since the arrest, Alice and Mamie had frantically implored Wallace's headquarters to release their beaux, but that seemed to be on the bottom of everyone's priority list.

"The last we saw of them," recalled the orderly, in one of those memorable images that all days of battle somehow create, "was their rapid crossing of the railroad bridge to the westward."

Judson Spofford, who was on that side of the river with the 10th Vermont that morning, "saw the young ladies, after the skirmishing . . . had commenced, hastening across what soon became a bloody battlefield." He watched as "the two weeping, heart-broken girls returned to the Thomas mansion and with the rest of the family took refuge in the cellar."

That cellar was filling up. At midmorning, Jim Gambrill's wife and sons, Richard and Staley, arrived at Araby to join Keefer Thomas and his wife, their daughters Alice and Virginia and son Frank and Mamie Tyler in the cellar, as the boots of federal sharpshooters pounded up the stairs, window sashes were thrown up and the bang of rifle fire reverberated through the halls.

Gambrill had stayed at his mill, and, unbeknownst to the women in the Araby cellar, he and the three lost lads were all down under his waterwheel.

As the skirmishing between Ramseur and the Maryland and Vermont boys around the blockhouse in the triangle grew hotter, agent Frank Mantz's wife and their children, Miller, Clarke, Lillie and William, had to run. They fled down the nearest road, Clifton's long drive along the riverbank, and arrived at the house in time to join the family and the slaves in the cellar with its boarded-up half-windows. Peering through the spaces between the planking, the refugees would soon see a large confederate armed force walking directly toward them from the west.

July 9, 10:00 A.M.—Frederick

Early himself had remained in Frederick, raising money. He had been met at the city outskirts that morning by Dr. Richard Hammond and escorted to the doctor's home on the northwest corner of Second and Market streets, where he set up headquarters. Despite such a warm reception from the city's "secesh," about one in every three citizens, Early levied a heavy ransom of $200,000 "in current money," five hundred barrels of flour, six thousand pounds of sugar, three thousand pounds of coffee, an equal amount of salt and twenty thousand pounds of bacon.

Negotiations with Mayor William G. Cole and his council opened with Early's army represented by the ordnance chief, commissary chief, chief surgeon and quartermaster. While that team stayed at the negotiation table, Early turned his attention to the developing battle. By the time he reached the field, Ramseur had moved both Massie's Fluvanna and Carpenter's Allegheny guns forward to the rail line south of the Washington road; along with Kirkpatrick in position to the north of the road, they added sixteen bronze Napoleons to the firepower directed against the triangle and bridges beyond.

July 9, 11:00 A.M.—Jug Bridge

At the Jug Bridge, Cook's Georgians made a strong advance against the left of Allison Brown's skirmishers and knocked them within a hundred yards of the bridge, opening firing lanes to the north along the federal line.

Brown called for help, and Tyler quickly sent three companies—B, G and I of the 144th Ohio. Brown ordered Co. B of the 149th Ohio to fix bayonets and charge to regain the lost ground. The brave boys who thought they would be spending the summer walking railroad tracks did their best, but they were quickly cut down and fell back. But on came the three companies of the 144th, and this time the Rebs had to give ground. Of the five officers and thirty-six men killed or wounded on this day from the two Ohio guard units, many fell in this spirited defense of the Jug Bridge.

July 9, Noon—The Covered Bridge Burns

The summer sun had been climbing swiftly toward the zenith, and the pleasant zephyrs of the cool morning had fallen to a hot stillness as the struggle intensified. Beyond a corn field, the J. Best house and barn stood just to the west of the tracks to Harpers Ferry, some three hundred yards to the left of Wood, Parker, Charles Brown and Davis in the triangle. Confederate sharpshooters had climbed into the barn and were reaping a harvest in the entire field from the turnpike to the railroad junction. Bullets kicked at the ground around Davis and his men, killing two and wounding several. As Johnston prepared to push his infantry forward once more, Alexander, from his height on the other bank, targeted on Best's barn.

"Our trouble," said Pvt. Frederick Wild, "was that we could not locate our enemies for some time until one of our officers noted small puffs of smoke from under the shingles of a barn, a half mile or more away; that barn was filled with sharpshooters, so we directed our attention to them. The second shot burst inside the barn, and so did the third and fourth; the barn was soon on fire and we had the satisfaction of seeing some of them being carried away."

Great, too, was the relief felt by Davis, but it was momentary. As Best's barn burned, Johnston's North Carolinians tried a flanking attack, moving northward across the tracks and attempting to get behind Davis and Brown by crawling south along the riverbank, hidden from view by the foliage. When Davis got wind of the movement from his scouts, he alertly withdrew his line to the west end of the railroad bridge and repelled the attack. While he was thus engaged, however, Wallace sent word across the covered bridge and withdrew both Wood's and Parker's New York companies. Thus, after Davis had gone forward to reclaim his original position, he found himself without support. Then a second pillar of smoke darkened the noon sky as a huge bloom of fire erupted at his rear. The covered bridge was burning.

Wallace had watched the action from a hilltop to the rear and had followed the retreat of the New York companies back to the rail line. He saw an ever greater force coming down the road behind Johnston: Lilley's Virginians and Lewis's North Carolinians, ten regiments of infantry with battle flags swaying in the dust and heat. About noon he sent down an order to Lt. Fish of Co. B, 9th New York heavies, stationed on the east bank, to burn the covered bridge. Privates Alvin Sova and Samuel Mack and Sgt. Albert L. Smith ran into a nearby wheat field and gathered up sheaves that they used as tinder under the southeast corner of the bridge.

Only then did Wallace realize that Davis and Brown were still out in the triangle.

"My God, what will become of them?" he asked Ross. His staff officer galloped down the hill and crossed the bridge to reach the forward lines in the triangle, but soon had to turn back. He reported to Wallace that he could not reach the forward positions; they were too far out and too exposed. It was deemed prudent to continue the order, and soon the fire had "wrapped the roof in flames like magic." Soon thereafter a huge column of smoke billowed into the high blue July sky, and great flaming timbers crashed into the water.

Davis looked back from his exposed skirmish line near the overpass and must have had only one thought—the bastards have burned the bridge without telling me! His 10th Vermont and Brown's Potomac Home Brigades were left stranded on the western bank.

July 9—Tiger John Finds A Ford

It was about that time that "Tiger John" McCausland appeared at the head of a long column of cavalry—the 14th, 16th, 17th and 22nd Virginia, perhaps a thousand men—coming up the road from Jefferson, where he had been tearing up the telegraph between Harpers Ferry and Washington. His scouts now turned off the road and began following a farm lane that led east along Ballenger Creek, which flowed southeast into the Monocacy and formed a dancing shallows of the Worthington-McKinney Ford. On the other side, in the deep shadows of large riverbank trees, were men in blue, the 8th Illinois, Co. B under Lt. George Corbit.

As the first horsemen splashed into the water, Corbit opened with his carbines, and the column recoiled. Reinforcements came up rapidly, forcing the crossing and giving Corbit no option but to fall back over the shoulder of Brooks Hill and through fields of wheat and corn, all the way to the Baker Valley road. The Confederates were soon crossing in force.

McCausland had found a way across the river, but the casual crossing and the nonchalant way he was going about the advance indicated that he was acting on old information. He had been ordered the previous day to turn to the Monocacy after breaking up the telegraph, cross it and "if possible occupy the railroad bridge" at Monocacy Junction, which, he was told, would be held only by weak 100-day men and national guards. A piece of cake.

The eastern bank was low, fertile bottom land inside a lazy loop of the river. McCausland and his troopers were screened from the federal view by the line of big trees that stood along the bank. Moving out of their cool shade, the horsemen came up into a sweetly-scented meadow, where they dismounted. A quarter of them gathered the horses and walked them back across the river. The rest walked along a fence that ran from the river up to the Worthington home.

The watchers in the basement followed their movements with pounding hearts.

As they approached the house, they climbed the fence to their left and jumped into a field of corn, only as high as a man's waist in this dry summer.

Ahead of them, beyond the corn, was the stout post-and-rail fence that divided the Araby and Clifton farms. Some large locust and walnut trees grew along the fence line, and the fence itself was obscured by the usual Maryland bramble, Greenbrier, Virginia creeper, fire cherry.

Three of Alexander's guns occupied the summit of the Thomas's hill field. It must have been from that vicinity that Col. Lynde Catlin, riding with Wallace, noticed movement at the far left of the federal line. He turned to Wallace: "Are those not skirmishers I see yonder?"

The commanding general's tongue had become dry with excitement and anxiety and he was "finding relief sucking a lemon" when Catlin addressed him.

"Where?"

"There, just south of the cornfield?"

Wallace looked a long moment through his scope, then sent a note to Ricketts:

> A line of skirmishers is advancing from the south beyond the cornfield on your left. I suggest you change front in that direction, and advance to the cornfield fence, concealing your men behind it.

Ricketts was now obliged to change front, to rearrange his army and face it south instead of west, which meant executing a complicated maneuver under fire. Massie's Fluvanna artillery had been moved forward to Best's farm, only eight hundred yards away across the river, and those guns opened on the moving masses of men of blue, inflicting "an unremitted enfilading fire." Wallace recorded that "the cannonading and noise of bursting shells were furious. Sympathy for the brave men under the iron rain racked me like a sharp pain." He would display in his memoir of the engagement the literary flair that he later brought to the composition of his popular novel of ancient Rome, *Ben Hur.*

Truex's brigade took Ricketts's left; the men ran eastward on the Washington pike and formed a battle line along, it facing south. The 14th New Jersey ended up at Araby's front gate, with the 87th Pennsylvania to its left and the 106th New York to its right. Truex's right flank was held by the 151st New York and the left by the 10th Vermont, whose troops found the road to be an "excellent natural breastwork" and extended their line "fully a quarter of a mile or more" down the Buckeystown road.

McClennan's brigade took their places on Ricketts' right, along the lower pike, and then up the steep hill field, with its right flank resting on the river. The 126th and 122nd Ohio, then the 138th Pennsylvania shared the hill with the 9th New York Heavy Artillery, with the 110th Ohio on the right flank. Ricketts's line was in the shape of a fish hook; from the covered bridge it ran southward and then bent sharply eastward with the road. Alexander responded to this new threat by sending two more guns over to the hill field, where three had been positioned since early morning.

Skirmishers moved quickly forward from Ricketts's line, running down the hill and through the pasture field to take up position behind the stout dividing fence. McClennan ordered Lt. Charles Gibson of the 122nd Ohio to take fifty men, Co. C and part of B, and add them to the line near the Worthington house.

McCausland's pickets had found the enemy, and now he prepared an attack, a prospect especially gratifying to the men of the 14th, most of whom were from the hills behind Roanoke and Lexington and Staunton in the far Valley. Some, like McCausland himself, were graduates of the burned VMI. Others were from farms and houses that had been torched and looted by Hunter's troops.

John Wise would write of them, "I had heard of their race . . . long before I went there; and now I was among them—those old McDowells, and McLaughlins, and McClungs, and Jacksons, and Paxtons, and Rosses, and Grahams, and Andersons, and Campbells, and Prestons, and Moores, and Houstons, and Barclays, and Comptons, and all the tribe of Presbyterians of the Valley. . . . Their impress was upon everything . . . the blue limestone streets . . . red brick houses with severe stone trimmings and plain white pillars . . . cedar hedges trimmed hard and close along straight brick pathways."

They were this kind of man: When 3rd Lt. William Fraiser Allen was killed at Gettysburg, his brother went there and buried him on the field. He threw his pocket knife into the grave so when the time came to take him to Virginia soil, however long it might be, he would have the right man.

They were this kind of man: The day after young John Hanger left Washington College and enlisted, a cannon ball came through the door of the stable where he was sleeping and took his right leg off below the knee. Union doctors completed the amputation—the first of the war.

These were the names advancing now toward Ricketts: McClung, McNutt, Poague, Bouldin, Feamster. Samuel William Newman Feamster, the first lieutenant of Co. A, had danced every dance with the 14th—South Mountain, Gettysburg, Dry Creek, Brandy Station, Droop Mountain, Lynchburg, Winchester, Martinsburg—and now Monocacy. None other than the union army's highest ranking officer, Maj. Gen. George B. McClellan, had said in exasperation and admiration, "That Newman Feamster can fight like the devil!"

One more time.

Wallace had a superb view as he watched the skirmishers disappear and a new line extending the length of the field climb over the fence and form up a line of attack. He noted guidons, flags with pale blue crosses on red fields, with white stars in the crosses. He told Ross that the flags meant regiments of cavalry.

"That's good!" said Ross.

"Why so?"

"Horsemen afoot are easy for infantry."

"But they may be mounted infantry."

"I don't know any difference. A horse always spoils a good soldier."

"I haven't observed that a horse has done you any hurt."

While they were thus bantering, gaps were being opened in the cornfield fence and two mounted officers, Lt. Col. John Alexander Gibson and Maj. Ben Franklin Eakle of the 14th, galloped through and took their places in front of the lines. Then the lines started forward.

Wallace never forgot it. "[S]uddenly . . . arms were shifted, and, taking to the double-quick, the men raised their battle cry, which, sounding across the field and intervening distance, rose to me on the height, sharper, shriller, and more like the composite yelping of wolves than I had ever heard it . . . a tempestuous tossing of guidons, waving of banners, and a furious trampling of the young corn that flew before them like splashed billows . . . was more than exciting—it was really fearful."

But fear yielded to astonishment when he realized what he was seeing. "I could not understand it. . . . I was lost in amazement, . . . not a man took time to stop, even for an instant, and fire a shot! . . . Did [the chief] not know what was before him?"

Wallace's eyes dropped involuntarily to the fence toward which the charge was coming. The soldiers appeared as daubs of blue pigment in the shade of the locusts. They reminded Wallace of hunters, lying in wait for deer speeding down upon them. Only one man was mounted, Ricketts himself, who "sat the horse like a block of wood, calm, indifferent." Wallace, knowing he might never see a sight like this in a hundred years, felt his flesh creep and wondered whether the coming fire would "hush the howling? Would it stop the rush?"

Then Ricketts's men all rose as one. "I saw the gleaming of the burnished gun-barrels as they were laid upon the upper rails . . . and for an instant, smoke interfered with the view."

Behind the smoke comes the crash of musket fire and the roar of angry men.

Down goes Col. Gibson, shot in the arm.

Down goes Maj. Eakle, shot through the body.

William Pitt Anderson of the 17th Virginia Cavalry topples, wounded. Private

Johnny Barger of Co. D goes down clutching his left thigh, unbelieving. It is the same goddamn leg that was shot at Second Manassas, when he was with the infantry!

Isaac Brady, 4th Corporal, Co. I, 17th Virginia Cavalry, is killed instantly.

Pvt. Jim Kirkpatrick tumbles over the wounded, and Pvt. George Knopp of the 17th staggers back with a ball through his lung. John Mills falls wounded, and Henderson Lucas hobbles sideways with a fractured leg.

James Scott Moore suffers his second wound of the war.

One of the McClungs, Alexander, falls mortally wounded, and another, the one they call "Grasshopper" also falls, but he will live. A third, George Alderson McClung, is flung backward as a ball shatters his shoulder.

Johnny Thompson from Blacksburg is down with a broken ankle, and he will lie on the field awaiting capture, as will others.

Back on the hill, the smoke clears and Wallace's aide, Maj. Max Woodhull, cries out, "My God! They are all killed!"

The line had disappeared, Wallace recalled, "not a man of it was to be seen, only the green of the trodden corn, horses galloping about riderless."

John Worthington was also watching, from an upstairs window of his house. His son Glenn recorded the family memory. "[T]he whole rebel line disappeared as if swallowed up in the earth. Save and except several riderless horses galloping about, and a few mounted officers bravely facing the storm, the attacking force had vanished."

"Give the fellows unhurt time to crawl along the furrows back to the fence and you will see they are not all dead," Wallace told Woodhull, and sure enough, the fence was soon so darkened with climbing bodies that whole sections of rail collapsed.

Making his way back to the ford, James McChesney, 14th Virginia, noted with disgust that, "Out of one hundred of our regiment that went into the fight, we had twenty-two men killed and wounded *in less than twenty minutes!*" He was sensitive about people getting killed; both his brothers were University of Virginia trained doctors, and one of them, Bob, had been the first officer and the first man from Rockbridge County killed in the war.

As McCausland's troopers withdrew from the bloody cornfield, Worthington watched them pass and thought he "never saw another such terrible sight as an army shocked and frightened as this one was. The men dragged their muskets by the muzzle and their faces depicted the greatest terror." He noted that "they were panic stricken by the deadly ambush into which they were unwittingly led."

A part of it, certainly, was in the realization that they had attacked not a lot of home guards and weekend warriors but dog-faces with Greek crosses on their caps; no one had to tell them that meant the VI Corps out of the Petersburg trenches. They could not help but feel they had been led into a slaughter.

From the hill, an exulting Wallace sent an orderly down with congratulations to Ricketts, consulted his watch, and thought to himself, so far—victory!

July 9—The Second Attack

Greek crosses or not, McCausland was not defeated. His officers tried to rally the men. John Worthington remembered, "They swore at them and threatened them with sword and pistol, but for awhile they would give them no heed." But eventually the panic subsided, and the retreat was halted below the Worthington house. And, as difficult as it was, the men formed up for another advance.

This time they angled away from the fatal fence, the 16th and 17th Virginia regiments moving rapidly to the southeast behind the Worthington house and toward the high saddle of the end of Brooks Hill. Down the opposite slope they went, toward a large wheat field. By the time the Yankees at the dividing fence saw the Virginians climbing that same fence several hundred yards to their left, saw them jumping down into the wheat field, it was too late, even though they ran that way in an attempt to stop the flanking movement. The troopers moved around Ricketts's left, and they hastened on through the wheat field and through a corn field below Araby's house and barn.

Samuel A. Abbott of the 10th Vermont, who was commanding Co. D while Davis was out in the triangle, watched them come, "shouting their ominous defiant battle cry. . . . The long swaying lines of grey in perfect cadence with glistening guns and brasses, and above all the proudly borne but to us hated banner of the Confederacy . . . was a spectacle rarely surpassed in the bright sunlight of a perfect summer day." Abbott regarded the spectacle with "mingled feelings of bitterness, dread, and awe," since the Virginians were "making directly for our part of the line," and he feared being cut off "when the shock of battle should come." Much to his relief, the charging infantry changed direction to their left.

Maj. Peter Vredenburgh of the 14th New Jersey watched as "the rebels now came in force from behind Thomas' house. They advanced over the crest, . . . the firing became brisk and then it opened as severely as I have ever heard from such a small force. . . . [O]ur boys fought as if they were fighting for their own homes and literally mowed down the first two lines of rebels."

A lone rider was now seen moving swiftly along the federal line, racing down the pike in full view of confederate sharpshooters and artillery, his bravery attracting every eye. It was Capt. W. H. Lanius of Truex's staff, and he carried orders from Wallace: the 87th Pennsylvania and 14th New Jersey to their right were ordered to charge across the fields and take the Thomas house.

They sprang to the attack. Vredenburgh wrote to his mother that "Our men at Thomas's gate then charged up his yard and across his field right up to his house, and drove the enemy around the corners, behind the barn. . . . [T]here was terrific firing."

Cpl. Roderick Clark of the 14th New Jersey recalled the large hawthorne hedge that continued the fence line from the barn yard that divided Thomas's lawn and drive from the surrounding fields. His company charged from behind the hedge and "drove them toward the river, killing and capturing many."

Once more, McCausland had to fall back, into the corn and wheat fields below.

There the 16th and 17th made a stand when they reached "the top of an eminence."

Nathaniel Harris of the 16th recalled forming a line that lay down until the pursuing Yankees approached. "As each charge was made, . . . the 16th rose and fired into the faces of those making the assault. . . . [T]here was a falling back of the enemy after each fire."

From their position on the hilltop, the regimental officers could not see the enemy below the brow. Lt. Col. William Cabell Tavenner of the 17th called for a volunteer to stand on his shoulders and see what the enemy was up to. A lieutenant promptly responded.

"The Colonel bent down and the Lieutenant climbed on his shoulders, and then the Colonel slowly rose. He had scarcely straightened himself out, and the officer above him had likewise risen up, where there came a sharp sound . . . and a volley was poured into the bodies of the two men."

By now the 106th New York had been ordered forward and was making a charge on a right wheel with the 14th New Jersey and 87th Pennsylvania. Peter Robertson said they captured a lieutenant colonel, captain, two lieutenants and twenty privates of the 17th. Nat Harris of the 16th wrote that "every field officer was killed or wounded."

This particular fight was finished as McCausland continued to withdraw over Brooks Hill and back to the Worthington house. That left Ricketts in complete command of the field. Truex's brigade had so advanced in pursuit of McCausland, that three regiments held a line of battle in the fields between Araby and Clifton that curved from the Baker Valley road toward the Monocacy and crossed over the dirt road between the houses. Behind them, the 10th Vermont and 151st New York still held the high Washington pike that commanded the ground to the south.

To an attacking army, Ricketts's position seemed strong. He now had two battle lines on elevated ground, strong enough to hold anything thrown at him and long enough to flank them.

He must have been pleased with the day's work thus far.

And across the river, Old Jube seemed equally pleased with what he seen. He had regarded Wallace's position on the hills with a river at his feet like a moat, as one that could be exceedingly difficult and costly to take a grip on, especially the crossing of the river in the face of enemy fire. But now he watched McCausland's flanking probe and said it had been "brilliantly executed. It solved the problem for me." Without further ado, he sent orders to Gordon to take his entire division, a tidal wave of two thousand, five hundred men, straight across the river at the Worthington-McKinney Ford.

July 9, Noon—Buckeystown Road

For John Worsham and his comrades in the 21st Virginia, this beautiful day had been only getting better as they halted along the road to Buckeystown and were told to fall out, stack arms and rest, as they would not be fighting that day.

The day was warming rapidly, so "the men took out blankets, oil cloths, etc. and stretched them in fence corners, on muskets, and on rails to make shelters from the sun."

Best of all, there promised to be entertainment. "We made ourselves comfortable and lay down under the shelter, to *look at* a battle. As Jackson's old 'foot cavalry,' this was something we had never done."

As the 21st watched McCausland's men dismount, climb the fence and begin the advance through the corn field, "it was very exciting to us old Confederates, and a yell went up along our line every few minutes."

The sport ended, however, as a courier came "riding up the road toward us, leaving a streak of dust behind him." They saw him stop where Gen. Gordon's headquarters were, then Gordon mounted his horse and with other riders headed out. Then came the call to attention, and Worsham and his comrades started to roll up their blankets and oil cloths.

"Take arms! No time now for blankets! Get into your places at once! . . . Right face! Forward march!"

It was a grumbling lot that made its way "through fields and over fences" until they came to the river and found "a small path on the river bank leading down to the water." Not only had they lost their promised day of peace; they had to leave their precious blankets and other things behind, probably not to be seen again.

Clement Evans's Georgians were in the lead and had stopped for a moment to remove their shoes (those precious shoes!) before fording the river, but there was John B. Gordon himself in his red shirt with the rolled up sleeves telling them, "Plunge right in, boys! no time for pulling off clothes!" Zebulon York then led his Louisiana units across. The Virginians under Terry were the last brigade to cross, and he told them to take off their shoes. On the eastern bank he said, "Put on your shoes and be in a hurry about it, but take time to tie them well. This being done, . . . we formed in line of battle facing north."

Gordon had ridden ahead. He had crossed Worthington's lower fields, keeping the limb of Brooks Hill between himself and the enemy, and found an old road through the woods to the top. There at the crest stood the post-and-rail boundary fence, climbing in a straight line but at an angle all the way up from the river. On the other side, on the Thomas farm, the woods had been cut out, and the slope was part of the forty-acre wheatfield that McCausland had crossed earlier.

What came into Gordon's mind was trouble. He had been properly enthralled at McCausland's bravery and at the same time properly annoyed. Gordon had, in fact, hoped to slip across the river concealed from "Wallace's watchful eye," and then "apprise him of my presence . . . by a sudden rush upon his left flank," but McCausland had blown that chance, and now Ricketts had already changed front and drawn up lines "in strong position to meet the assault" from the south. Instead of "giving my isolated command the immense advantage of the proposed flank attack," Gordon now found himself "separated from all other confederate infantry, with the bristling front of Wallace's army before me."

Worse yet was the field he now looked down upon and across which the assault must be carried: "[S]trong farm fences, which my men must climb while under fire . . . fields thickly studded with huge grain-stacks . . . so broad and high and close together that . . . every intelligent private . . . must have known before we started that my battle-line would become tangled and confused." Wallace's guns on the opposite ridge were positioned to "rake every foot of the field," and he had a passing and terrible vision of "my lines broken and tangled by fences and grain-stacks at every rod of advance" as the fire poured in.

He turned his horse back to the lee of the hill, consoling himself that "if any troops in the world could win victory against such adverse conditions," they would be his.

Gordon formed his strategy. He directed Evans to follow the contours around to his right and then cross over the lower slope of Brooks Hill through the woods, climb the boundary fence and attack Ricketts's left across the wheatfield. York and then Terry would follow *en echelon* (each a bit to the left rear of the other), so when the movement was completed, the entire division would have pushed Ricketts in from his left.

Isaac Bradwell, a Georgian, recalled Evans's orders to his troops. "We are now on the flank of the enemy. Their left rests on the edge of this wood in front of you. You must advance quietly until you strike them, then give a yell and a charge!"

Evans formed his column in the big meadow by the river and duly made his way across the fields east of Clifton, then up the slope and through the woods to the crest of the hill, where the troops soon appeared in the open sunlight of the wheatfield. Gordon, watching from the woods, reported that "they were met by a tempest of bullets, and many of the brave fellows fell at the first volley. But over they climbed or tumbled, and rushed forward. . . . Then came the grain-stacks. Around them and between them they pressed on."

Roderick Clark of the 14th New Jersey saw the Rebs coming from half a mile away; there was not "a tree or obstruction of any kind to hide them. It was certainly a grand sight as they advanced, in good order, with their numerous battle flags waving in the breeze. We began firing at once, but it made no difference. On they came with quick step until they got within three hundred yards. . . . Then our regiment and the 87th Pennsylvania was moved by the left flank and changed front to prevent them from flanking us."

Alexander's shells fell among the rushing men, and from the windows of Araby the Pennsylvania and New Jersey sharpshooters began reaping an awful harvest, especially among the mounted officers. A minié ball hit Evans on his left side, right at a pocket containing a number of sewing pins in a folded paper; as the ball entered his side it drove the pins before it and Evans went down as though struck with a sledge-hammer. He was carried back into the woods and presumed dead. His staff officer, Maj. Eugene C. Gordon, fell next, badly wounded.

So galling and accurate was the fire from Araby that five successive color bearers of the 12th Georgia were felled. The sixth to take up the standard, Lt. James Mincy of Co. D, was instantly shot through the lung but lived to tell about it.

The 61st Georgia was being ravaged. First its young and popular colonel, John H. Lamar, and then its lieutenant colonel, David Von Valkenburg, were killed in their saddles by murderously aimed balls. A particularly gruesome wound was suffered by Thomas Nichols of Co. A, whose skull was grazed by a ball just enough to slice it open it, and he found himself wiping his brains on his sleeve. The poor man lived in agony for 12 hours.

Lt. Col. John Baker of the 13th Georgia toppled wounded from his horse.

Leaderless, the advance milled in confusion. "It was one of those fights," said Gordon, "where success depends largely upon the prowess of the individual soldier." One of the survivors, Isaac Bradwell, confirmed that opinion when he remarked that "this battle, as far as Gordon's Georgia Brigade was concerned, was conducted by private soldiers, each man acting independently."

July 9, 3:00 P.M.—The Georgia Regiments Attack Truex

Truex's brigade had so much ground to cover in the large fields south of the Thomas house that its battle line was badly strung out. Col. James A. Stahle of the 87th Pennsylvania called it "no more than a thin skirmish line." Chaplain Haynes of the 10th Vermont used the same phrase, said that Truex's line "had been attenuated until it was little stronger than a skirmish line." Lt. Osceolo Lewis of the 138th Pennslvania said that the whole division "was stretched out into a single line of battle, without support, and with the left flank totally unprotected."

As the 126th Ohio, in the middle of McClennan's line, prepared its defenses, Bill McDougal and eight others went down the hill into the little valley to bolster the skirmish line. The men noticed "a large washout, with a stiff growth of weeds on its banks, [that] extended up the hill." McDougal and his comrades ran into the washout, anticipating that they would surprise the advancing Confederates by firing into their flanks as they passed.

With Evans down, the brigade command had passed to Col. E. N. Atkinson of the 26th Georgia, and he soon had the regiments organized in a double line of battle, with the 13th and his own 26th on the left, the 31st and 12th on the right, and the 38th, 60th, and 61st in the center.

At three o'clock, he ordered a general attack on Truex's position. The regiments on the right were aimed at the Thomas house and would have to overrun the 87th Pennsylvania, 14th New Jersey and, less directly, the 10th Vermont. A soldier told George Nicols of the 61st Georgia that as the 26th passed through the brightly sunlit field, "a Yankee shot at them from behind a shock of wheat, and they hit that Yankee with eighteen balls."

As Stahle recalled it, "We had hardly got into place before, out of the woods and through an oat field, came our foes charging in two lines. They moved in splendid order and excited our admiration by their splendid marching. Orders were at once given that not a shot should be fired until the enemy had reached a large oak three hundred yards distant from us due west. And as that point was reached the cheers, the firing began."

On the federal left, Col. William Henry told his Vermonters, "Wait, boys, don't fire until you see the C.S.A. on their waist belts, and then give it to 'em."

The Georgians came on, battle flags waving. They reached the oak. Volleys thundered from the federal defense. The attacking line stopped, staggered. More volleys poured in, and the line "fell back in broken ranks to the woods by the Worthington house."

Maj. Edwin Dillingham of the 10th Vermont was "swinging his saber and yelling, 'Give it to them, boys! We have them on the flank! Pitch it into them!' "

But before long the intrepid Georgians had reformed and again "came marching down the slope" toward the oak tree. Again the Federals waited, and again there was a tremendous exchange of musket fire.

The federal line suffered as well. The 14th New York lost its commanding officer, and then his replacement. Peter Robertson of the 106th New York, whose regiment was to the right of the 14th New Jersey, recalled that as the Georgians came on, "The command 'fire!' rang out along our line; then 'load and fire at will,' and such a fire was kept up that no mortal power could face and cross that field. At one time I counted five riderless horses."

Again the brigade had to fall back.

Then, as Gordon planned, Zebulon York and his Louisianans came charging through the haystacks. Isaac Bradwell noted with sadness that this famous brigade, "Lee's Tigers," that once numbered more than ten thousand, were now represented by these few hundred men charging through the Maryland wheat. As Lt. Col. John Hodges of the 9th Louisiana broke into the open, a ball hit him on the right arm, shattered the humerus and forced him to withdraw to the Worthington house.

Concerned with this new pressure on Truex, Ricketts sent three hundred men—the 138th Pennsylvania and Maj. Charles Burgess's battalion from the 9th New York—running to the extreme left of McClennan, where it bolstered the 106th and 151st holding Truex's right. As York's Louisianans now entered the field and aimed their line of attack between Truex and McClennan, they hit the 138th.

Osceolo Lewis recalled that "their three formidable lines came boldly up, with flaunting banners and bristling steel, as if by one grand demonstration to sweep us from the field. When they approached within one hundred and fifty yards, our troops poured into their well-closed ranks a withering fire which being continuously kept up soon shattered, demoralized and scattered the first and alike the second column . . . the third line of rebels came forward and the battle raged."

Then the unthinkable happened. Gordon himself, a veritable god of war, so far immune to the singing balls, went down. "In that vortex of fire my favorite battle horse . . . which had never hitherto been wounded, was struck by a minié ball, and plunged and fell in the midst of my men, carrying me down with him. . . . By his death, I had been unhorsed in the very crisis of the battle. Many of my leading officers were killed or disabled. The chances for victory or defeat were at the moment so evenly balanced that a temporary halt or slight blunder might turn the scales."

There was a mad scramble for a horse until an unidentified officer sent one to Gordon (probably his own), and the general was quickly remounted. But the momentum of the charge had been spent, and the union line still stood firmly in place.

Gordon had reached far south and east around Ricketts's line, and, though he was inflicting many casualties, he was also paying a dreadful price. He could see, ahead and above, Ricketts's strong position on the Washington pike. He knew the outcome was hanging in the balance. The day was not won and not lost. The war was not won and not lost. It was still forty miles to the White House, and Jubilee was still in Frederick, and the high July sun was riding down the ecliptic from the zenith toward the southwest; the only certain thing was that it would not wait to see who won.

Much needed relief from the Araby shooters arrived as confederate guns from Lt. Col. J. Floyd King's battery were brought over the ford and wheeled into place in the Worthington yard, at the south end of the house. There they were joined by Gen. Breckinridge, stepping on his first battlefield since being injured at Cold Harbor. When the first field piece opened fire, "a big rooster with a flaming comb and throttle, and withal, a big voice," gave out a lusty crow. After the second shot, it crowed again and continued to match each departing shell's explosion with a clarion call.

The third shell hit the side of Araby at the dining room, crashed through the brick wall, landed on a table still set with silver and exploded, hurling the silver in every direction. Other shells quickly followed, smashing great holes in the walls.

As this bombardment whistled overhead, Gordon galloped to the front. "Forward!" he cried, "and forward they went. . . . I recall no charge of the war, except of the 12th of May against Hancock, in which my brave fellows seemed so swayed by an enthusiasm which amounted almost to a martial delerium; and the swell of the Southern yell rose high above the din of battle."

There was no denying this third advance. The reluctant federals began a withdrawal to the pike. As the 14th New Jersey retreated, Cpl. Roderick Clark was hit by a ball in the left ankle, "completely crushing the joint." Two of his comrades made a seat of a rifle; Clark put his arms around their necks and they started back up the hill with him sitting on the gun. "But ere they got twenty steps I was struck with another minié-ball under the right shoulder blade just to the right of the backbone, penetrating the right lung, stopping just under the skin in my breast. It felt about the size of a cannon ball."

Clark fell to the ground unconscious, and his friends had no recourse but to save themselves.

July 9, 3:45 P.M.—The Thomas House

Pvt. Joseph Stonesifer of Co. I, 87th Pennsylvania, had been the first man to reach the Thomas house when McCausland withdrew. He and Spangler Welsh of Co. F and a few others had stayed in the house to snipe from the windows, but they stayed too long at the fair. As the shells crashed in, they ran out only to meet the first of the Georgia advance arriving at the Thomas barn; they were taken prisoner in hand-to-hand fighting.

As he ran toward the Thomas house, Maj. Vredenburgh of the 14th New Jersey had seen the shells pouring in. "In less time than I write it, they had sent a half dozen shells into it," and he became concerned for "the family who had extended to me so many acts of kindness. . . . I rushed into the house." He saw a basket of silver that had been packed and forgotten and carried it down to the cellar, where he found the family. They entreated him to stay, but he could not, for the good major had had some disturbing news from a wounded confederate prisoner: Lee, with his army, was near Urbana.

On the way out he locked the house.

July 9—Georgetown Pike, 10th Vermont

No sooner had the Georgia regiments overrun the grounds of the Thomas house than they broke in and hustled sharpshooters to the upstairs windows, who quickly opened fire on the federal positions along the pike. Col. William Henry of the 10th Vermont called Sgt. Lyman Pike, who had one of the best eyes in the regiment and, looking through a glass at the house, directed Pike to return fire as guided by Henry's observations.

"Soon I saw a head and gun coming in sight around one of the window casings, and directed Pike where to look, and almost at the same instant both fired. I felt a bullet go under my skin, and the reb pitched out of the window. The brave Color Sergeant, Billy Mahoney, was watching us and in a moment he caught me by the coat tail and pulled me to the ground, saying 'that will do, Colonel, the blooming rebs mean you,' and a moment after the brave Sergeant Pike dropped upon us, shot dead."

Still the brigade would not yield the pike.

George Nichols of the 61st thought the pike and its fences and cuts provided "as fine a breastwork as I ever saw. Here our brigade suffered as bad as it ever did in battle for the amount of men and length of time engaged. . . . We advanced to within thirty yards of the line, but we would have to fall back, for our men were killed and wounded until we had but a mere skirmish line. . . . It made our hearts ache to look over the battlefield and see so many of our dear comrades, friends, and beloved officers killed and wounded. Our loss was terrible."

Gordon described the narrow ravine that ran between the hostile lines, carrying a small stream. "In this ravine the fighting was desperate and at close quarters. To and fro the battle swayed across the little stream, the dead and wounded of both sides mingling in its waters. . . . Nearly one half of my men and large numbers of the Federals fell there."

James Stahle of the 87th Pennsylvania vividly recalled the slaughter. "Lt. John Spangler of Co. A stepped between us to make a request of some kind when he received

Vermont Historical Society

GEORGE DAVIS

his death wound. Just beyond, poor Dan Walsh lay. Close by him Cpl. Sheeds of F, John Bittinger of Co. A. Now Adjutant Martin is down. Lt. Hawk mortally wounded. Capt. [W.H.] Lanius shot in the arm. Lt. Deadrich dead. Lt. Walt Meyer gone. Nat Thompson shot through the body. Billy Harris dead. Sgt. Thorger terribly wounded. Sgt. Busey of K and a hundred others dead, dying, or captured."

Unable to dislodge Ricketts from the pike, Gordon sent word to Early, asking that Echols's division be brought up to help.

July 9, 4:00 P.M.—West Bank Triangle

It was only four o'clock, and the July sun, high in its radiant sky, still had four hours to burn searingly before the long, orange smoulder of a warm sunset, but the game was up. Out front, on the forward skirmish line around the overpass bridge where they had been all day, George Davis and his veteran Vermonters and Charles Brown's green Marylanders looked behind them at Ricketts's left being rolled up in smoke and cascading gunfire. Men were running northward, up the steep slopes toward to the Georgetown pike, not the other way. Directly behind them the covered bridge was billowing black smoke as it continued to burn; its entrance, which had looked like the mouth of a blast furnace, gaped black with wisping smoke.

At that point, Davis remembered it as being around three-thirty, "the enemy came upon us with such overwhelming numbers and desperation it seemed that we must be swept into the river." His position had been compromised by the departure of the 9th New York, and now Brown's hundred-day men on his right were, as he put it, "melting away" and running for the railroad bridge, the only remaining crossing. Before he left, however, Brown evacuated and fired the blockhouse, the black roiling smoke adding to the drifting white clouds from Ramseur's cannon, which were now in Best's farm fields.

The Vermonters stood their ground for another hour, an impressive demonstration

Deeds of Valor

10TH VERMONT INFANTRY CROSSING THE IRON BRIDGE

of courage and discipline, until they were on the verge of being completely overrun, and Davis realized that "we must leave now or never."

Davis asked Cpl. John G. Wright of Co. E to go through the cornfield to their left and report any enemy movement in that direction. Wright called Daniel Freeman of Co. G, who had spent the day firing from a rifle pit near the overpass, and told him to come along and relieve the vidette outpost, who was on duty some two hundred yards into the corn.

"As we came to this comrade," Freeman recalled, "Wright stretched up to take observations and was shot through the head. We carried him back to the reserve and

I returned to the outpost alone, just in time to see in the distance across the river the enemy on their fourth charge, with as many lines of battle. On and on I saw them come."

Freeman heard Lt. Wilkie urgently calling him in. He ran back across the pike, down the embankment and along the tracks toward the iron bridge, on which the reserve was already moving in column. Freeman looked behind him and "saw one of my comrades under the Pike Bridge, fighting a dozen Johnnies charging down the railroad toward him. He was riddled with lead."

The 10th Vermont would lose five killed and twenty wounded in this defense, and most of them were falling now. The name of the man under the bridge was not recorded, but Freeman, who considered his own escape "a miracle," would never forget "the heroic comrade covering my retreat, who . . . sacrificed his life there under the Pike Bridge that I and others might be spared."

It was an amazing scene as the soldiers "wormed themselves off the field," as Lew Wallace described it, until "they sprang up, and unmindful of exposure, made a dash for liberty."

The dash was across the railroad bridge. Its iron supports held cross-ties on which two tracks were laid, some forty-five feet over the river. There were no railings of any kind and only a narrow footway of boards down the middle. The distance between the ties made walking hazardous, and a slip meant a broken leg or a fall to the river below.

As Wallace and others on the high ground watched "spellbound," the fleeing Vermonters and Marylanders, Wallace saw perhaps two hundred, formed up in column order, "not crowding or pushing or struggling to pass or yelling," and came stepping across in perfect order.

It must have resembled a shooting gallery, with the soldiers crossing in single file against a blue sky in full view not only of sharpshooters who were firing from a bend on the bank a few rods below, as Freeman recalled, but of much of the rebel army. "Now and then we could see one stop short, let go his musket, throw up his hands, and with a splash disappear in the stream beneath," Wallace recalled, "Fortunately, though holding the moving files in plain view, the artillerymen mercifully refrained from firing."

Whose hand stayed the artillery fire that would have butchered the crossing men, Early's or Ramseur's, is not recorded, but it was ever after gratefully remembered.

When they reached the comparative safety of the west bank, some of the men swung their caps and cheered and some swung their guns up and fired back at the enemy, then they "reformed and in perfect order marched away. . . . I have not words to express my admiration. . . . From every point of view it was heroism."

Wallace asked an aide, Col. Catlin, to "hurry down and meet those men. That man in command is brave. I should like to know his name."

It was George E. Davis.

July 9, 4:00 P.M.—Terry Turns the Flank

Gen. Gordon sent another messenger to Early; then he realized it would take too long to get help from that quarter, and he turned to Terry.

Gordon concluded that by shifting his strength to meet the challenge to Truex, Ricketts had so weakened his right that a hard and swift thrust might turn it in and cut the Georgetown pike, trapping the entire division. Having spent all day in a laborious assault on Ricketts's left, Gordon would now strike swiftly at his right for a victory.

By the time Terry's Virginians had crossed the river and moved into line awaiting their turn, Evans and York, by the echelon movement, had moved north. Now Terry began *his* march north along the low river bank with orders to come out behind Ricketts's flank.

At about the same time, the two battalions of the 9th New York on the Thomas hill field were ordered forward. The regimental historian, Lt. Alfred Seelye Roe, recalled that Col. Seward "sat on his horse as erect as a centaur" as they moved south. "Our alignment is excellent, and the colors stream along as we advance." As they moved in such grand style toward the dividing fence, they saw the Virginians coming at them through the western side of the cornfield plowed up by McCausland's attack that morning, "firing as he comes." Resting their rifles on the fence, as Ricketts's skirmishers had several hours before, the New Yorkers fired into the corn field. Roe thought the position could be held indefinitely.

Col. Randolph Barton, with Terry's advance, had his horse shot from under him. Running to Worthington's stable, Barton's orderly found the only horse not carried away to Sugarloaf, the carriage horse, Old Davy. The tack was quickly transferred, and Old Davy galloped to war under Col. Barton, a short career, alas, as he, too, was soon felled by a ball. A third horse was obtained from those galloping loose over the battlefield, and Barton again was in the charge.

Pvt. James Hutcheson, with Terry's old Jackson Brigade, recalled that "we started at them at a double-quick, when General Terry said, 'Stop running and walk or you will break yourselves down and will not be able to fight the enemy when you get to them.'

"We slowed down and walked to the fence, the enemy still lying on the ground behind it, shooting at us for all they knew how. We stuck our guns between the rails and put a volley into them and those that didn't get shot jumped up and ran like wildfire, and we went over the fence after them."

Roe, falling back up the hill, noted "the rebels . . . climb[ed] our fence in a surprisingly brief time after we [left] it."

At the top of the hill, Lt. Daniel Harmon of the 9th was restoring the line and yelling, "Rally round your flag, boys!" which Roe noted was "the refrain of Root's 'Battle Hymn.'" The new line was based on an old sunken road that ran across the hill field and down toward an ancient spring next to the river.

Then Terry discovered that he had turned up from the river too soon. He needed someone farther north, behind Seward. He sorted out Col. J.H. Funk's old Stonewall Brigade veterans (the 2nd, 4th, 5th, 27th and 33rd), told the men to fall back again across the cornfield to the river. Then Funk led them at a run, concealed by the river bank, until they reached the damp and cool hollow where the spring issued. They again turned to the right and climbed up from the river bottom, and, as Worsham recalled, "There was Gordon. I shall recollect him to my dying day. Not another man was in sight. He was sitting on his horse as quietly as if nothing was going on. He was wearing his old red shirt, with the sleeves pulled up a little, the only indication that he was ready for a fight."

Gordon spurred his horse down to meet Funk's brigade. They could hear all hell breaking loose away to their right, in the fields around Araby, and behind them as well, from across the river, where Davis and Brown were fighting their way across the railroad bridge.

"Hurry up, boys!" Gordon said, and turned his horse to lead the column. Soon they were at the northern end of the boundary fence and could see another fence, that of Thomas's hill field, about two hundred yards ahead and "a line of Yankees" running for the riverbank beside it at "right-shoulder-shift arms," which made Worsham think it looked "more like a drill than a movement in battle."

It was the 110th Ohio, moving at a dead run, trying to prevent Terry turning the flank. The Ohioans and the two battalions of the 9th New York to their left had spent most of the day "laying . . . on the brow of the hill." Starting as the farthest left regiment of Ricketts's initial line, the 110th had become the farthest right when the division changed front to face south.

Now that it was engaged, however, it found itself in a pickle, subject, as Col. Binkley said, to the "murderous fire of musketry and artillery, the latter coming obliquely from the front and rear and directly from the right." As the last unit, the 110th's right flank was wide open, fully exposed to confederate cannon across the river. Pvt. Henry Robinson Berkeley of the Amherst Artillery recalled that "about three forty-five P.M. we heard, on our right, some heavy fighting in a big field of corn. We immediately opened on the Yanks in our front." And now came Funk up the hill from the river.

The fired-up Virginians in front started yelling, "At them, boys!" but Gordon restrained his troops. "Keep quiet! We'll have our time presently." He asked the boys to pull down the fence so he could step his horse through. A hundred men had followed him through, and Gordon lost control as the troops sent up a shout of "Charge! Charge!" Worsham reported that the men, knowing that he who fired first would have the distinct advantage, "were perfectly wild when they came in sight of the enemy's column." He thought that "nothing but a shot through each man" could have prevented the charge.

"With a yell," Worsham said, "we were at the fence." Gunfire sprang northward and the federal line quavered.

One fence.

One red shirt.

Its position untenable, the 110th rapidly "retreated a few rods" over the hill to the

Georgetown pike, leaving uncovered what was left of the 9th New York's right flank. There, as Terry's battle lines advanced, Seward's horse was shot. It rolled as it went down, injuring him severely. Two of his men had rushed to hold him up so he could continue to direct the unit when they saw, down the hillside ahead of them, Lt. Col. E.P. Taft of the 9th pitch forward from his black horse as a ball hit his leg; the horse bolted toward the rear as Taft's men carried him to the shade of a tree. As Seward shouted out orders for the rescue of Taft, the confederate line engulfed the tree and Taft disappeared from view. One of Seward's men grabbed a riderless mule that was running by. It had no bridle, so they tied a silk handerchief to the mule's mouth and hoisted the colonel aboard. He turned up the hill toward the Washington road.

July 9, 4:30 P.M.—Sound the Retreat

Hit with flanking fire and unable to form a line against Terry's attack, McClennan's brigade began to buckle. Now the whole of Gordon, those still living from 2,500 men, was pushing up the hills from the south. Sensing victory, the ranks began a cheer which was answered from across the river by observing troops as the federal line began to vanish from the hill field and drain rapidly toward Gambrill's mill and the farm roads beyond.

"This was the most exciting time I witnessed during the war," Worsham wrote afterward. For Porter Wren of Co. F, it was also the last. The retreating Yanks stopped at the road and fired back; Wren was hit in the breast. He managed to walk all the way back to the fence, started to climb it, and fell over dead.

July 9, 4:00 P.M.—Along The Fence

Cpl. Roderick Clark, who had been wounded and abandoned earlier, regained consciousness and managed to crawl about twenty feet, to the protection of a rail fence on the west side of Araby's lower field. He lay under intense musket fire from the units along the Washington road above. "I never heard miniés fly so fast or sound so spiteful . . . cutting the weeds and throwing the dirt all over me."

Two soldiers came up and threw themselves down just behind Clark, whom they assumed dead, and "as they fired, the muzzles of their guns were within a few inches. . . . To prevent burning my face, I put my hat over my eyes. I had just taken my hand away when a ball . . . struck the hat and . . . burned my forehead, passed on, and killed a Rebel stone dead," hitting the man just over the eye.

The galling fire that Truex was pouring down from the Washington road toward the hapless Clark also greeted the Georgians, who by now had pushed past Araby. As Capt. B.S. Boatwright of the 12th Georgia Battalion came up beside a young man who was prone in the grass and peering toward the Thomas gate, a ball whizzed straight through the grass and hit the boy in the forehead, killing him instantly. Boatwright covered him with his blanket and left him there. He and a four others jumped up and started for the gate; a volley from there killed two and wounded two, left only the captain standing, his coat riddled with bullet holes.

In the next moment, the battle was over. Terry came up the hill field, and the union line simply unrolled and disappeared to the north. One moment less and the boys would have lived.

July 9—Escape From the Ravine

As Terry's Virginians from the riverbank were turning Ricketts's right and the Georgia and Louisiana brigades were swarming irresistibly down the hill toward the pike, McDougal and his comrades in the 126th Ohio were still crouched in the ravine. Two of them had been badly wounded. "Judge of our surprise when . . . it was discovered that the Rebs had flanked us on the right and gobbled up the most of our regiment." He began to crawl back through the ravine, looking in vain for a place to escape, as the gray infantry poured up the hill on either side of him. Despite the heart-pounding excitement, it occurred to him that "I could not surrender with a loaded gun." He noticed on a nearby knoll "a confederate flag surrounded by some fifteen or twenty of its followers. . . . I raised my gun and sent my best wishes into their midst." Then he threw down the rifle and sat down to await capture. But he couldn't stand the thought—"it was the most horrid thought that had ever entered my mind"—and he jumped up, grabbed his gun and made a run for it across the field and up the hill toward the Washington road. He heard voices ordering him to halt and heard the banging as they "sent shot after shot after me, till the air appeared alive." One Confederate made a desperate attempt to run him down, but McDougal abandoned his knapsack with his diary and a picture of his girl friend, and made good his escape.

July 9, 4:30 P.M.—The 10th Vermont Runs For Its Life

Col. Henry's 10th Vermont had anchored Ricketts's far left all day, and now they had to double-time up the steep, wooded slope behind them under intense fire to avoid being cut off and captured as the line to their right collapsed under the weight of the confederate advance. Up they ran, leaving their screaming wounded behind. In the tangled woods above Gambrill's mill, both Vermont color bearers collapsed. Cpl. Alexander Scott picked up both flags, no mean feat, and carried them for eight more miles, until the exhausted soldiers stumbled into Monrovia Station and saw sitting on the track a steaming locomotive and empty passenger cars.

July 9, 5:00 P.M.—Along the Fence

Painful reality became a nightmare for the wounded Clark as his comrades disappeared from the crest and the pursuing rebel infantry paused to plunder. One large man stopped and pulled off his boots, causing Clark "almost unbearable" pain. The man then saw the bullet hole in the left boot and threw them to the ground, swearing, "What a god damned shame to spoil so good a boot!"

The next man took his watch—"you won't be able to see what time it is for very long, Yank"—his empty pocketbook, knife and picture album. On the latter, Clark held out his hand, saying, "Please . . ." The Reb threw it back.

Next appeared "a mere boy." Clark, "dying with thirst," asked for "water, please."

The boy stopped and put his hand on his bayonet.

"Water? I would rather give you this!" He walked on ten steps, then returned, his hand still on the bayonet. Clark decided his life was about to end, "but I did not care much, for I thought it was impossible for me to live long anyway."

Instead, the lad handed Clark his canteen.

"We are not as bad as you think us," the boy said.

July 9, 5:00 P.M.—Pursuit

Perhaps Early's artillery held its fire because the Confederates, too, needed the bridge as the formidable army before them began to dissolve and drain rapidly away from the landscape, almost disappearing before their eyes.

After waiting all day for the chance, Johnston's North Carolinians were now seized with the mania of combat. Col. Tom Toon of the 20th North Carolina Infantry grabbed the regimental flag and led his troops across the railroad bridge, devil take the hindmost. As the Carolinians poured onto the east bank, they overran the field hospital at Gambrill's mill and captured three hundred Federals in the woods to the east of the mill.

Old Jube, sitting in the catbird seat with a wagon train that stretched nine miles behind him and $200,000 piled up in one of the wagons, didn't need a lot of prisoners, and he called in the pursuit. But the day was gone, and, as Keats said, all its sweets were gone—those sweets for Early being the minutes and hours that might have been better spent on the road to Washington.

In the failing light, Gordon rode over to the small creek and fence line just below Araby, where very hard fighting had occurred, and took notice in his official report of what he found. "So profuse was the flow of blood from the killed and wounded of both these forces that it reddened the stream for more than a hundred yards below."

The stream still flows in the same place and same manner, coiling around the foot of the ridge before emptying into the Monocacy, and there cows rest on hot afternoons in the shade of its trees, and flies hum and wasps drone and a meadowlark sings and is gone.

X.
Aftermath of Battle

Saturday, July 9, 6:00 P.M.—The Jug Bridge

With the retreat from Araby, the scene of action began to shift northward. The federal army moved rapidly toward the Baltimore pike (and the B&O and transportation) by way of a narrow county road that ran from Gambrill's mill. Alexander's ammunition was almost gone, and he knew he might need it on the retreat, so he, too, wheeled his guns out of their hilltop positions and took them up the county road.

When the head of the retreating column came out onto the pike, Wallace galloped to the Jug Bridge and told E.B. Tyler that the whole federal army would soon be passing behind his back. He must hold the bridge at all hazards, even until the enemy appeared in his rear, and at all costs, until the last of the retreating units had come out onto the pike and gone down it to New Market. Tyler saluted and, with his aides, captains F.I.D. Webb and E.Y. Goldsborough, went to the bridge to assume command.

Not long afterward, around six P.M., Rodes moved in force against Allison Brown's positions on the west bank. Tyler sent Goldsborough down the east bank a few miles, to a meadow at Reich's Ford, just below the hamlet of Bartonsville, to tell Col. Landstreet to take the 11th Maryland out of there and head for New Market immediately. Goldsborough watched the Baltimore city boys scamper up the country road toward the pike, then found Tyler watching the struggle east of the bridge from the vantage of a hill on the west bank.

"They're gone," he reported. "The only troops left on the Monocacy field are these," and he gestured toward the smoke and firing across the stream.

"Get them out as well," Tyler ordered. As Brown's men began to run back across the bridge, an orderly galloped up to Tyler with distressing news. "General, the rebels are in our rear at Bartonsville."

All hell broke loose as an artillery shell hit the bridge while men were running across; they panicked, wanted to break and run. On the west bank, Col. Brown ran up a hill to an orchard, where he rallied his retreating command, and they made a stand. The volleys they fired across the river into the advancing infantry caused a pause there but, even more importantly, they changed fire to their south, on their own side of the river, where a skirmish line was closing in on what was left of Tyler's flank. In this brave manner Brown was able to depart the field in order with about three hundred of his command intact and make his way to New Market, Maryland. Others broke their guns and threw them down and looked for a place to hide or escape.

Tyler rode toward Bartonsville with his staff of six to estimate the depth of penetration on his flank, and he quickly realized his error in judgement. His party had just reached the top of a hill at the entrance to the road leading to a house owned by N.O. Cline, when a party of confederate cavalry charged from the orchard at Bartonsville.

Cut off from an escape route to the east, Tyler had no option but to race up the road past Cline's house, then down past the mill near Hughs's Ford, with the yelping Confederates directly on his heels. The chase continued up the east bank toward the Liberty road, the route that Bradley Johnson had taken that morning. The panting riders saw clouds of dust rising above the Woodsboro road, which led to the Liberty road and Frederick. It was more confederate cavalry, whose movement would surely cut them off.

Undaunted, Tyler and his group spurred ahead madly, reaching the Liberty road ahead of the Confederates and opening some distance between them and the pursuit. Turning eastward, toward Baltimore, hope of escape sprang up.

Their luck was bad, however, for at the village of Mount Pleasant they rode squarely into a squad of confederate cavalry plundering a store. After a sudden and sharp exchange of fire, only Tyler, Webb and Goldsborough continued out of town, but not far. After a mile, the officers saw that they were being pursued and knew their flagging mounts would carry them no farther. They turned into the woods, where Webb's horse collapsed. Tyler and Goldsborough dismounted, pulled up Webb's horse, and then whipped all three animals down the road. The pursuers, who were chasing the dust, followed the animals.

Winded, shaking with fatigue and covered with dust, the three officers, with Webb limping badly from his spill, went deeper into the woods and there by chance met a "colored man named Ridgley, who piloted us to a safe hiding place in a dense thicket." Probably upon Ridgley's advice, Tyler and Goldsborough helped Webb to the house of Ephriam Creager, "a Unionist" who took him in, and then made their way, like wild animals, to their hiding place in the wildwood.

July 9, 6:00 P.M.—Road to Urbana

Wallace's retreat to the north had, in effect, abandoned the 8th Illinois Cavalry that stood far down on his left flank. The companies that had gone down river in the morning to burn the bridges were completely isolated. Two companies under Levi

Wells made their way along the hilly and narrow roads on the skirt of Sugarloaf Mountain and then eastward through Dickerson and Beallsville, knowing they would fight another day.

Five miles north of Wells, and still south of the main line of retreat, Clendenin pulled the remaining three companies of the 8th Illinois away from the collapsing federal front and down the Washington road, pursued by McCausland. Although McCausland had suffered terrible losses early in the day, he was in motion again with a thousand troopers, the 17th Virginia in the lead, pounding down the Washington road. He had it in his mind to drive through Clendenin and turn north to New Market by way of Monrovia to cut off Wallace's retreat.

When the first unit of the 17th reached Urbana, the riders paused at the temptation of Cockey's store and the thought of a cool drink to wash the hot dust from their throats. They must have forgotten whom they were chasing when they dismounted and tied up their horses, for Clendenin, watching the proceedings from the porch of the Dixon house at the intersection of the Urbana and Monrovia roads just east of town, was in his saddle in an instant and leading a party down the hill. In the ensuing melée of pistol fire and swinging sabers, Clendenin himself seized the "Night Hawk Rangers" battle flag of Co. E and captured the color-bearer.

As the rest of the 17th came up, Clendenin withdrew and formed a line.

Unit historian Abner Hand reported: "[Maj. Smith] rode boldly forward of his regiment and fired his pistol into our ranks. . . . The rear guard of the 8th, under Lt. [J. Wayland] Trask of Co. K, stood their ground. . . . Sgt. [Harrison] Hakes of Co. B and Cpl. Mighell of Co. K were in front of our line, exchanging shots with the rebel Major and one of his men, when Mighell gave the reins of his horse to Hakes and dismounting leveled his carbine at the Major and killed him at the first fire, and the second brought down his companion."

Clendenin withdrew in good order toward Monrovia, where he provided Wallace's rear guard. McCausland, having had enough of this day, broke it off. His intention was not to chase Glendenin toward Baltimore but to head out in the morning down the wide open Washington road.

July 9—Evening

As the great noise subsided and the tide of battle flowed northward, John Worthington climbed out of his cellar and went into the yard, where he saw Gen. Breckinridge, who had observed the battle from there. As he walked toward him, Breckinridge dismounted and extended his hand. It is likely that Worthington had voted for him four years earlier. When Maryland went to the polls in November of 1860, Breckinridge carried the state with 42,497 votes, following closely by John Hood Bell with 41,177. Lincoln received a paltry 2,294, one reason he never felt secure about Maryland sympathies.

As Worthington extended his right hand to shake the general's, a bullet knocked his cane out of his left hand.

"Mr. Worthington, it is not safe for you to be here. Bullets are still flying."

"It is just as dangerous for you, General!"

"But it is my duty to be here."

Worthington went back to his cellar.

July 9, Late Evening—Araby

The Worthington family emerged from their cellar later that evening, into a scene lifted straight out of hell. The fields of Araby were darkened by a great crop of the dead. The once bucolic summer landscape of their gentle river valley was littered with dead and wounded, and in their cornfield, their pasture, their wheatfield, their yard and their garden men screamed in pain, groaned in agony. Here and there the dry wheat stubble blazed, ignited by gunfire, burning the wounded men who were unable to escape the spreading flames.

A stricken soldier in gray lay bleeding to death in the back yard, in the angle made by the wings of the house. Mrs. Worthington went to him to hear his last words, later to be sent to his wife and children.

A Yankee lay propped against a tree in the front yard, bleeding internally. John Worthington found a confederate doctor at work among the wounded and sent him to give the man morphine; he died that night.

At the rear of the house they found Lt. Col. John Hodges of the 9th Louisiana, his right arm shattered by a minié ball but still standing. The Worthington sons, Glenn and Harry, were sent into the wheatfield to gather sheaves to make a bed, and Hodges was made to lie down near the fence until an ambulance carried him into Frederick.

Field hospitals were set up at the Worthington and Thomas houses, at Gambrill's mill and along the Washington road near the Yaste house. Some lucky officers were dispatched to nearby homes. Capt. Chauncey Harris of Co. C, 14th New Jersey, had been struck twice—once in the shoulder by an enemy taking deliberate aim and again while lying in an ambulance by a stray ball that shattered his knee. He was carted down Baker's Valley road to the Baker farm and turned over to Miss Clementine.

Lying in agony near the fence, Cpl. Clark was, incredibly, still alive. A confederate battery had moved up quite close to him. One of the gunners went down to the river for water for his horse and on his way back noticed Clark.

"What is your regiment?" he asked.

"Fourteenth New Jersey."

"That was the regiment that guarded about nine hundred of us to Fort Delaware after the battle of Antietam. You used us well, and I will do the same for you."

He propped Clark on knapsacks and blankets and left a bucket of water near his hand. Later, during the night, both federal and confederate doctors came to call, and the confederate gave Clark a drink of whiskey.

Clark was not carried from the field on a confederate stretcher until ten o'clock the following morning. He was placed in an ambulance with two wounded Rebs. Since the bridge had been burned, the wagon had to ford the river; as it climbed the steep western bank, Clark was almost thrown into the river, going into the water (with his broken ankle) up to his knees. He saved himself by hanging onto hoops inside the ambulance.

As they passed through the depot, Clark noticed that the station house and water tower and other buildings had been set afire, and two guns were banging away at the railroad bridge to knock it down.

Garrett's beloved bridge that had practically caused the battle of Monocacy, the one whose destruction he feared so deeply, could not be destroyed! Early's artillery hammered away at point blank range, but could not knock it down or faze its iron shoulders. They finally gave up.

Counting the Dead

Clark finally arrived at the federal hospital in Frederick at eleven A.M., some seventeen hours after he was wounded. There were no nurses, all having been sent away to prevent their capture, but the ladies of Frederick had nobly come forward to fill in, and one, Miss Lissie Ott, soon had Clark in her gentle care.

Slowly they rolled into old Frederick, the wagons and carts and ambulances with the dead, the dying, and the wounded—more than seven hundred men who were torn, broken, gashed by shot and shell and knife and bayonet, stinking from sweat and fear and excrement, grimed by heat and dirt and clay and river mud. And the surgeons in their blood-spattered aprons worked in their butcher shops, sawing on legs and arms, feet and hands. Col. Taft of the 9th New York had his wounded leg sawn away.

Lt. John Spangler of Co. A, 87th Pennsylvania, badly wounded by a ball that hit him in the breast and took a bad turn downward, was taken to the home of the widow Ruth Doffler, who wrote to John's father in York that his son was not expected to live.

No one can be sure of the size of the harvest as that great gray grim one lurched and swayed through the summer fields—snick-snap, snick-snap, boys tumbling, heads rolling, arms cracking. Some regiments suffered far more than others. On the morning after the battle, as Maj. John Patterson of the 14th New Jersey recalled, only ninety-two rifles were stacked from a unit that had sent 256 men into the fight. Of their fifteen officers, two were dead (captains Henry Conine and Henry Stults) and eight wounded. Of the color guard, two were dead, including the color sergeant, and eight wounded.

Many of the 14th's missing had been captured or wandered off to regroup later, but twenty-four had been killed and eighty-seven wounded, according to Capt. Goldsborough, who later produced a history of the battle. The only unit to suffer casualties so high was the 9th New York, which fought in the western triangle and on the eastern hill field and lost thirteen dead and eighty-nine wounded. The 106th New York counted sixteen dead and seventy-three wounded, the 151st New York twenty-four dead and forty-five wounded.

Altogether, Goldsborough estimated that Wallace's army had suffered 123 killed, 605 wounded and 668 captured—1,294 lost to further service.

The confederate losses, it is now thought, were under-reported. Gordon alone admitted his loss in killed and wounded was "by tabular report of brigade commanders" only two shy of seven hundred. George Nichols, of the badly battered 61st Georgia, said that Evans's brigade alone had lost over five hundred men killed and wounded.

Federal estimates by body-count and by those carried wounded to the homes and hospitals of Frederick were 275 Confederates killed and 435 wounded, a total of 710. But since Gordon's loss alone was about that number, and there were uncounted and unreported losses among Ramseur's and Rodes's divisions, the estimate is too low.

On the centennial of the battle, local historian Albert E. Conradis concluded that "it is not inconceivable that the Confederates lost between thirteen and fifteen hundred killed and wounded."

July 9—Night

After corralling seven hundred prisoners along the roads eastward, Early called in his cavalry. It had been a long day for the infantry, and he still had forty miles to march with a force down to eight thousand foot soldiers, a thousand cavalry and forty guns manned by seven hundred men. While confederate camp fires sprang up along the Monocacy, the roads to New Market and Urbana were filled with exhausted but desperate survivors walking east. In Washington, a light burned in the study of Henry Halleck, who was running the war for Lincoln. He had already agreed with Grant that the XIX Corps, coming up from Louisiana, should keep moving to Washington. Now, late at night, he summoned an aide to send another telegram to Grant, asking for the other two divisions of the VI Corps. But Grant had long before issued the order, and as Early's army walked away from the Monocacy on Sunday morning, July 10, the veteran remaining soldiers of the Greek Cross corps were already walking over the gangplanks of steamers docked at City Point.

It would be a race for the capital.

July 9—City Point, 5:30 P.M.

Grant still had Hunter on his brain, believing that Hunter could somehow get back into the Valley and cut Lee's supply lines at Charlottesville and cut Early off from a retreat, but Halleck was now insisting: "If you propose to cut off this raid . . . we must have more forces here." He wanted Grant to forward the XIX Corps, then due to arrive in Virginia from New Orleans, directly to Washington. If he did that, Grant said, he wanted that corps back before the end of the month.

The seriousness of the situation finally registered on the reluctant Grant when Halleck told him that he believed that a full third of Lee's army was with Early. My

God—had Lee so outsmarted and outmaneuvered him? Had he actually slipped a third of his army around Grant's back? Was it possible that Lee could capture Washington before Grant could take Richmond? Was this really happening?

Without further hesitation he ordered the rest of the VI Corps, three thousand men under Maj. Gen. Horatio Wright, to Washington by fast steamer, ordered the six-thousand-man XIX Corps to keep on moving to Washington, and promised they would all be there to defend the city and defeat Early by Monday night, July 11. He told Halleck that he himself would be ready to leave with an hour's notice if Lincoln wanted him there. Lincoln thought it would be nice if he came, but Grant changed his mind. He thought it might not look good.

July 9—Evening, Westminster

It was late in the afternoon when mad Harry Gilmor's little unit of twenty men formed up, drew sabers, and charged into Westminster, and found a few sympathizers applauding, but mostly drawn shutters and locked doors in the nearly empty streets. When Bradley Johnson later came up with the column, "secesh" families brought out bread and crackers for those lucky enough to get them.

July 9, Evening—The Battlefield

As John Gordon slowly walked his horse away from the scenes of death and harm, the former vice president of the United States, also making his way back to Frederick, fell in beside him.

"Well, John," he said, "if you never fought another fight, you've just fought one that will immortalize you."

Gordon's reply is not recorded.

July 9, Night—Gambrill's Orchard

John Worsham's 21st Virginia had been among Terry's men who had marched fourteen miles from Middletown that morning and fought all day. They had run a short way after the fleeing Yanks and then called it a day, setting up camp at sunset in Gambrill's apple orchard near the Washington pike. Several of the men had gone to the mill pond for a bath. Lord, how they needed one.

Worsham spied around among the slain until he found a dead Yankee with a full haversack, which he pulled off him. He was sitting by his campfire, eating what was in the pack, when he heard a wounded man asking for water.

Worsham went over to him, a Yankee.

"You have a canteen?" he asked.

The man shook his head. "One of your boys took it."

Worsham took one of his two, filled it at the pond and gave it to the "poor fellow." He then offered him dinner from the haversack.

"Thank you, I have my own," the man replied.

"You listen," said Worsham, "if anybody tries to take away that canteen, you tell 'em how you got it. You tell 'em where you got it. You tell 'em the 21st Virginia gave it to you."

He went back to his fire, still somewhat angry about the broken promise of the morning. "We thought we would *witness* the battle," he told his journal, "but instead our little army saw our division of twenty-three hundred men whip Wallace's force of ten thousand." After that day's work, Worsham "went to bed for the night."

July 9, Night—Death Visits Woodlands

Wallace directed Ricketts and Alexander and the main units of his army to retreat eastward along the Baltimore turnpike because he knew he could pick up the B&O at New Market and outdistance any pursuit. From Baltimore, troops could hasten as well by rail down to Washington by way of Relay and Annapolis Junction. The 8th Illinois had been forced backward along the Washington pike as far as Urbana, but there were other, parallel roads to Washington. Farthest south, in the shadow of an old Indian trail, the Mouth of Monocacy road ran to the east from Dickerson, through Beallsville, Dawsonville, Darnestown and Hunting Hill to Rockville. Between that route and the National Road was a third way to Rockville, from below Sugarloaf and Mt. Ephraim to Barnesville, Blocktown, Boyds, Germantown, Clopper and Gaithersburg, where it, too, joined the National Road.

It was along this middle route, the most direct to Washington from where he had been cut off from Wallace's army, that Capt. Levi Wells directed companies C and I of the 8th Illinois. Right behind him came the completely dogged McCausland, who had the crippled 17th chasing Clendenin and the mauled 14th chasing Wells.

Toward close of day, Co. D from the 14th came riding down into the cool, oak-sheltered Great Seneca Valley along the road from Germantown to Clopper and its mill. They stopped for water and what supper they could scavenge at the roadside house of Joseph Taney. As they stood on the front porch, a scout from the 8th Illinois appeared like a blue wraith on the road. A musket banged, and Billy Scott, a young private, crumpled over clutching his stomach.

The only place to get help in the neighborhood was at Woodlands, the Clopper's big manor house in the nearby woods. The wounded man managed to stay astride his horse long enough to reach Woodlands, where he crawled onto the porch. The black servant who found him ran screaming into the house.

Woodlands had been built in 1811 for Francis Cassatt Clopper (among whose decendants would be the Pennsylvania Railroad Cassatts, including the artist, Mary) and his Irish wife, Ann Jayne Byrne. In 1834, Clopper had built the grist mill beside which the town of Clopper had grown. Woodlands was now managed by William Rich Hutton, who would become a famed engineer (Annapolis Water Works, C&O Canal, Western Maryland Railroad, Washington Bridge over the Harlem). In 1855, upon his return from several years in California, he had married Francis and Ann's daughter, Mary Augusta,

It was Hutton who ordered that the young trooper be carried from the porch to the parlor, where he was laid on the floor, and had a doctor summoned.

Billy Scott was twenty-one years old. He had grown up on a farm in West Virginia's Greenbrier County. His elder brother, Rankin, who also served in the 14th, would fight through the whole war and get back home.

Mary Augusta asked if the lad had a religion.

"Yes, ma'm, my folks are Baptists."

"Have you been baptized?"

"No, ma'm."

"Do you want to be baptized?"

"Yes, ma'm. I do."

Fetching a bowl of water, Mary baptized the young man in the name of the Father and the Son and the Holy Ghost, and he died.

That night a coffin was cut and nailed, and the body was carried up the hill to the graveyard of St. Rose of Lima Catholic Church, where it was buried secretly, in an unmarked grave. Accounts differ as to whether the trooper ever revealed his name.

July 9, 5:15 P.M.—Washington

Lincoln to Garrett:

> What have you heard about battle at Monocacy today? We have nothing about it here except what you say.

July 9, 7:30 P.M.—Baltimore

Garrett to Lincoln:

> Word from a Wallace aid at Monrovia telegraph is that Wallace was beaten at Monocacy. This is hearsay.

July 9, 11:40 P.M.—Near Monocacy

Wallace to Stanton and Halleck:

> From Crossing of the Baltimore Pike and Railroad: You will have to use every exertion to save Baltimore and Washington.

July 9, 11:57 P.M.—*Washington*

Halleck to Wallace:

> The President orders you to rally your troops and retard the Confederate advance toward Baltimore.

Obviously, for Washington, Halleck was turning elsewhere for help.

Sunday, July 10, 12:30 A.M.—*Washington*

Halleck to Grant:

> Wallace has suffered a serious defeat at Monocacy Junction. He reports twenty thousand enemy.

July 9, Night—The Battlefield

Rodes's men had seen some hot action in fits and starts near the Jug Bridge during the day, but now the quiet smoke from the campfires and still-burning fields blended with the lingering haze of the day's own heat, all of it smudging the summer stars. The corpses owned the night, and doctors and hospital orderlies moved with painstaking slowness among them on the battlefield. Lt. Col. Theodore O'Hara, who served with the 12th Alabama although he was a Kentuckian, must have recited at least a few lines of his fitting poem, written after the Mexican War's battle of Buena Vista, in 1847. "The Bivouac of the Dead" became a Civil War favorite.

> *The muffled drum's sad roll has beat*
> *The soldier's last tattoo;*
> *No more on life's parade shall meet*
> *That brave and fallen few.*
>
> *On Fame's eternal camping ground*
> *Their silent tents are spread,*
> *And glory guards, with solemn round,*
> *The bivouac of the dead.*

XI.
The Road to Rockville

Sunday, July 10, Morning—North of Baltimore

The tracks of the Northern Central that connected the port of Baltimore to the farms and mines of Pennsylvania ran through the valley of Jones Falls and then north through the hamlets of Padonia and Texas to Cockeysville and Ashton. From a few miles north of the city, it was roughly paralleled all the way into Pennsylvania by the old York road.

Coming from Westminster to the northwest of Baltimore, Bradley Johnson's troopers rode as far as Reisterstown along the Baltimore-Westminster road but then angled off across country through Glyndon and the Worthington and Green Spring valleys. Dirt farm roads took them to the Northern Central tracks at Texas.

Gilmor's 2nd Maryland had reached Texas earlier, so when Johnson and his command came up the York road to Cockeysville around nine A.M., a pillar of black smoke already stood over the railroad bridge across the Gunpowder River, three miles to the northeast. They spent the morning cutting the telegraph and tearing up the tracks as far north as Ashland.

Johnson, with an eye on his rendezvous at Point Lookout, consulted with Gilmor and divided the command. The railroad to Philadelphia and New York, the Philadelphia, Wilmington and Baltimore, lay twenty miles to the east of Cockeysville; its most vulnerable point was at the mile-long wooden bridge over the mouth of the Gunpowder River. Johnson told Gilmor to ride over there and cut the railroad and the telegraph, and he would swing west around Baltimore and strike for the rail line between Washington and Baltimore at Laurel, then head for Point Lookout.

Thinking he would have a command of five hundred men, Gilmor was put out when Johnson seconded to him only fifty men from the 1st Maryland under Lt. W.H. Dorsey; with his own serviceably mounted troopers, that made only one hundred thirty-five. But, as always, Gilmor was game.

The emerald valleys to the northwest of Baltimore were the setting for many of colonial Maryland's largest and wealthiest estates. The Ridgely's huge Hampton (now a national historic site), built in 1790 in the Dulaney Valley, was surrounded by five thousand acres, as was Charles Carroll's Clynmalira up near Monkton. Nearby My Lady's Manor, a gift from the third Lord Baltimore to his fourth wife, counted ten thousand acres. Charles Carroll's the Surgeon's Home in west Baltimore, Mount Clare, built in 1754, had terraced gardens and walks running for a mile down to Gwynn's Falls. The Dorseys, Hansons, Worthingtons, Hammonds and their ilk and kin enjoyed a way of life impossible without slaves, so secession ran rampant through this baronial region. At Lamb's School, four miles up the road from Cockeysville, John Wilkes Booth and his brother Edwin were educated. Just beyond was Gorsuch Tavern and the stone barn where Edward Gorsuch traded slaves. Thirteen years before, two slaves had escaped from him and made their way via the underground railroad to Lancaster. Gorsuch went after them and was shot dead for his trouble by the family that protected them.

As Gilmor led his command southward, toward Towson, Johnson turned his horse northward and then westward along Shawan Road to Hayfields, the estate of his friend John Merryman. In the southern way, they were cousins. A Philpot had married a Johnson in 1796, and one of their sons had married Sarah Merryman of Monkton.

John Merryman was already a famous prisoner and personage in the annals of the law. In 1861, on April 19, the eighty-sixth anniversary of the battle of Lexington, a Baltimore mob had assaulted troops of the 6th Massachusetts who were being transported in horse-drawn cars from the President Street Station to Camden Yards to board a locomotive for Washington. An angry mob had thrown sand and ship's anchors over the rails, cutting off four companies, about two hundred twenty men under Capt. A.S. Follansbee, who then attempted to march his detachment along the tracks. They were assaulted with rocks and bottles and finally fired upon with pistols. The Yanks returned fire, and when the smoke cleared four soldiers and twelve civilians were dead and more than fifty people gunshot.

One way to prevent such incidents was to keep troops away from the city, so the next day Merryman, a militia officer, helped to burn the railroad bridges over the Bush and Gunpowder Rivers. On May 24, at two A.M., he was awakened at his home, arrested and held without charge. To obtain his release, his lawyer obtained a writ of *habeas corpus* from none other than the chief justice of the United States, Roger B. Taney, who journeyed to Baltimore to issue it in person. Taney had been looking for such a test of the lawfulness of Lincoln's suspension of *habeas corpus* by executive proclamation when the war began. Gen. George Cadwallader, who was holding Merryman, asserted that he had authority to suspend the writ. Taney held him in contempt; Cadwallader ignored the summons to appear. Taney then issued in writing his opinion that the president, even as commander-in-chief, was not empowered by the Constitution to suspend *habeas corpus*, a common law protection for Englishman and American for centuries (*Ex Parte Merryman* Fed. Case no. 9487). That right, Taney argued, resides only with the Congress. In 1863, the Congress did delegate that power to the president, but with considerable reluctance. Before the year was out,

Baltimore's mayor, chief of police, thirty-one state legislators and a dozen Maryland congressmen, plus assorted judges and newspaper editors, were behind bars in Fort McHenry, charged with nothing and unable to bail themselves out. Federal troops occupied the city and held it under practical martial law throughout the war.

For Johnson, those few hours at Hayfields, amid "the charming society, the lovely girls, the balmy July air, and the luxuriant verdure" of the estate was a return to a gentler time of his life. Some forty miles south of there, along the road to Rockville, Early's exhausted troops were falling in the roadsides.

July 10—Road to Rockville

The men who made that march remembered it all of their lives. Many of them had walked half way around the world behind a mule and a plow, breaking and riding over great morsels of red clay, and many had walked long miles to find a place where deer would, maybe, be found in the fall, but this march was an endless treadmill in a brown, gritty cloud, where the dust clotted bloody wounds and the throat hawked up gobbets of dark spittle and each crease of skin was sanded raw.

Worsham remembered that day as "terribly hot, and the men straggled a great deal" even though word swept the column that Yankee cavalry from Harpers Ferry was right behind them, sweeping up stragglers. There was some truth in the rumor. Henry Kyd Douglas was in the rear with Ramseur, who had instructions to destroy the Monocacy railroad bridge. Douglas, like the wounded Clark before him, "noted a ludicrous attempt on the part of a battery of artillery to knock it to pieces with solid shot. This delay threw us much in the rear of the rest of the column," so much so that they were soon being annoyed by enemy cavalry.

The sun reached ever higher in the hot July sky and the humidity seemed to clot the brown air as the columns went on, over hill and dale. McCausland's troopers led the way, their mounts walking head down with flagging tongues, through roadside hamlets like Urbana and Hyattstown and Clarksburg . These little towns had long known the tread of soldiers. Clarksburg, on elevated Parr's Ridge, was named for an Indian trader who established himself where the old Seneca trail running north-south crossed the path to Frederick and the west. A tavern had been built by Michael Ashford Dowden as early as 1752, and it was there that Gen. Edward Braddock camped in a snow storm in April of 1755 and where Andrew Jackson dined in 1829 on his way to his inauguration as president.

The Washington road sounded like an important thoroughfare, and it was, historically, being one of the earliest roads in Maryland, linking the Frederick and Cumberland valleys with the Tidewater at the Potomac. But in reality, it was a narrow dirt pathway about eight feet wide that wound through farmland, past humble cabins and houses whose front porches were only four or five feet from the road. It was a land of small farmers and scattered slaves. Of the 18,322 people who lived in Montgomery County in 1860, seven thousand were black. Of that number, fifteen hundred were free. (The Quakers around Sandy Spring had long since freed their slaves). The 5,421 slaves were scattered among many small farms; only one in every five farmers owned more than ten slaves.

It was a favored country they were marching through, even though they could not see much of it through the dust and sweat. The settlers called it sugarland because of the maples. Drained by big creeks like Bennett's and Seneca, rolling pastures swept past islands of oak and beech, and stout brick farmhouses with wooden porches peered over fields of corn.

Between the America those scenes represented and the America that would emerge from this war would be the real rip in American history. The little places they passed through had grown around grants of land from an English king to a favored subject. Colonial life depended upon rolling the tobacco in huge hogsheads down to market, and moving the produce by wagon to feed the upstart towns like Georgetown and Montgomery Court House.

The bottom line was that the economy was built on one person enslaving another. It was the Banquo's ghost at Philadelphia in 1776, this question of one person enslaving another because the welfare of the majority demanded it. It was the great debate that never took place. It was the language written by Jefferson for the Declaration of Independence, charging the English king with responsibility for this odious system—language struck out of that document at the insistence of the southern colonies.

The colonial fabric woven in 1776 ripped apart in 1860 because it had that terrible weakness in it from the beginning, and no one was willing to do anything about it. Once the question came down, it had to be faced; our civil war became institutional, motivated not by the American but by the Industrial Revolution; the fatigued men who marched up and down the dusty roads of the 1860s were more spiritual kin to the doughboys of 1918 than the rebels of 1776.

So here they were, exhausted, choking on the dust of little places named Urbana and Hyattstown and Clarksburg, shuffling along on the hinge of history.

July 10—Glen Ellen

That afternoon Johnson dispatched Capt. James C. Clark, a trusted Marylander, to Baltimore to gather information and left two couriers at Hayfields to await Clark's report. He then gathered his command and rode back across the valley, toward John Carroll's estate, The Caves, where he intended to camp.

Harry Gilmor also had connections north of Baltimore, far closer to him than Brad Johnson's. He led his small command down to the toll gate at Towsontown and then eastward on the Timonium road and down into the steep valley of the Gunpowder and the crossing at Meredith's Bridge on the Dulaney Valley road. There he told his men to wait—and he went home.

Home was Glen Ellen, two miles down Loch Raven Road from the Dulaney Valley road. Designed in 1834 by A.J. Davis, a Hudson Valley architect, for Harry's father,

Robert, the house was a replica of Sir Walter Scott's home in Scotland and displayed high mullioned windows and battlemented towers. Harry kiddingly reported that he "captured the whole party on the front steps."

July 10, Late Morning—Rockville Pike

Between Rockville and Washington lay a rolling countryside of large farms and plantations with fenced fields and pastures, a pretty and rich country. About halfway between the towns, a landmark stood on a high hill on the west side of the pike, a white wooden church with four square columns and gothic windows whose red, blue and yellow panes glinted in the sun. Rebuilt in 1850 on the foundations of an 1820 church that had burned, the church served a Presbyterian congregation organized in the previous century. This Bethesda Meeting House would give its name in 1871 to the community that was growing even then around the Darcy Store post office. Its other, even older name, Capt. John's Meeting House, would also survive in corrupted form in the familiar local place name, Cabin John. The church included a slave gallery over the sanctuary.

Virginia Campbell Moore and her father were attending services in the stuffy church on this warm Sunday morning when a federal officer burst through the door.

"The Rebs are coming! Get these horses away from here! Get to your homes!"

The Moores hastened to their home across the pike, climbed down into the cellar and closed the doors over them. From the suddenly quiet road at the foot of their steep drive, they could hear an occasional horseman pass, but it was not until late in the afternoon that they harkened to distant booming from the west, exactly the sound of an approaching July thunderstorm.

July 10—Washington City

Washington had been suffering one of the most tenacious hot spells in its history—forty-seven days without a drop of rain. The temperature had hovered in the nineties each day of July, as one muggy dawn after another yielded to a blistering afternoon. The heat and humidity seemed, in fact, a greater present danger than even Early's army. On July 4th, as Early was enjoying the Dutch generals' barbecue at Harpers Ferry, the Congress had adjourned and gone home. On the very day that the armies were struggling along the Monocacy, Lincoln's postmaster general, Montgomery Blair, and his father, Francis Preston Blair, sent their families to the Jersey shore and themselves went fishing in Pennsylvania, in full knowledge that if Early persisted, the Blair homes of Silver Spring and Falkland, near Sligo Post Office, out the Seventh Street road from town, might lay in his path.

Even the president got out of town, or as far as he could go, which was to the cooler heights of the Soldier's Home to the northeast, some three hundred feet above the city's zero sea level. The five hundred acres of the home had been authorized by Congress in 1848 (using the $100,000 tribute money that the U.S. had extracted from Mexico City) at the suggestion of Winfield Scott and upon the formal introduction of the bill by the chairman of the committee on military affairs, a senator from Mississippi named Jefferson Davis. The rolling grounds were countryside in 1864, with large stands of oak and beech forest and meadows and grazing pastures. A start had been made in 1852 on the main building (which would not be completed until 1891). Nearby was a gray stucco homestead known as the Anderson Cottage, and here the president and his family were spending this hot but quiet Sunday, unsure like everyone else exactly what was going on beyond the

Harper's Weekly

GEN. ALEXANDER McCOOK

blue hills to the west. It was reassuring to know that nearby were two of the great forts that ringed the city.

There were a few cool heads in the sweltering swamp below. The assistant secretary of the navy, Gustavus V. Fox, ordered a small steamer to stand by in the Potomac to take off the president if worse came to worse.

When Lucius Chittenden arrived for work at the Treasury Department, he found officials stuffing certificates into mail sacks to be sent out on the steamer.

As refugees from Frederick and Montgomery began trickling and then flooding into the western perimeter, some driving their farm animals before them, Washingtonians typically began assigning blame. Gen. Edward Bates, Lincoln's attorney general, wondering how such a large force could get this close to the capital, answered his own question: "Wallace and Seigel *et cetera* are helpless imbeciles, . . . Stanton . . . [as] stupid . . . [as Halleck]!"

In fact, both those worthies had assigned to different people the various tasks of defending the city, as did Grant. But Grant's man, E.O.C. Ord, had ended up in Baltimore. Halleck and Stanton rummaged through the available officers—the most

Leslie's Illustrated Newspaper

GEN. CHRISTOPHER AUGUR

able, physically fit and undisgraced were with Grant—and found two who were capable and only slightly tainted. Halleck's man, Maj. Gen. Quincy Gillmore, had been disciplined for conduct at Petersburg; he was now given command of the northeast sector of forts. Stanton's man, Maj. Gen. Alexander McCook, had misperformed at Chickamauga, but he now rode out Fourteenth Street to the reserve camp near the Blagden farm, where he set up a command post, even though command of the northern part of the defense had already been given to one-armed Martin Hardin.

Overall command of the Military District of Washington and the XXII Corps defending the city was given to Christopher Augur, who had served in both Virginia and Louisiana. What Augur had on paper in his department was daunting—thirty-one thousand troops with a thousand cannon in more than one hundred sixty forts, batteries and rifle trenches in a forty-mile ring around the city.

Where Early's army was aimed, there were eighty-seven forts and batteries north of the Potomac, holding 484 heavy and thirty-three field guns, and a total of 518 officers and 13,986 soldiers. From the Anacostia around to the Potomac, a twenty-mile swath had been cut through the woods for a mile out from the fortifications, creating barriers of felled logs and open fields of fire.

At the gates of the city, where major arteries pierced this defensive line, major forts loomed at the skyline: Reno, overlooking the Rockville road, the main artery west; Lincoln, overlooking the Philadelphia turnpike and B&O tracks; and Stevens, astride the Seventh Street road to the northwest.

As a screening force, the six companies of the veteran 8th Illinois who had remained in the city were now scattered in front of the northern defenses.

But the whole thing was a perfect paper tiger.

Gen. John G. Barnard, Grant's engineering officer, knew the defenses well since he had helped design and build them. As he went through town he noted that about twenty thousand troops were actually at hand, and most of them were not fit for true soldierly duty. They were beat-up veterans reserves, bridge and barracks and paddock guards, novice gunners, dismounted cavalry. As the heavy gunners from the forts had been shipped south to Grant as infantry, their places had been taken by Ohio national guardsmen on one-hundred-day enlistments. These soldiers, Halleck had said, could "scarcely fire a gun."

At Giesboro Point, on the Anacostia's south bank, just where it joined the Potomac, a huge cavalry depot had been erected. Camp Stoneman was filled with men who had lost their mounts and were waiting for replacements. The city's hospitals, Columbia College and Garfield out Fourteenth Street, Clifbourne near Rock Creek road, Mt. Pleasant, were filled with convalescing men who might be able to fire a weapon again. But overall, Barnard's considered opinion was that the number of real soldiers who could be put into line against Early was not thirty-one thousand but nine thousand, six hundred.

The true situation was that on this hot Sunday, the northern forts of Washington were defended by only two regiments of raw militia, spaced out in earth-banked forts, between which the rifle pits were empty. If Jubilee could move fast enough, Washington, and maybe the war itself, would be his.

July 10—Gaithersburg

John T. De Sellum's Summit Hall farm stood just south of the village of Gaithersburg, right on the road to Washington. The fine federal house, built of weatherboard on log, reposed on a hill five hundred feet above sea level, skirted by fifty-eight acres of fenced pastures and yards and lawns on every side. It was part of a three-hundred-acre parcel owned by DeSellum, a substantial bachelor on the board of the Gaithersburg Milling and Manufacturing Company, a trustee of the Presbyterian Church, and a man of opinion with a controversial political history.

The Democrats of Montgomery county, led by George Peter, William Veirs Bouic and William Brewer, wanted out of the Union. The county newspaper, Matthew Fields's Sentinel, supported that view. At the war's beginning, many men had slipped south to ride with fellow countian Ridgely Brown or with Col. Elijah Veirs White of Poolesville, who formed the 35th Battalion of Virginia Cavalry, of which Co. B, "Chiswell's Exile Band" under Capt. George Chiswell, was made up of men from Montgomery.

There was a pro-union party, the Whigs. Prominent among them were Allen Bowie Davis and Richard Johns Bowie and DeSellum, who had already suffered for his beliefs. When the military draft was instituted in 1862, DeSellum, as a prominent citizen of Gaithersburg, reported that he was "earnestly requested to draw the names. I replied it would be putting my character, property and life in imminent danger. But the Country demanded personal sacrifices. . . . I drew the names from the box. . . . My stockyard was burned and I was ostracized from Society."

DeSellum left an odd memoir of the war years, including the events of July 10. He recalls that after the sound of firing to the west on Saturday and again on Sunday morning, "for hours an ominous silence prevailed in the afternoon." During those hot hours, a squadron of union cavalry under Maj. William Fry had appeared on the Washington road and deployed briefly on DeSellum's farm, with a skirmish line starting back west, in the village of Gaithersburg.

In Washington, Fry, of the 16th Pennsylvania, had been ordered to pull together a command from the troops at Giesboro Depot as quickly as he could. By Saturday night, as the corpse of Billy Scott was being carted up the hill toward Rose of Lima, Fry had thrown together five hundred mounted men and was on the way to reconnoiter the country above Rockville. On Sunday morning he fell in with Levi Wells of the 8th Illinois coming out of the Clopper road at Gaithersburg. They felt strong enough together to move past Gaithersburg, where they soon greeted the van of McCausland with enough musket fire to give them pause. But only pause.

Fry withdrew through the village to the DeSellum farm and put up another skirmish line, which as quickly evaporated when the head of McCausland's column appeared through the trembling heat waves. Fry disappeared eastward; in his place came a confederate officer who rode up to DeSellum's door and told him that Gen. Early would be dining there.

"General Early arrived," writes DeSellum, "and *I tried* to be polite while my sister superintended the preparations for supper." His sister was Sarah Ann, born in 1812. Like John, two years her elder, she would never marry, and, like John, Sarah Ann was a substantial spinster. She owned, when the place was bought out by a cousin Fulks in 1885, no less than four beds, two sofas, tables, twenty-two chairs, two stoves and sundry other material goods. They also owned slaves, even though the worldly estates of both the bachelor brother and spinster sister went to the Union Theological Seminary in New York and the Princeton Theological Seminary in New Jersey.

DeSellum reported that "Early and staff sat down to the table. A conversation commenced about the war and its cause. They saw I was a slave holder, and my remarks about John Brown's raid suddenly caused a Colonel Lee to abruptly demand of me 'whether I was for coercing the south!' As I did not intend to lie or act the coward, my reply was 'I wanted the south whipped back under the Constitution, union, and government of the United States—with the rights and privileges she had before the war.' Again abruptly, Lee in a rage told me, 'You are an abolitionist—it is no use to blame the devil and do the devil's work,' and was very insulting."

All well and good—but who is this Col. Lee, Robert E., Jr., had gone back to Richmond with Early's written report to Robert E.

Now there rose from the table in the DeSellum house a figure "with the dignity and politeness of a gentleman, . . . his polished manners . . . an indirect reproof for Lee's violation of common politeness in the presence of my sister."

That dignified character bringing politeness back to the DeSellum table, said the host, was "Arnold Elsey"—by which DeSellum must have meant Brig. Gen. Arnold J. Elzey, who was at that moment two hundred miles away in Richmond. Although

DeSellum could not remember who was at his table during this most memorable meal, his memoir marks his own position on both sides of the question—a slave-holder four-square for the union.

Even as they spoke, the diners could hear the sound of looting outside as the farm was stripped for food and fodder; horses and cows, beef and dairy, disappeared; tons of hay and barrels of corn were loaded into wagons; fences were torn down for firewood. On the nearby farm of Ignatius Fulks, one thousand, eight hundred cavalrymen and their animals were camped with an equally destructive result.

DeSellum accosted Early. "Do you intend, sir, to give me up to be indiscriminately plundered?"

"It is plain where your sympathies lie," Early replied. "You cannot expect favor or protection." Sarah Ann had already decided that, and had sequestered $3,000 and some government bonds in a safe haven—under her skirt.

July 10, 4:00 P.M.—Rockville

By late in the day, McCausland had chased Fry all the way to Rockville and down the Georgetown road. Fry paused at a hill east of the little country seat and dashed off a note to Augur:

> Washington Road
> Two miles from Rockville
> July 10, 1864 – 4 p.m.

> General:
> I have taken position and formed. My rear guard is fighting the enemy near Rockville. I have been joined by a squadron Eighth Illinois Cavalry and expect to be engaged in a few moments. I would respectfully suggest that the forts in the vicinity of Tennallytown be strongly guarded as the enemy's column is a mile long.

> Very respectfully,
> Your obedient servant,
> Wm. H. Fry,
> Major, Commanding

The head of McCausland's column quickly brushed aside Fry's pickets in Rockville. He broke off the pursuit; as the main force came up they were directed to the open grounds to the east of town, where the county fairs were held in peaceful times.

Rockville had been the seat of Montgomery County since its formation in 1776. Named at first Montgomery Court House, the settlement of seventeen houses became the little town of Rockville, named for the fallen hero of Quebec, in 1801, when eighty-five lots were laid out on six streets; they quickly filled up with people drawn to the court—judges and lawyers and lobbyists and services attending to their needs. Two lively hotels did a brisk business during court sessions, as did the livery stables. In 1860, a city ordinance declared that "no horse, hog, shoat, goose . . . or goat shall be allowed to run loose . . . under penalty of one dollar." By the time McCausland appeared, the streets between the B&O station and the town were paved, and the Montgomery House and Washington hotels were competing with Kilgour's Oyster Saloon for the dinner trade.

McCausland honored the Montgomery House with his patronage. He summoned the regimental band, which assembled in the street outside the hotel and played martial music to the delight of the citizens, many of whom, including the mayor and leading citizens like Allen Bouic, were known southern sympathizers. McCausland paid his bill in confederate money.

July 10, 11:00 P.M.—Gaithersburg

The DeSellums, angered but powerless to stop the looting of their farm, stayed in their rooms, watchful and awake, as the sounds of movement of a large body of troops echoed from the direction of the village. It was Ramseur and the last of the rear guard, who had finally scattered the pursuing federal cavalry and come up to join the main encampment at Gaithersburg.

July 10, Midnight—Washington City

Martin Hardin arrived at midnight to take command of Fort Reno. During the small hours of the morning, soldiers from the veterans reserve arrived constantly. There also arrived three companies of stragglers from the camp at Alexandria.

Montgomery Meigs, the quartermaster general of the union army, had hastily assembled his corps of file clerks and warehouse workers, and by Sunday night was able to offer Gen. Augur nearly two thousand men. Augur politely accepted them.

Out on Piney Branch, an arm of Rock Creek, Gen. Alex McCook was followed into camp by some veteran reserves, the 2nd District of Columbia Regiment and two batteries of guns, but they had no one to report to—McCook had gone out to inspect the defenses he now commanded and which he had never before seen. And what he saw deeply distressed him.

The five miles of the line of batteries and pits and forts between Rock Creek and Bladensburg were garrisoned by a single regiment of Ohio boys who had not gone to the Monocacy, the 150th Ohio hundred days men. In Fort Stevens, the centerpiece of defense, there was but a single company. Also in the fort that Sunday night was a battery of artillerymen and a few veteran reservists. Total strength: 209 men.

McCook realized that had Early reached Washington that day, the city would have fallen. And it might fall yet. All that could save it now were the troops from Grant, and he knew not where they were.

July 10, Midnight—Soldier's Home

While McCausland's tired troopers were wrapped in their blankets in Rockville, a squad of federal soldiers emerged from the darkness surrounding the Anderson Cottage and woke their commander-in-chief. Stanton had sent word, had, in effect, ordered him to return to the executive mansion. The president did not appreciate the concern, but even as he complained about it, he and son Todd dressed and took the carriage back to the city, along the dark roads in the gloom of a hot midnight.

July 10, Night—East of Glen Ellen

Twenty miles north of Baltimore, Harry Gilmor had taken leave of his family at Glen Ellen, one of whom he later reported "uttered the not very cheering prediction that I would never return alive. I said, in reply, that I was much of the same opinion myself." He then led his exhausted troopers along the road through Dulaney's Valley, intending to cross the ridge by Morgan's mill. But "I fell asleep on my horse, and did not wake till I came to a gate farther on, when the barking of dogs aroused me."

Gilmor knew that his men desperately needed sleep, "for they were actually so suffering for it that they were falling from their horses on the road, and I was beginning to lose some of them." He turned into Joshua Price's estate, at the juncture of the Mountain and Joppa roads in Harford County, where there was an old stage stop. His men simply fell from their horses and slept.

July 10, Midnight—The Caves

It was near midnight when Bradley Johnson turned off Caves Road to the splendid country house built in 1730 by Charles Carroll the Barrister, who framed the Declaration of Rights incorporated in the Maryland constitution. Now The Caves was home to John Canon, Esq., with whom Johnson was dining when the messengers arrived:

> Colonel Clarke reports that every rail car in Baltimore is waiting at Locust Point and transports off the point are debarking General Emory's corps, the XIX from Grant.

"Then General Early will soon be facing both Ricketts and Emory, two full corps, with Hunter somewhere at his back. He must know his situation at once."

Johnson quickly named a party of six men to ride south to find Early's army. It wasn't a difficult task, for at that moment the confederate army lay in thousands of pieces, like a disintegrated serpent stretched beside the Washington road for a good ten miles between Gaithersburg and Rockville.

XII.
The Road to Washington

Monday, July 11, Dawn—Theatre of War

At dawn the air was stale and warm and already singing with flies. Early noted that "the heat during the night was oppressive and but little sleep had been obtained." His unrested army began to stir in its camps around Gaithersburg and Rockville, knowing that by nightfall they might be in Washington.

On the previous day, Col. Charles Russell Lowell had crossed the Potomac from Falls Church with his 2nd Massachusetts Cavalry; now he was moving out from Fort Reno, jangling through the morning twilight with three squadrons and an attached company of the 8th Illinois, moving along the pike toward Rockville.

North of Baltimore, Harry Gilmor's tireless troopers were already cutting the telegraph wires along the Harford road.

In the Green Spring Valley, Bradley Johnson, who planned to ride that day around the western side of Baltimore and then travel east to reach the rail line north of Washington, had a higher priority—revenge. He detailed a war party under Lt. Henry C. Blackiston of Co. B, 1st Maryland Cavalry, C.S.A., to make even what had happened in Lexington. Blackistone led his troop down silent North Charles Street to the opulent summer residence of Maryland's governor, Augustus Bradford. The governor was in Baltimore, but Mrs. Bradford was awakened by the sound of smashing furniture, her first indication that her house was about to be burned down.

And in the White House, the president was standing by a south window with a long spyglass, peering anxiously down the Potomac in the thin morning light for a smudge on the horizon—the smoke of the big steamers carrying two divisions of the VI Corps to Alexandria and the southwest waterfront of Washington at Sixth Street. Lincoln was fully aware that the safety of the capital at stake.

July 11, Dawn—Fort Stevens

Maj. Gen. Christopher C. Augur, commanding, his great handle-bar mustache and huge side whiskers giving him a look of ferocity, reined up at Fort Stevens at first light, the beginning of an inspection of the city's northern and western fortifications. For days the defense of the city had been slowly organizing. Under Augur, Brig. Martin D. Hardin had been asked to command the thirty-six hundred effective troops north of the Potomac, which included eighteen hundred infantry, eighteen hundred gunners and only sixty cavalry. Brig. Gen. Augustus DeRussy, south of the river and presumably closer to the enemy, counted four thousand infantry, eighteen hundred gunners and fifty cavalry.

The northern half of the city was divided by Rock Creek. East of the creek, Lt. Col. Joseph Haskin commanded the 1,250 men manning 126 guns in forts Stevens, Slocum, Totten, Slemmer, Bunker Hill, Saratoga and Lincoln. Most of these troops were in three regiments of Ohio national guard and two companies of heavy artillery. West of the creek, Col. J.M. Warner of the 1st Vermont Heavy Artillery had a hundred guns manned by a thousand men—mainly Ohio hundred-dayers and a single company of regular artillerists—in forts DeRussy, Reno, Kearny, Bayard, Simmons and Sumner.

Gen. Hardin, at age twenty-seven, had already been badly mauled by the war. He'd racked up three wounds, including the loss of an arm to a confederate guerilla ambush. Even so, he hurried to confer with McCook at the Piney Branch camp and soon discovered that McCook, Stanton's man, intended to exercise the northern command. Hardin did not protest when he was asked to direct the defenses at Tennallytown, where the major attack would probably come. He had gone directly there, arriving at Fort Reno at midnight, and by the pink dawn of what promised to be another hot day he and Warner had moved into the lines west of Tennallytown a number of the units feeding out of the city—Ohio guards, veteran reservists and convalescents, with a few regular artillerists such as the 2nd U.S.

All this was in Augur's mind as on a map when he inspected Stevens and found its puny complement of 209 men. There were a bunch of boys from Ohio in the 150th National Guard, including those from Oberlin College in Capt. A.A. Safford's Co. F, who had joined up on the promise they would not be sent to combat. After watching the dreary parade of refugees from western Maryland pass during the night, James Cannon spoke for them all. "The front has come to us."

There were also a few men from the 13th Michigan Battery under Capt. Charles du Pont and some of the inevitable convalescents gathered up by Lt. Henry Turner.

Augur took one look and sent a message to Col. Gamble at Camp Stoneman to round up every cavalry soldier he could find and send them forward at once, horse or no horse. Those found set out without breakfast, but the grateful and apparently sleepless citizens of Washington quickly lined the roads with bread baskets. Augur also called out the Washington militia, two companies of about six hundred men commanded by a grocer aptly named Peter Bacon, whose brother, when asked by the provost marshal where the unit's headquarters was, replied: "Damned if I know!"

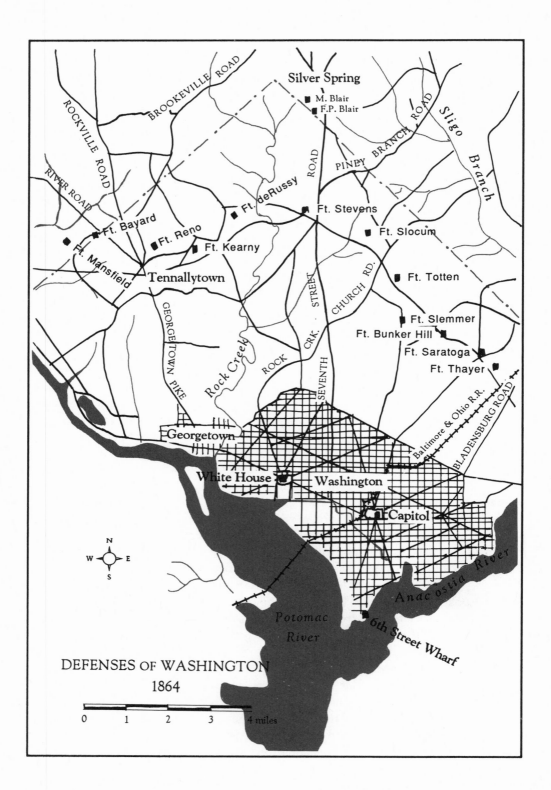

BROOKEVILLE ROAD

Silver Spring

M. Blair
F.P. Blair

ROCKVILLE ROAD

RIVER ROAD

PINEY BRANCH ROAD

Sligo Branch

Ft. deRussy

Ft. Stevens

Ft. Bayard

Ft. Reno

Ft. Kearny

Ft. Mansfield

Tennallytown

Ft. Slocum

Ft. Totten

Ft. Slemmer

Ft. Bunker Hill

Ft. Saratoga

Ft. Thayer

GEORGETOWN PIKE

Rock Creek

ROCK CRK.

SEVENTH STREET

CHURCH RD.

Baltimore & Ohio R.R.

BLADENSBURG ROAD

Georgetown

White House

Washington

Capitol

Potomac River

Anacostia River

6th Street Wharf

DEFENSES OF WASHINGTON
1864

0   1   2   3   4 miles

Finally, Montgomery Meigs's little army of paper pushers was summoned to action. They were much as Maj. John Brinton described them: "orderlies, messengers, military riffraff, invalids . . . indeed, every man in government employ who could put on a uniform, or carry a musket."

July 11, Early Morning—Jerusalem Road

As they were crossing over to the Bel Air road on the old Jerusalem road near Kingsville, Gilmor's point riders noticed a union flag flying from the home of one Ishmael Day. They stopped and ordered him to take it down. When Day ran inside, Ordnance Sgt. Eugene Fields dismounted to do it himself. Day came back out, leveled a shotgun at Fields, fired it and ran into the woods. Gilmor galloped up with four men and rushed to Fields's aid. It was a sight he would never forget.

"There lay Fields, his head thrown back, and a deathly pallor fast overspreading his countenance, flecked here and there with dark bluish-purple spots, where the buckshot had entered. His shirt was thrown open and his manly breast was literally covered with these purple spots. He bled very little. The men stood around us at some little distance, in violent gesticulation, swearing terribly."

Gilmor put Fields in one of Day's carriages and sent him to Wright's Hotel on the Harford road, where he later died. Day's house was soon in flames, then his barn and out-buildings. Gilmor was certain that he could not have saved Day's life had his men caught him. Fields, ironically, was a Baltimorean.

July 11, Early Morning—The Old Georgetown Road

Old Jube had a choice. From Rockville he could follow the Frederick road straight on through the hamlets of Montrose and Darcy Store (later called Bethesda) before crossing into the District of Columbia a mile west of the commanding height of Fort Reno at Tennallytown, beyond which lay Georgetown and Washington City. Or he could avoid that well-guarded approach and take his army east, by way of New Cut Road, past Samuel Veirs's grist and saw mill which stood on Rock Creek. That road joined the old Union turnpike at Leesborough, which continued south through Sligo Post Office to the northern corner of the District, where it became Washington's Seventh Street.

Early chose to do both, dispatching the faster moving McCausland to the south, down the Georgetown pike toward Montrose, while he prepared to take the main force eastward. The marching orders put Rodes's division in the van of the column, with Col. George Smith's cavalry (Imboden's brigade, the 18th, 23rd and 62nd Virginians; he was ill with typhoid in Winchester) on the point. Then came artillery, Ramseur, more artillery, Gordon, the wagon train and provisions, with Echols bringing up the rear. In Rockville, the passing troops noticed that horses killed in the cavalry skirmishing still lay in the streets, bloating and stinking in the rising heat.

Leslie's Illustrated Newspaper

CAPTURE OF THE TRAIN AT MAGNOLIA STATION

July 11, 8:30 A.M.—Magnolia Station

The Jerusalem, Mountain and Magnolia roads led east toward the Chesapeake Bay and the railroad station at Magnolia, on the north side of the Gunpowder River. Luck had the morning train from Baltimore to Philadelphia and New York sitting at the station when Gilmor came thundering down the road about 8:30 A.M. The engineer saw him coming, disabled the controls and fled, but the surprised, not to say amazed, passengers were all captured; among them was a genuine prize, a federal major general, William B. Franklin, who had been a corps commander at Fredericksburg and was home on leave from Louisiana.

Since Gilmor could not move the train, he set it afire and waited for the next one, which appeared on time an hour later and, unwarned, fell intact into his hands.

A mile to the southwest of the station, the long bridge that carried the tracks over the wide mouth of the Gunpowder River was defended by a pick-up crowd of fifty thirty-day enlistees from Delaware under the command of Capt. Thomas Hugh Sterling; as panic spread from the confederate raids, they had arrived at three that morning to join the thirty-two men from Co. F, 159th Ohio National Guard, under Lt. Robert Price. Price took the Baltimore end and Sterling the Philadelphia end of the long bridge. Of far more serious consequence to Gilmor was the bridge's main defense, the gunboat *Juanita* lying at anchor three hundred yards downstream.

Leslie's Illustrated Newspaper

MAJ. GEN. WILLIAM B. FRANKLIN CAPTURED

Gilmor sent Capt. Bailey and his sharpshooters up ahead to clear out Sterling's force and immobilize the gunboat. Then he set fire to the second train, and when she was burning good, he backed her onto the bridge. One of Sterling's men fell over the side, wounded, and others leaped into the river as the flaming train rolled toward them. Sterling retreated over the ties to the center of the bridge where he was joined by a detachment under Lt. Price coming at a run from the other end. As the train lost momentum, these men managed to uncouple two cars not yet aflame and roll them to safety.

Behind them a segment of the bridge itself was now engulfed, the draw span went out, and the span with several cars crashed down into the water. And from *Juanita* came—nothing, not a single shot. She was caught so completely by surprise that Ensign William J. Herring had no steam in his boilers, but he did maneuver her so as to avoid being set afire by the sparks now flying from the burning bridge. Gilmor calmly motioned Herring to come ashore and take aboard the stranded railroad passengers.

Gen. Franklin was loaded with a few other choice captives into a coach, and Gilmor turned his column down the Philadelphia road toward Baltimore, fully intending to ride directly *through* the city on his way to rejoin Johnson. But as they approached in mid-afternoon, a sympathizer waved him down and said, "You can't get through, Harry. They've barricaded the streets," so he turned off once more on the Joppa road to Towsontown. When he arrived there, he did what any Baltimore gentleman would do after such a strenuous morning. He tied up his horse, went into the bar of Ady's Hotel and ordered a drink.

July 11, Morning—Rockville Pike

Maj. Fry's provisionals, stung by the action in Rockville, had spent the night on a hill about a mile east of that town. Outnumbered and almost out of ammunition, they began an orderly withdrawal as McCausland came out toward them. They kept riders in front of him all the way to the Old Stone Tavern, near modern Bethesda, where Lowell appeared with his reinforcement and took command.

At the village of Montrose, with its school for black children and Mrs. Ball's popular tavern, the pike intersected with the old Georgetown road opened by Gen. Braddock in 1755. That road branched to the south and paralleled the pike until they joined again at Darcy Store.

Wanting no surprises on his flank, McCausland dispatched a column to follow and clear the old road. As the riders followed the big bend in the road to the east, they passed a 500-acre farm owned by the widow Matilda Riley. Here the hungry and thirsty troopers stopped at a little brook to gather calamus roots. They were observed by a young girl from the loft of a cabin that stood nearby. It was not any cabin but actually *the* cabin. Uncle Tom's cabin.

A black male child named Josiah Henson, born in 1789 in Charles County, was sold at age ten to Adam Robb, a tavern keeper in Rockville. Young Josie, as he was called, had come to Montgomery County because his mother had been sold to George Riley, whose farm was east of town on the Old Georgetown road. Robb later agreed to reunite the pair by selling Josie to Riley, whose son Isaac managed the labor. There the adult "Si" Henson lived for 25 years and became an overseer. One fine day he went to Newport Mill (also known as Duvall's) on Rock Creek near the hamlet of Kensington and was so moved by the words of an itinerant preacher, John McKenney, that he determined to become a preacher himself. In 1825, Si was sent to Kentucky with Riley's brother who was emmigrating there. From Kentucky he escaped to Canada and was later admitted the Methodist Episcopal Church as a minister. He lived to the age of 94 in Canada, operating a farm called Dawn, and a school for former slaves. He traveled to England, where he filled every hall in which he spoke and met Queen Victoria, who gave him a portrait of herself in a gold frame.

One of the people interested in Si Henson's story was a woman author who interviewed him in Boston. She produced a series of articles for the Washington *National Era*, which were later became a book. Her fictional Montgomery County characters became famous in the struggle against slavery: Topsy, Little Eva, Simon Legree.

Harriet Beecher Stowe's *Uncle Tom's Cabin, or Life Among the Lowly* was translated into twenty languages and sold six million copies. Later, Si wrote his own book, *Uncle Tom's Story of His Life,* with vivid recollections of the days spent near old Rockville, which he knew as Montgomery Court House, and of his trips to Georgetown and Washington.

Could the soldiers have known the history of the cabin they passed that day? and if they did, what might they have thought of it?

July 11, Morning—The Road to Washington

Only a few hundred men blocked their path to immortal military glory, but as the hours and the miles dragged by—it was twenty miles from Gaithersburg to Fort Stevens, a dozen from Rockville—it became clear that the column, imprisoned in the mid-90s heat and dust of the march, was reaching a state of collapse. It began spewing bodies as exhausted men fell out.

Early described the day. "[It was] an exceedingly hot one and no air stirring. When marching, the men were enveloped in a suffocating cloud of dust and many of them fell by the way. . . . I pushed on as rapidly as possible . . . , [but later, with heat waves shimmering and men gasping,] it became necessary to slacken our pace."

Ramseur would later write to his wife that "the heat and the dust were so great that our men could not possibly march further." John Worsham, whose unit was with Gordon, said the entire division was stretched out so thin from straggling that it looked like a line of skirmishers.

July 11, Morning—Owings Mills

Just beyond Owings Mills, Brad Johnson's troopers came upon two wagons on their way to the Baltimore markets containing a substance that almost none of them had ever seen. It was some kind of "frozen mush" or some kind of beer, they thought, but far too cold. They passed it around in their hats and in cups and tins, and a few yelped in pain when they held too much of it too long in their mouths, until the Painter's Vanilla Ice Cream finally melted. When Blackiston and his torch party returned, the united command moved on toward Woodstock to tear up the tracks of the Baltimore and Ohio railroad and cut the telegraph wires.

July 11, Morning—Rockville to Leesborough

Isaac Bradwell was with Gordon, in the column of march behind Rodes and Ramseur. "When we were several miles from the city, the enemy in the works around the town opened on us with their big guns. As these big shells passed high over our heads, our boys in the ranks laughed at the marksmanship of the 'melish' behind the guns. We knew then that our enemies were a set of fellows untrained and badly frightened."

Bradwell commented that the guns might be deliberately aiming for the wagon trains "far in the rear," but his comrades replied, "Then why haven't they hit any?"

As the struggling marchers neared the Seventh Street road, the brown cloud kicked up by those thousands of shuffling feet was clearly visible to the lookouts at Fort Reno, seven miles to the south, and Fort Totten, on the high ground near the Soldier's Home. Capt. James F. Berry of the 8th Illinois Cavalry, stationed out on the Union turnpike near Leesborough, also saw it coming his way and dispatched a rider to McCook's camp at Piney Branch. McCook immediately started his entire little force for Fort Stevens, before which he shook out a curtain of veterans reservists and Ohio volunteers, with some dismounted cavalry men from the 25th New York. McCook noted that his command now included invalids, convalescents and government clerks. "There was never before a command so hereogeneous [*sic*]."

July 11, Morning—Old Georgetown Road

Not very far beyond the Riley farm, McCausland's detachment soon collided with a number of Fry's cavalry troopers and a sporadic but not very lethal fire-fight started.

In the steaming and nervous city, the newspapers were going mad with extra editions. The *Stars* that hit the streets around noon described the Rebel's capture of Rockville with a force of between fifteen hundred and two thousand men (less than a fourth of Early's real strength), and reported on the morning fight "in the vicinity of Rabbitt's Creek Post Office between Tennallytown and Rockville."

There was no Rabbitt's Creek Post Office, but there was a Rabbitt's Store on the Old Georgetown road, near where Bells Mill road joined it, and near the old Mount Zion Baptist Church known as the Spider Hill church. The neighborhood was home to country families with familiar names; all of the farms between there and Montrose were owned by Wilsons or Rabbitts. Isaac Rabbitt's farm adjoined that of Osborn Sprigg Wilson, which was across the road from Samuel Clark Veirs's place. So it was here, about where the Wildwood Shopping Center stands today, that the defense of Washington began on July 11.

July 11, Late Morning—Silver Spring

As Kyd Douglas was riding down the pike, a soldier hailed him and informed him that nearby Silver Spring, Francis Preston Blair's country estate, was being looted. Douglas quickly collected a squad and found the house deserted, "not a servant . . . to be seen," and a party of stragglers "hunting for booty and things to eat and drink." He cleared them out, posted a guard and went to report to Early, who took possession of the grand house for his headquarters.

And grand it was. The twenty-room country manor, a kind of rustic brick chateau with porches and big gables, boasted eight white marble fireplaces and four baths and was set in five hundred wooded acres that included an artificial lake. Two large kitchens and a laundry room shared the basement with a wine cellar in which stood huge spiggoted casks, symbols of lavish entertaining.

The estate had been erected in 1842, twelve years after Blair had come to Washington at Andy Jackson's request to edit *The Globe* newspaper. His town home was (and is) across the street from the White House. It is said that he came upon the location of the estate by accident when his fractious horse, Selim, threw him while he was riding the countryside; Selim was captured when his bridle caught up in a bush near a crystal spring whose beauty so captivated Blair that he bought up the land around it. At one time he owned a thousand acres, which included much of present Takoma Park and large tracts of Rock Creek Park.

Blair was a native of Virginia but later, like Breckinridge, a Kentuckian. In fact, the families were distantly related, and Breckinridge had often been a guest at Silver Spring when he was vice president. In time the road out front became Eastern Avenue, and the bridal paths turn into the Piney Branch and Blair roads.

Nearby, toward Rock Creek, stood another fine Blair family home, Falkland, the country home of Francis Blair's son, Montgomery, who had been counsel to Dred Scott in that controversial case before chief justice Roger B. Taney.

July 11, Noon—Seventh Street Road

All night long the young Ohioans from the 150th National Guard who were on picket in front of Fort Stevens had watched frightened farm families hurrying past on their way toward Washington. There were some others, not-so-frightened civilian stragglers, "who only stopped at the third 'halt' and click of the lock," recalled John Amos Bedient. Then, with the rising heat of the day, had come a silence and a strange emptiness, an anxiety beyond foreboding.

There were only four of them at the "chestnut station" where the Piney Branch road, coming from the northeast, joined the Seventh Street road. In the junction was a toll gate and a small white toll house with a single door and window. Another three young men were on a hill about a mile out from Stevens, and a few more in a third vedette farther still, near the district line.

About noon, the head of Smith's Brigade, in the form of Lt. Col. David Lang's 62nd Virginia mounted infantry, suddenly appeared through the shimmering heat waves, gray figures moving in brown dust, moving cautiously but relentlessly toward them, the hot sun glinting off obscure weapons. The pickets bolted toward the fort, firing as they ran.

It was then, or shortly thereafter, that William Leach of Co. K, 150th Ohio, fell, the first of many who would die in these sunny fields. As shots rang out, a startled George Hobbs and his family leaped from the table where they were enjoying their noon meal and sought safety.

On the skirmish line below the fort, in dozens of rifle pits scattered between and before the major works a heterogenous group awaited. There were a lot of green kids from the Ohio guard units, but also some experienced and steady veteran reservists and genuine fighting soldiers from the 25th New York Cavalry. In reserve were five hundred newly-arrived cavalrymen pulled together from various units and led by a 7th Michigan officer, Maj. George G. Briggs.

These men watched as Smith's cavalry approached, coming on in column and then dismounting and filing out left and right into the fenced fields. In the hazy distance, the head of Rodes's division began to materialize in the dust and haze. Parties of sharpshooters could be seen dashing toward several of the big wooden farm houses that sat back from the road, framed with trees and grassy meadows belonging to families named Carberry and Shoemaker and Reeves. All the while the big guns growled and roared behind them, from DeRussy and Slocum and Totten as well as Stevens.

Along the front of both lines there now bloomed the white puffs of musket fire and there could be heard a nonrhythmic beat, like the sound that young children make when playing with drums.

July 11, Noon Until 1:30 P.M.—Fort Stevens

Early himself "rode ahead of the infantry and arrived in sight of Fort Stevens on this road a short time after noon." What he saw through his glasses was daunting: Slocum's great bulk was to his left, with its attendant strong battery. To his right, Rock Creek cut a "deep ravine," made impassable by felled trees. Milkhouse Ford road crossed the ravine and forded the creek below the imposing Fort DeRussy with its attendant batteries, Kingsbury and Smead. Farther around the circle rose Gloria Point, near which Fort Reno dominated the skyline. Early noted that these works were "connected by breastworks, with ditches, palisades, and abatis in front, and every approach swept by a cross-fire of artillery." He noticed something else. "I discovered the works were but feebly manned."

He had won the race! Almost within his grasp—those union warehouses bulging with food and clothes, those arsenals full of new guns and ammunition, the Treasury itself with the union's gold and good money, all within the reach of his hand! One good blow and he would be in, rolling down the Seventh Street road straight to the White House and grabbing Abe Lincoln by the nape of his neck, collecting the whole Congress in wagons and carting them off to Virginia to be auctioned off. Remember what he said when asked whether he would send the abolitionist Thad Stevens to prison? "Hell, no. I'd cut him up into little pieces and send his bones out to every state as a curiosity."

Cavalry scout John Opie was of the opinion that a yell, a shot and a charge at that point would have delivered Washington.

But . . .

But the Army of the Valley District, Second Army Corps, Army of Northern Virginia, was strung out for miles, lying all along the road, prostrate with the heat, with breathing the damned dust; hundreds had staggered out of ranks and fallen over or wandered off, thirsting for water. Said Early, "When we reached the . . . enemy's fortifications, the men were . . . not in condition to make an attack."

On his cool Rock Spring farm near Sandy Spring, Quaker farmer Roger B. Farquhar recorded in his diary that the temperature had reached ninety-four degrees fahrenheit.

New York war correspondent Sylvanus Cadwallader, who thought Early could have swept through the federal line "with the loss of a few hundred men," noticed how lackluster the army's approach was; rather than rushing forward to form order of battle, men sprawled in the shade of trees and stacked arms and flopped next to cooking fires.

But that bobcat Newman Feamster had not fallen out and flopped over. He was "with some sharpshooters on the right," and had an opinion of the feebly manned works ahead far different from his commander's.

"We now have to stop as their fort and fortifications are too strong. We can dissern the U.S. flag on many of the fortifications. It is now 12 o c and both lines are at a stand. Sharpshooting is all that can be heard. Their fortifications are strong and well guard[ed]."

Nonetheless, Early had to do what he could, and he ordered Rodes to bring his division into line "as rapidly as possible, throw out skirmishers and move into the works if he could."

Without waiting for his whole division, Rodes built a scattered line from his advance units in the shallow valley before the fort, through which ran a little stream, and began an advance, hoping for a surprise entrance. McCook sent word to his people out in front, the Ohio hundred-day men and a portion of the 26th New York, "to fall back slowly, fighting until they reached the rifle pits." At one P.M. a frantic signal was sent from Stevens that "the enemy is within twenty rods."

Early noticed "a cloud of dust in the rear of the works toward Washington, and soon a column of the enemy filed into them." These were six hundred dismounted men from the second division of the cavalry corps hustled forward by Maj. Briggs. They did not hesitate. Early noted that "artillery fire was opened on us from a number of batteries." The cavalrymen came out of the fort to join the others in the pits and by one-thirty had driven the Confederates back until the federal line was "well established at 1,100 yards in front of the works."

"This," said Early, "defeated our hopes of getting possession of the works by surprise."

Opie was of the opinoin that "Early was about the only man in that army who believed it impossible to accomplish."

July 11, Noon—The White House

At just about the time Jubilee Early was taking his first good look at the defenses around Fort Stevens, Abraham Lincoln saw through his spyglass what he had been looking for, the sudden loom of the big transports in the heat mist hanging over the Potomac. He ran down the stairs, grabbed his hat and called for his carriage. He had already mentally rehearsed a quip with which he planned to greet the soldiers when they reached the Sixth Street wharf: "You can't be Late if you want to get Early."

July 11, 1:00 P.M.—Gordon

Gordon had moved his command to Rodes's left, and now, while firing sputtered along the skirmish line in front of Stevens, he spurred his horse forward and found himself "at a point of those breastworks at which there was no force whatever. The unprotected space was broad enough for the easy passage of Early's army without resistance. . . . Undoubtedly we could have marched into Washington."

But was it politic to do so? Would they be able ever to march out again? To a man, the army realized that men in blue under Hunter were beginning to close up the roads behind them. Already Frederick and its wounded was in their hands. They also knew that Grant, by now, was sending battle-hardened divisions up from City Point.

So Gordon, as at Monocacy, sat alone in his red shirt in the blazing sun atop the federal breastworks and looked south, toward the city, before he finally turned his horse's head back the way he had come.

July 11—Confederate Line

Isaac Bradwell reported, "Out in front of Fort Stevens, we halted and formed our line. Skirmishers were thrown out and the usual preliminaries of battle began. . . . General Gordon ordered up a battery of Parrott field pieces. . . . These brave gunners unlimbered in front of the brigade out in the open field in full view of the Yanks, about four hundred yards away, and replied, knocking up the red dirt around the muzzle of the big fellows in the fort while the enemy continued to aim at the moon and stars."

July 11, Early Afternoon—Fort Stevens

As the sun wheeled slowly away from the zenith, baking the men in the rifle pits and along the lines, there was no forward movement from either side. But a murderous fire now began to rake the federal line from sharpshooters in the Rives house, surrounded by an orchard and large shade trees on the east side of the Silver Spring road, and the Carberry house on the west side. So deadly was the shooters' aim that they killed and wounded no less than thirty men during the afternoon.

From his vantage high in Fort De Russy, Col. John C. Marble, commanding DeRussy, Smead and Kearny, saw the consternation along the federal line and "a considerable movement of the enemy in the vicinity of Wilson's house on the Seventh Street road. We deemed it advisable to send in a few shells." Marble later boasted (contrary to what Bradwell reported of the accuracy of the fort guns) that "the enemy were surprised at the accuracy of our fire at such distance," and claimed that the artillery and skirmish line "contributed largely to deter them from making the intended assault."

One action may have been a deterance. Brig. Gen. Martin Hardin, commanding that section, thought the line in front of DeRussy was the weakest of the entire front. It had been made a lot weaker by the continuous fire of sharpshooters from a barn in Rock Creek valley. As Hardin looked on, a single company of veteran reservists under a Capt. Clark charged the barn. Clark quickly tumbled over wounded as did most of his company. Such stiff resistance, Hardin thought, made Early realize it would take "a desperate assault to carry that portion of the line."

The forts began a systematic obliteration of any nearby structure that could harbor a nest of sharpshooters. Nearest to Fort Stevens, the houses of Richard Butts and W.M. Morrison to the east of the road, and of W. Bell to the west, shuddered and smoked and splintered under the rain of hot metal; they would soon be fully afire.

July 11, 2:00 P.M.—Worsham

John Worsham recalled that it was two or three P.M. before "the head of Gordon's division passed the toll gate about four or five miles from Washington." The forts were shelling the road with their big guns. Worsham looked ahead at the fortifications on the heights of the Soldier's Home and decided that "we were really in Washington" when he saw that men marching into the forts "had on linen dusters." One house between the skirmish lines was already afire, smoke rising into the warm afternoon air.

Worsham's division stacked arms on the side of the road, and he walked over to Silver Spring, "a splendid home," in search of water, which he quickly found, a pond full. Then he went back and examined the front of the house with a practiced and professional eye.

"As far as my eye could reach to the right and left were fortifications, and the most formidable looking I ever saw!" He noted that the trees had been felled with their sharpened ends and limbs pointed toward him, so that "the enemy had a full sweep of the ground for at least a mile in their front." He concluded that "if their works were well manned, our force would not be able to take them."

July 11, 2:00 P.M.—Sixth Street Wharf

Lincoln had been waiting at the Sixth Street wharf to wave his hat and greet personally the boats bearing the first of ten thousand men in two divisions of soldiers. Tanned to a man by a hot Virginia sun and wearing uniforms laundered by the weather, they carried arms at the ready and wore on their caps the famous Greek cross of Horatio Wright's veteran VI Corps.

The first to step ashore were Pennsylvanians in Frank Wheaton's brigade (93rd, 98th and 102nd Pennsylvania infantry, with the 62nd New York) who had departed

City Point in the transports *Dictator* and *Guide* at dawn of the previous day and steamed since then down the James, up the bay and up the Potomac.

Wright's First Division was like a Yankee map with William Penrose's brigade of New Jersey units (4th, 10th, 15th); Emory Upton's New York (65th, 67th, 121st) and Pennsylvania (95th, 96th), with the 2nd Connecticut Heavy Artillery; and Oliver Edwards's mix of Maine (6th), Massachusetts (37th), Pennsylvania (23rd, 82nd, 119th), New York (49th), Rhode Island (2nd) and Wisconsin (5th) infantry.

Brig. George W. Getty's Second Division counted, in addition to Wheaton's Pennsylvanians, Lewis Grant's brigade of all Vermont regiments (2nd, 3rd, 4th, 5th and 6th) and Daniel Bidwell's New Yorkers (43rd, Bidwell's own 49th, 77th, 122nd) with one Maine (7th) and the 61st Pennsylvania infantry.

George T. Stevens of the 77th New York recorded the event. "At 2 o'clock we touched at the wharf at the foot of Sixth Street. President Lincoln stood on the wharf chatting familiarly with the veterans and now and then, as if in compliment to them, biting a piece of hardtack which he held in his hand."

"Hurrah!" the gathering crowds yelled. "Hurrah for the Sixth!"

"You better hurry if you want to catch Jubal Early!"

Corps commander Wright was an engineer who had helped to build the defenses of Washington, but he now directed Wheaton to march off in the wrong direction, toward the Chain Bridge. The Pennsylvanians had reached the avenue named for their state before Col. Taylor, chief-of-staff of the Department of Washington, caught up to Wheaton with Gen. Augur's instructions to march at once to Fort Stevens, where "the enemy were driving in our picket line and seriously threatening" the fort. Turning up Eleventh Street, Wheaton was soon passed by Wright himself, who told him to mass his command "near Crystal Spring, in the neighborhood of Fort Stevens, where we arrived at four o'clock in the P.M."

A growing mob of citizens tagged along with the troops, including the chief one, as a clattering cavalry patrol, sabers drawn and held over the shoulder, escorted his carriage and cried out, "Give the road to the President!"

It seemed the whole town, including Abraham Lincoln himself, was on its way to war.

July 11, 3:00 P.M.—Fort Stevens

Wright learned, probably with some surprise, that his veteran corps would be held in reserve while the lines and pits continued to be filled with the reservists. The strategy was to have his large and capable force ready to maneuver to any point where a confederate breakthrough seemed imminent, and be ready to counter-attack and destroy Early's entire force if possible.

Moving ahead of his troops, Wright reported to McCook at Fort Stevens about three P.M. Whatever Halleck and the war department brains might think, however, McCook "directed him to furnish a force of nine hundred strong of his veteran corps for picket duty during the night."

July 11, 5:00 P.M.—*Fort Stevens*

By five o'clock the intense heat and excitement of the long afternoon was beginning to take its toll on the men in the rifle pits and along the skirmish line, which began to show gaps and to waver backwards. At the same time, sharpshooter fire from an orchard to the north of the fort suddenly found the range and so swept the gun platforms that it was impossible to man them. This went on for twenty minutes. A determined charge at that moment might have taken Stevens. Something had to be done quickly.

Wheaton, whose command had arrived only an hour before, was ordered "to recover the line." Three of his Pennsylvania regiments, the 98th, 102nd and 138th, with the 93rd and 62nd New York in support, moved up to the works, formed up in lines of battle and moved out down the slope toward the creek. The firing grew more intense as the lines closed on Rodes's skirmishers, who now began in turn to fall back, but grudgingly.

The land rose gradually from the swale to the north and northwest and then rapidly lifted and rounded off into a small range of three-hundred-foot hills. Somewhere up the road and behind that higher land was Early's entire force.

As soon as Wheaton felt comfortable with his defensive circumstance, about a thousand yards out from the fort, he stopped and dug in. It had taken two hours, and the sun was already gone from behind the wooded hills to his left and front. Early's last chance to mount an attack was rapidly draining away with the daylight.

This action provided Lincoln with his first witness to a battle in which blood flowed and men died. While accounts are muddled about his presence on the 11th, tradition places him at Stevens, and a contemporary sketch shows his long legs astride a horse prancing about to the east of the fort. A unit to his right is moving up to the battlefield, and in the swale below the skirmish lines, silhouetted in clouds of musket fire, they face each other in the positions they held on the afternoon of the eleventh, before Wheaton's recovery.

July 11, Evening—*At the Patuxent*

In the warm evening, BradleyJohnson's column passed along the Triadelphia road, making its way south toward the Patuxent River, the boundary between Howard and Montgomery counties. This upper Patuxent country is lovely, rolling, high country. In the 1720s English colonial civilization had reached here from southern Maryland. That meant land grants with English-only names like Gittings Ha! Ha! and New Year's Gift and, in that rising country, Far View and Prospect Hill and Walnut Hill.

Tobacco was the crop, the farms were big and families were Maryland rooted, grown and connected: Bowie, Bradford, Claggett, Clark, Davis, Dorsey, Gaither, Griffith, Linthicum, Magruder, Owings, Riggs, Snowden, Worthington. It was a conservative colonial culture, far closer to that of Richmond than to Philadelphia, for with the families and the tobacco had come their slaves. The tobacco had burned out many a field, and these had been replaced with pasture for thoroughbred horses and tawny fields of wheat, corn, hay, oats and rye, averaging about fifty dollars an acre in value. But slavery still existed, and the political sentiment was southern.

It was often overt. One of the colonial holdings above the Patuxent was Elton, a huge stone manor commanding the summit of a knoll with a stream at its foot. Built by a Gaither, it was the home of Amos Brown and his wife, Sarah Ridgely Griffith. Among their children was Ridgely Brown, who was named first captain of the 1st Maryland Cavalry of the Confederate States of America, which he helped to organize with 18 men at Richmond on May 15, 1862.

Johnson's bone-weary column—they had ridden thirty miles that day—completed the crossing of the Patuxent about nine o'clock in the evening and camped in the unique riverside village of Triadelphia. Named for its founding "three brothers," (actually brothers-in-law who had married daughters of the Quaker settler Roger Brooke IV and started to build the little town in 1810), the settlement by 1864 boasted a cotton mill, blacksmith and wheelwright shops, stables, store, dairy, granary, a saw and grist mill that ground most of the grain grown in this part of Montgomery, tobacco house, church, school house, post office and many fine homes. Many of these edifices were built with substantial, square-cut stone walls that gave a look of permanence and prosperity, a false one, it proved, for only three years after Johnson's visit a huge flood swept away most of the three-hundred-acre village.

A general on the move can dine where he chooses, and Johnson and his officers went on down the road toward Brookeville to dine at Allen Bowie Davis's famous old home, Greenwood. The Davis family had lived there since 1755, when it was inherited by Allen Bowie's grandfather, Ephraim. Today, as when Johnson stopped by, the three-part U-shaped house displays its history. The north wing is of stone and was built as early as 1735 by a Davis uncle, Larkin Pierpont. Ephraim Davis built the central section of brick; it has a porch and three antique dormer windows in the gambrel roof. Thomas Davis III and his wife Elizabeth Bowie built the third wing, of stone, about 1800.

These Davises were go-getters. Allen Bowie's father, Thomas, raised a regiment to accompany George Washington to Pennsylvania in 1794 to suppress the whiskey rebellion. He was an elector of the Maryland senate, magistrate, surveyor and judge of the Montgomery County court. Allen Bowie was no slouch himself. Elected to the board of the Brookeville Academy at age twenty-four, he was a member of the board of public works of the state of Maryland, president of the board of the Agricultural College (that became the University of Maryland) and president of the Montgomery Manufacturing Company and the Montgomery County Agricultural Association. He chartered the Brookeville and Washington Turnpike Company, was elected president, served sixteen years, finished the road and resigned.

In the course of this dynamic life, Davis had changed the old farm's name from Hygham to Greenwood and enlarged it to three thousand acres. The home acres ran for a mile on either side of the Westminster pike north of Brookeville. The old manor house with its family graveyard was on the east side, but he held parcels north to Roxbury Mills and south to Rockville. For that, of course, he needed slaves, about a hundred of them. Supplying supper to a confederate general and his staff was not a cause for panic, since Hester Ann Wilkins Davis, Bowie's second wife, kept a housekeeper, a cook, three upstairs maids, three parlor maids, three dairy maids and three laundresses.

When Lincoln issued the Emancipation Proclamation, Davis had assembled his entire holding of slaves, read it to them and explained it. "You are now free men and women. You may go where you wish and do as you please." Many slaves leaped for joy and ran away, but many others, such as Dick Powell, the gardener, Wilson Johnson, the miller, Rube Lynn, the coachman, and Ike Wallace, the wagoner, simply went back to work.

Johnson's supper on this muggy July Monday was rudely interrupted with news of a federal cavalry unit encamped at Brookeville, just two miles away. Johnson ordered horses saddled and prepared his boys for a night attack, but scouts reported that the federal force had wind of the men at Triadelphia and chosen the better path of wisdom by withdrawing toward Washington.

What a journey through American history these Virginia boys made that day, although none of them knew it. *Ex parte* Merryman surely meant nothing to them. Carroll the Barrister and Carroll of Carrollton's heir and would-be governor of Maryland were famous for patriotic contributions to the founding of the United States, for the Declarations of Rights and the like, and the Davis family seemed to be good and prosperous farmers—but what the cavalrymen noticed was that none could exist without slaves.

July 11, Evening—Silver Spring

While Johnson dined in one notable Maryland manor house, Early prepared to dine in another. He assembled his commanders, Rodes, Breckinridge, Gordon and Ramseur, at Silver Spring for a council of war, deliberations aided and abetted by the discovery of the large wine casks in the cellar. The conversation turned somewhat jocular. One officer suggested that they put Breckinridge at the head of the attacking column for "escorting him to the Senate chamber and seating him again in the vice-president's chair."

As the officers bantered over their wine glasses in the house, the privates who were enjoying the blackberries and the cool waters of the pond had their own opinions. A conversation recorded by Gordon went this way:

"What do you suppose we're going to do with the city of Washington once we take it?"

"Reminds me of Simon's dog. Tony Towns asked him, 'Simon, ain't you afraid of losin' your dog after chasin' every train that comes through here?' Simon says, no, he ain't afraid of losin' his dog, he's just wonderin' what that dog's going to do with that train once he catches it."

The officers agreed with that basic assessment for, as Gordon reported, there was not a single dissent "to the impolicy of entering the city." The conversation turned to a serious discussion of the options.

"We must do something at once, for we cannot linger here. The passes of South Mountain and the fords of the upper Potomac will soon be closed against us, if they are not already. An army will be placed against our backs and another against our front."

"The works ahead are substantial. Every possible approach is swept by a crossfire from heavy artillery."

"The men are obviously exhausted."

"The success of an attack will depend upon the character of the soldiers manning the works. Are they one-hundred-day men or veteran troops from Grant?"

"If only we had been able to get into those works this afternoon, to see how well they are manned, and in what number."

"Well, we didn't. We will examine the works at daylight and make an assault on them if they are still feebly manned."

That order did not survive the night, however, for out of the dark came, at length, the small troop dispatched by BradleyJohnson from The Caves at midnight Sunday, with the report that two entire corps were being landed.

It meant to Early and his generals that at least one of their objectives had been attained: Grant was having to ease the pressure against Richmond to save Washington. It also meant that an attack would be suicidal.

July 11—York Road, Baltimore

In Towsontown, Harry Gilmor learned that a column of cavalry was coming north from Baltimore up the York road. He told Capt. Nick Owings to take the prisoners and a squad of a dozen troopers up to the Ten Mile House in the Green Spring Valley and wait there. He then sent Lt. William Kemp and fifteen men down the York road with orders to charge straight at the federal advance and then retreat, drawing the column into an ambush. Kemp found the enemy to be a force of about seventy-five mounted volunteers under a Capt. Haverstick. He willingly hit them head on, and "a good many shots were fired but nobody hurt," as a witness told Madge Preston, a secessionist. Kemp chased the volunteers as far as Govanstown, inside the city limits, before turning back.

The 2nd Maryland Cavalry, had by now been in the saddle for forty-eight hours with little or no sleep or food, so it was not completely unexpected when Gilmor and Kemp arrived later that night at the old stone tavern on the Reisterstown pike to find every last man, including the guards, sound asleep and the prisoners, including Gen. Franklin, gone.

Gilmor was sensible enough to let the men sleep while he went on to the Seven Mile House in Reisterstown and slept for a few hours himself.

Leslie's Illustrated Newspaper

GEN. FRANKLIN ESCAPES

July 11, 9:00 P.M.—Fort Stevens

McCook reported on the pick-up defense forces. "At 9:00 P.M. Brig.-Gen. M.C. Meigs reported at Fort Stevens with about 1,500 quartermaster employees armed and equipped. They were at once ordered into position near Fort Slocum, placed on right and left in rifle pits. At 10 P.M. Col. R. Butler Price reported with about 2,800 convalescents and men from hospitals, organized into a provisional brigade composed of men from nearly every regiment in the army of the Potomac. They were ordered into position in the rear of Fort Slocum."

A soldier in Wright's corps observed that "there came out from Washington the most unique body of soldiers, if soldiers they could be called, ever seen during the war."

July 11, 10:00 P.M.—Washington City

Charles A. Dana, assistant secretary of war to Gen. Grant at City Point:

> Five boatloads of General Wright's troops have arrived and one of the XIX Corps. General Wright and his troops have gone to Fort Stevens.

July 11, 11:40 P.M.—Washington City

W.G. Raymond, assistant adjutant-general, to Maj. Gen. McCook, commanding reserve, Fort Stevens:

> The chief officer of pickets says the enemy are apparently making every preparation for a grand assault, tearing down fences, bands playing, cavalry moving to our left. Cannot a part of the VI Corps be hurried up at once?

July 11, 11:45 P.M.—Fort Stevens

C.C. Augur, major-general, U.S. Volunteers, to Gen. H.C. Wright, commander, VI Corps:

> General Halleck thinks your corps should all be assembled near Fort Stevens.

XIII.
The Battle at Fort Stevens

Tuesday, July 12, Dawn—Confederate Line

Whether or not he was suffering from an overindulgence of the contents of Blair's wine casks, tradition puts Jubilee Early in the saddle at first light. He rode forward to examine the federal works and saw at once that Johnson's report was correct; the rifle pits teemed with blue uniforms; figures and faces filled the gunnery ports in the forts; corps and army flags flew overhead.

George Stevens of the 77th New York watched the scene from the other side, and what he saw was a bucolic field before battle, "a scene of surpassing loveliness, with its rich green meadows, its fields of waving corn, its orchards and its groves."

Early pondered the probable destruction of his army if it became trapped inside the city, and the subsequent destruction of Johnson's cavalry. He knew his advance was at high water.

Rodes and Gordon formed battle lines, not to launch an attack on the works but to make sure the retreat, done more safely under the cover of night, would be orderly.

Capt. Thomas Lewis Feamster, Newman's brother, had slept on the line facing Stevens, prepared to charge at dawn. He was a little surprised, and probably much relieved, when the order came not to charge but to move into the valley of Rock Creek and take up a position. He would be there most of the day as the armies exchanged long distance blows by sniper and cannon fire.

The thirty-pound Parrott rifled cannon at Stevens opened by hurling shells toward the Carberry house, the beginning of a steady artillery barrage from DeRussy's eleven guns, Stevens's twenty-three guns and Slocum's twenty-five that would rain over 225 shells on confederate positions. The gunners probed at every target from a thousand yards outward, bodies of troops moving against distant woods, houses from the windows of which came the spit of fire, even the Blair houses, well over three thousand yards up the pike.

July 12, Morning—Rockville Pike

Since the previous evening, the cavalry troops of Lowell and Fry had been holding a skirmish line so near to Fort Reno's 420-foot height that its guns were rendered useless for fear of hitting Federals as well as enemy soldiers in the close lines below. Now, in the dim light of early morning, Lowell began a flanking movement by sending two squadrons down the old River road from Reno's height, endangering McCausland's column on the Rockville pike. He moved another squadron directly forward, giving McCausland no choice but to withdraw, a movement that carried the lines back about a mile and a half. But here the movement stopped, and the morning wore away with only sparring fire.

July 12—Mosby at Seneca

With Early drawing universal attention near Washington, Mosby seized an opportunity on July 11 and crossed into Maryland at Conrad's (now White's) Ferry and proceeded into Poolesville. He led his command down Partnership Road to Seneca Mills on the River road, where big Seneca Creek flowed into the Potomac and powered the Mitford mill, which he burned. Beyond, on a turning basin of the Chesapeake and Ohio canal, stood a cutting mill which provided the distinctive red sandstone that was barged down the canal for the building of many public works in Washington, such as the Smithsonian tower.

Moving toward the east from Violette's Lock along the canal tow-path, Mosby burned a frame building in the canal-side community of Rushville and then the square fort that gave modern Blockhouse Point its name. Beyond, at the mouth of Muddy Branch, he found the hastily abandoned camp of the squadron of the 8th Illinois that Clendenin had hustled out to Point of Rocks on the morning of the fifth. Everything was still in place, "tents standing, with bales of hay, bags of oats, saddles, bridles, and every description of camp equipage lying around. These we burned."

They also rounded up "thirty head of fine cattle" found grazing near the camp, in the meadow near the foot of the stream, which they herded across the Potomac, driving them toward a camp near Dranesville, Virginia.

July 12—Beltsville

When Capt. Thomas Griffin rode out from Triadelphia with Co. A, he had a new recruit in a saddle behind him, a young man stuffed full of old Maryland names. Gassaway Watkins Warfield was home from Rock Hill College for the summer vacation of his junior year and unable to resist the lure of the saddle and the great game of war. He came from deep American roots. He and his brother, Albert Gallatin Warfield, Jr., were the sons of Margaret Gassaway Watkins, daughter of that famed

Gassaway Watkins who was the last surviving officer of the Old Maryland Line that had fought so gallantly for George Washington. When he died in 1840, he was the president of the Maryland Society of the Cincinnati.

From Triadelphia, the rural roads still run straight eastward through Brighton, Ashton, Spencerville and Burton's to Laurel, on the railroad track between Baltimore and Washington, which Johnson intended to tear up. As Johnson's long column moved slowly eastward during the morning, another hot one, word came that Laurel was closely guarded. He turned south on Powder Mill Road and followed it into Beltsville, where he found what he was looking for—seven cars on the main track, a camp train with its construction crew and two gondolas and eleven ballast cars on a siding. They went up in roaring flames as the troopers hacked down eight poles carrying the telegraph lines.

Washington's connection with the outside world suddenly went dead. The pillar of dense smoke rising on the northern horizon attracted the attention of lookouts on the Washington forts fronting northeast. A column of five hundred cavalry, fearing they might confront Early's whole corps, was sent out. These were veteran cavalry troops of Maj. Gen. James Harrison Wilson's division, men who had long been in hot action in southside Virginia and the Petersburg front and had been sent up to Washington to get new mounts.

As the riders in blue approached, Johnson watched from a hilltop with two of his scouts. The Yanks dismounted, and put out a line of skirmishers in the little vale where the tracks crossed the Paint Branch of the Anacostia. The good horseman Johnson noticed what the Yanks already knew: their horses were fresh, but green. Johnson told his battery, the Confederate Baltimore Light Artillery, to lob a few shells toward the animals; the cannon fired, the shells flew and so did the horses, in a hot hurry all the way back to the Washington stables. Capt. Wilson Nicholas took off after them with companies E and F in a vain attempt to "gobble up a few stragglers," while the rest of the command rounded up several hundred "government issue" mules that had been found at Beltsville. Johnson intended to mount his freed prisoners on them once he reached Point Lookout, but he was not far along the road to Upper Marlboro when a scout from Early reached the column with orders to abandon the plan and return to the main army.

Johnson may have been relieved. He had sent word ahead to ask sympathizers to provide fresh mounts for his troopers as they raced toward the prison, but it was all a piece of daring-do that depended upon absolute luck. He now halted the column and asked his adjutant, George W. Booth, to find men in the unit who had lived in the region before the war to lead them over to Silver Spring. Booth set out in front, and Johnson took up the rear of the column with its captured mules and wagons and artillery. Having to cross directly in front of the coastal guns mounted in the Washington forts, they crept along the country roads, crossing from Adelphi to Riggs to Piney Branch, picketing each crossroad as they passed, moving as slowly as they dared to keep the dust down, and expecting to have shells fall on them at any moment.

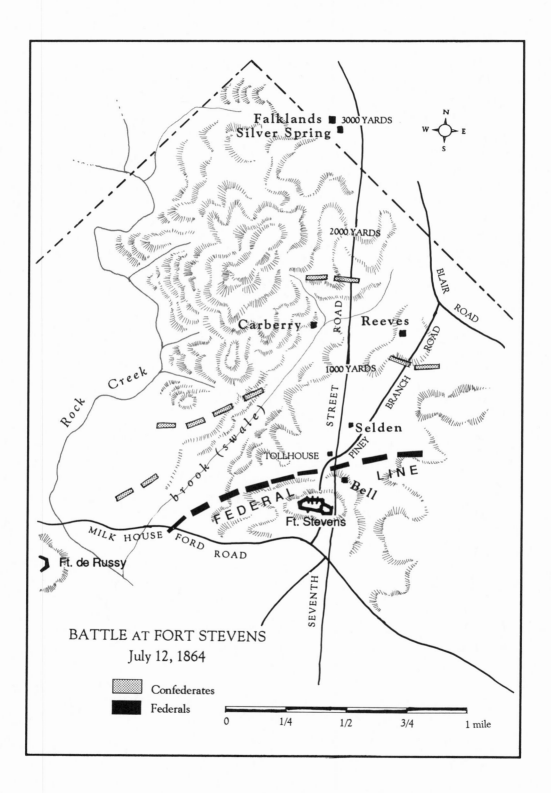

Falklands ■ 3000 YARDS

Silver Spring ■

N
W · E
S

2000 YARDS

Rock Creek

Carberry ●

Reeves ●

1000 YARDS

BLAIR ROAD

STREET ROAD

BRANCH ROAD

Selden ●

brook (swale)

TOLLHOUSE ●

PINEY

Bell ●

FEDERAL LINE

Ft. Stevens

MILK HOUSE FORD ROAD

Ft. de Russy

SEVENTH

BATTLE AT FORT STEVENS
July 12, 1864

▦ Confederates

■ Federals

0   1/4   1/2   3/4   1 mile

July 12, Afternoon—Fort Stevens

All morning the whistle of minié balls and the scream of descending shells and the crackling rattle of musket fire and the bam-bam-bam of repeating rifles had punctuated the terrific din of engagement in the vale below Stevens, but there had been no battle. Early's artillery had not come forward to slug it out with the big forts, except for the unit sent by Gordon. His lines had not surged forward in an attempt to find a weakness in the works while soldiers in blue had steadily streamed toward the front all day, collecting a reserve in the piney woods behind DeRussy and in the camps of Brightwood.

Many of Washington's more prominent citizens and politicians made, or tried to make their way up the Seventh Street road to witness the action.

Lucius Chittenden of the treasury left the Willard Hotel in a carriage with a few friends around three-thirty and started out Seventh Street toward the battlefield. There was a mob of curious citizens milling around on the summit of Meridian Hill, beyond which no civilians were allowed, but Chittenden talked his way through. There were so many VI Corps soldiers on the march toward Stevens that the carriage took to the open fields, where the civilians encountered "many soldiers in the lively stage of drunkenness, all armed with loaded muskets," who reacted to their presence. "Skedaddle white livers!" "Comin' out here to get up another Bull Run, aren't ye!"

Through two toll gates, and past "picket after picket," they finally arrived at Fort Stevens. Chittenden noted that the ground sloped down to the brook for one-half a mile, then rose for another mile and one-half toward Silver Spring, bringing the opposite slope of hill and field and woods into plain and full view of those standing at the fort.

The ground between the fort and brook had been swept bare or left with stands of tree stumps. Beyond the brook to the north were substantial farms, a "fine wooden mansion two stories in height, with a cupola," where lived a Mr. Lay of the post office department, and beyond that the bare chimney of a house burned out the previous day.

To the northeast there was a field of corn, a peach orchard, an open field with a few large trees, the brook and a bridle path that wound its way through a field of brush from the Seventh Street road and up a hill to a house surrounded by a large meadow and cultivated grounds, the whole scene framed by "a large forest of original growth."

In the brushy field between the brook and house, "not a man was visible but from every square rod of it as it seemed to me we could see the smoke and hear the report of musketry."

July 12, Afternoon—Lincoln Under Fire

At eleven-thirty that morning, before Johnson cut the line, the president had sent a telegraph to Grant (the message traveled north, then across the bay and down the

David Hunter Strother
Virginia State Library & Achives

ABRAHAM LINCOLN AT FORT STEVENS

eastern shore rather than directly south from Washington) passing on rumors about Longstreet joining Early. At noon Lincoln conducted the regular Tuesday cabinet meeting. Thus it was sometime after lunch that Lincoln invited his wife and Secretary of War Stanton to accompany him as he took a carriage with cavalry escort out to the lines at Fort Stevens. Gen. Wright and his wife met the party at a hospital behind the lines, and the men went on to the fort where they were challenged by Sgt. Hiram Thompson of the 49th New York.

They walked through the open interior and up a ramp to the parapet where Lincoln looked out at a genuine battlefield. The seemingly calm countryside baked in the hot summer sun, but he could see jerked clouds of white smoke and blurs of motion along a line where men in butternut crouched, stood briefly and fired their muskets—toward him!

Fire was coming from the windows of houses in the fields below the fort as well, keeping men pinned down in the rifle pits. The tall Lincoln was such a conspicuous target, especially if he still wore his high, black stovepipe hat—that Wright must have been very uneasy about his exposed position on the parapet.

As Lincoln watched, a minié ball whizzed into the parapet, ricocheted and knocked down surgeon C.V.A. Crawford of the 102nd Pennsylvania. Maj. Thomas Hyde was serving in the fort, and he saw Crawford "suddenly keel over." As the officer was helped from the parapet, it was reported the wound was in his ankle, not mortal but painful enough. The rumor was nearly true; Crawford had sustained a serious wound in his thigh.

What happened next, quite naturally, has never been clear. What is not to be doubted is that a chorus sprang up to get Lincoln out of danger. Gen. Wright recalled ordering his commander-in-chief to step down or be forced to. Years later, Oliver Wendell Holmes claimed that he had been a young captain at Stevens that day, and he had simply yelled at Lincoln, "Get down, you fool!" Also years later, Pvt. John A. Bedient of the 150th Ohio National Guard claimed that it was he who shouted the warning. Thomas Hyde probably had it right when he said "a lot of people persuaded Mr. Lincoln to get down out of range, which he very reluctantly did."

All agree that on this hot summer day, Abraham Lincoln could easily have been killed by his own curiosity.

Sixth Corps veteran James Bowan told a story with a ring of truth to it. "In the fort were gathered cabinet officers and citizens of both sexes who had come out from the city to see the VI Corps whip Early. In an abrasure beside Gen. Wright, the corps commander, and a surgeon, stood the six-foot tall form of President Lincoln. Gen. [David] Russell, commanding the 1st Division, with two of his brigade commanders, Gen. [Emory] Upton and Col. [Oliver] Edwards, just entered the fort and mounted the parapet to select positions for their troops in order to join with the second divison in an attack on the enemy. The turning of their field glasses toward the hostile line was a signal for the Confederate sharp shooters to open fire, and one of their bullets almost immediately entered the embrasure, struck a wheel of the siege gun and wounded the surgeon standing almost behind it, close to the president. The latter was then induced by Wright to sit down out of range and a chair was placed for him close to the parapet."

Somewhat later, one of his cabinet pointed toward the field of battle and said, "Mr. President, if you will look over in that direction, you can see just where the rebels are." Lincoln replied, "My impression is that if I am where I can see the rebels, they are where they can see me."

July 12, 5:00 P.M.—The Battle of Fort Stevens

There were other important civilians gathered at the fort. In fact, one can place almost the entire cabinet there by combining the recollections of old men. The navy secretary Gideon Welles was definitely there. It was said that the secretary of state, William Henry Seward, arrived accompanied by his son, William Henry, Jr., commander of the 9th New York Heavy Artillery, who had been wounded on the Monocacy and escaped by riding that mule with the silken hackamore back to his command. Secretary of War Edwin M. Stanton was said to have arrived with Lincoln. A Wisconsin soldier, B.T. Plugh of the 1st Heavy Artillery, recalled that Lincoln had visited Fort DeRussy in the company of the head of the secret service, Col. Lafayette C. Baker, while a second Wisconsin veteran, Will Langford, remembered that the postmaster general, Montgomery Blair, had been there. And C.E. Enos of the 122nd New York claimed he was the one who had quieted Mrs. Lincoln's fears when word spread that someone had been wounded on the parapet. She was supposedly sitting in a carriage outside the fort with the secretary of the treasury, Salmon P. Chase!

Because of this convergence of personalities in so many memories, enough people of importance were gathered in the vicinity of Stevens that something had to be done to assure their safety, especially after the close call with Mr. Lincoln. McCook turned to Wright and asked that a full brigade be readied for an attack, with the object of clearing out the confederate skirmish line and putting an end to the sharpshooter fire from the nearby houses.

Wright conferred with his commanders and assigned the attack to Brig. Frank Wheaton, commanding the Second Division. Wheaton's own First Brigade would follow the attack-leading Second Brigade under Col. Daniel D. Bidwell of Buffalo. In reserve, on the field before the fort, was Col. Oliver Edwards's Third Brigade from the First Division.

What a theatrical scene it was. With the president of the United States and a covey of cabinet-rank politicians looking on, Bidwell deployed his troops into battle lines. The 49th New York, 77th New York and 7th Maine formed the front line, with the 43rd New York, 122nd New York and 61st Pennsylvania making up the second. The big guns of forts Stevens and Slocum were to soften up the enemy positions and neutralize the fire from the houses with three salvos, with the shelling ending after the thirty-sixth shot. Then the charge would be made.

Bidwell was a rock, a general officer who had enlisted as a private three years before.

Leslie's Illustrated Newspaper

THE BATTLE AT FORT STEVENS

He had spent three lifetimes at the Seven Days and Malvern Hill and Antietam and Gettysburg and the Wilderness, and he was now one tough nut. His men went up in perfect order toward the battlefield.

As soon as they entered the field below the fort, they came under withering fire from the confederate line and shooters in the houses. Most of the men hit the ground. From Stevens and nearby DeRussy, long-throated cannon roared to life; two houses along the pike vanished in explosions that blew out clouds of powder, dust, shattered glass and splintered wood. Daniel Bee of the 61st Pennsylvania, while awaiting the order to charge, counted twenty-five shells that slammed into the Carberry house alone. Five men jumped from the upstairs windows as the house began to burn.

At last came the command to charge. Bidwell's lines rose and sprang forward in "as fine a bayonet charge as could be," and quickly overran the small ridge used by forward confederate marksmen. Pushing over fences and fields, the blue lines on the left flank advanced easily against that sector held by Grimes's brigade of Rodes's division. The 32nd and 53rd North Carolina, holding the right flank, and a passel of sharpshooters were driven sharply in.

Capt. Feamster of the 14th Virginia Cavalry noted that "the enemy repulsed us from both points on the right and drives us entirely back. I received a severe wound in the head & mouth, Shattering my teeth & gold plugs in all directions, cutting and mangling my tongue."

One of the boys who went down amid that hail of balls was Billy Henry McClung, and he went down because he was trying to carry his wounded brother, Johnny

Thomas, off the field.

Rodes, now under pressure, sent the 42nd and 45th North Carolina regiments forward. Col. E.N. Atkinson in Gordon's division said "they went up beautifully . . . cheerfully and confidently," and halted the union charge just below the range of hills between the pike and Rock Creek.

The 122nd New York had reached a forward position north of the Reeves house, but it had taken such an effort to get there that men like Pvt. William Eugene Ruggles found themselves out of ammunition. They had no choice but to fall back. Rodes was on their heels, and they realized that in flight lay death. They again had no choice but to stop, fix bayonets and charge the pursuing Confederates—without ammunition.

This affair was developing into a full scale fight, something neither side seemed anxious or willing to undertake with darkness coming on. Wright decided to try to stabilize the situation and ordered forward not only Wheaton's reserve brigade, but the Edwards's Third Brigade of the First Division as well. Kyd Douglas watched the movement of this mass of veterans of the VI Corps and anticipated capture. "I saw it coming and thought we were 'gone up,'" he later wrote.

The battleground now reached a mile out from the works, and the excited spectators could not see the distant action in the dusk and smoky haze. Lucius Chittenden thought he could make out a charge by mounted men against Bidwell's front and a bloody repulse of same. Heavy firing went on well after the sun had set and the full buck moon illuminated the scene of carnage.

At length the firing quieted and finally died but for the occasional nervous sentry challenging a shadow.

To the cool, pale moonlight was added the pulsing orange glow of burning houses. Chittenden made his way onto the battlefield below Stevens and approached a flaming house. "On all the floors, on the roofs, in the yards, within reach of the heat, were many bodies of the dead or dying, who could not move, and had been left behind by their comrades. The odor of burning flesh filled the air; it was a sickening spectacle!"

Men with stretchers made their way through this eery light, collecting the dead and wounded. A soldier in the Vermont brigade confided a smug opinion to his diary, that "the dignitaries in the fort returned to their homes, having witnessed as pretty and well-conducted a little fight as was seen during the whole war." The New Yorker Ruggles, reflecting on the same subject, concluded, "I suppose they think it was a splendid sight, but we poor fellows could not see much fun in it."

At least he was alive. Of the thousand men in Bidwell's brigade, 280 certain and perhaps 375 had been killed or wounded. Ruggles's comrade in the 122nd New York, S.A. McDonald, later calculated that over thirty-five percent of the brigade had been killed outright, compared to sixteen percent killed or wounded at Antietam, Chancellorsville and Gettysburg. Every single regimental commander in the entire brigade had fallen.

Chittenden, in his tour of the field, came upon a fallen sharpshooter who still clutched a fine English rifle and cartridge box and wore body armor, "the only things about him which did not indicate extreme destitution." Here was the face of the enemy at last, real and up close: A sprawled, bony body that had marched more than three hundred miles in six weeks and fought on many fields, his haversack containing "a jack-knife, a plug of twisted tobacco, a tin cup and about two quarts of coarsely cracked corn, with, perhaps, an ounce of salt, tied in a rag."

It took a soldier like Thomas Hyde to see such men for what they were. "That is as fine a corps of infantry as ever marched to the tap of a drum."

July 12, Morning—Pikesville

As Johnson scared horses and tore up tracks at Beltsville, and federal cannon blew up houses in front of Fort Stevens, Harry Gilmor led his exhausted command into Pikesville, with every intention of burning down the huge old (1816) federal arsenal.

He was intercepted by a distinguished gentleman, Benjamin O. Howard, a former congressman, who rode up and told him, "You can't do that, Harry! You know the people here are sympathetic to the South, but the Yankees know that, too, and they'll come in here and burn us all out in retaliation. Listen to what I'm saying."

Gilmor listened and replied, "All right, Uncle Benjamin."

His uncle having talked him out of his prize, Gilmor led his command into Randallstown for the night. Had he known that Early's army was, at that hour, preparing to withdraw from the front gates of Washington, Gilmor might have prompted his exhausted men to move farther south. As it was, he now faced the real possibility of being trapped and killed or captured many miles north of the Potomac.

July 12, Night—Early's Field Headquarters

When Kyd Douglas reported to Early on the battlefield, it was "some while after dark." Breckinridge and Gordon were planning an orderly withdrawal. Early "seemed in a droll humor, perhaps one of relief," and he greeted Douglas in his falsetto drawl.

"Major, we haven't taken Washington, but we've scared Abe Lincoln like hell!"

"Yes, General," Douglas replied, "but this afternoon when that Yankee line moved out against us, I think some other people were scared blue as hell's brimstone!"

Breckinridge was amused by the remark and prodded Early. "How about that, General?"

"That's true," piped Early, "but it won't appear in history!"

Douglas made sure it did.

He was given the unenviable assignment of commanding the two-hundred-man detail being left on the picket line. He was to "remain with them and keep them there until after midnight, unless driven in or ordered away before that time, and then march them away as rear guard until cavalry fell in behind."

As Douglas rode forward to the line, the vast, moving shadows in the summer night behind him revealed the stirrings of an army preparing for a long dash to safety.

Johnson's van under his adjutant, Capt. Booth reached Early's headquarters at Silver Spring around nine P.M. Three hours later an exhausted Johnson appeared, only to be told abruptly that the army was moving out now, and he was to take up the rear guard.

Leslie's Illustrated Newspaper

BLAIR MANSION IN RUINS

July 12, 11:00 P.M.—Falkland

Toward midnight, the damp massed darkness of the creek valley was split with a huge bloom of fire and light that leaped over the tree tops, the unmistakeable signature of a great house succumbing to the torch. It was Montgomery Blair's Falklands. What led to the destruction—simple mob vandalism, calculated revenge for Hunter's deprivations in the valley, a specific injury to one of Lincoln's cabinet, a stray shell—will never be known, but each possibility was offered in the heated public discussion that followed. (When Ben "Beast" Butler heard of the burning of Falkland, he sent a gunboat to burn down the house of the Confederate Secretary of War James Seddon near Fredericksburg, occupied or not.)

Leonidus Polk of the 43rd North Carolina said that it was Marylanders serving under Early who "struck a match to it." That would implicate Johnson's cavalry, the only Maryland troops in the vicinity late at night on the twelfth. Kyd Douglas, with his two hundred pickets, was also in the vicinity.

As they withdrew up the Seventh Street road, Douglas sent a courier to collect the guard at Silver Spring, who soon appeared. Then, "a mile or two beyond, my attention was called to a bright light behind us, which proved to be the burning house of Mr. Blair. By whom it was burned is mere conjecture. It was not destroyed by anyone's order. I feel confidant the cavalry guard, in charge of a reliable officer, did not do it."

Douglas made the point that the great flame "notified the enemy that we had gone, and . . . we were pursued and annoyed several hours before we would otherwise have been."

If it was not deliberate arson, then artillery fire from Fort Stevens was the most popular explanation. Union artillerists claimed hits on several other homes along the Brookeville pike.

Silver Spring survived but was vandalized, its furniture broken up, its library and wine cellar pillaged. A note was found enscribed on the fly-leaf of a book:

Near Washington, July 12, '64

> Now Uncle Abe, you had better be quiet the balance of your administration,
> as we only came near your town this time to show you what we could do,
> but if you go on in your mad career we will come again, soon, and and then
> you had better stand from under.

Yours respectfully,
the worst rebel you ever saw
58th Virginia Infantry

By eleven P.M. on the twelfth, Early's army was fully on the move toward Rockville. Bradley Johnson's advance had come in from the affair at Beltsville and was already moving to close the column, with Brig. Gen. W.L. "Mudwall" Jackson's cavalry at the rear guard. After their brief conference with Douglas, the generals, Early, Breckenridge and Gordon, had moved on up the road. The gray tide was ebbing north and west, and it is possible that stragglers set fire to Falklands because it represented a direct link to the enemy. It is also possible that a Maryland cavalry officer, remembering far happier times and a certain Miss Mason he somehow associated with Silver Spring, had stood guard over it as he stood guard over that memory and left a note before riding off into the dark.

Capt. Aldace F. Wallace of the 1st Vermont heavies found these words penned on a visiting card in the Blair mansion:

> Taken from a pilferer for old acquaintance sake with Miss Emma Mason,
> and left at 11 p.m. here by a Rebel officer who once knew her and remained
> behind to prevent this house from being burned by stragglers as was the
> neighboring one, 11 p.m., and no light, July 12, 1864.

XIV.
Withdrawal from
Washington

Wednesday, July 13—Dawn

There lay on the land at sunrise the awful peace of a Civil War battlefield, a benign country morning in which the gentle lowing of cattle counterpoints the distant boom of guns, and the clear blueness of the sky is marred by roiling smoke from burning houses, and the meadows and groves are adorned by prone men, stiffened in death.

"The gray dawn spread over the landscape widely extended in sight," Montgomery Meigs recalled. "An occasional shot from a suspicious picket and the low of a cow or bray of a mule alone broke the stillness of the morning, and at last the sun arose and all remained quiet."

McCook sent forward two companies of infantry flanked by cavalry to probe up the pike and discover Early's skirmish line. They went out cautiously and moved slowly over the ground, sending back a report that McCook passed on. "The rebel pickets in front of Fort Stevens were changed in the night from infantry to cavalry, and the cavalry departed just before daylight."

The people along the pike said that some units had moved out as early as seven o'clock the previous evening, and the last of the cavalry had departed before five A.M. If his main force had marched quietly away around midnight, Early had at least an eight hour jump on any possible pursuit.

Continuing up the pike, the detachment came upon Rodes's field hospital at Sligo Post Office and captured eleven surgeons and orderlies and seventy wounded, including Thomas Feamster. Farther on they found another fifty-eight wounded, and still others, until they had almost two hundred south of Leesborough.

But Early's army was gone, and so relieved was everyone that no one thought of chasing after it until it was too late.

July 13, 10:00 A.M.—Washington City

Charles A. Dana, assistant secretary of war, to Grant at City Point:

The enemy have disappeared along the entire line.

July 13, Morning—Rockville

Col. Lowell's 2nd Massachusetts Cavalry had filed out from the defensive line at Fort Reno soon after sunrise and probed up the Rockville pike until, around nine o'clock and a few miles below Rockville, it made contact with a confederate force that had been withdrawing all that morning from near Bethesda Church. The sparring began instantly. As Lowell came within a half mile of Rockville, he realized that Early's whole army had already passed by way of the old city road from Leesborough and was heading out through Rockville toward Darnestown, Poolesville and the Potomac River crossings.

Lowell's troopers moved in to harass and annoy Johnson's rear guard under Mudwall Jackson. As the riders in blue peppered the retreating column with fire from Spencer repeating rifles, Johnson found that matters were "getting disagreeable." He put in a squadron from the 1st Maryland under Capt. Wilson Cavey Nicholas and Lt. Thomas Green on a yelling charge along Commerce Lane. Many of the 2nd Massachusetts turned and bolted for the safety of the rear, but many others dismounted and, as Johnson recalled, "stuck to the houses and fences and poured in a galling fire. The dust was so thick that the men in their charge could not see the houses in front of them."

Nicholas and Green both were hit, their gunshot horses staggered and went down. Men in blue quickly surrounded them. Johnson, watching from farther west on Commerce Lane as his officers were seized, organized a second charge that drove Lowell backward along Montgomery Avenue and again filled the street with billowing dust, milling horsemen and blazing guns. James Hill of the 2nd Massachusetts, wounded and dismounted, ran to a nearby house; Margaret Bell opened her door, and he fell inside with bullets singing.

In the melée, Green was taken back from his erstwhile captors, but Nicholas, the young inspector general of the confederate Maryland line, had already been put on a horse and led from the field. As Johnson once again withdrew, Lowell followed, until the action spilled into the little valley of Watts Branch, where that stream crossed the Darnestown Road. Here Johnson's waiting picket line came under such galling fire from the Spencers that he again drove hard against Lowell, this time making him fall back all of the way through town and two miles down the Rockville pike, where the 2nd Massachusetts pulled up, content to join forces with Fry's provisionals and the 8th Illinois Cavalry before resuming the chase.

Accounts of the action at Rockville note that "many men were killed," but realistic figures are impossible to come by. Certainly Johnson thought himself "treated with more respect" as he continued down the road toward Poolesville, with sixty new prisoners in tow.

July 13—Rockville Pike

Early's army left bizarre examples of death in its wake. Three miles from Fort Reno, near the present Naval Medical Center, a soldier with a crushed skull was found lying next to a shell fragment that had flown those miles and struck him. Amazingly, he was still alive and was carted to Lincoln Hospital, where he died July 17.

Others had also died from the rain of big shells in the vicinity. At least that was the conclusion they came to on the morning of the thirteenth, when Louis Rohrer and his wife emerged from their home, where the tower of the center now stands, to find the confederate encampment on their farm deserted and freshly dug graves under the locust trees down by the road.

And at Silver Spring, a descending shell knocked the foot off a statue that ornamented the pool by the spring; it killed a confederate soldier who was drinking there at that moment. He was buried nearby.

July 13, Morning—Fort Stevens

Abe Lincoln must have given a vivid report to his family, for on Wednesday morning his son Robert Todd and Robert's pal, John Hay, the president's personal assistant, went sightseeing on the battlefield. They were met a young captain, Oliver Wendell Holmes, who escorted them out to the "gypsy style" encampment where Early's troops had been but a few hours before. Hay was not impressed with his own army, which he found to be soldierly enough but otherwise "dirty, careless."

They looked out from the parapet of the fort and then went to McCook's headquarters in the Mooreland Tavern on the Seventh Street road and had a beer with the staff. Lunch was served at Montgomery Meigs's field headquarters, after which the young men watched as a burial detail of fifty freedmen, their faces covered with handkerchiefs to filter some of the stench of death, walked the battlefield, bringing in the Reaper's harvest.

July 13, Noon—Great Seneca Valley, Dawsonville

Beyond Rockville, the long column shuffled forward through the summer morning, the infantry swaying along in its loping stride with prisoners from Monocacy, creaking artillery and long lines of cattle and horses kicking up dust. As the miles went by, those able to find a stray horse to rest their legs did not hesitate to climb up, so much so that chaplain James B. Sheeran declared the column looked like "demoralized cavalry."

At midday, the long line of march had snaked its way down into the broad valley of Great Seneca Creek between Darnestown and Dawsonville and, mercifully, a halt was declared. The men had been on the march since midnight, twelve hours before.

John Worsham, like many others, was "still barefooted; my feet were too sore to wear my boots." The scars would remain with him for the rest of his life. Many of his comrades were "barefooted and footsore, and we had made a terrible campaign since we left our winter quarters." In the thirty-one days since they left Lee's army at Richmond, Worsham calculated, they had "marched 469 miles, fought several combats, and one battle, and threatened Washington, causing the biggest scare they ever had."

July 13—Pursuit

Montgomery Meigs was nonchalant about the possibility of pursuing and perhaps defeating Early. "We remained in position until full daylight, and then sent the men to their breakfast," he noted. Afterward, they "completed our entrenchments." Did Meigs actually believe Early would return?

Meigs may be excused for thinking that the pursuit of Early was not the affair of his desk-soldiers but the professionals, Wright's Greek cross veterans, were also slow to react to the retreat. For one thing, Wright was not convinced his ten thousand troops were a match for the thirty thousand that he thought Early had. For another, to whom did they report in this capital city—McCook, Hardin, Secretary of War Stanton, Grant through his chief of staff, Henry Halleck, or Lincoln himself?

Grant wanted his troops back. He was for "promptly punishing the enemy," and Wright could chase Early as long as there was "any prospect of punishing" him, but the sooner they showed up at Petersburg the better.

Lincoln refused to second guess the command structure, but he let it be known that if someone would hustle down River Road, they could cut off Early's approach to a Potomac crossing.

With that very thought in mind, and also because some Potomac fords were suitable for cavalry but not for infantry and artillery, McCausland occupied the River Road and retreated down it. It led, eventually but directly, to Edward's and Conrad's (now White's) ferries, both of which he could cross.

Wright finally organized his pursuit of Early by way of the roads from Fort Stevens, and of McCausland by way of River Road and the Rockville pike. He sent Stanton a message:

> I can assure yourself and the President that there will be no delay on my part
> to head off the enemy, and that the men I have will do all that the number
> of men can do.

But it was three-thirty P.M., and Early's army was sleeping in the afternoon shade of the Great Seneca Valley, some twenty miles from the White House as the crow flies.

By the time Wright's lead regiments reached Offut's Crossroads,, modern Potomac, on the River Road, it was dark. They had marched the ten miles from the defensive perimeter of the city quite manfully, but the heat and dust affected them as it had Early's troops, and their column was strung out for miles behind them. They had no choice but to camp at the crossroads just as Early's men began their march to White's Ford.

July 13—Gilmor On the Road

From Randallstown in Baltimore County to Poolesville in Montgomery it is forty miles, a powerful day's ride on horseback. Gilmor, unaware that Early was in full flight toward the Potomac, followed Johnson's tracks across Howard County as far as Brookeville, where he, too, called at Greenwood and bowed to the trio of Allen and Hester Davis's daughters, Miss Mary, age twenty-two, Miss Rebecca, age twenty, and Miss Esther, age seventeen. Here he learned that he was running far behind the army and would have to ride hard all night, cross-county toward Poolesville.

Rebecca found young Gilmor and his officers "a most independent set, in highest spirits, easy and affable in their manners." She had learned from Bradley Johnson's visit of the burning of Governor Bradford's home in Baltimore and protested it even as a retaliation. Why, she wondered in her innocence, could they not "return good for evil?"

"We have tried that three years, Miss," she was told. "Been twice to Pennsylvania respecting private property, and what have we in return?" But politics were laid aside, and Rebecca and her sisters charmed the men by singing "Annie in the Vale" and other sentimental tunes; in appreciation, the officers bestowed upon the ladies buttons from their tunics and then, in a classic romantic departure, rode off into the sunset.

July 14, Dawn, Poolesville

At sunset, it had been rise and march again for Early's footsore legion. Bradley Johnson recalled that "all night long we marched and stopped, and stopped and marched, with that terrible tedious delay and iteration so wearing to men and horses."

At daybreak, while the rest of the army passed along the road leading to White's Ford above Mason Island, Johnson deployed his artillery and set out a "strong skirmish line in front of Poolesville."

Soon a column was seen advancing. It was Harry Gilmor, having ridden all night, returning to the army command. Later in his career, when Gilmor was offered a regiment, he said that he "preferred [his] battalion to any regiment in the army; it was the right kind of stuff."

Harper's Weekly

RETREATING ACROSS THE POTOMAC

Johnson welcomed him warmly, saying he was sure Gilmor had been captured.

"I felt very well pleased myself to be where I was," Gilmor wrote later, "having made, without doubt, a rather venturesome trip."

July 14, Morning—White's Ford

Harper's *Pictorial History of the Great Rebellion* displays a sketch of the army crossing at White's Ford, and it looks more like a scene from a Chisholm Trail cattle drive than from the Civil War. In the foreground cattle are descending a slight slope and wading into the shallow river, part of a long line that runs across to the steeper hill on the Virginia side. Upstream is the wagon crossing. Three wagons, drawn by teams of four horses, are in the river and seven are preparing to enter it. Even farther upstream, a column of captured horses, many but not most of them with riders, makes an easier crossing. Somehow the picture conveys a sense of relief.

Said G.W. Nichols, "We were all glad to get back to Dixie land."

Said J. Kelley Bennette, "Heaven be praised, we are once more in the Old Dominion."

July 14, Sunset—Poolesville

Sometime during the afternoon a long line of soldiers appeared in Johnson's front, their line stretching far beyond each end of his own. He summoned General Ransom, and the two men watched "the advancing line through our glasses, which showed their cartridge boxes and canteens plainly, puff! puff! puff! went their fire all along the line. There was no mistaking the sound. The swish of the minié-ball was so clear and so evident that it could not possibly come from carbines." In other words, infantry. And time to go.

Johnson looked back on his tremendous effort. "We had been marching, working, and fighting from daylight, July 9, until sundown, July 14th, four days and a half, or about 108 hours. We had unsaddled only twice during that time, with a halt of from 4 to 5 hours each time, making nearly 100 hours of marching.

". . . [H]aving been notified that everything, including my own ordnance and baggage train, had crossed, I withdrew comfortably and got into Virginia about sundown."

Early's great raid against the union capital, which had profoundly shaken men's hearts and minds, was over. In his own assessment, "I had then made a march, over the circuitous route by Charlottesville, Lynchburg, and Salem, down the valley and through the passes of the South Mountain, which, notwithstanding the delays in dealing with Hunter's, Sigel's, and Wallace's forces, is, for its length and rapidity, I believe, without a parallel in this or any other modern war. . . . [The] wonder [is] not why I failed to take Washington but why I had the audacity to approach it as I did."

Friday, July 15—Harpers Ferry

David Strother: "General Hunter received a telegram from Halleck directing him to put his troops under command of Crook or send them to Wright or to join Wright personally and serve under his orders. . . . The General asks to be relieved of command, considering himself insulted. . . . The enemy has made his raid and is gone scot-free without a fight. . . . [T]he disgrace is unspeakable."

Saturday, July 16—Harpers Ferry

Strother: "The General showed me a telegram sent by himself to the President asking to be relieved of command, giving as reason General Halleck's order of yesterday. . . . [H]e will not be made the scapegoat for other people's blunders. . . . At dinner General Hunter showed me a dispatch from President Lincoln apologizing for the order . . . saying no offence was meant and it was only temporary. . . . I have begged off Charles Town from being burnt for the third time.

Monday, July 18—Near Harpers Ferry

Strother: "The house of Andrew Hunter was burned yesterday."

Tuesday, July 19—Near Harper's Ferry

Strother: "Orders given to burn the houses of E.J. Lee and Alex Boteler. Martindale went forward to execute it. His description of the women and the scene is heart-rending."

Tuesday, August 2—Thomas House, Monocacy

Strother: "We took headquarters at the house of a Mr. Thomas, the center of the battleground of Monocacy. The trees, hedges, shrubs, all bear marks of battle more decidedly than any place I have seen."

Friday, August 5—Monocacy

Strother: "I spoke to the General concering my intention of leaving the service and find there will be no difficulty on his part. I will get ready and tender my resignation immediately."

August 5—Araby

In the fullness of time, U.S. Grant himself finally appeared at the Monocacy. He must have realized how wrong his intelligence had been about Early's movements, and how close Early had come to bringing England into the war against the Union, and that had it not been for Lew Wallace, the object of Grant's scorn after Shiloh, who put the Potomac home brigades and a lot of raw Ohio guards between Early and Washington, Grant might have been made to look a complete fool.

Early was safely in the Shenandoah, free to raid into Pennsylvania and Maryland, and Grant was now "determined to put a stop to this." In early August he went by steamer from City Point to Baltimore, then rode the B&O to Monocacy Junction, by-passing Washington and Lincoln and the war department and Stanton and Halleck entirely.

Waiting for him at Monocacy was David Hunter and his army, back from their long sojourn through the hills of West Virginia. They were encamped all over the former battlefield, on both sides of the river. Frederick Junction's side tracks were filled with railroad cars that Garrett had put there for safe keeping.

The meeting was held at Araby, in an upstairs room over the library. Grant had called in eight major generals, including Hunter, Wright and Crook. His *Memoirs* record the conversation when he asked Hunter, "General, where is the enemy?"

"I do not know, General Grant. The fact of the matter is that I am so baffled by orders from the War Department in Washington, moving me right, then left, then right, that I have lost all trace of the enemy."

GEN. GRANT MEETS GEN. SHERIDAN AT MONOCACY JUNCTION

Grant went downstairs and directed an aid to telegraph to Washington an order for Gen. Philip Sheridan to get out to Araby, immediately.

Waiting for Sheridan meant that Grant had to spend the night at Araby. On the morning of August sixth, at breakfast, Grant lifted little Virginia Thomas, then five, onto his lap and asked her, "Well, Virginia, are your mother and father rebels or Yankees?"

To which Virginia honestly replied, "Mamma is a Rebel, but Papa is a Rebel when the Rebels are here and a Yankee when the Yankees are here."

After a long moment of deep silence, Grant put his head back and roared with laughter.

August 6—Monocacy

Strother: "Went to the Monocacy Depot in an ambulance with General Grant. His manner of speech is Western and Yankee. His face indicates firmness and his manner is cool and quiet. His general appearance is most unsoldierly.... At dinner sat opposite Major General Sheridan. The General wished he had a drink. I went upstairs and got a bottle and carried it down to him. . . . Sheridan is short, broad-shouldered, and of an iron frame. Very short legs and small feet and naturally cannot be a good horseman."

In the course of that year, Sheridan went into the Shenandoah Valley, where he made his famous ride at the battle of Cedar Creek, rallying a beaten army for a decisive victory. Within months he had burned two thousand farms, won four battles and driven Early and his army into the ground, a major event in the winning of the war for the Union.

XV.
Afterword:
Afterward

Honors

Almost thirty years after the battle, on May 27, 1892, when men remembered what he had done that blistering day, the name of George E. Davis, Co. D., 10th Vermont Volunteer Infantry, who brought his men in fine order through a murderous field of fire across the Monocacy railroad bridge, was recorded on a Congressional Medal of Honor.

As was the name of Cpl. Alexander Scott, also of the 10th Vermont, on September 28, 1897. Scott had not saved lives nor killed the enemy, but had carried the regimental flags, those sacred emblems, to safety. Tell me that war was not a game.

Capt. Henry du Pont also won a Medal of Honor—at Cedar Creek, firing his guns into the morning mist as the Confederates surprised the federal flank, and managed to save two of his three sections by leap-frogging them off the field, as he had done after New Market. He later served two terms in the United States Senate, and lived until 1926.

Love Triumphant

As the great gray grim one passed over the horizon, following the armies eastward, forever unsatisfied, his hood disguised as summer cloud, more gentle spirits emerged.

Imagine the joy that flashed through such general anguish when the young ladies of Araby looked up from their damaged home to see their missing beaux, Julius Anderson and Hugh Gatchell, hastening down the driveway. For Cupid had also flown on the wings of war to the young men hiding under the big wheel of James Gambrill's mill and they now rushed down the drive to Araby, past the dead and wounded, and into the arms of their courageous young ladies, who had twice braved the iron bridge on their behalf. Both these attachments resulted in marriage.

Cpl. Roderick Clark of the 14th New Jersey, some seventeen hours after being wounded, had been placed, more dead than alive, in the care of Miss Lissie Ott. For three long months she nursed him back to life, sitting by him hour after hour, fanning him in the summer heat, speaking soft words of cheer.

"Do you blame me for falling in love with her?" Clark asks us rhetorically. Hell no, Rod. He married the lady, and they lived happily in Point Pleasant, New Jersey, where he wrote a memoir of his experience in 1886.

Capt. Chauncey Harris, also of the 14th New Jersey, who had been so unfairly wounded in the knee while lying in the ambulance from a previous shoulder wound, had been turned over to another compassionate hand, that of Miss Clementine Baker, at her father's farm a mile below Araby. Compassion warmed to love, and Chauncey and Clementine were married. He was brevetted colonel for bravery on the field and took Clementine back to Elizabeth, where he served as postmaster for many years.

Lt. John Spangler of the 87th Pennsylvania, with that terrible chest and stomach wound, was placed in the care of the widow Doffler, who wrote to his father in York. The father hastened to his son's side and was there when he died on July fifteenth. After the burial in York's Union Cemetery, the father returned to thank and, in time, to marry the kindly Ruth.

Thus, for the Clark, Harris, Spangler, Gatchell and Thomas families, the bitterness of the loss and destruction at Monocacy was sweetened by the chance for lasting love.

Death Triumphant

The truly gallant could not survive a war such as this was, a certainty that makes their gallantry even more remarkable. The closing month of 1864 claimed several of the best: Thirty-four-year-old Col. James J. Mulligan of the 23rd Illinois "Irish Brigade" fell with three mortal wounds at Kernstown on July 24. His last command: "Lay me down and save the flag."

Young Lt. Henry C. Blackiston, who had torched Governor Bradford's home in Baltimore, was killed August 12. Partisan John H. MacNeill did not have a chance to become a living legend as did Mosby; he died of a gunshot wound suffered on October 3 while about his old practice of attacking a wagon train near Mount Jackson. Charles Russell Lowell of the 2nd Massachusetts Cavalry was shot from his horse by a sniper at Cedar Creek on October 19.

Brigade commander Col. Joseph Thoburn and Col. George D. Wells of the brave 34th Massachusetts were also killed at Cedar Creek.

Confederate Col. George S. Patton of the 22nd Virginia died on September 19, on the battlefield at Winchester, of wounds from a shell fragment—but his ferocious blood lived on. His son George was nine when the colonel was killed; when grown, George also had a son he named George S., the celebrated commander of the American Third

Army in World War II. This general had a grandson born on May 15, 1947—the 83rd anniversary of the battle at New Market.

Death Slumbering

The dead sleep in many places. Within a week of the battle at Fort Stevens, forty-one soldiers had been buried pratically where they died, in a little stonehenge of two circles of white tombstones around a flag pole in a one-acre plot along the Seventh Street road. It was dedicated by Lincoln as Battlefield National Cemetery, the smallest of all and, today as then, one of the most compelling—and unfortunately neglected. Beyond a rubble wall, the circles of graves remain, and a superintendent's lodge built in 1865 of dressed fieldstone with a handsome slate mansard roof. A marble rostrum and columns lend dignity to the place, and monuments to the 98th Pennsylvania Infantry, the 122nd New York, Co. K of the 150th Ohio National Guard and the 25th New York Cavalry.

Farther up Georgia Avenue, in the corner of the grounds of Grace Episcopal Church, a monument stands over seventeen confederate dead, moved there from their first resting place when a trolley line was laid out along the old pike.

The union dead from Monocacy were carted all the way to Antietam for burial; eighty-seven of the Confederate dead were buried at Mount Olivet Cemetery in Frederick. Some years after the battle, the Ladies' Confederate Memorial Association of Frederick employed a crew to go over the field and collect the bones of the fallen for reburial in Mount Olivet. These were placed in a common grave, it being impossible to identify so many, and a tablet erected in the 1870s marks "the last resting place of 408 Confederate Soldiers." Thus we are certain that almost 500 of Early's army stayed forever in Maryland.

Young Billy Scott still sleeps in the yard of Rose of Lima Catholic Church on Clopper Road, a long way from home, buried among friends he made once, if only for a moment. Those last earthly friends, William Rich Hutton and Mary Augusta Clopper Hutton, and her parents, Ann Jayne and Francis Cassatt Clopper, also sleep in the churchyard. On the Clopper's marker is written:

"Blessed art thou, O Lord. Thou has taught me Thy justifications."

Roger Farquhar, who knew three of the Hutton children (who, amazingly, still lived in the manor house in 1950), said it took a careful search of confederate records over a period of years to establish young Billy's identity, for he was buried in an unmarked grave. Some say the trooper never revealed his identity; others feel the grave remained unmarked because of lingering hostility. In any event, the United Daughters of the Confederacy eventually erected a small headstone that stands near the church today: Pvt. William D. Scott, Co. D, 14th Virginia Cavalry, July 10, 1864.

Valley Memories

The VMI cadets who gave their lives in the taking of Kleiser's field gun will live forever in the memory of the institute. Their charge is depicted in a painting twenty-three feet tall that hangs in a place of high honor in Jackson Memorial Hall on the campus.

Capt. Thomas Feamster, shot in the mouth at Fort Stevens, survived, but for a long time he could not eat and could drink only by immersing his entire head in a pail of water. He became the postmaster of Lewisburg, in the West Virginia mountains, and died there on the last day of 1906.

William "Billy" Henry McClung, who had fallen while carrying his wounded brother from the field, was a classic American hard-ass. Hit in the face and presumably captured at Cedarville in November, his third war wound, he leaped onto a horse and rode it through the federal lines into the Shenandoah River, which he swam three times to shake off pursuit, slept in the mountains and rejoined his command the next day. Billy fared well, was elected to the West Virginia house of delegates for eight years, owned three thousand acres of coal, timber and grazing lands, and lived until 1915.

Years after the war, the former sergeant Cyrus Creigh of the 14th Virginia Cavalry, who had surrendered at Appomattox and who believed his father had been hanged with Hunter's approval near Lexington, was dining with friends in Staunton when word came of Gen. Hunter's death. He took a pistol from his coat pocket and laid it on the table, saying, "Then I will have no further use of this. Had ever I met Hunter face to face, I would have shot him down." He never again carried a pistol.

Maryland Memories

Stories and tales of course lingered on for years after the passage of the armies through Maryland. Two rural hamlets through which the armies moved were renamed after the war.

The citizens of Leesborough were so happy to be delivered by the occupying forces that they later voted to rename their town in honor of the union general commanding the liberating forces—Frank Wheaton—and so it remains.

After the war, Montgomery Blair rebuilt Falkland, and he and his descendants lived there until 1958, when the great house and grounds gave way, as was the rule for such places in expanding Montgomery County, to a tawdry shopping mall named Blair Center. Nearby stand the two-story, red brick, fifty-year-old apartments named for Falkland, the only residue. The even greater house of Silver Spring, the name of which Sligo Post Office adopted for its own, was razed in 1955.

Other places have had their historical identities erased by development or covered by change. The booming little town of Triadelphia met a dismal fate, drowned by the ten-mile lake backed up in 1943 by the Brighton Dam. The place below the range of hills between the old pike and Rock Creek, where the North Carolina boys halted the union charge on July 10, is now the grounds of Walter Reed Medical Center; only a single reminder, the tablet marking the location of a sniper's tree, remains.

The lovely locale around Pennyfield Lock on the C&O Canal, where the 8th Illinois once abandoned its camp to Mosby's torch, is a favorite birding place for Washingtonians, and its past is recalled in the name of the bluff—Blockhouse Point.

In Baltimore, the future inhabitants of the arsenal that Gilmore spared that July day had reason to thank him, for it became in 1888 the Association of the Maryland Line's home—the "old soldier's home" for Confederate veterans. In 1932 it became headquarters of the Maryland State Police.

For Bradley Johnson, the raid into Maryland had been a visit to his own landed class, one so secure in the legal protections of property that no war, however it came out, could cause them fatal harm. And it didn't. After the war he returned to Maryland, prospered and became a state senator.

Other secessionists in Maryland faced harder times; the nine hundred acres in three farms owned by the widowed Sarah Griffith Brown were sold to her former slave, Enoch George Howard, whose descendants are still numerous in the region. Family tradition has it that he bought all of the surrounding land, but not the manor house parcel, because he did not want to embarass the family. His daughter, Martha, married John Murphy, who founded in 1892 the oldest black newspaper in the nation, Baltimore's *Afro-American,* still managed by his family.

County historian Roger Brooke Farquhar tells us that according to local lore, Si Henson, the inspiration for *Uncle Tom's Cabin,* visited the Riley farm long after the war. A grandmother, very old, nearly blind and hard of hearing, refused to believe it was the former slave until she felt his shoulder, once broken during a beating by a neighborhood gang.

"Why, Si," she said, "it is you. You are quite the gentleman now!"

"I always was, madam," was his reply.

Harry Gilmor

Harry Gilmor resonates through minor American history like one of the innumerable Irish chieftains who fought bravely and died for a lost cause and are forgotten.

And like those later and real Irish patriots, he was, in the end, betrayed. Severely wounded by a superior force under Sheridan at Darkesville in September of 1864, he had returned to service in December. Early, his hands full with a relentless Sheridan, ordered Gilmor to take the 2nd Maryland Battalion into Hardy County in western Virginia to seize and destroy the B&O line.

Gilmor had become such a notorious figure that Sheridan had men tracking his every move, especially Maj. Harry Young of the notorious Jessie scouts, union soldiers dressed in confederate uniforms who operated "sting" operations. When Archie Rowand tracked Gilmor to Morefield, an elaborate trap was designed to take him. Young and Rowand and twenty men were uniformed as Maryland volunteers, a contingent of which Gilmor was expecting. Young then arranged to have his group chased by three hundred union cavalry—no mere gesture, as the two columns rode for fifty-eight miles through severe winter weather, an exercise that took all day and all night.

So convincing was this demonstration that Young was able to ride right up to the house of William Randolph, where Gilmor and his cousin, Hoffman Gilmor, were asleep, and capture both men. And so convincing was Harry Gilmor's reputation that Harry Young personally escorted his prisoner all the way to Boston, where he was once again incarcerated, this time in Fort Warren, until July 24, 1865.

After the war, Gilmor, like many other restless Confederates, moved to New Orleans, where he married, finally, a Miss Mentoria Strong. He found success as a business man, then returned to his native state, where he prospered. He was elected colonel of cavalry of the Maryland National Guard, the members of which had fought on both sides in the late war, and served as Baltimore City police commissioner.

When he died on March 4, 1883, after an operation, he was only forty-five years old. The monument over his grave on Confederate Hill in Loudon Park Cemetery reads:

> OUR GALLANT HARRY
> DAUNTLESS IN BATTLE
> SPLENDID IN SUCCESS
>
> This Dashing Cavalry Chief
> Outrode the Storm of War
> And In The Noontime of Life
> Entered The Valley of Death
> Where He Was Conqueror.

The Generals

Franz Sigel: Sigel resigned his commission in May of 1865 and wandered over to Baltimore to take a job as an editor on a German-language newspaper. He soon went on to the great immigrant port of New York, where he became through political connections the first pension agent, then city tax collector, as well as publisher and editor of the *New Yorker Deutches Volksblatt*. It must be said of Sigel that his instincts were republican, patriotic, and his immense popularity with the the German minority helped place them solidly in the Union camp. He lived until 1902, busy lecturing and writing to the end of his seventy-eight years. In 1907, sculptor Karl Bitter erected along Manhattan's Riverside Drive a bronze equestrian statue—Franz Sigel on a bronze horse, ever acting ever victorious.

John Brown Gordon: Gordon,"the most purtiest thing you ever saw on a field of battle," led the last charge of Lee's army at Appomattox, "taking the Union breastworks and capturing artillery." In 1873 and 1879 he was elected to the United States senate from Georgia, but he resigned the following year to guide the fledging Georgia Pacific Railroad. He then was elected governor for four years and, in 1891, again to the senate, a position he would hold until 1897, when he declined to be a candidate. He spent the remaining seven years of his life in literary work and lecturing.

Some old, lost moments haunted his final years: Grant's flank in the air at the Wilderness, that undefended breastwork at Fort Stevens, those never-fired artillery guns and the last push at Cedar Creek that would have sealed the great victory. In each instance it was Early who had cost the victory. While Gordon was too much a soldier not to have served under his commanding officer without complaint, he was historian enought to know that his final words on the subject were also to be honored, and Early was the subject of his reprimand.

Sometime in the 1890s, Lew Wallace stopped by the senate to visit this most admired and distinguished of all Georgians. They sat on a large overstuffed sofa in the senate chamber.

"What I most remember about that day at Monocacy," said Wallace, "was watching McCausland's charge across the cornfield through my binoculars. It was a spectacle I will never forget."

"I was watching, too. From the other side of the river—*'uth-a side of the riv-a' is how it sounded to Wallace, of course*—and I too was taken aback with the audacity of that movement."

"General Gordon," said Wallace, deliberating addressing the military and not the political figure, "why did he do it?"

"He didn't know. He didn't know it was Ricketts and the VI Corps. He was acting on old orders. He thought all he had to do was blow a bugle at those hundred-day boys and they would disappear."

"I understand he went back to the farm after the war."

"Yes, he took Lee's advice and took up the plow. You know there was bad blood between him and Bradley Johnson after the Chambersburg raid. Johnson thought that McCausland's men had behaved atrociously, and then Averill chased them down and captured and shamed both commands. I think McCausland had enough. He was, you may know, only twenty-seven years old.

"Clement Evans became, of all things, a preacher. And Bill Terry was here in congress, on the house side, in the Forty-second and Forthy-fourth Congresses. He drowned in '88, trying to ford Reed Creek down there in Wytheville, Virginia, where he is from and is buried. And yourself, General Wallace?"

"I am writing as usual."

"Another *Ben Hur?*"

"No, I am starting an autobiography. That is one of the reasons for this visit. I am thinking now about the Monocacy. It was the battle to save Washington, and it really did."

Lew Wallace: Wallace, born in Indiana in 1827, lived a life full of interest and literary achievement. After the war, with the wanderlust that affected so many soldiers on

GEN. JUBAL EARLY
"Whipped Near Winchester"
July 1864

both sides, he went to Mexico, where he had served in the Mexican War, and dabbled in politics and researched for his first novel, *The Fair God*, a story of the Spanish conquest of Mexico, published successfully in 1873. The enormously best selling *Ben Hur* (two million copies) followed in 1880 and then *The Boyhood of Christ* eight years later.

Wallace sustained a political career along with his literary one. He served as territorial governor of New Mexico from 1878 until 1881, when he began a four year appointment as United States minister to Turkey, from which experience came *The Prince of India* in 1893, a turgid story based on the wandering Jew.

The autobiography he discussed with John Gordon was unfinished at his death in 1905; it was completed by his wife, Susan Arnold Wallace, herself an author, who published it in 1906, a year before her own death.

Jubal Early: An unreconstructed rebel until his dying day in 1894, Early at first refused to live in the Union, choosing to be "a voluntary exile rather than submit to the rule of our enemies." Disguised as a farmer, he made his way to Texas, looking in vain for Kirby Smith and a confederate force to continue the fight, and then to Mexico, and on to Cuba and finally to Canada before returning, at last, to Lynchburg, Virginia, where in 1869 he resumed the practise of law and continued the war with words, as the head of the Southern Historical Association. He remained unmarried, caustic and embroiled in controversy with one-time colleagues Longstreet and Gordon over the action at Gettysburg.

In reply to those critics who wondered why he failed to take Washington, he said they should instead wonder "why I had the audacity to approach it as I did, with the small force under my command." He noted that the march of his corps in that summer of 1864 "is, for its length and rapidity, I believe, without a parallel in this or any other modern war."

David Hunter: After being replaced by Sheridan, Hunter was one of those unemployed generals again, but his old association with the White House surfaced after the Lincoln assassination, when he was detailed to stand at the head of the slain president's coffin and to accompany the body to Springfield. That summer he was named by Judge Advocate General Joseph Holt to be presiding officer at the court martial of the presumed assassins; also serving on the eight-person panel were Lew Wallace and Col. Clendenin of the 8th Illinois. Holt knew his man; Hunter could be relied on "to exclude all testimony favorable to the defense and unfavorable to summary execution." Margaret Leech characterized the evidence as "extorted, perverted, and, where necessary, manufactured," but Hunter hurried them all to the gallows. He lived on in Washington City until his death at age eighty-four.

GEN. DAVID HUNTER
in Winchester
September 1864

Appendix: Military Commands

BATTLE AT NEW MARKET

FEDERAL: Maj. Gen. Franz Sigel

First Infantry Division
Brig. Gen. Jeremiah C. Sullivan

First Brigade, Col. August Moor
18th Connecticut—Maj. Henry Peale
28th Ohio—Lt. Col. Gottfried Becker (not engaged)
116th Ohio—Col. James Washburn (not engaged)
123rd Ohio—Maj. Horace Kellogg

Second Brigade, Col. Joseph Thoburn
1st West Virginia—Lt. Col. Jacob Weddle
12th West Virginia—Col. William B. Curtis
34th Massachusetts—Col. George D. Wells
54th Pennsylvania—Col. Jacob M. Campbell

First Cavalry Division
Maj. Gen. Julius Stahel

First Brigade, Col. William B. Tibbits
1st N. Y. (Veteran)—Col. R.F. Taylor
1st N.Y. (Lincoln)—Lt. Col. Alonzo W. Adams

1st Md. Potomac Home Brigade (detachment)
—Maj. J. Townsend Daniel
21st New York—Maj. C.G. Otis
14th Penna. (detachment)—Capt. Ashbel F. Duncan, Lt. Col. William Blakely

Second Brigade, Col. John E. Wynkoop
15th New York (detachment)—Maj. H. Roessler
20th Penna. (detachment)—Maj. R.B. Douglas
22nd Penna. (detachment)—1st Lt. Caleb McNulty

Artillery (22 guns engaged)
Md. Light, Battery B—Capt. Alonzo Snow (6 rifles)
30th Battery, N.Y.—Capt. Alfred von Kleisar (6 Napoleons)
1st W. Va., Battery D—Capt. John Carlin (6 rifles)
1st W. Va. Light, Batt. G—Capt C.T. Ewing (4 rifles)
5th U.S., Batt. B—Capt. Henry A. duPont (not engaged)

CONFEDERATE: Maj. Gen. John C. Breckinridge

First Brigade, Brig. Gen. John Echols
22nd Virginia—Col. George S. Patton
23rd Virginia Battalion—Lt. Col. Clarence Derrick
26th Virginia Battalion—Col. George M. Edgar

Second Brigade, Brig. Gen. C. Gabriel Wharton
30th Virginia Battalion—Lt. Col. J. Lyle Clark
51st Virginia—Lt. Col. John P. Wolfe
62nd Va. Mounted Inf.—Col. George H. Smith
Attached to 62nd: Co. A, 1st Missouri Cavalry—Capt. Charles H. Woodson

Small Attached Commands Fighting As Infantry
VMI Cadet Corps—Lt. Col. Scott Shipp
23rd Virginia Cavalry—Col. Robert White
Davis's Md. Cav. Battn.—Capt. T. Sturgis Davis

Hart's Engineer Co.—Capt. William T. Hart

Cavalry, Brig. Gen. John D. Imboden (not engaged)
18th Virginia—Col. George W. Imboden
2nd Maryland Battalion—Maj. Harry Gilmor
Partisan Rangers—Capt. John H. McNeil
43rd Virginia Battalion—Lt. Col. John S. Mosby

Artillery (18 guns), Maj. William McLaughlin
Chapman's Battery—Capt. George B. Chapman (4 howitzers, 2 rifles)
Jackson's Battery—1st Lt. Randolph H. Blain (1 Parrott, 3 Napoleons)
McClanahan's Battery—Capt. John McClanahan (4 rifles, 2 howitzers)
VMI Battery Section—Lt. C. H. Minge (2 rifles)

Sigel estimated Breckinridge's command at 5,000, with 4,816 engaged; William C. Davis's modern count is 4,087 engaged. Sigel estimated 6,500 in his own command, with 5,150 engaged; Davis estimates 8,940, with 6,275 engaged. Sigel counted Confederate losses at 522 (42 K, 522 W, 13 MIA); Davis estimates 531 (43 K, 474 W, 3 MIA) or 13%. Sigel counted Federal losses at 831 (93 K, 552 W, 186 captured); Davis estimates 870 (96 K, 520 W, 225 MIA) or 13+%.

FEDERALS IN THE VALLEY

Maj. Gen. David Hunter
Aide-de-camp David Hunter Strother

First Infantry Division
Brig. Gen. Jeremiah C. Sullivan

First Brigade, Col. August Moor/Col. George D. Wells
34th Mass.—Col. George D. Wells/Capt. George W. Thompson (transf. from 2nd Brigade, June 8)
28th Ohio—Lt. Col. Gottfried Becker (sent back with prisoners, June 8)
116th Ohio—Col. James Washburn
123rd Ohio—Col. William T. Wilson
5th New York Heavy Artillery, A, B, C and D—Lt. Col. Edward Murray

Second Brigade, Col. Joseph Thoburn
18th Conn.—Col. William G. Ely (transf. to 2nd Brigade, June 8)
1st West Virginia—Lt. Col. Jacob Weddle
12th West Virginia—Col. William B. Curtis

Second Infantry Division
Brig. Gen. George Crook

First Brigade, Col. Rutherford B. Hayes
23rd Ohio—Lt. Col. James M. Comly
36th Ohio—Col. Hiram F. Duval
5th West Virginia—Col. A.A. Tomlinson
13th West Virginia—Col. William R. Brown

Second Brigade, Col. Carr B. White
12th Ohio—Lt. Col. Jonathan Hines
91st Ohio—Col. John A. Turley/Lt. Col. Benjamin F. Coates
9th West Virginia—Col. Isaac Duval
14th West Virginia—Col. Daniel D. Johnson

Third Brigade, Col. Jacob M. Campbell
54th Pennsylvania—Col. Jacob M. Campbell/Maj. Enoch D. Yutzy (transf. from 2nd Brigade, 1st Div., June 9)
3rd and 4th Penna. Reserves, Battn.—Capt. Abel T. Sweet

11th W. Va. (6 companies)—Col. Daniel Frost
15th W. Va.—Lt. Col. Thomas Morris
Brigade Artillery:
  1st Kentucky—Capt. Daniel W. Glassie
  1st Ohio—Lt. George P. Kirtland

Artillery, Capt. Henry A. du Pont
Maryland Light, Battery B—
30th New York—Capt. Alfred von Kleiser
1st West Virginia, Battery D—Capt. John Carlin
5th United States, Battery B—

First Cavalry Division
Maj. Gen. Julius Stahel

First Brigade, Col. William B. Tibbits
1st New York (Lincoln)
1st New York (Veteran)
21st New York
1st Md Potomac Home Brigade

Second Brigade, Col. John E. Wynkoop
15th New York
20th Pennsylvania
22nd Pennsylvania

Second Cavalry Division
Brig. Gen. William W. Averell

First Brigade, Col. James M. Schoonmaker
8th Ohio
14th Pennsylvania

Second Brigade, Col. John H. Oley
34th Ohio (Mounted Infantry)
3rd West Virginia
5th West Virginia
7th West Virginia

Third Brigade, Col. William H. Powell
1st West Virginia
2nd West Virginia

Prior to his rendezvous with Crook at Staunton, Hunter had about 8,500 men at arms under his command; the combined commands numbered about 18,000.

Opposing this force before the arrival of Jubal Early's Corps and its combination with Breckinridge were various forces under W.E. Jones (killed at Piedmont), J.C. Vaughn, John McCausland, W.L. Jackson, and J.D. Imboden.

BATTLE AT THE MONOCACY

FEDERAL
Middle Department (VIII Corps): Maj. Gen. Lewis Wallace, Commanding

First Separate Brigade, Brig. Gen. Erastus B. Tyler
1st Md. Potomac Home Brigade—Capt. Charles J. Brown
3rd Md. Potomac Home Brigade—Col. Charles P. Gilpin
11th Maryland Volunteer Infantry—Col. William T. Landstreet
144th Ohio National Guard (3 companies)
149th Ohio National Guard (7 companies)—Col. Allison Brown

Cavalry
8th Illinois Volunteer Cavalry (7 companies)—Col. David Clendenin
Loudon (Va.) Rangers (Cos. A, B)—Maj. Thorpe
159th Ohio Mounted Infantry—Capts. Edward Leib, Henry Allen
Mixed Cav. Detachment—Maj. Charles A. Wells.

Artillery
Baltimore Light Artillery Battery—Capt. Frederick W. Alexander (6 guns)
At Blockhouse—1 howitzer

Third Division, VI Corps: Brig. Gen. James Ricketts

First Brigade, Col. William S. Truex
14th New Jersey—Lt. Col. C.K. Hall
106th New York—Capt. Edward M. Paine
151st New York Vol. Inf.—Col. William Emerson
87th Penna. Vol. Infantry—Lt. Col. James A. Stahle
10th Vermont Vol. Inf.—Col. William W. Henry

Second Brigade, Col. Matthew R. McClennan
6th Maryland (not engaged)

9th N.Y. Heavy Artillery (2 Battns)—Col. William Seward
110th Ohio Volunteer Infantry—Lt. Col. Otho H. Binkley
122nd Ohio, part (not engaged)
122nd Ohio (detachment)—Lt. Charles Gibson
126th Ohio—Lt. Col. Aaron W. Ebright
67th Pennsylvania (not engaged)
138th Pennsylvania—Maj. Lewis A. May

Casualties: Wallace lost one quarter of his command to death, injury or desertion. Most estimates place the number killed outright at around 125 (Goldsborough 123, *Battles & Leaders* 98), the number wounded at around 600 (594-605), the number captured at 700 (668), and the number missing at around 500. Total of killed, wounded, captured and missing, between 1,880 and 1,968.

CONFEDERATE
The Second Army Corps, Army of Northern Virginia, Army of the Valley District
Lt. Gen. Jubal A. Early, Commander

Breckinridge's Corps: Maj. Gen. John C. Breckinridge

Gordon's Division: Maj. Gen. John B. Gordon

Evan's Brigade, Brig. Gen. Clement A. Evans (W) /Col. E.N. Atkinson
13th Georgia—Lt. Col. John Baker (W)
26th Georgia—Col. E.N. Atkinson
31st Georgia
38th Georgia

60th Georgia
61st Georgia—Col. J.H. Lamar (K)/David Van Valinburg (K) (lost 98 of 152 men engaged)
12th Georgia Battalion

York's Brigade, Brig. Gen. Zebulon York
Harry Hayes's old "Louisiana Tigers" Brigade, 5th,

6th, 7th, 8th and 9th La., fragments—Col. W.R. Peck

Stafford's old brigade, 1st, 2nd, 10th, 14th and 15th Louisiana, fragments—Col. E. Waggaman

Terry's Brigade, Brig. Gen. William Terry
The fragmentary remains of fourteen of the regiments of Edward Johnson's division, most of which was captured by the enemy May 12th, 1864.

Jackson's old 1st or Stonewall Brigade, 2nd, 4th, 5th, 27th, and 33rd Virginia—Col. J.H.S. Funk

21st, 25th, 42nd, 44th, 48th, and 50th Virginia —Col. R. H. Dungan

Steuart's old brigade, 10th, 23rd, and 37th Virginia—Lt. Col. H.S. Saunders

Ramseur's Division
Maj. Gen. Stephen D. Ramseur

Lilley's Brigade (Early's old brigade), Brig. Gen. Robert D. Lilley
13th, 31st, 49th, 52nd, and 58th Virginia

Johnston's Brigade, Brig. Gen. Robert D. Johnston

5th, 12th, 20th (Col. Thomas F. Toon) and 23rd North Carolina

Lewis's Brigade, Brig. Gen. William Lewis
6th, 21st, 54th, 57th North Carolina, fragments
1st N.C. Battalion Sharpshooters

Rodes's Division
Maj. Gen. Robert E. Rodes

Battle's Brigade, Brig. Gen. Cullen A. Battle
3rd, 5th, 6th, 12th, and 61st Alabama

Grimes's Brigade, Brig. Gen. Bryan Grimes
32nd, 43rd, 45th, 53rd North Carolina
2nd North Carolina, Battalion

Cook's Brigade, Brig. Gen. Philip Cook
4th, 12th, 21st, and 44th Georgia, fragments

Cox's Brigade (Ramseur's old brigade), Brig. Gen. William R. Cox
1st, 2nd, 3rd, 4th, 14th, and 30th North Carolina

Echol's Division
Brig. Gen. John Echols

Breckinridge's old command, given temporarily to Elzey at Lynchburg and then temporarily transferred to Vaughn at Staunton. Echols got it back in Maryland.

Wharton's Brigade (was the 2nd Brigade at New Market), Brig. Gen. Gabriel C. Wharton
30th (Battalion), 45th, 50th, and 51st Virginia

Echol's Brigade (was the 1st brigade at New Market), Col. George S. Patton
22nd, 23rd (Battalion), 26th (Battalion) Virginia

Vaughn's Brigade, Brig. Gen. John C. Vaughn
36th, 45th, 60 Tennessee, fragments; Thomas's North Carolina

Artillery,
Brig. Gen. Armistead Long
Maj. J. Floyd King

Maj. Carter M. Braxton
Allegheny Artillery—Carpenter (Virginia)
Lee Artillery—Hardwicke (Virginia)
Stafford Artillery—Cooper (Virginia)

Maj. William McLaughlin
Wise Legion Artillery—Lowry (Centreville Rifles, Lowry's Artillery)

Lewisburg Artillery—Bryan
Monroe Battery—Chapman

Maj. William Nelson
Amherst Artillery—Kirkpatrick
Fluvanna Artillery—Massie (Virginia)
Milledge Artillery—Milledge (Georgia)

Cavalry
Maj. Gen. Robert Ransom

Brig. Gen. John Imboden/Col. George Smith
18th Virginia Cavalry
23rd Virginia Cavalry
62nd Virginia Mounted Infantry
McClannahan's Horse Artillery

Brig. Gen. John McCausland
14th, 16th, 17th, 25th, 37th Virginia Cavalry

Brig. Gen. Bradley T. Johnson
1st Maryland Cavalry Battalion
8th Virginia Cavalry
21st Virginia Cavalry

22nd Virginia Cavalry Battalion
34th Virginia Cavalry Battalion
36th Virginia Cavalry
Griffin's Baltimore Light Artillery (2nd Md)

Brig. Gen W. L. "Mudwall" Jackson
2nd Maryland Cavalry Battalion
19th Virginia Cavalry
20th Virginia Cavalry
46th Virginia Cavalry Battlion
47th Virginia Cavalry Battalion
Lurty's Virginia Battery

Casualties: By modern estimates, Wallace commanded about 7,500 troops—2,500 men and cavalry in the VIII corps, and 4,500 to 5,000 in Ricketts's Division. They were organized in seventeen infantry regiments (some in parts), four cavalry units, one battery of field guns, plus the unattached howitzer. Wallace lost 17% of his command, killed (c. 125), wounded (c. 600) and captured (c. 700).

Early commanded sixty-seven infantry regiments, six battalions of infantry (or fragments), plus eleven regiments and nine battalions of cavalry, as well as three battalions (nine batteries) of field artillery and seven batteries of horse artillery. The force may have numbered as many as 20,000 when it started out, although Early claims to have had only 10,000 before Washington.

There were sixty-one Virginia military units in the fight, including thirty infantry; the cavalry and artillery was entirerly Virginian. There were twenty North Carolina units, all infantry; eleven Georgian, some fragments; ten Louisiana regiments, all fragments; and five Alabama. It is interesting that with their disproportionate share of the army, Evans's Georgians and York's Louisianans got to do the lion's share of the fighting, along with Terry's veteran Virginians, and as a result took the heaviest losses.

Those losses are obviously underreported, the estmated total of 710 (275 killed, 435 wounded) equalling what Gordon himself lost in his division. Conradis concluded that Early may have actually lost between 1,300 and 1,500 killed and wounded.

Select Bibliography

General Histories

The foundation document for all Civil War history is the monumental *War of the Rebellion: A Compilation of the Official Records of the Union and Confederate Armies* compiled by the U.S. War Department and issued by the Government Printing Office between 1880 and 1901. The seventy sections of the "O.R.'s" are in 128 volumes, plus Atlas and Index. The U.S. Navy Department's companion work on the union and confederate navies, issued between 1894 and 1927, runs to thirty volumes. Of particular relevance for the Monocacy is O.R. Volume 37, Part 2.

Frederick H. A. Dyer's *A Compendium of the War of the Rebellion*, Thomas Yoseloff, New York, 1959, in three volumes, offers thumbnail histories of every federal regiment and naval unit and listings of every engagement by state among other information.

Battles and Leaders of the Civil War, in four volumes, consists of "accurate, unbiased" accounts of engagements written by confederate and federal officers involved; it was created by editors Robert Underwood Johnson and Clarence Clough Buel of *Century Magazine* in 1883 for a series that ran until 1887 (reprinted, New York, Castle, 1956). Of particular interest for *Season of Fire* are the accounts in Volume IV by generals John D. Imboden (Newmarket), Franz Sigel (Valley campaign), Jubal Early (march to Washington, Monocacy) and in Volume I by James A. Mulligan (Lexington, Mo.), who wrote it before he was killed.

Even though they viewed these events from a distance and in the midst of a great number of other, more pressing concerns, both Lee and Grant provide a necessary backdrop for the general movement of the armies, in the standard *R.E. Lee, A Biography* in four volumes by Douglas Southall Freeman, New York, 1934-35 and the incomparable *Personal Memoirs of U.S. Grant*, New York, 1885, two volumes.

Douglas Southall Freeman's *Lee's Lieutenants*, Charles Scribner, New York, 1942, in three volumes, (Vol. III, Chapter XXIX, pp. 557-570) was the predecessor for the popular historical narratives, covering the entire war, of Bruce Catton and Shelby Foote, both of whom cover in one degree or another the Early campaign. (Catton's *A Stillness at Appomattox*, Chapter Five, New York, Doubleday & Co, 1954; Shelby Foote's *Civil War: A Narrative*, New York, Random House, 1974.)

Among more recent popular narratives, the twenty-four volume set covering the entire *Civil War* by Time-Life Books are well written, researched, and very well illustrated, including the 1987 volume by Thomas A. Lewis that covers events of *The Valley Campaign of 1864*.

One of the first and still useful collections to present the voices of the common soldiers as well as the officers is Henry Steele Commager's *The Blue and the Gray* in two volumes, Bobbs-Merrill, New York, 1950. Biographical summaries of general officers are readily available in Ezra Warner's volumes: *Generals in Gray: Lives of the Confederate Commanders*, Baton Rouge, 1959, and its counterpart, *Generals in Blue*, 1964. The technique is carried downward in rank by Roger Hunt's *Brevet Brigadier Generals in Blue*.

The Civil War, Day By Day, An Almanac 1861-1865, Garden City, Doubleday, 1971, was compiled by E.B. Long, the editor of *Grant's Memoirs* and Director of Research for Bruce Catton's *The Centennial History of the Civil War*, New York, Doubleday, 1961, 1963, 1965. Intended as a companion volume to the history, it gives a quick reference to every action of the war, but better yet contains a 110-page bibliography with an invaluable guide to the manuscript collections of the war.

The actions that won Congressional Medals of Honor for several men who appear in this book —Davis, Scott, Stahel, du Pont—are described in *Deeds of Valor from Records in the Archives of the United States Government*, ed. by O.F. Keydel and W.F. Beyer, Detroit, Perrien-Keydel Co.,1906.

A useful compendium for Bradley Johnson, Harry Gilmor, and other Marylanders in gray is W.W. Goldsborough's *The Maryland Line in the Confederate Army, 1861-1865*, Baltimore, 1869 and Guggenheimer, Weil, 1900.

<hr>

Particular Histories

<hr>

Specific to the Early campaign itself are Frank E. Vandiver's brief and somewhat cursive *Jubal's Raid*, McGraw-Hill, New York, 1960, reissued in paperback by the University of Nebraska Press in 1992, and Benjamin Franklin Cooling's far more elaborated *Jubal Early's Raid on Washington, 1864*, the Nautical & Aviation Publishing Company, Baltimore, 1989, which has many useful appendices of army compositions and an extensive bibliography. Also useful was Jedediah Hotchkiss's *Make Me a Map of the Valley: The Civil War Journal of Stonewall Jackson's Cartographer*, edited by Archie P. McDonald and published by the Southern Methodist Press, Dallas, 1973.

New Market:

    E. Raymond Turner's 1912 work *The New Market Campaign, May, 1864*, has some enduring qualities but it cannot compare to the new standard, *The Battle of New Market*, by William C. Davis (Breckinridge's biographer), Doubleday, New York, 1975. Davis makes apt use of the Franz Sigel Papers held at Western Reserve Historical Society in Cleveland and the extensive VMI files and offers by far the best summation and distillation of source materials that Davis correctly calls "legion." Also see:

    Bruce, Daniel H., "The Battle of New Market, Virginia," in *Confederate Veteran*, XV, 1907

    Imboden, John D., "The Battle of New Market, Va., May 15th, 1864," *Battles and Leaders*, IV, p. 480

Piedmont and Aftermath:

    Boley, Henry, *Lexington in Old Virginia*, Richmond, Va., Garrett & Massey, 1936, reissued 1974 by Liberty Hall Press, Lexington, and in 1990 by Rockbridge Publishing Co., Berryville, Va.

    Driver, Robert J., Jr., *Lexington and Rockbridge County in the Civil War*, Lynchburg, Va., H.E. Howard, Inc., 1989

    Kimball, William J., "The Battle of Piedmont," *Civil War Times Illustrated*, January, 1967

    Vaughn, Brig. Gen. John Crawford's report, O.R., 50, Pt. 2, p. 990

    David Hunter Strother's account (see below) is also very informative.

Lynchburg:

    Blackford, Charles M., *The Campaign and Battle of Lynchburg*, Lynchburg, J.P. Bell, 1901

    Southern Historical Society Papers, XXX, Richmond, Va., 1902. pp. 279-332.

Frederick:
>   Thomas J. Scharf's classic *History of Western Maryland*, first issued at Philadelphia in 1882 and reprinted in 1968 at Baltimore, Regional Publishing Co., in two volumes, describes the action at Frederick and at the Monocacy and contains reports by Capt. F.W. Alexander, Brig.-Gen. E.B. Tyler and Capt. Charles J. Brown.

Monocacy: The classic eyewitness account is Glenn H. Worthington's 1932 *Fighting For Time or The Battle That Saved Washington and Mayhap the Union*, Frederick County Historical Society, Shippensburg, Pa., Beidel Printing House, an amateur history of the Early campaign with particular attention to the battle by a man who was there as a child of six years and who watched it from the basement window of his father's house. Worthington's history was reissued in 1985 by the White Mane Publishing Co. and edited by Brian C. Pohanka, who adds six very informative eye-witness accounts. Worthington also contributed a brief article, "The Battle of Monocacy," to *Confederate Veteran*, XXXVI, January 1928.

>   The 100th anniversary of the battle was commemorated in 1964 with "Monocacy, The Battle That Saved Washington," a magazine format program issued by the Frederick County Civil War Centennial Commission containing a 24-page history by Albert E. Conradis.

>   On the 125th anniversary of the battle, in 1989, the Historical Society of Frederick reissued E.Y. Goldsborough's 1898 *Early's Great Raid and the Battle of the Monocacy*. As aide-de-camp to Gen. E.B. Tyler, who commanded Wallace's right wing, Goldsborough was an adult eyewitness to the fighting at the Jug Bridge; but his narrative is little more than a paraphrase of sections of the O.R.

>   Two old government documents focus on the battle and battlefield: John Gross Barnard's 1871 *Report on the Defenses of Washington*, Government Printing Office, has a detailed description of the battle at the Monocacy; also The U.S. Congress, 70th, 1st Session, House Of Representatives, Hearings before the Committee on Military Affairs, *To Establish A National Military Park at Battlefield of Monocacy, Maryland, April 13, 1928*, Goverment Printing Office, 1928.

>   Among unpublished accounts of the battle, Cooling cites three at the Army War College written 74 years apart:

Pickering, Abner, *Early's Raid in 1864, Including the Battle of the Monocacy*, AWC, 1913-14

Fenton, Charles Wendell, *Early's Raid on Washington*, AWC, March 1916

Minney, Elton D., *The Battle of Monocacy; An Individual Study Project*, AWC, 1988

Lewis cites an unpublished 1972 manuscript, "The Battle of Monocacy," by Brian Pohanka. I am indebted to Monocacy National Battlefield Superintendent Susan Moore and historian Kathy Beeling for a copy of the unpublished National Park Service manuscript composed under the direction of Edwin C. Bearss, Chief Historian, National Park Service, detailing events in the battle almost hour by hour.

Urbana:
>   *History and Legends, Urbana District, 1976*, compiled by the Urbana Civic Association, has the story of the Meyers's downspout slate that turned out to be Major Smith's gravestone.

Gaithersburg:
>   The John T. DeSellum Papers in the Montgomery County Historical Society, Rockville, describe the scenes with Early.

Washington and Fort Stevens:

> Carl Sandburg's *Abraham Lincoln: The War Years*, in four volumes, Harcourt Brace, New York, 1945, in Volume 3, Chapter 53, "Washington Beleaguered and Tumultuous," provides the national political setting for the events of the summer of 1864, as Margaret Leech's *Reveille in Washington 1860-1865*, Harper & Brothers, New York, 1941, "Chapter XVI, Siege in the Suburbs," provides the local situation. Other accounts of similarly placed individuals are in Secretary of the Navy Gideon Welles's *Diary* in three volumes, edited by John T. Morse, Boston and New York, 1911, and Treasury Registrar Lucius Chittenden's *Recollections of President Lincoln and His Administration*, New York, Harper & Brothers, 1891. A separate manuscript of Chittenden reminiscences of the battle is in the collection of Frank E. Vandiver, who quotes it extensively in his *Jubal's Raid*.

> "The Defenses of Washington: General Early's Advance on the Capital and the Battle of Fort Stevens, July 11 and 12, 1864," by William V. Cox in *Records of the Columbia Historical Society*, IV, (1901), 135-165 is an old but still useful account. The standard for the defenses of Civil War Washington is B.F. Cooling's *Symbol, Sword and Shield*, Hamden, Conn., Archon, 1975.

> The cavalry skirmishing to the west of the city is described in Hard's history of the 8th Illinois Cavalry (see below) and *Life and Letters of Charles Russell Lowell* by Edward W. Emerson, Boston, Houghton, Mifflin Co., 1907.

The Johnson-Gilmor Raid to Baltimore:

> Gen. Bradley T. Johnson told the story twice, in Vol. II, "Maryland," of the *Confederate Military History* in 12 volumes, edited by Gen. Clement A. Evans, Atlanta, Ga., the Confederate Publishing Company, 1899, and in "My Ride Around Baltimore in Eighteen Hundred and Sixty-Four" in *Southern Historical Society Papers*, XXX, 1902, pp. 215-225. Col. Harry Gilmor's lively account is in his biographical *Four Years in the Saddle*, New York, Harper and Brothers, 1866.

> Details of the Rockville skirmish are in *Civil War Guide to Montgomery County* by Charles T. Jacobs, Montgomery County Historical Society, Rockville, Pacemaker Press, 1983, and in *Maryland in the Civil War* by Harold R. Manakee, Baltimore, Maryland Historical Society, 1961.

Specific and Unit Histories

And legion are the Civil War regiments that have had someone tell their story. The Virginia Regimental Series from H.E. Howard, Inc., Lynchburg, Va., is a constant and consistent source for the kind of personal, detailed individual histories that personalize and personify the war. For this campaign, Robert J. Driver, Jr.'s *14th Virginia Cavalry*, and *The Staunton Artillery— McClanahan's Battery*, provided such special material for, among other things, those memorable Feamsters and McClungs.

The story of the Baltimore Battery, Light Artillery, "Alexander's" that stood all day in the center at the Monocacy is told in *History and Roster of Maryland Volunteers, War of 1861-5* by Allison Wilmer, J.H. Jarrett, and George W.T. Vernon.

Some regiments stand above others for heroism and color, and their histories seem to reflect that. I am partial to William Lincoln's *Life With the Thirty-fourth Mass. Infantry in the War of the Rebellion*, and also made extensive use of Abner Hard's 1868 *History of the Eighth Cavalry Regiment, Illinois Volunteers, During the Great Rebellion*, since that regiment was so prominent in the events leading to the Monocacy. Almost as a counterpoint is James J. Williamson's 1896 *Mosby's Rangers, A Record of the Operations of the Forty-third Battalion Virginia Cavalry*, reprinted 1982 for the Time-Life Collector's Library of the Civil War. This should be supplemented with the 1981 *The Memoirs of Colonel John S. Mosby*, edited by Charles Wells Russell.

Unit histories:

12th Alabama: Park, Robert E., "Diary," *Southern Historical Society Papers* I, 1876
——, "The Twelfth Alabama Infantry, Confederate States Army," *Southern Historical Society Papers*, XXXIII, 1905

18th Conn.: Walker, William C., *History of the Eighteenth Regiment Connecticut Volunteers in the War for the Union*, Norwich, 1885

26th Georgia: Murray, Allen J., *South Georgia Rebels: the True Wartime Experiences of the Twenty-sixth Regiment Georgia Volunteer Infantry, Lawton-Gordon-Evans Brigade, Confederate States Army, 1861-1865*, St. Mary's, Ga., by author, 1976

31st Georgia: Isaac G. Bradwell, a veteran of the 31st, became a prolific contributor for a long period of years to *Confederate Veteran*, always on the same themes:
——, "First Valley Campaign of General Early," XIX, 1911, pp. 230-231
——, "Early's Demonstration Against Washington in 1864," XXII, No. 10, October 1914, pp. 438-4439
——, "Early's March To Washington in 1864," XXVIII, No. 5, May 1920, pp. 176-177
——, "Cold Harbor, Lynchburg, Valley Campaign, 1864," XXVIII, 1920, pp. 138-139
——, "In the Battle of Monocacy, Md.," XXVI, No. 2, February 1928, pp. 55-57
——, "On to Washington," XXXVI, No. 3, March 1928, pp. 95-96
——, "The Battle of Monocacy, Md.," XXVII, No. 10, October 1929, pp. 382-383

38th Georgia: United Daughters of the Confederacy, Georgia Division, Oglethorpe County Chapter, *This They Remembered: The History of Four Companies Who Went From Oglethorpe County ... etc.*, Washington, Ga., Washington Publishing Co., 1965 (Includes *Diary of George H. Lester* of Co. E, the "Tom Cobb Infantry")

61st Georgia: Nichols, G.W., *A Soldier's Story of His Regiment (Sixty-First Georgia) and Incidentally of the Lawton-Gordon-Evans Brigade, Army of Northern Virginia*, Kennesaw, Ga., Continental Book Co., 1961

8th Illinois: Hard, Abner, *History of the Eighth Cavalry Regiment Illinois Volunteers During the Great Rebellion*, Aurora, Ill., By author, 1868

Louisiana (York's Brigade): Bartlett, Napier, *Military Record of Louisiana*, Baton Rouge, Louisiana State University Press, 1964
Jones, Terry L., *Lee's Tigers: the Louisiana Infantry in the Army of Northern Virginia*, Baton Rouge, Louisiana State University Press, 1987

14th Louisiana: Durkin, Joseph T., ed., *Confederate Chaplain: A War Journal of Rev. James B. Sheeran, c.ss.r., Fourteenth Louisiana, C.S.A.*, Milwaukee, Bruce Publishing Co., 1960

Maryland (Artillery): Wilmer, Allison, J.H. Jarrett, and George W.T. Vernon, *History and Roster of Maryland Volunteers, War of 1861-5*, Baltimore, Guggenheimer & Weil Co., 1898

Maryland (Cavalry): Booth, George Wilson, *Personal Reminiscences of a Maryland Soldier in the War Between the States*, Baltimore, 1898

Mettam, Henry C., "Civil War Memoirs: First Maryland Cavalry, C.S.A.," *Maryland Historical Magazine* 58, No. 2, June 1963

11th Maryland.: James, William H., "Blue and Gray; A Baltimore Volunteer of 1864," *Maryland Historical Magazine*, Vol. 36, #1, March 1941

34th Mass.: Lincoln, William S., *Life With the Thirty-fourth Massachusetts Infantry in the War of the Rebellion*, Worcester, Mass., Noyes, Snow & Co., 1879

14th New Jersey: "9 July 1864: the 14th New Jersey Infantry at the Battle of Monocacy," *Military Images Magazine*, May-June 1980

   Clark, Roderick A., "Reminiscences," *National Tribune*, April 15, 1886 (per Pohanka in Worthington)

   Terrill, J. Newton, *Campaigns of the Fourteenth Regiment New Jersey Volunteers*, New Brunswick, Daily Home News Press, 1884.

1st New York Cavalry (Lincoln): Stevenson, James H., *Boots and Saddles: A History of the First Volunteer Cavalry of the War, Known as the First New York (Lincoln) Cavalry*, Harrisburg, 1879

106th New York: Robertson, Peter, "Monocacy and the Gallant Stand of the One Hundred and Sixth New York," *National Tribune*, January 24, 1884 (per Pohanka in Worthington)

6th North Carolina: Iobst, Richard W. and Louis H. Manarin, *The Bloody Sixth: The Sixth North Carolina Regiment Confederate States of America*, Raleigh, North Carolina Confederate Centennial Commission, 1965

14th North Carolina: Smith, W.A., *The Anson Guards: Company C, Fourteenth Regiment North Carolina Volunteers, 1861-1865*, Charlotte, Stone Publishing Co., 1914

123rd Ohio: Keyes, Charles M., *The Military History of the 123rd Regiment of Ohio Volunteer Infantry*, Sandusky, 1874

126th Ohio: McDougle, W.T., (Co. K), "Account of Monocacy," *National Tribune*, February 21, 1884 (per Pohanka in Worthington)

149th Ohio: Perkins, George R., *A Summer in Maryland and Virginia, or Campaigning with the One Hundred and Forty-Ninth Ohio*, Chillicothe, 1911

22nd Penna.: Farrer, Samuel C., *The Twenty-Second Pennsylvania Cavalry and the Ringgold Battalion, 1861-1865*, Pittsburgh, 1911

87th Penna: Prowell, George R., *History of the Eighty-Seventh Regiment, Pennsylvania Volunteers*, York, Press of the York Daily, 1901

138th Penna.: Lewis, Osceola, *History of the One Hundred and Thirty-eighth Pennsylvania*, Norristown, Wills, Tredell, and Jenkins, 1866

U.S. VI Corps: Hyde, Thomas W., *Following the Greek Cross: or, Memories of the Sixth Army Corps*, Boston, Houghton-Miflin, 1895

   Stevens, George T., *Three Years In The Sixth Corps, A Concise Narrative of Events in the Army of the Potomac*, New York, D. Van Nostrand, 1870

10th Vermont: Abbott, Samuel A., *Personal Recollections and Civil War Diary, 1864*, Burlington (Vt.) Free Press, 1908

   Freeman, Daniel B., (Co. G), "A Day's Skirmish," *National Tribune*, March 18, 1897 (per Pohanka in Worthington)

   Haynes, Edwin M., *History of the Tenth Vermont*, Rutland, 1894

Virginia (Artillery): Driver, Robert J., Jr., *Staunton Artillery and McClanahan's Battery*, Virginia Regimental Series, Lynchburg, Va., H.E. Howard, Inc., 1988

   Fonerden, C.A., *A Brief History of the Military Career of Carpenter's Battery*, New

Market, Va., Henkel and Co., 1911

Runge, W.H., ed., *Diary of Private Henry Robinson Berkeley: Four Years in the Confederate Artillery*, Chapel Hill, University of North Carolina Press, 1961

Virginia (Cavalry): Bennette, J. Kelly, *Diary* (manuscript), Southern Historical Collection, University of North Carolina, Chapel Hill.

Driver, Robert J., Jr., *14th Virginia Cavalry*, Virginia Regimental Series, Lynchburg, Va., H.E. Howard, Inc., 1988

Opie, John N., *A Rebel Cavalryman with Lee, Stuart, and Jackson*, Chicago, Conkey, 1899

Russell, Charles Wells, ed., *The Memoirs of Colonel John S. Mosby*, Millwood, New York, Kraus, 1981.

Williamson, James J., *Mosby's Rangers, A Record of the Operations of the Forty-third Battalion Virginia Cavalry*, 1896, reprinted 1982 for the Time-Life Collector's Library of the Civil War.

Virginia (Stonewall Brigade): Casler, John O., *Four Years in the Stonewall Brigade*, Girard, Kans., Appeal Publishing Co., 1906 and Dayton, Ohio, Morningside Bookshop, 1971

Douglas, Henry Kyd, *I Rode With Stonewall*, Chapel Hill, University of North Carolina Press, 1940

Robertson, James I., *The Stonewall Brigade*, Baton Rouge, Louisiana State University Press, 1963

Worsham, John H., *One of Jackson's Foot Cavalry: His Experience and What He Saw During the War 1861-1865*, New York, Neale, 1912 and Jackson, Tenn., McCowat, 1964

5th Virginia: Wallace, Lee A., *Fifth Virginia Infantry*, Virginia Regimental Series, Lynchburg, H.E. Howard, Inc., 1988

62nd Virginia: Delauter, Roger V., Jr., *Sixty-Second Virginia Infantry*, Virginia Regimental Series, Lynchburg, Va., H.E. Howard, Inc., 1988

Individuals

Almost every prominent figure who was engaged in the actions described in this book left their own memoirs or have had capable biographers—Breckinridge, Wallace, Early, Gordon, Gilmor among them. In addition, diarists and commentators abound; important among these for *Season of Fire* is David Strother, whose journal contributes heavily to my account of the Hunter campaign: *A Virginia Yankee in the Civil War: The Diaries of David Hunter Strother*, edited by Cecil D. Eby, Jr. I also particularly relied on John H. Worsham's *One of Jackson's Foot Cavalry*, edited by James I. Robertson, Jr., Jackson, Tenn., McCowat-Mercer Press, 1964, and on Samuel A. Abbott's *A Personal Recollection and Civil War Diary*, 1864, Burlington, Vt., Free Press, 1908. Other resources:

Breckinridge: Davis, William C., *Breckinridge: Statesman, Soldier, Symbol*, Baton Rouge, Louisiana State University Press, 1974

Crook: Schmitt, Martin F., ed., *General George Crook: His Autobiography*, Norman, Okla., 1946

Early: "The Advance on Washington in 1864," in Southern Historical Society Papers, IX, Nos. 7 and 8 (July/August 1881), pp. 297-312

Bushong, Millard K., *Old Jube: A Biography of General Jubal A. Early*, Boyce, Va., Carr Publishing, 1955

Early, Jubal A., *A Memoir of the Last Year of the War for Independence in the Confederate States of America*, Lynchburg, Va., C.W. Burton, 1867

——*Autobiographical Sketch and Narrative of the War Between the States*, Philadelphia, Lippincott, 1912

"Early's March to Washington," *Battles and Leaders of the Civil War*, Vol. IV, The Century Co., New York, 1887

Vandiver, Frank, ed., *War Memoirs of Jubal Anderson Early*, Bloomington, Ind., Indiana University Press, 1960

Gordon: Gordon, John B., *Reminiscences of the Civil War*, New York, Charles Scribner's Sons

Johnson: Booth, George Wilson, *Personal Reminiscences of a Maryland Soldier in the War Between the States*, Baltimore, 1898

Ramseur: Gallagher, Gary W., *Stephen Dodson Ramseur: Lee's Gallant General*, Chapel Hill, University of North Carolina Press, 1985

Sigel: Sigel, Franz, "Sigel in the Shenandoah Valley," *Battles and Leaders of the Civil War*, IV

Strother: Eby, Cecil D., Jr., *"Porte Crayon": The Life of David Hunter Strother*, Chapel Hill, The Univ. of North Carolina Press, 1960

Eby, Cecil D., Jr., ed., *A Virginia Yankee in the Civil War: The Diaries of David Hunter Strother*, Chapel Hill, The Univ. of North Carolina Press, 1961

Wallace: McKee, Irving, *Ben Hur Wallace, The Life of Lew Wallace*, Berkeley, 1947

Morsberger, Robert E. and Katharine M. Morsberger, *Lew Wallace, Militant Romantic*, McGraw Hill, 1980

Wallace, Lewis, *Autobiography*, 2 vols., New York, 1906

Regional Histories

Jewels are often found in the smaller regional and county histories that abound. In Roger Brooke Farquhar's *Historic Montgomery County, Maryland, Old Homes and History* are found the story of Uncle Tom (Josiah Henson) and those of the Allen Bowie Davis, Ridgely Brown and Carroll families. T.H.S Boyd's 1879 *History of Montgomery County* supplements the material.

Collections

The Library of Congress Manuscripts Division holds the papers of Jubal Anderson Early, some 5,000 items including official correspondence, and those of Maj. Jedediah Hotchkiss, cartographer to Stonewall Jackson, Gen. Richard Ewell and Jubal Early—20,000 items on sixty-one reels of microfilm. Early's papers include the typescript diary of Capt. W.W. Old, Early's aide-de-camp, kept from June 13, 1864 until August 12. The Breckinridge Family Papers number 200,000 items. Finding aids are available to these large collections.

Thanks are due to Dr. Richard J. Sommers, archivist of the wonderful U.S. Army Military

History Institute, Carlisle Barracks, Pennsylvania, in particular for calling to my attention the James A. Stahle papers relating to the 87th Pennsylvania Infantry.

Cartography

Jedediah Hotchkiss's map of the battlefield at Monocacy is at the Map Division of the Library of Congress. Goldsborough's small but eyewitness history also includes a battlefield map, as does Worthington, where it appears as an end paper. *Battles and Leaders of the Civil War* and *Lee's Lieutenants* have useful maps. EDAW, Inc., of Alexandria produced in 1978 a series of large scale maps for the National Park Service showing the troop movements hour-by-hour at the Monocacy.

Index

A